THE GOSPEL ACCORDING TO PAUL

THE GOSPEL ACCORDING TO PAUL

The Creative Genius Who Brought
Jesus to the World

ROBIN GRIFFITH-JONES

HarperOne
An Imprint of HarperCollinsPublishers

HarperOne

To Tethys

FIRST HARPERCOLLINS PAPERBACK EDITION PUBLISHED IN 2005

Library of Congress Cataloging-in-Publication Data is available upon request.
ISBN: 978-06-073066-6

10 11 RRD(H) 10 9 8 7 6

CONTENTS

THE JOURNEYS OF PAUL

IN THE SAILING SEASON, mid-March to mid-November (with the window of greatest safety open only May 27–September 14), the prevailing winds in the Aegean and Eastern Mediterranean blow from the north or northwest. Travelers such as Paul did best to journey overland, if they could, when going west from Asia or north from Greece, and to sail to the east or south. With a good following wind, a ship might travel at 4–5 knots, straight as a die, 100 nautical miles in a day. In the face of a contrary wind, a ship might be held up for days. A ship caught in a storm could well sink with all hands lost (see The Mission [Acts of the Apostles; hereafter Miss.] 27:9–44.)

Major Roman roads were furnished with hostels, set apart at distances that a foot traveler could expect to cover in a day, about 20 modern miles. To travel by road—unless protected by imperial troops or private retainers—was to be forever on the alert for robbers or gangs of robbers, for wolves, or for press-gangs seeking slaves. On smaller roads the dangers multiplied. Often enough Paul used the great roads: the Egnatian Road (in Macedonia), for instance, or the Augustan Road (in southern Galatia). The Augustan Road linked a cluster of Roman colonies; Paul traveled much of its length, probably on foot, on his first journey. The northern arm of the Augustan Road was part of the ancient "general road" of Asia Minor, from Antioch-in-Syria in the east to Ephesus in the west. Paul came to know it well. On the second journey he walked its eastern part; and on the third, from one end to the other.

Parts of the story in The Mission are told in the first-person plural, "we": perhaps 11:27; a short section near the start of the Second Journey,

16:10–18; two sections of the Third, 20:5–15 and 21:8–18; and the journey under arrest from Caesarea to Rome, 27:1–28:16. Luke may well have based these parts of his narrative on a travel journal kept by a companion of Paul's.

Paul traveled some 10,000 miles on these journeys. Others journeyed much farther. A tombstone has survived that marked the grave of a merchant who traveled from Phrygia to Rome seventy-two times.

Some approximate distances on Map 1: From Antioch-in-Syria by sea to Salamis, 125 miles, and from Paphos to Perge, 175 miles. Overland from Perge to Antioch-in-Pisidia, 125 miles, and on to Iconium, 110 miles.

The present maps are highly selective. A standard map of the Roman province of Asia would show, between Antioch-in-Pisidia and Ephesus (blank on our Maps 2 and 3), sixteen other cities, fourteen of them sufficiently important to mint coinage of their own. Paul passed through or near them all.

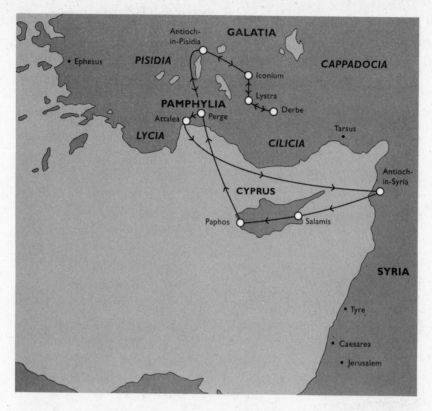

MAP 1. PAUL'S FIRST MISSIONARY JOURNEY, EARLY 40s, AS RECORDED BY LUKE

The assembly at Antioch-in-Syria, a center second only to Jerusalem for Jesus' followers, commissions Barnabas and Paul for mission.

They take ship for Barnabas's home, Cyprus, and head across the island to Paphos, seat of the Roman commander (proconsul) Sergius Paulus (Miss. 13:4–12).

They sail north to Perge, and carry on northward to the Roman colony of Antioch-in-Pisidia. (The family of Sergius Paulus had estates nearby.) Here Luke has a major scene on the response of Jews to the good news (Miss. 13:13–52).

They then proceed east along the new Augustan Road to the colonies Iconium and Lystra (Miss. 14:1–19); here Luke has a major scene on the response of pagans.

They go eastward to Derbe, then back through the same cities and by sea to Antioch-in-Syria.

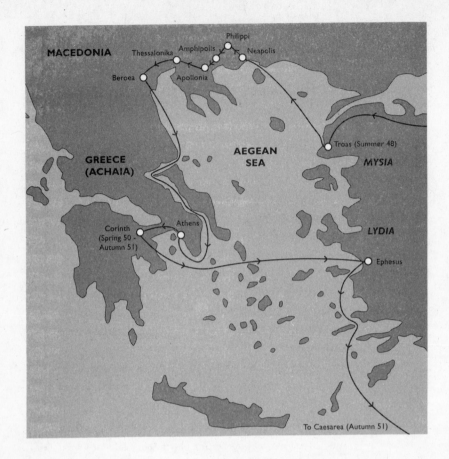

The map contains the following labels:

MACEDONIA · Thessalonika · Amphipolis · Philippi · Neapolis · Beroea · Apollonia · Troas (Summer 48) · MYSIA · GREECE (ACHAIA) · AEGEAN SEA · LYDIA · Corinth (Spring 50 - Autumn 51) · Athens · Ephesus · To Caesarea (Autumn 51)

MAP 2. PAUL'S SECOND MISSIONARY JOURNEY, 46–51

Note: Luke tells in The Mission of the Jerusalem Council, convened to discuss the conditions on which Gentiles might be admitted to membership of the assemblies. He places this council right at the center of his narrative. He tells next of Paul's second journey. Luke may well have combined into this story of a single council decisions made over several years and perhaps at several meetings. Paul's journey likely took place before and not after one such meeting in Jerusalem, in which Paul took part and of which he speaks in Galatians 2:1–10.

April 46: Paul sets out from Antioch-in-Syria; without Barnabas, but with assistant Silas. They head northwest through the Cilician Gates (mountain pass) and westward.

46–48: Again to Derbe, Lystra, Iconium (Miss. 16:1–5). Timothy circumcized at Lystra, to become another assistant. Is Paul making, initially, for Ephesus?

Winter 47–48: Paul seriously ill in Galatia (Gal. 4:13).

Summer 48: Paul avoids the province of Asia. He turns north through Phrygia and Galatia toward Bithynia, then turns westward (across wild country) to Troas (Miss. 16:6–10). (We cannot be sure what route Luke is claiming for Paul here.) He takes ship to Macedonia.

Autumn 48–Spring 50: Paul and assistants in Macedonia: at Philippi (Miss. 16:11–40) and along the Egnatian Road to Thessalonica (Miss. 17:1–9). Paul is opposed, so they go on to Beroea (well away from the Egnatian Road) and then, leaving Silas and

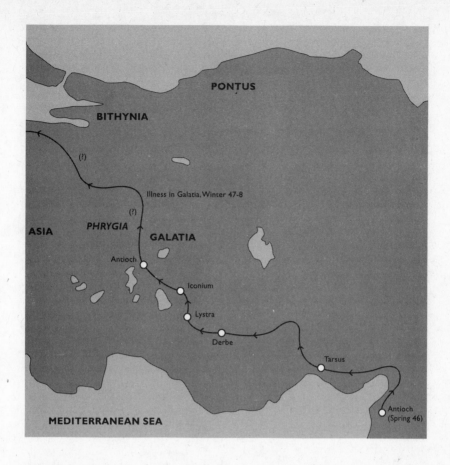

The map shows the following labels: PONTUS, BITHYNIA, ASIA, PHRYGIA, GALATIA, MEDITERRANEAN SEA, and route points: (?), Illness in Galatia, Winter 47-8, (?), Antioch, Iconium, Lystra, Derbe, Tarsus, Antioch (Spring 46).

Timothy behind, Paul moves hurriedly out of Macedonia and goes by sea to Athens (Miss. 17:16–34).

Spring 50–Autumn 51: Paul is in Corinth, for eighteen months the center of his western mission. He is joined by Silas and Timothy. Among his converts is Crispus, leader of the prayer house (Miss. 18:6) and perhaps Sosthenes, Crispus's co-leader or successor (see Third Missionary Journey, below). Paul is arraigned before the proconsul Gallio, summer 51 (Miss. 18:1–16). He sends Timothy to Thessalonica (1 Thess. 3:2) and on Timothy's return writes 1 Thessalonians (from "Paul, Silas, and Timothy"). Second Thessalonians, by Paul, a close assistant, or a worried ally, follows on soon after.

Autumn 51: Paul sails eastward with allies from Corinth (and exiles from Rome), Aquila and Prisca, leaves them in Ephesus, and sails on to Antioch or Caesarea, capital of Judaea, arriving before the winter storms (Miss. 18:18–22). Apollos, from Alexandria in Egypt, arrives in Ephesus and is instructed by Aquila and Prisca; he is sent on to Corinth by the Ephesian assembly, probably in spring 52 (Miss. 18:24–28).

Late Autumn 51: Paul is in Jerusalem with Titus (whom he refuses to have circumcized; Gal. 2:1–3). The Jerusalem council takes place; its leading figures are James, Peter, Barnabas, and Paul (Miss. 15:5–29). Barnabas and Paul return to Antioch-in-Syria.

Winter 51–52: Paul is in Antioch. Representatives of James arrive. A fierce dispute occurs, which is lost by Paul (Gal. 2:1–10). Paul leaves Antioch, never to return.

MACEDONIA

GREECE
(ACHAIA)

Troas

Late Summer 54

Corinth
(Summer 54,
short visit)

Summer 54

Ephesus
(Summer 52 -
Summer 54,
Autumn 54)

MAP 3. PAUL'S THIRD MISSIONARY JOURNEY, 52–56: FIRST PART, 52–54

Note: The details of Paul's journeys to and from Corinth are famously hard to reconstruct with confidence.

Spring–Summer 52: Paul heads west overland to Ephesus, revisiting old foundations on way.

Late Summer 52–54: Paul is based for two years or more in Ephesus, the center of his Asian mission (Miss. 19:1–20:1). Aquila and Prisca are still there. Apollos returns from Corinth. Paul writes his first letter (now lost) to Corinth (1 Cor. 5:9). Paul writes Galatians in 53.

Spring 54: Paul hears more news of Corinth from Chloe's people (1 Cor. 1:11): factions are emerging. He sends Timothy to Corinth (1 Cor. 4:17, 16:10) and hears further news from Stephanas, who brings a letter and perhaps leads an "official" delegation (1 Cor. 16:17). Paul writes 1 Corinthians (from "Paul and Sosthenes") before the Jewish feast of Pentecost, June 2 (1 Cor. 16:8). He is planning an overland trip via Macedonia, to reach Corinth for the winter (1 Cor. 16:5–9).

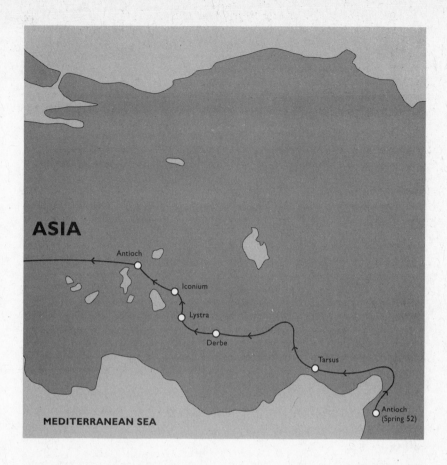

Late Summer 54: Timothy reports back from Corinth with bad news. Paul now sends Timothy to Macedonia (Miss. 19:22) and goes himself straight to Corinth. It is a disastrous visit; Paul goes back north to Macedonia to check on Timothy's welfare. Paul next plans a return to Corinth, but instead travels on back to Ephesus. From Ephesus he writes a fraught letter "through many tears" to Corinth (2 Cor. 2:4), which is taken by Titus.

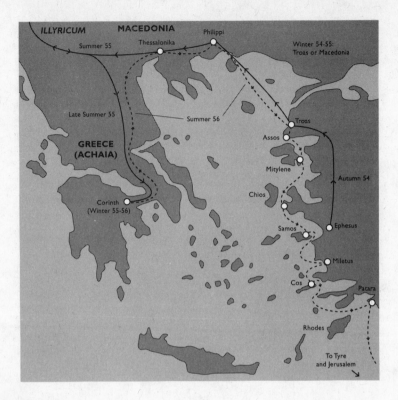

MAP 4. PAUL'S THIRD MISSIONARY JOURNEY, 52–56: SECOND PART, 54–56

Autumn 54: Trouble in Ephesus. Paul retreats north to Troas and winters there or in Macedonia.

Spring 55: Paul in Macedonia to intercept Titus (2 Cor. 2:13). He hears the news from Corinth and writes 2 Corinthians 1–9 (from "Paul and Timothy"), which is delivered by Titus and two others (one a representative of Macedonia, to confirm Paul's probity in the collection; 2 Cor. 8:16–24).

Summer 55: Paul is probably in Illyricum, traveling westward from Thessalonica along the Egnatian Road (Rom. 15:19). He writes 2 Corinthians 10–13.

Late 55–Spring 56: Paul is in Corinth. (Aquila and Prisca go back to Rome and write Paul with news?) Paul writes Romans, which is taken by Phoebe, Paul's patroness in Cenchreae (a harbor south of Corinth).

Summer 56: Paul goes to Jerusalem with the collection, leaving Corinth with delegates from Macedonia, Galatia, and Asia (Miss. 20:4) and traveling overland through Greece and Macedonia. They then go by sea down the coast from Troas, perhaps picking up additional contributions (Miss. 20:7–16). Paul avoids Ephesus, where he might still be unwelcome, and sends for the leaders of the Ephesian assembly to Miletus for a farewell (Miss. 20:17–38). He is keen to reach Jerusalem for Pentecost (Miss. 20:16). He is arrested in Jerusalem.

The New Order contains three other letters written as if to the assistants we have encountered here. Two are addressed to Timothy. One Timothy has Timothy in Ephesus, where Paul had left him to carry on the work in Paul's absence. Second Timothy (the one of the three that may be by Paul himself) is written as if from imprisonment in Rome. The third is addressed to Titus in Crete as the place where Paul had left him.

PREFACE

To write about Paul is to owe large debts. Thinkers have devoted themselves to Paul for nearly two thousand years, historians for two hundred. All of us, writers and readers, have learned from this great tradition.

The tree of Pauline scholarship has now grown beyond all bounds. The trunk has divided into branches and these have divided, over and over, in their turn. The process is unending. Some readers will want to know where on the tree should they expect to locate *The Gospel According to Paul*. Which branches does it grow from?

The book falls into two sections. The first, Parts I–IV, draws upon various texts outside the New Testament: from the Old Testament, Qumran, and visionary texts of the centuries either side of Paul's. Here I have ample debts: to the work, for instance, of John Ashton, Margaret Barker, Richard Bauckham, Crispin Fletcher-Louis, Seyoon Kim, Andrew Lincoln, Christopher Morray-Jones, Carey Newman, Christopher Rowland, and Alan Segal. The overall direction of my thought, however, is a direction that none of these has taken. Our routes converge, stay together, and part again. I am immensely grateful for the inspiring company of their work on the roads we share. And I realize how often I have been led by their work to discover, explore, and finally to adopt routes they themselves are unlikely ever to pursue.

The second and longer section of this book, Parts V–X, has fewer forebears. My concern throughout is to discover: What did Paul want his text to achieve? We will be watching, on page after page, to what Paul is saying and, just as important, what he is *doing*. On this road, rarely traveled, I recognize my more personal and deeper debt to three people, professors at Cambridge and Oxford.

Ernst Bammel, German to the core despite decades in England, introduced me seventeen years ago to the study of the New Testament. He forbade me, through my first semester, to read for my New Testament work anything but the text itself in Greek. I once asked him cautiously about translations; I never asked again.

John Sweet combines the most exact scholarship with a gentle and generous Christian ministry that I can only hope one day to emulate. I started, in Cambridge in 1988, to write for John a paper on Paul. I have finished it at last.

Chris Rowland (a pupil, many years before me, of both Ernst and John) was a friend and mentor for the seven years I spent as a chaplain at Oxford. He demands of all scholarship that it be written to serve the world and its needs today. He has encouraged me to explore—and to test and refine and improve—ideas quite foreign to most modern scholarship.

Behind this book lie other allies too, in particular my agent, Felicity Bryan, and my editor, John Loudon, his colleague Kris Ashley, and their team at Harper San Francisco. In 2000 Harper San Francisco published my book on the gospels, *The Four Witnesses*. I had written it at Lincoln College, Oxford, in the study from which John Wesley launched the Holy Club and so the revival that would become the Methodist Church.

Four years later I am writing this preface in the Temple, in the center of London, midway between St. Paul's Cathedral and Trafalgar Square. Twenty yards away is the Temple Church, built over eight hundred years ago by the Knights Templar in their London headquarters. Through my window comes the sound of our choristers rehearsing. Across the courtyard work the judges and attorneys whom I am here to serve, as challenging and supportive a congregation as any in the land. On Sunday our regular congregation will gather again, alongside visitors from all over the world, in one of the most ancient and beautiful churches in London. We will hear the oldest Anglican service sung by one of the finest choirs in the country to music written over the course of five centuries.

Nowhere could our debt to the past be more clear. And from here, in a few minutes, I will e-mail the manuscript of this book across the world to serve the people of a new millennium.

London
November 1, 2003

INTRODUCTION:
PAUL THEN, PAUL NOW

PAUL. TWO THOUSAND YEARS AFTER HE WAS BORN his name still conjures up a conversion that changed his own and every Christian life forever. And not just Christian lives. For centuries the churches dominated the thought, education, and politics of Europe and America. Even today, no one with Christian forebears escapes the ancestral influence of those churches. And where the churches have influence, so has Paul. He still affects us all in all parts of our lives: our thoughts and feelings about guilt and innocence, the standing of women and of men, our bodies and sex, the political and social order in this world, and our destiny in the next. We may be grateful for his teaching, we may be its unconscious heirs, or we may be its vigorous opponents, but, like it or not, that teaching is in our bones.

Paul is forever fascinating. His thought has shaped the Western world. But it has for centuries been disputed exactly *what* he thought. His letters are vividly personal. But they raise the question ever more sharply *what sort of person* he really was. As modern readers we ask important modern questions. Did Paul really do justice to Jesus' teaching and example? Or did he found a Christianity that its Christ would have disowned? As a missionary did Paul combine Judaism and Christianity? Or did he abandon his Jewish roots? Had he perhaps even grown to hate the Law that had bound his Jewish life—the life from which, it seems, he so dramatically broke free at his conversion?

Such questions are already personal, and they lead to others more intimate still. When we speak of "the road to Damascus" or "a Damascus experience," we invoke Paul's conversion as a model of sudden and radical change. But what happened at Paul's conversion on the road to Damascus? Did it free him from some psychological torment? Or was there a pain in Paul too deep to be dug out? Something surely did afflict him as an emissary. He said, *There was given me a thorn in the flesh,* and God refused to remove it (2 Cor. 12:7). Did some psychological thorn—of sexual or some other guilt perhaps—drive his thought and his frenetic life? How strange it would be, if the Western mind has been molded by a troubled man whose sickness distorted—perhaps beyond recognition—the teaching of the Lord he claimed to follow.

These are modern questions, to which we rightly look for modern, secular answers. To find them, however, we should first hear a quite different set of questions: those that confronted Paul himself, his converts, and his opponents. This book removes the layers of overpainting that later piety and fashion have applied to Paul's portrait; readers can see at last the man his converts saw. It is a sight without parallel. No wonder the later church dulled its colors with a thick, dark varnish of timeless doctrine. This treacly portrait has been baffling enough to those who study it. The original is far stranger, and far more exciting. It is time to bring this masterpiece back to light.

RAISE A HAND, ANY READER who would read Paul's letters for fun. For a church group, yes, or for school or college. And quite right too. I hope this book will itself be of real value to students of all kinds. But all that feels like work. When you think of books to take on vacation or an airline flight, do you think of Paul's letter to the Romans? If you do, you are one in a million.

And if you did, what would you expect to find? History, for one thing. Unforgettable snapshots of life in the early church, written by one of its leaders within thirty years of Jesus' death. And doctrine. Paul's views on God and Jesus, on God's promises and demands, on daily life in this world, and on the rewards and punishments stored up for the next.

You won't be disappointed. But to find in any of Paul's letters just history and doctrine is to eat the buns around a burger. Of course Paul wrote to inform his addressees. But far more than that. He wrote to transform them, to lead them, even as they heard his letter, into the new life of which the letter spoke. Paul did not want his addressees to just hear his letter—but to undergo it.

This Paul is far more than a teacher of doctrine, dry, methodical, and stern. Paul has been granted an apocalypse, the unveiling of a truth hidden from all normal view. He is awed by the majesty and beauty of the disclosure granted to him. The question always in his mind is: How is he to reveal to others what has been so mysteriously revealed to him? Paul is a *poet*. Modern readers, so alert to literature and style, have good reason to enjoy the riches of Paul's writing. Paul does not use his skills just to add icing to the cake of his serious message. He has an unveiling to disclose to his churches. Here, Paul believes, are truths that no ordinary form of teaching can hope to impart. Many modern readers find Paul's gospel alien and hard to grasp. This is just what Paul would have expected. It took a vision of Jesus to bring these truths home to Paul himself, and it will take an instruction just as strange and dramatic to reveal them to his audience. To do so, Paul uses every technique he can. Some of his tactics are so radical that modern readers have quite lost sight of them. In *The Gospel According to Paul* these tactics are brought back to light.

When we think of Paul, we think of a collection of letters. When his churches thought of him, they thought of their founder, father, and friend. We have never had Paul among us and do not miss him. Paul's churches had been founded by Paul in person, and it was the person Paul that they wanted back. Leadership was as important then as now. In *The Gospel According to Paul* we will watch Paul's thought and his life together, each shaping the other. Paul was throughout at the center of a whirlpool of conflicting loyalties and beliefs. As a story, his career was as dramatic as Jesus' own: the fervent adversary of the church became its most determined preacher. He became its most contentious preacher too; wherever Paul went, his distinctive claims for the faith stirred listeners for and against him in equal measure.

Paul was a leader who claimed an extraordinary authority within his communities. Each of those communities was, he believed, dependent for its very survival on reciprocal love and responsibility among its members—and between those members and himself. And so he worked tirelessly to heal divisions. But Paul was himself an ambiguous figure whose gospel was fiercely contested. His authority was challenged, his integrity was questioned, his pleas for unity were flouted. How was he to keep control? He warned and wheedled, threatened and cajoled. No, more than that. He maneuvered and bullied his addressees. And it didn't help. He deepened the divisions he worked to heal.

Paul's intentions and effects, successes and failures will fascinate any reader interested in the nurture and cohesion of communities, in leadership and the exercise of power.

THE CURTAIN RISES. On the darkened stage we can see just the shadowy outlines of a cast, clustered into groups. Up comes a single spotlight, shining with ever greater power on a single figure. It follows him as he walks from group to group on the stage, as he talks, smiles, hugs, frowns, argues, gesticulates, bids farewell, and heads on. Against the dazzling light in which he moves, the rest of the cast looks darker still. However crowded the stage, we are watching a one-man show. And a strange man he is bound to seem. We hear just his voice, see just his movements, watch just his reactions to the actions of others that we can hardly distinguish in the gloom. This is the Paul of tradition.

In *The Gospel According to Paul* we will illumine the whole stage, shedding some light at last on those shadowy figures around Paul. We will hear of those forms of Judaism that most deeply influenced Paul. We will hear of the dominant pagan cultures with which he jostled day by day. Three times in the course of the book, for a good few pages, we will take up the likely viewpoint of his gentile addressees, and from there we will compare Paul's claims and community with those of rival teachers and cults. At one such point we will follow the grand words and strategy of a famous orator graced with all the social standing that Paul lacked. At another we will watch a novel's hero being admitted, near Corinth, into the cult of the goddess Isis. And finally we will wonder how a Roman household, after conversion to Paul's faith, would have looked upon the statues of the household gods that had protected the family for generations. Among all the religious claims that vied for attention, respect, and reverence, we want to know what made Paul's good news attractive, and to whom.

We will be hearing all sides of the arguments with which Paul and his allies shaped—and shocked—the early church. In these years the churches were alive with assurance and hope. Their members were struggling for the words and images in which to say what seemed to need saying about Jesus. Words and images would be taken on, explored, and remixed. New thoughts became possible, were tested, and taken on in turn. New assurance was felt, and new hope. A deepening spiral of language and belief was bringing these converts to the convictions that still underlie the churches' life today. Different groups found value in Jesus' different legacies, in his teaching, for instance, or in his death. Different groups spoke of this value with different images. Images, for instance, of his effect: Jesus the perfect sacrifice. Or of his vindication: Jesus raised to heaven. Or of the role this gives him: Jesus enthroned as judge.

We are speaking here of images, of the attempts by Jesus' first followers to express the significance and rationale of events that came near to confounding their understanding. But an "image," for our generation, suggests a thin substitute for reality. The heavenly scenes the Bible speaks of—so often of pomp and rituals strange to us now—are as fugitive as a castle in the clouds. Not so, for the seers we shall encounter and those who heard or read the records of their visions. The seers, we shall see, thought visually. They dwelt on the layout of the court of heaven, and so could make the subtlest distinctions in its occupants' rank and power. They dwelt on the Temple in Jerusalem as a model of all creation and on its sanctuary as heaven itself, and so could speak precisely, in terms of the Temple, about God's nearness and distance and about the knowledge we can have of him. Among these seers was Paul himself.

The authors of the New Testament knew only too well the distinctions between this world and the "next," this world and "heaven." Heaven was not less real than earth; it offered the truth about earth. And for that very reason it must never be confused with earth. The early church knew of all such categories and the distinctions between them. And it deliberately overturned them. The barriers were crumbling between heaven and earth and what the followers of Jesus could know of each. Not least among the glories of the New Testament is this revolution, to which its authors subjected the categories their history had bequeathed to them.

THIS BOOK IS THE STORY of arguments bitterly contested between different missionaries and different churches. Paul was in the thick of them. The conduct of these arguments is as gripping as their content.

They throw into sharp relief the questions that still face any community growing in numbers and independence.

Different churches, then as now, sent out emissaries with different—and conflicting—messages about Jesus. City after city heard varying messages as the emissaries competed, sometimes bitterly, for allegiance, loyalty, and love. And different cities heard in quite different ways even one and the same missionary. We can see why. The culture of a city—its history, style, and ethnic mix—affected what teachers said there and what listeners heard. As New York, Boston, and San Francisco differ from each other now, so Rome, Athens, and Corinth differed two thousand years ago.

The followers of Jesus were not alone in building a community on a claim to knowledge, a way of life, and the leader who inspired them. Other such communities offered their members, as the churches did, an intellectual, emotional, and spiritual home. In any one city Jesus' followers were compared with these well-known groups and took on, in the eyes of an onlooker or follower, something of their contour. As then, so now. We too assimilate the new and the strange to the old and familiar, and in our modern melting pot we see around and within us the mixing and merging of different cultures.

Each of the empire's great cities was home to a marketplace of religions. A wide range of claims to truth, drawn from a wide range of traditions, fought then, as now, for allegiance. They might attract adherents by their age-old familiarity or by their recent arrival from an exotically ancient or faraway culture. Among them, then as now, were those sects that claimed access to some strange knowledge. Outsiders viewed them with suspicion or fear. In its first decades the church was just such a sect. And in *The Gospel According to Paul* we hear of its struggle to be respected, accepted, and genuinely heard against heavy opposition. This story from so long ago and far away is ready to be brought alive for modern readers. The world of Paul is as new as it is old.

Some of those faiths were more easily domesticated than others. Paul's was more bizarre than most, and he knew it. Those who heard Paul then and those who read him now are confronted by one claim before all others: that the objects and categories of knowledge valued by current culture do not embrace all that is the case, for there are other and deeper truths to which we can have access—but only by forms of learning that outsiders condemn, quite reasonably, as childish or illusory. The poet Wordsworth made such a claim when he saw in nature the glimpse of something more than itself. He was trying to evoke such a recognition in his readers too, to stir them through his poetry to see what they had not seen before.

> I have felt
> A presence that disturbs me with the joy
> Of elevated thoughts; a sense sublime
> Of something far more deeply interfused . . .
> "*Tintern Abbey*," LL. 93-96)

Was the poet right? How would we ever know? It is extraordinarily hard to define or prove. What Wordsworth sensed in nature, others have sensed elsewhere: in human relations, in the prospect of death, or (variously but closely linked, as Christians see it, with all three) in a relation with God. Readers of any or of no religious belief will find food for endless thought in Paul's sustained attempts to unveil God's truth—and to equip his addressees to see it.

PAUL HIMSELF BEARS VIVID WITNESS to the tensions to which his gospel gave rise. On the one hand is God's eternal law, God's greatest gift to his people Israel. On the other is Paul's own gospel of Jesus, the Anointed of God, rejected by that people of God and offering its gentile enemies a gift even greater than the Law. Paul was not alone in such a proclamation. A gap opened between most of the Jews among Jesus' followers and most of the Gentiles. At quite different speeds in different places this gap widened into a gulf between gentile churches and Jewish synagogues.

We hear of Paul's missions from his own letters and from the narrative of The Mission (Acts of the Apostles), the story compiled by Luke in the 80s as the sequel to his gospel. Luke follows a pattern we will get to know well. His Paul preaches first to the Jews in a city. Sooner or later his message is unacceptable in the synagogue, so he turns his attention to the Gentiles. We will see in the following pages how effectively Luke has constructed his story to meet his own needs. (Here I will be taking up a thread that readers may have encountered in my earlier book, on the four gospels, *The Four Witnesses*.) Luke must reassure his readers. This Christian faith, he insists, is no new religion; it is the true full fruition of Judaism. And if by Luke's day the churches and synagogues are notoriously hostile to each other, it is, as Luke would have it, only because the Jews have resisted the churches' proclamation. The bitterness of the 80s has poisoned all history since. It is time to understand the origins of this ancient fight between synagogue and church, to draw its vicious sting, and so to lay it, once and for all, to rest.

It is a good time to do so. Pauline study has enjoyed an exciting thirty years. Christian scholars have come to a new understanding of the promises, in Jewish tradition, that God has made to the Jews and the demands he has made of them. Christian thought was for centuries dominated by a pernicious contrast between the regime of love established by Jesus and the supposedly cold and casuistic application of Mosaic Law among the Jews. It was Christian thinkers of the sixteenth century, with an important agenda of their own, who erected the mirror in which these opposites have ever since been seen. But the glass was warped from the start. The angles of reflection were determined by Christians alone, with Christian priorities and interests. The result was a cruel parody of Judaism.

Our agenda has changed. The mirror has at last been taken down. We are better placed than any generation for centuries to hear of God's loyalty to his people the Jews, and so of a vivid, startling danger—that Paul's gospel denied that loyalty. Paul has a real challenge to meet. His God is not obviously just. What Paul attempted in letter after letter, the poet Milton knew, sixteen hundred years later, must be attempted still:

> Of Man's first Disobedience, and the Fruits
> Of that Forbidden Tree, whose mortal taste
> Brought Death into the World, and all our woe,
> With loss of Eden, till one greater Man
> Restore us, and regain the blissful Seat,
> Sing Heav'nly Muse. . . .
> That to the highth of this great Argument
> I may assert Eternal Providence,
> And justify the ways of God to men.
>
>   *Paradise Lost* l. 1-6, 24-27

• • •

THIS BOOK IS WRITTEN for general readers; no knowledge of the Bible or the early church and no religious faith is assumed. Although biblical terms and titles are used, from the outset they are freed up from the deep religious patina with which centuries of church use have darkened them. We do well to hear these words with the freshness they had for Paul and his converts. We will translate "Christ"; it means "Anointed." (Even that makes Jesus sound grander than he would have to a pagan who heard of "Christ" or "the Christ" for the first time. Paul's contemporaries expected men to "anoint" themselves with oil for the sports that were central to Greek education and life.) We will speak of the "Old and New Orders," not "Old and New Testaments," so that we, like the later church, can use the same word for God's arrangement ("order" or "covenant") with his people and for the texts that speak of it. We nowadays only ever hear of the "gospel" in connection with Christian churches; subjects of the Roman Empire heard other "gospels" too, official statements of political "good news"—so "good news" is the phrase we will use.

"Churches" we will call "assemblies"; Paul's term had for centuries been used for civic and military gatherings. When we speak of Paul's addressees in any one city, we shall generally speak of "the (one) assembly" there. This may be misleading. It may well be that disagreements over belief and practice—or just differences in background and nationality—had given rise in single cities to more than one group of Jesus' followers meeting in different places, even if all were accessible to Paul's instruction. We will often speak too of "Paul's converts," but need to bear in mind those converted by his assistants, allies—or rivals. When Paul writes to the area of Galatia he writes to *the assemblies* there; Galatians is a letter that was expected to circulate in one or more copies. Paul rounds off his letter to Rome with a series of greetings in which we may be able to trace the outlines of five or more assemblies in Rome, meeting separately. This would not have involved five or more buildings formally dedicated to worship. Historians have long thought that the early assemblies followed a practice of the synagogues and met in the houses of patrons; there were few or no buildings allocated to the business of an assembly alone. And the synagogues themselves? They will be "prayer houses" here, a Greek term used in the first century; we do well to be reminded that many of Paul's converts were breaking their links with the prayerful, faithful communities of a flourishing Judaism. We will speak of Paul the "emissary," an agent sent out on a grand task, rather than Paul the familiar and sainted "apostle."

The word for "law," *nomos,* is a common Greek word for custom and habitual practice as well as for formal statutes. The definite article is not used in Greek quite as in English. *Nomos,* with no article, can mean "a custom" or "the custom," "a law" or "the law." With the article the reference is likely to be quite specific: "the custom" or "the law we are speaking of," almost "that custom" or "that law." Paul speaks of *nomos* sometimes without and sometimes with the article. Is he drawing a distinction between accepted practice settled into law, on the one hand, and the Jewish Law of the Old Order, on the other? The question has rumbled on now for over seventeen hundred years. To avoid losing a possible clue to the word's meaning in any one case, we will be giving a visual hint to readers like the verbal hint Paul may have been giving to his listeners: when Paul uses the article, *nomos* will be translated as "the Law"; when he does not, as "law" or "the law."

The same principle will be applied for *pneuma,* normally translated as "spirit." The translation is misleading, but is not easy to avoid. The Greek word behind it means "wind" and "breath" and so the being-alive that our breathing represents. Now the wind is all around us and not only at the service of ourselves. This "breath," then, speaks of far more than just human life. Long before Paul, it had been adopted by philosophers to denote an invisible power that accounts for any and all life in living things; different thinkers had used it with widely different nuances. We never hear of "spirit" now outside a religious setting. I will be translating the word as "breath" where it does not have the definite article and "Breath" where it does, and must ask readers to bear with some clumsy translations of its adjective as "filled with the Breath" or "enlivened by the Breath."

And, finally, we hear that Jesus "rose" or "was raised" from the dead. Two quite different word stems provide the vocabulary for this. *Anisteemi* means "I set (something) up" or "I make (something) to stand up." Linked with this is the noun *anastasis,* "a raising up." This quickly became the Christian word for Jesus' resurrection. For God's raising

Jesus, however, Paul often uses the verb *egeiro,* "I wake up" or "I rouse." I will be keeping the distinction between "raising" and "rousing."

One change I have not made. For the blue expanse above us, we nowadays use "sky"; for the imagined home of the Anointed and his followers from past ages, we use "heaven." The same Greek word was used in the New Order for both. Yet it feels crude to refer over and over to "the kingdom of the sky" or "a journey to the sky." We would by our language itself be condemning, as a journey into fantasy, what the seers understood as a journey to the truth. The "sky" of our astronomers is not linked, as the vault of heaven once was, to the possibilities of knowledge and a precious route toward it. We will come in this book to value the horizons open to this old topography of knowledge. If we used "sky," we would be closing ourselves off from a whole realm of insight and imagination. We have found no other language yet in which to speak of the seers' themes; and we cannot understand Paul—and are immeasurably the poorer ourselves—if we have no language in which to speak of such themes at all.

FROM PAUL WE HAVE JUST A HANDFUL OF LETTERS, a few more than a hundred pages in all, but what a dense, difficult text each letter seems to be. "Paul," wrote Porphyry, a fierce critic of Christianity in the third century, "shows the ignorant person's habit of constantly contradicting himself, feverish in mind and weak in reasoning." We set out from home at each letter's start. Within a page we seem to have lost our bearings and our place on any map. Paul is conducting a dialogue about which we know nothing with people whose voices we never hear. By the time we reach the letter's end we barely know which road we are on or which town we have come to. In *The Gospel According to Paul* we will be reading each of Paul's major letters closely, and we will find within the letters themselves all the guidance we need to help us through their complexity.

From one viewpoint, therefore, my procedure in this book is very simple. I present the material of each letter with just the accents and emphases that make clear to modern readers the connections between its different parts. They are not the connections we nowadays listen for. If you have not ventured through a letter of Paul's before, I hope you will enjoy the action-packed journey on which he takes us. If you are in a library and hemmed in by books on Paul, I hope you will lay them aside and open your ears to the melodies and rhythms of the letters themselves. Paul is a Beethoven, not a Schoenberg. He wants his addressees, with no technical expertise or insiders' knowledge of their own, to follow his music; and we can.

The parts of every letter are marked out by Paul and tied together by a web of verbal and thematic links. You may find it odd that I pay them so much attention. When we survey Paul's theology, we are surely offered a view through the window of his letters onto a great landscape beyond. To concentrate on the shape of the letters themselves is, you may think, to focus our gaze on the window itself, its scratches, dust, and wrinkles. And so we can fail to see the real object of our attention: the landscape outside. Wrote the English poet George Herbert:

> A man that looks on glass,
>   On it may stay his eye;
> Or if he chooseth, through it pass,
>   And then the heaven espy.
>   *"The Elixir"*

Should we not pass through the glass to the heaven opened before us by Paul? I hope that my answer to such questions will become clear during the course of this book. Here are just two quick comments in advance. First, it is from the texture of Paul's letters that we can discover what he is trying to achieve, what he wants his letters to *do*. He has far more in mind than simply to instruct or inform his assemblies. Second, if Paul succeeds in his purpose, he will have shown his addressees the landscape beyond the glass. Or better still, they will be in that landscape for themselves. Paul is not inviting his addressees just to gaze at a distance from this side of the window upon the truth about the Anointed.

And finally, a note about this book itself. A book on Paul may do one of many things: it may tell a gripping story, analyze the letters, pose acerbic questions, or watch Paul's thought with gratitude and awe. Or it may do all four. The different parts of such a book will have different styles and tones. *The Gospel According to Paul* is such a book. I hope readers will enjoy the invitation to approach Paul, in a single book, from different viewpoints and with different questions in mind. The voice you are hearing throughout is the voice of an author pacing round Paul and reporting on the view we gain from every angle. I hope you will enjoy coming with me.

IN PAUL'S LETTERS WE ENCOUNTER a world both old and new. We must never pretend we can bridge the gap between Paul's day and our own, but there is much in common too. The concerns of our own time were the concerns of his: concerns about leadership and power, communities and their cohesion, new movements in an unsettled world, and the ways to knowledge and its limits.

Perhaps, after all, a bridge is not what we need to span the distance between us and him. Paul stands at the headwaters of a long tradition. Most of us—whether Christian or not—are still embarked on its river. We are not looking on from the bank, comparing the waters now with a far-distant source we cannot hope to see. Our own ship joined the river many miles upstream and has been part of its flow ever since. We are way downstream now, and the waters of its first springs can hardly be identified in the weight of the river that has amassed over two thousand years of life and teaching and culture. But within this Mississippi those headwaters are not lost. We are not cut off from them by thousands of years or miles. They set the river's direction at its source and still flow in every current around us. Their springs feed the river even now and add pressure to its flow. This makes the river more difficult to map as a critic, but as a mariner far easier to navigate.

The Gospel According to Paul is aimed at any readers who have ever looked back across the centuries and wondered what inspired this famous—and famously contentious—figure. I will be glad if such readers leave this book with a vivid sense of the driven, difficult person so well hidden behind the varnish of the churches' piety. This book is aimed too at any readers who wonder what influence Paul should really have today. Those readers will be fascinated just to discover how bold, poetic, and personal were Paul's strategies.

As with *The Four Witnesses,* however, so here: there may be readers keen as well to take the opportunity to discover for themselves what Paul summoned his audience to see. Readers can find here again a new *sort* of book—one that enables them to undergo for themselves, if they so wish, something of the transformation to which an author invited his addressees two thousand years ago. It is not helpful to be naïvely optimistic. We will, at this distance, more likely distort Paul's purpose than fulfill it. But in the attempt there may be the best opportunity we will ever have to understand that purpose for ourselves. Here is our chance to bring Paul and his letters to life.

This is a heartening task for those committed to study or to worship. But as important as any curriculum is the enjoyment to be had from Paul's letters. And this is not for students alone. If you cannot imagine taking Paul's letters on your next vacation or next flight, perhaps instead you will take *The Gospel According to Paul.* You will find here, in Paul himself, a man as gripping as any leader in the world today.

PART I

PARADISE
REGAINED

CHAPTER 1

"CAUGHT UP TO PARADISE"

In the beginning God created the heaven and the earth. And the earth was invisible and unformed. And darkness was over the deep. And the breath of God was borne above the water. And God said, "Let there be light." And there was light.

THE BEGINNING [GENESIS] 1:1-3, GREEK VERSION

"As I was going to Damascus, in the middle of the day on the road I saw from heaven a light shining around me with a brightness greater than the sun's."

THE MISSION [ACTS] 26:12-13

THE STORY OF THIS BOOK does not start with Paul's conversion or with Jesus' death. It opens at the start of all things in The Beginning when God spoke over the chaos on day one of creation and said, *"Let there be light."* This is not the light of sun or moon, created on the fourth day, but the light with which God dispelled the darkness at the very start of creation with his first word of command. For six days, says the Old Order, God created. And when he came to the sixth day he said, *"Let us make man—adam—in our image."* And *in his image* he created him (1:26–27). (The Hebrew word *adam* means "human being"; Hebrew has no capital letters.) Adam was the crown of creation. His heel, said rabbis, outshone the sun; far brighter still was his face. But Adam and Eve disobeyed God and were expelled from Paradise. At this Fall, said

17

the rabbis, Adam lost the glory of God, and only at the last times will
he recover it.

But humanity, once created in the likeness of God, did not lose that
image at the Fall. This likeness fueled the thought and visions of the
prophet and seer Ezekiel. Ezekiel· is granted a vision of the chariot-
throne of God. He writes cautiously of what he saw. At the heart of a
dazzling light he saw the likeness of a throne. Upon this throne he saw
the *likeness as the appearance of a human being*—or of *adam* (1:26). God
had made humankind in his own image and likeness; conversely, his
own image would have the appearance of humankind. Here was the
form in which a human, an *adam* on earth, could know just something
of God. This was not a specific, individual person to be recognized as
such—that thought would have been grotesque and tantamount to blasphemy—but, rather, the assurance that something of God is accessible
to human knowledge. For like knows like; and we who are made in the
image of God are offered just a glimpse in ourselves—however sullied
and distorted—of that image in which we are made.

Paul too, centuries later, was a visionary, trained in the ways of the
Jewish seers. He himself, he believed, was once taken up to the third
heaven, to Paradise. On such a journey a seer would be shown the
secrets of heaven; and as he drew nearer to the presence of God, the
seer would be transformed into the glory of the inhabitants of heaven.

But the journey is for us less important than the long training that
made it possible. This was an intense study of scripture and in particular
of the visions recorded by earlier seers. Visions, that is, of the court of
heaven and of the one seated on God's own throne who had the *likeness
as the appearance of adam*. Paul journeyed to Paradise years after his conversion. The training, however, that would eventually lead to that journey had already borne fruit on the road to Damascus—in the vision
that changed Paul's life.

ENTER THE FOLLOWERS OF JESUS. They were making grand claims for
their leader. This Jesus too had been a seer—and, as they would have it,
far more than a seer. It would be one thing for Jesus to be a human
who visited heaven and saw there the glory of God; quite another, to
be an inhabitant of heaven who had visited earth to unveil that glory
here among us. The first follows the tradition of unveilings familiar for

centuries; the second turns that tradition upside down. Jesus' followers were already, before Paul, developing the second claim out of the first. There had been angels enough, in the Old Order, who implemented God's will on earth and represented him. These could offer a template against which to measure Jesus and refine claims made for him. But what status had this Jesus now that he had gone or returned to his heavenly home? Jesus' following was increasingly confident that Jesus' status was far higher than the status of any agent or subordinate. These followers seemed close to seeing in their leader a second, human god. The greater these claims for Jesus became, the more appalled and angry the visionary Paul would be. A seer squares up to the followers of another seer. Their abhorrent error must be fought at every turn.

Unless those followers were right. Unless the seer Paul must abandon every expectation vested in *the appearance of adam* upon the throne—and see there the features of a particular individual Adam. Unless, more devastating still, the features were those of the false seer Jesus. Here is the core of the explosion in Paul's thought.

What happened, then, on the road to Damascus, when Paul was struck blind by a dazzling light and heard the voice of Jesus? This was no bolt from the blue. It was the result of many years' work. Intellect and imagination, nurtured and disciplined in the traditions of the seers, bore fruit in a single overwhelming insight. The premises and categories of the ancient traditions inherited by Paul had to be overturned. In defiance of all the conditions that made thinkable any thought of God, Paul was convinced that the one seated on the throne of God in a human likeness—was Jesus.

Jesus, condemned and crucified, was the image of God himself, untarnished in glory, the perfect and total disclosure of God's plan and faithfulness to that plan. And on the road to Damascus Paul saw this glory face-to-face. *God,* writes Paul, *who said "Light shall shine out of darkness" is the one who shone in our hearts, to bring about enlightenment, the knowledge of the glory of God in the face of Jesus Anointed* (2 Cor. 4:6).

At his conversion Paul saw the face of the Anointed—and recognized in its brilliance the light that shone at the start of creation when God said, *"Let there be light."* This brilliance was due to be seen again only at the time of God's final intervention in the history of his world. And on the road to Damascus it shone again, on Paul. So Jesus was not a blasphemer, killed as a blasphemer should be. His was the figure who sat upon the throne of God, the likeness of the glory of the Lord, unveiled at last to humankind. Adam himself had been restored to his former glory and once more outshone the sun. So the time of God's last intervention was at hand: as Adam had been restored, so all humanity, all creation was in the throes of restoration.

In Jesus, then, had been the ultimate self-disclosure of God. God had disclosed himself in an *act,* in the fulfillment of his promises and plan. The seers' visions had been linked with the Temple in Jerusalem and its sanctuary, the Holy of Holies. To enter the Holy of Holies was to enter the court of heaven. Only one person, once a year, went in, the high priest on the Day of Atonement with the blood of the atoning sacrifice. The Anointed descended from heaven; and as the atonement sacrifice he passed with his blood into the Holy of Holies and so returned to heaven. Atonement, central to Paul's thought, was inseparable from the rituals of the Temple.

How does this affect the followers whom Jesus' preachers will introduce to the mysteries of heaven? The Anointed has brought them in his atonement the purity they need if they are to encounter without death the purity of God. And so he can take them with him through the hanging that keeps the Holy of Holies from view and separates the world from the court of God. The descent of the Anointed to earth makes possible his followers' ascent to heaven. This is the movement by which Paul describes the mechanics of our deliverance.

God had revealed himself in the life and death of a single man, put to death by the enemies of God's people. It was an unruly life and a shameful death; what was unthinkable in principle was scandalous in detail. The disclosure was easily missed. But its sight required no travel to heaven. It needed the viewers only to open their eyes and see.

Such visions as Paul was trained for—rare, dangerous journeys for the privileged few—were redundant now. Most people had no hope of them; no one now needed them. The mysteries of heaven had been laid bare in the death and rising of Jesus. The glory of heaven shone in the transformation here and now of Jesus' followers.

All the images, categories, and language of Paul's training had been designed to prevent any such link between an individual and God from

being made. But the flow of thought was reversed. And all the mecha-
nisms that worked against such a link were now working in its favor.
Paul's thought could never be the same again.

AND HOW WAS ANYONE TO LEARN THIS MYSTERY? From preachers. But
words are a weak vehicle for such a truth as this. God had disclosed
himself in an individual. Paul recognized an individual on the throne of
God. And in an individual this disclosure would be offered to the
world. Paul the emissary, as he himself believed, re-presented Jesus. Not
in his words alone, but in his whole life and person. Jesus is the perfect
disclosure of God; Paul is the frail, partial disclosure of Jesus. For his
converts to see and understand this disclosure with all its implications
was for them to be transformed, gradually and imperfectly, into the
glory of the life of heaven.

Jesus' followers and their assemblies—they themselves were now
Holy of Holies, the site of God's presence on earth. Paul, then, makes
nothing of his own or others' visions. It is not the story of such journeys
that his converts need. They need only Paul himself: the good news,
which he brings in his own person. Here lies the route of their transformation. And when Paul himself cannot be present? Then he writes. He
writes letters designed to transform his addressees as in an easier world
his own presence would. We nowadays read Paul's letters to hear what
he says. We need as well to watch what he is setting out to *do*.

And so a community was born, a community of small assemblies
scattered across the eastern Mediterranean, founded and nurtured by
Paul. They were under constant threat. The gentile members were still
influenced by the pagan ways that had shaped their former lives. The
Jewish members—and some Gentiles too—still hankered after the
ancient and well-loved norms of Jewish life. Paul himself was a maverick. The mother assemblies in Jerusalem and Antioch came to distrust
his every move. If they could undermine him, they would. Some rival
preachers urged a fuller obedience of the Jewish Law; some spoke with
pride and allure of such heavenly visions as Paul had left behind.

Paul fought back. He was a father to his converts. He felt threatened
and insecure in their loyalty and love. Paul's converts needed him, he was
sure. And every page of his letters makes it clear he needed them too.

THE THIRD HEAVEN

Paul's experience on the road to Damascus was not a fluke; it grew from long training in an ancient tradition. If we want to investigate that tradition, Paul himself can give us the most vivid introduction to it. From his conversion in 33 C.E. we must fast-forward several years, to a far stranger journey that took Paul, he himself believed, much farther than Damascus. We must follow Paul on this journey to see with him his destination.

Paul was not alone in his visions and unveilings, but he knew how dangerous was the authority they gave to those who claimed them and the arrogance that followed it. Such visions had been, for him, a ladder he could climb and then discard. They had revealed to him their own redundancy. The Anointed would not be revealed to Paul's converts by visions of heaven, but by the person and preaching, here on earth, of Paul himself.

This Paul would have to defend himself, nonetheless, from other missionaries who laid claim to visions and boasted of the standing they gave. He tells, in his own defense, of his deepest experience, his journey to Paradise. It had been so strange that he does not even claim it as his own. We know from later texts of a convention that forbade the public discussion of such experiences; the convention may well have been observed in Paul's own day. More likely, he just finds it hard to account for the experience. Other seers too were confused over the nature of their journey and their apparent departure from the body, taken as they were where the body surely could not (and, according to any earth-bound witness, did not) go.

Paul's rivals wished to boast? Then he had to too. In 55 he says about himself:

Boasting is necessary. There is nothing to be gained by it, but I will come to visions and unveilings of the Lord. I know a person in Anointed, four-teen years ago—whether in the body I do not know, or out of the body I do not know, God knows—caught up, the person in question, as far as the third heaven. And I know the person in question—whether in the body or apart from the body I do not know, God knows—that he was

caught up to Paradise and heard uttered things unutterable, which it is not
permitted a person to speak.

2 CORINTHIANS 12:1–4

Nothing in what Paul describes—and nothing in the way he says it—would surprise another seer. What did Paul reach? The third heaven was in some traditions the highest of all; in others it was just the third heaven out of seven. In several texts it is the site of Paradise.

Paul gives a two-stage account. His visit to Paradise may have been a second ascent, but more likely it was the climax of the first. What will he have seen there? Paradise, in the seers' tradition, is the home of God. So it is the home as well of the knowledge that only the presence of God makes possible. No wonder the Temple, home of God on earth, bore as decoration the trees and cherubim of Paradise. This Paradise, the Temple, was the setting for the great rituals of the Day of Atonement. As God and humankind had once been "at one" in Eden, so on the Day of Atonement they were again.

It is no surprise, then, that in later rabbinic literature Paradise is the destination of the just after death, a place for God and humankind alike. Paul is clear that there is more to follow for the dead, when the final resurrection comes and the corpses are awakened at death's ultimate defeat, but this interim glory is enough. Paul has seen the reward of God's faithful after their death, and he will offer it to his converts in their lifetime—a part in the life of heaven.

It is worth wondering why Paul tells the Corinthians of this journey. At this stage in the letter he is describing his weaknesses, not his strengths. He may, then, be stressing the limits of his ascent. Perhaps he got only as far as—that is, to the entrance of—the third heaven. He will go on to say that he was given a thorn in the flesh *so that he should not be overelevated,* perhaps, that is, so that he should not ascend on his journey too high. But Paul knows how high a value the Corinthians put on such special disclosures. Rival leaders have reached the assembly and attracted a following. They are making grand claims for their own status as visionaries and for the authority it gives them. How is Paul to bring them down to size?

Paul is being belittled in Corinth for his earthbound preaching, belittled too as a puny figure who exposes himself to humiliation unworthy of the good news. Paul turns the tables deftly. He accounts first for his sufferings: as evidence of a brave resilience. And next, for the visions. He talks down the privilege that God has given him, but expands on his account of it. He leaves the Corinthians, by the end of the passage, in no doubt that he has heard in heaven itself such wonders as they could never hope to learn. These new leaders speak openly of what they have heard. What they have heard, then, is less deep a mystery than the unutterable truths that had been granted Paul himself.

In or out of the body, the third heaven, Paradise, things unutterable: Paul is steeped in the language of the seers. We will be hearing more of such journeys as his. For the moment we will listen to just one famous story, which will be enough to convey the hopes—and the dangers—involved in these experiments. Enough too to show how uncertain for outsiders was the diagnosis and description of such a strange experience. The story was first told in the second century C.E. It grew over time; its later editors enriched its meaning. We can be grateful that we can draw on Paul to help us trace, back into the first century C.E., the tradition in which this story belongs.

We are going to hear what four visionaries underwent in a "garden" and what the other stories that have reached us reveal about each of the four. They were not weird figures on the fringes of Judaism, even if one of them was a notorious heretic. They—and their successors who told their story—expected to study scripture, to apply it in their own lives and in their teaching, and within that study to dwell on Paradise, the garden of heaven. As Paul had before them.

FOUR RABBIS IN PARADISE, THE GARDEN OF HEAVEN

Let's follow, then, these four seers into the garden of heaven. In its earliest version, which may have been known in the second century, our story is sparely told. Four rabbis entered a garden. "One looked and died. One looked and was struck. One looked and cut the plants. One entered in peace and came out in peace." This is likely a parable, warning about the dangers to which the study of the Law can lead. The garden is the garden of scripture, planted and nurtured by God. Rabbis are intended to enter it, but they are not safe there. They can become obsessed with its most dangerous elements.

Later versions expand the story. Let us follow the fullest of these. In it the great Rabbi Akiba gives the others a command at the start, which sets the story's tone:

> Akiba said to the others, "When you approach the stones of pure marble, do not say "Water, water," for it is written, *Those who speak lies will not tarry in my presence* [Ps. 101:7]."

We will hear of this marble again, which could be mistaken for water. There were walls in the Temple in Jerusalem of blue and white marble, resembling the sea. As on earth, so in heaven: to approach the presence of God was to approach his sanctuary, past the Temple's outer glories to the Holy of Holies itself.

The rabbis are going to a garden. Where is it? It is the garden of Paradise. But not earth's Eden. The rabbis are traveling to the garden of God, the heavenly counterpart to the garden lost by Adam and Eve, for the earthly Eden is matched by the heavenly. And at the consummation of all things, according to the Bible, such an Eden will once more be accessible on earth. In the New Order's book of Unveiling [Revelation] its seer imagines the New Jerusalem, which will descend from heaven. At its center is the garden: *a river, bright as crystal, of the water of life . . . and on either bank a tree of life, bearing twelve crops a year, each giving its fruit once a month, and the leaves of the tree are for the healing of the nations. . . . [Here is] the throne of God and of the lamb, and his slaves will serve him and will see his face* (22:1–4). The seer of Unveiling sees fulfilled, before his eyes, the Old Order's greatest prophecies: the created order is restored, and Eden is regained, in which God and humankind can be in unity once more.

But the seers of our present story did not have Paradise to hand. They had to travel. There were dangers along its route, as we have seen, and dangers in its destination. We hear what happened to the first of the four:

> Simeon son of Azzai looked and died. About him scripture says, *Precious in the sight of the Lord is the death of his saints* [Ps. 116:15].

Other stories have reached us of all these seers. We should be wary of the names attached to wise sayings or exemplary tales, but it remains worthwhile to sketch such a portrait as the tradition makes possible. In another story of Akiba and Simeon, Akiba, the hero of the garden journey, was once told that fire had surrounded Simeon when Simeon was expounding scripture. Akiba drew the natural inference that Simeon had been expounding Ezekiel's great vision of God's throne and the figure upon it. But Simeon insisted that was not so; he had just been drawing connections between different parts of scripture, as any other rabbi might.

We should not take any such story quite at face value. It is told as a warning with a polemical edge: do not assume, as Akiba did, that the study of one—famously and dangerously appealing—passage is the source of special blessings. Fire had indeed blazed in the vision of Ezekiel, but there was fire also on Mt. Sinai when God gave the Law to Moses and through him to the people of Israel. What mattered was scripture as a whole and its loyal, disciplined interpretation.

Simeon died in the garden. What of the second seer?

The son of Zoma looked and was struck. About him scripture says, *Have you found honey? Eat what is enough for you, lest you be filled with it and vomit* [Prov. 25:16].

Another rabbi once met the son of Zoma. The son of Zoma was so preoccupied he did not greet his colleague. At last he explained that he had been meditating on the account of creation in The Beginning. We must imagine, for a moment, the blue of the sky as a solid vault keeping safely above us a sea, unimaginably vast, from which the rain is released and falls. *God said, Let there be a vault through the middle of the waters, and let it divide water from water. And it was so. And God made the vault, and divided the waters under the vault from the waters over the vault, and he called the vault heaven* (1:6–8). The son of Zoma said: "I was reflecting on the work of creation and there is only a width the width of a hand-breadth between the upper and the lower waters." How did he know? The Beginning speaks of the Breath of God *hovering* over the waters. In The Second Law [Deuteronomy] 32:11 we read of an eagle *hovering* over the nest of its young. A bird hovers only inches above its nest. This second use of the word clarifies the first. This was the distance between the two waters, those same few inches.

Here is an intense meditation on the greatest and most mysterious of all God's acts, creation itself. In one version of that story the son of Zoma says, "I was looking at the space between the waters," and in two others, "I was having a vision of the work of creation." This is the vision of a mystic, but it remains tightly disciplined. The son of Zoma—like Simeon in the story we heard above—is comparing passage with passage in the Old Order. These mystics were rabbis, trained in and loyal to rabbinic ways.

But such visions were dangerous. That rabbinic colleague of the son of Zoma went on to tell his pupils that the son of Zoma was "outside." Had his preoccupations driven him mad? Was he in ecstasy? Or had he moved in his speculation beyond the bounds of responsible study? Once more a warning is being sounded, for within a few days, we are told, the son of Zoma died.

And so to the third of the four:

Aher cut the plants. . . . About him scripture says, *Do not allow your mouth to bring your flesh into sin* [Eccl. 5:6].

Elisha son of Abuyah was a heretic. Instead of his name, rabbis used the cipher Aher, "Another," to refer to him. At the end of this book we shall hear more of the most notorious story about him, the story of his ascent to heaven, where he saw a figure on a throne and identified him as a second power in heaven, a power to rival God himself. Of the four who entered the garden, Another is the only one who actually damages the garden. Three of our four versions of the story gloss this odd account, that he "cut the plants." Another, they say, was infamous for discouraging children—young plants—from studying scripture. The story had more likely referred, in its early tellings, to speculation about the heavenly world that led Another into errors fatal to faith.

And so finally to Akiba:

Rabbi Akiba went up in peace and came down in peace. About him scripture says, *Draw me; we shall run after you* [Song of Sol. 1:4]. The ministering angels tried to push Rabbi Akiba away too, but the Holy One, blessed be He, said to them, "Leave this elder alone, for he is worthy to avail himself of my glory."

Akiba came down in peace. Out of the four rabbis, he is the only one of whom we do not hear, in the story's earliest version, that he "looked." He knew what to avoid. He faced, nonetheless, dangers enough. The angels try to prevent Akiba from reaching the presence of God; other seers too faced such obstruction and needed God's own intervention to secure their passage. But *the King,* continues the Song of Solomon, *has brought me into his chambers.* Akiba went to Paradise and survived.

So did Paul. In all these various stories of the four rabbis we are hearing of Paul's successors. These are seers who knew and traveled in their generation what Paul had known and traveled in his—the way to heaven. Their stories were told to warn others against their emulation. Paul told his story to make clear that the assembly in Corinth—and chiefly within it the new leaders with their grand claims—could not emulate him even if they wanted to. To these converts Paul declares his lack of strength by speaking of the extraordinary privileges granted to him. *If I do want to boast, I will not be without good sense, for I will be speaking the truth. But I refrain, in case anyone imputes to me more than they see in me or hear from me, and thanks to the extraordinary unveilings* (2 Cor. 12:6–7). Never has modesty admitted greater grounds for pride.

Rival preachers are belittling Paul. He is losing his influence over the Corinthians. His position in the assembly is fragile. But would anyone among the Corinthians dare denigrate a seer who has been to Paradise?

CHAPTER 2

RE-PRESENTING THE ANOINTED

PAUL THE SEER HAS LEARNED all there is to learn from journeys to heaven such as his own. And he offers to his converts, earthbound and untrained, all the blessings the journeys have brought him.

There were seers who simply saw, and there were seers who were transformed by what they saw. As they drew near to the glory of God, their own faces took on the glory before them. The faces of Paul's converts do likewise. *All of us,* says Paul, *gazing as in a mirror on the glory of the Lord, are being transformed into the same image, from glory into glory* (2 Cor. 3:18). Adam lost the glory of God at the Fall, but thanks to the Anointed we can now *boast in the hope of the glory of God* (Rom. 5:2). To see the glory of the Anointed is to become glorious in one's turn. Paul imparts to his converts and addressees, here and now, the first glow of that glory their faces will one day reflect from the glory of the Anointed himself, when they see him face-to-face. When present, Paul imparts this gift himself. When absent, he brings it through his letters. And so he does not simply talk of transformation; he sets out, when writing, to effect it.

In 2 Corinthians 4 Paul refers to his conversion and to the insight it unveiled to him. It is part of an argument that covers pages in Paul's letter. He is evoking, as he writes, the converts' lifelong movement from glory to glory that he is describing and fostering through half the letter.

The whole passage is shaped by a contrast with the great prophet Moses. Moses had caught a glimpse of the glory of God and his face had been suffused with glory. But his splendor faded. Paul too has seen the glory of God. He knows from the inside the tradition of visionary journeys to heaven. His own conversion had much in common with such journeys. It triggered a transformation in him whose glory, far from fading, is growing ever brighter. And it is a glory that his converts are called to share.

But how? There is more to the good news than is readily seen. Paul himself before his conversion had heard the good news often enough, but had fervently resisted it. Trained and experienced as he was in the ways of the seers, he was brought to grasp and accept the good news only by a vision, an unveiling of divine truth. What will bring others to grasp and accept this truth in their turn? Paul expects them to need an unveiling too. He must, through his own person and letters, effect in others what a vision from heaven effected in him. What did such transformation involve or achieve? And how, in detail, was Paul to effect it? When we ask these questions, we are looking for the key to all Paul's thought. When we find the answers, we will see the door swing open and walk into the mansion of his life and thought and imagination.

Paul's converts must have the knowledge that had previously been given to just a handful of seers. Those seers had relayed it to their followers—or as much of it as others were allowed to know, for the seers rarely relayed all that they had learned. Some knowledge had to remain secret until the last times.

And Paul is sure those last times have dawned. The great secret of God's plan has been disclosed. Not through some privileged intermediary to his privileged followers, but in the death and rising of Jesus.

PAUL'S LETTERS ARE SHAPED by the same insight that informs the gospels of Mark and John. The evangelists are working with a story. They present the most important of all knowledge as unveiled here on earth, in the person of a single human being. A warrior of heaven and his battles, once seen only in visions, has come down to earth to be seen by all. All the categories and expectations of unveiling are deployed—and turned upside down. No longer is any heavenly journey needed, for what would be seen in heaven now stands revealed on earth. So strange is the sight and so easily missed that Mark and John must work, in section after section, to make it possible for their addressees to see what is there to be seen. In this way their gospels themselves, the texts as read and heard, become the place of unveiling.

Most striking of all is the parallel between Paul's aims and John's. John aims to bring his readers through the new birth of which he speaks in and through their reading of the gospel. And Paul, in his letter to the Romans, sets out to heal the minds of his audience in the course of the letter's reception—and so to heal the community, the Body of the Anointed that has been riven by disputes. Paul and John were not alone in the needs and possibilities they saw for an insight and transformation that defied all normal forms of learning and life. The genius of Paul and John was in their attempt—their sustained, all-consuming attempt—to take their addressees into that insight and through that transformation in the reception of their texts themselves.

Paul is not telling the story of the Anointed; he is nurturing the Body of the Anointed—here on earth. His assemblies have no access to visions like Paul's. And they do not need them, for the emissary Paul re-presents the Anointed and they are themselves the Body of the Anointed. Paul will draw upon his sight of the throne in everything he writes, but he will not write about the sight itself. That is the ploy of his rivals, who trade openly upon the privilege and power to which such visions have entitled them. For Paul, the most important of all knowledge is unveiled here on earth in the assemblies themselves and in the emissary who founded them.

VISIONS LIKE THESE were not randomly given. They were nurtured by years of training from other seers, by the study of earlier visions, by physical discipline, and above all by the study of scripture. To be a visionary was not a hobby, to be taken up in the occasional spare moment after work. In the architecture of Paul's personality, we are not dealing here with an annex extraneous to the main shape of the building. This is the heart of the house, the central hallway that is our route—our only route—to every other room.

The geography and population of heaven provided the vocabulary in which the seers thought. The seers thought visually. They sought *knowledge* visually. Their imaginative world was as full and coherent as any conceptual world of our own today. Journeys to heaven, then, and visions there—is our Paul a mystic? The word is misleading, and I will be avoiding it. The terms "mystic," "mystical," and "mysticism" evoke a world of strange, esoteric experiences where normal forms of knowledge fade away. What is learned by the mystic is a paradox: the individual is so close to the divine that she or he can see, with the clarity of love utterly given and returned, that the divine is infinitely beyond our comprehension. In the secular world the mystic's mental processes are readily contrasted with our own. We engage in thought and reason to acquire knowledge. But mystics, as we see them from the outside, undertake strange training, prayer, and meditation to achieve an inexplicable and paradoxical union.

The effect of using any such contrast, as we read Paul, will be clear. If we call Paul a mystic, we seem to be denying that he argues rationally or offers "real" knowledge. Paul would have resisted the charge. Yes, he called upon the imagination of his converts to envisage his own visionary experience as the model for their transformation and that ongoing transformation in turn as the basis for their self-understanding. And he sought to describe and affect with that new understanding far more than their intellect. But his converts and those around them could fruitfully test Paul's claims no less than any other claim to truth. They could, and did, ask if Paul's thought as a whole was internally consistent, if it was refuted by any better established claims, and if it affected its believers as Paul said it did. However strange the knowledge Paul offered and the route he offered to it, both were open to effective public scrutiny. We might be tempted to claim Paul is drawing his converts into the dark, private world of the mystic, but he does so by drawing such mysticism out into the public and brightly lit world of his converts.

Paul himself traveled a route to this knowledge that was rare in his day, but was known to exist and was trusted by those who had never trodden it themselves. It is a route now so overgrown that we must be archaeologists to trace its path. It was suited to traffic so unfamiliar to us now that we are hard put to recognize in its remains the evidence of a road at all. But, as we have already seen from the story of the four rabbis in the garden, it was a well-mapped route that would be charted by generations of explorers. We close ourselves off from any hope of understanding Paul if we divide the roads of rational thought and mystical experience and then force Paul onto one and away from the other.

Paul addresses the same questions in the 50s that the gospel writers will face in the following decades: How to make this knowledge genuinely and deeply accessible? What Paul knows of Jesus on the throne is the basis for all that he believes about his good news and about himself. But it is not the vision that his converts need. Paul himself—and not the court of heaven—is to be the object of their gaze.

The Way to Heaven

It pleased God to unveil his son in me (Gal. 1:15–16). It is not Paul's words that will evoke the Anointed; Paul himself, in his own person, will re-present the Anointed to his audiences, converts, and addressees. Paul may have to write, but he knows before he starts that words are not enough.

Here is a standing for Paul higher than that of any other seer. We need to take as much care in its description as Paul took in its exercise, for it invested him with untrammeled authority—and could bring his assemblies dangerously close to idolatry. Paul is forever aware of the peril. *It is not ourselves that we preach, but Jesus Anointed as Lord, and ourselves as your slaves on account of Jesus* (2 Cor. 4:5).

Paul is re-presenting the Anointed. We need a term for Paul's role, and "re-presenting" is less misleading than any other. Exactly what Paul does and how, we shall come to see during the course of the book. But we are likely to ask straightaway: Are we really just speaking of an exceptionally vivid preaching? No, more than that. Does his lifestyle echo the death and rising of the Anointed? Yes, but more than that. Does he come armed with the power of the Anointed? With part of it, yes: he prophesies, heals, and speaks in tongues. But the power that matters is the power of the good news: *the power of God for deliverance* (Rom. 1:16). He brings it with him in his words and in his person; the challenge, threat, and promise of the good news are all active and at work in his own presence. Paul is inseparable from the good news he brings; and his good news—as he sees it—is inseparable from the Paul who brings it.

Yet the good news brings more than just challenge, threat, and promise. Converts were enfolded in a community. It offered all the security, friendship, esteem, and sense of belonging that converts jeopardized when they abandoned the faith of their forebears and their city. Paul will speak of himself as his converts' father (when he needs to instruct or upbraid them), as their brother (when he stands beside them with encouragement), even as their mother (when they are struggling with their new life's demands). He insists that they need him.

What authority this gives to Paul! To visit heaven and see its truths is to have an authority beyond all challenge. To offer converts, here and now, the blessings of heaven is to detach those converts from this world. It is to make them wholly dependent, in this isolation, upon their emissary the seer. Everything in Paul's presentation of himself and his good news articulates and strengthens his power.

Paul re-presents the Anointed to the communities. These communities in their turn re-present the Anointed to those within and around them. They are the Body of the Anointed. Does Paul have access to a single motif that will sum up for himself and his churches his own unparalleled role? Yes, he does.

Amid a grand sweep of prophecies promising Jerusalem that God's rescue is at hand, the prophet Isaiah had told of a Servant of God, commissioned to bring light to the nations. Rejected and despised by those around him, he bears their wrongdoings; ill-treated and killed, he makes many just by taking their guilt upon himself. The churches have naturally seen in this Servant the figure of Jesus. Paul himself draws over and over, when he speaks of Jesus, on Isaiah's promises to Jerusalem and on his Servant. He does so as well when he speaks of himself. Paul too, like the Servant, has been called from his mother's womb; he fears he has worked in vain; he is commissioned to bring good news to the nations. Paul too is the Servant of God.

Paul's converts themselves are more than observers in this strange drama. *"Israel,"* says Isaiah's God in one passage evoking the Servant, *"you are my slave, and in you I shall be glorified"* (49:3). A whole nation is involved in the suffering of the Servant and its effects. This is now the nation, Paul insists, that he himself is helping to bring into being: *the Israel of God* (Gal. 6:16), the followers of Jesus that include the assemblies of Paul himself. The assemblies themselves are the Servant of God.

The Anointed, Paul, and his assemblies may seem to be separate strands in God's plan for salvation, but they all bear the colors and textures of the Servant. And he, Paul himself, is the knot at which their threads are woven into one.

Presence and Absence

Paul re-presents the Anointed. What happens, then, when Paul is not present in person? He must write to evoke the unveiling that his presence would be. In every letter the tension lurks that the letter is a poor substitute for Paul's presence. Or is it? *His letters*, said the Corinthians, *are weighty; in person his presence is feeble and his speaking is contemptible* (2 Cor. 10:10). In a final irony, his letters may have turned out to be more effective than Paul's own presence. At this distance, we can believe it. The letters are incomparable roller-coasters of heartfelt care, whose expression twists and turns (and occasionally loses its way!) as Paul hurtles onward through his line of thought or exhortation. By the same token, and in a different image, the letters are not quarries from which we can mine a couple of handy doctrines. The letters are effectively poetry. Paul develops metaphors on a Shakespearean scale, for he has more to say than any prose can capture or convey. We must, then, hear each letter—each giant poem—as a whole.

We must hear each letter too in the setting of Paul himself and of the assemblies to whom he is writing. Paul is not offering the mellow thoughts of an armchair theologian; he is writing passionate, urgent letters to assemblies facing immediate decisions that will affect every aspect of their members' lives: at work, at home, in the market square. Paul is confronted by crisis after crisis and hammers his thoughts and words into the shape that will best address each danger in its turn. The assemblies, forming together just a tiny sect within Judaism, are growing into independent life. These communities, thinly scattered across the eastern empire, are under threat from the suspicion of imperial Rome, from opposition in the prayer houses, and from disagreements among and within themselves.

Each of Paul's letters has a character quite its own. His prose even has a different tone in the different letters as he writes in anger, concern, or open-hearted fondness. How much we lose, when sentences are extracted from their setting for special scrutiny. We must let the symphony play through and so see the part each passage plays in the driving, carefully orchestrated whole. Let's listen, very briefly, to the melodies of each letter, which we shall hear developed in the chapters to come.

Paul writes 1 Thessalonians to foster the assembly's faith, love, and hope. Each is fragile, and for reasons Paul addresses at length but never quite admits. His converts are wondering whether they can any longer trust their father who never visits them. Paul reminds them of his love for them; how can they have come to suspect him of false prophecy, of a wicked deceit? The grounds for the suspicion emerge: the Thessalonians are scared by deaths among them. Paul had not warned them of such danger. Should not Jesus have returned before such deaths to rescue his own followers from the looming wrath of God? Paul must strengthen their faith, love, and hope, but above all he must strengthen their trust in him and their loyalty to him.

Paul is less relaxed in 1 Thessalonians than he pretends to be, but he abandons all such delicacy when he writes to Galatia in palpable anger and fear. He has lost the most important argument of his life, with the leaders of the mother assemblies in Jerusalem and Antioch. He is on his own. And his converts are susceptible to the claims and demands of those who outrank and outmaneuver him. The letter is shaped by the danger presented, as Paul sees it, to his converts from those who are now telling them to be circumcised into the lineage of ancestral Judaism.

Paul redefines the whole lineage of faith and its proclamation, and so he redefines his converts themselves. As the Galatians change the way they see themselves, they will be freed to change themselves, to grow into the new definition that Paul holds out before them. Paul insists that he and the Galatians are answerable not to any human authority, but directly to God's. Paul is making a virtue out of necessity, a new stature out of his enforced isolation. It becomes a virtue for his converts too. They are the children of God, brothers and sisters of the Anointed, freed from all the demands of Jewish ancestry or formal adoption. Here we first see the grandeur of Paul's metaphors. Everywhere we look, there are vivid images of ancestry and parenthood.

In 1 Corinthians Paul explores the power of his own writing. The

Corinthians have grown confident in themselves and their right and capacity to assess their various missionaries. For at least some of the Corinthians, Paul does not come out on top. In a tour de force of encouragement, flattery, sarcasm, attack, and demand, Paul reduces his addressees to an infancy as extreme as the childishness he has deplored in them. By the time he issues a trenchant command in chapter 5, he, *absent in body but present in the Breath* (v. 3), can expect the Corinthians to have been shamed into obedience. And then he rebuilds what he has just demolished. He shows them how the judgments they have been getting so wrong should be made. Paul works to regenerate a community of "spiritual" converts reenlivened by the Breath during and by their hearing of the letter. Within the limits of their present life, the addressees can by the end of the letter be in practice what in principle they were at its start. Here, for the first time, Paul discovers how much he can effect within the course of a single letter. Far more than mere persuasion is under way.

In 2 Corinthians 1–9 we can hear echoes of the trouble Paul faced in Thessalonica. The Corinthians have come to distrust their ever absent teacher. Paul constructs a magisterial defense. He will bring the Corinthians to see that *we are the ground for your boasting just as you too are ours in the day of the Lord Jesus* (1:14) This program shapes all of chapters 1–9: shared pride and shared dependence are to bind the Corinthians to their Paul. The balance proves immensely hard to keep, for Paul, as he knows only too well, has an authority that the Corinthians can never match. They are his children and will forever be subject to their father's correction and teaching. Paul speaks of his weakness, but a weakness that imitates Jesus' weakness gives to Paul the strength of Jesus too. An enthralling relationship between Jesus, Paul, and the assemblies is unfolding before us.

Three times in 2 Corinthians 1–9 Paul refers to the Breath. First, to remind his converts of their baptism in the past. Second, to point out their ongoing transformation in their gaze upon the Anointed. And finally, to hold before them their destination, when they put on their robes of glory and all that is mortal about them will be swallowed up by life. Paul evokes their movement toward glory. And the letter itself is designed to take them along the road into the glory he speaks of.

To recover the trust of the Corinthians, Paul insists in the letter's first half on his own openness. How telling it is, then, that he keeps quiet until its second half about his other reason for writing: his need for their money, to support his great collection for Jerusalem. 1 Corinthians had battered his converts into submission; 2 Corinthians 1–9 maneuvers them into compliance. These letters from Paul are weapons of real power.

The greatest of Paul's surviving letters is his letter to the Romans. Paul sets out to heal the Romans' delinquency and the dissolution of their churches in and through their hearing of the letter itself. The good news is the power of God for deliverance—and here is that power in action, even as readers read or listeners hear. Paul is not expounding a system of doctrine; he is taking his audience of baptized Christians once more through the mystery of baptism, which alone can heal their deformation.

As they have not reckoned to keep God in their awareness, God himself has consigned them to an unreckoning mind, to do all kinds of wrong (Rom. 1:28). By using "they," not "you," Paul at first skirts round the divisions that are splitting the assembly in Rome. He soon homes in. In the course of the letter Paul will, he hopes, heal each recipient's mind, and so in turn each recipient as a whole—and so finally the community of which they are members. His technique is no more to duplicate baptism than Paul himself duplicates Jesus. We need subtler words to say what needs saying. Paul knows as much himself: he is again straining the limits of our normal forms of learning and growing, so as to unveil truths beyond such apprehension. At the center of the letter the Romans are to undergo again the death to death—and so the rising—that Paul has described. *Do you not know that all of us who have been baptized into Anointed Jesus have been baptized into his death? So we were buried together with him through that baptism, into that death, so that just as Anointed was raised from the dead through the glory of the father—so we too might walk in newness of life* (6:3–4). Here is the New Order's grandest account of baptism and its uncanny gift: the Breath of God.

The choice is stark—to be dead from wrongdoing or to be dead to it. Paul draws his addressees from the first to the second. It is a turbulent, personal process. Exactly halfway through the letter the inner person is ready to endorse God's law, but sees a rival law at work in the body battling against *the law of my mind*. The result is impasse. Once more Paul turns to the mind: *So then I myself serve the law of God with my mind—but with my flesh the law of wrongdoing* (7:22–25). All the powers God has given us have done their work of healing, powers of understanding and of will, but the law of wrongdoing still dominates the flesh. And so Paul comes to his climactic turn. The dominion of wrongdoing was unraveled at Jesus' death and rising. All is well. *There is therefore now no condemnation for those in Anointed Jesus. For the law of the Breath of life in Anointed Jesus has freed you from the law of wrongdoing and death* (8:1–2).

By the letter's end, therefore, the healing is to be complete: its recipients are to have risen to new life as members of the Anointed's reunited Body. We shall be asking, rather bluntly, what the cash value of this transformation was. How did it differ from the moral amendment that any teachers might wish to arouse in their followers? But first we need to hear Paul on his own terms, fitting into place the last pieces of his all-embracing jigsaw puzzle. *Stop fashioning yourselves as at one with the present age. Keep up your transformation in the renewal of your mind, so that you might reckon aright what is the will of God: what is good and well-pleasing and perfect* (12:2).

Paul's poetic instinct never deserts him. In writing to the Philippians, divided by a competitive suspicion, Paul once more offers his converts a new understanding of themselves. He redefines them in terms of the Anointed: as the Anointed moved through humility to glory, so the Philippians are moving now. Paul urges them to live as a commonwealth grounded in the example and the effects of Anointed Jesus, *who, being in the form of God . . . made himself empty; . . . and in fashion being found as a human he humbled himself, and was obedient unto death. Therefore God has highly exalted him and has given him the name above every name* (Phil. 2:6–9). We are listening here to a hymn, to words said or sung in assemblies within thirty years of Jesus' death. Yet again Paul's letter is a grand symphony. It will return in its last movement to these opening themes. The transformation of Jesus into his humble form will be followed by the transformation of his followers. *For us, our commonwealth is in heaven, from where we are waiting for a deliverer, the Lord Jesus Anointed, who will refashion our humble body to be conformed to his glorious body, in accordance with his power to subject everything, yes everything, to him* (3:20–21)—the power of which we have heard in that opening hymn, *that at the name of Jesus every knee should bow* (2:10). Paul speaks of transformation in the future, and so fosters transformation here and now.

We are seeing the re-presentation of Jesus, the life of heaven, and the transformation of converts within the course of the letter itself. To grasp Paul's purpose we need to set aside our normal categories and expectations. It should not surprise us, perhaps, that the character of his aims has been lost to view. In our generation it is ripe for rediscovery. Now again, in the West, we are faced with a range of religions, all of which compete for attention. Exotic routes to enlightenment and self-understanding are advertised. Traditional Christianity seems dry, formalized, and alien. It is time amid the hubbub to hear Paul's outlandish voice—as strange and exciting now as it was two thousand years ago.

CHAPTER 3

"MADE IN THE IMAGE OF GOD"

FROM GLORY TO GLORY

Three times Luke tells the story of Paul's conversion, once as a narrative and twice in speeches that he has Paul giving. But Luke is writing in the 80s, forty years or more after the event. Paul himself, in his surviving letters, does not tell the story of his own conversion, but we hear some of the hints he gives of it, to remind his converts of a story they had heard before. We will be looking back to the Old Order to hear more of the stories that shaped Paul's thought and experience. And we will glance at more of the descriptions from Paul's own time of experiences that might have been similar to his own. In each case we find just a point or two where Paul has found inspiration and where others of his culture found inspiration too.

In every one of these stories and descriptions we are offered a small piece in a large jigsaw puzzle. In the end we will never be able to complete the puzzle. We cannot hope to know as much about Paul's change as we would like to know, but we can learn enough to follow its consequences through all his letters. All the problems and challenges that Paul faced—and all the answers he gave—were shaped by one awesome insight to which, after years of thought, he finally came, if Luke is right, in a single blinding flash.

To understand Paul, we must furnish ourselves with some of the furniture of his mind. Or perhaps this picture is too static. We must let some of the trees grow in our minds that were deep-rooted in Paul's, the trees that defined his mental landscape and provided its landmarks, destinations, viewpoints, and shade. The trees, above all, that were growing. As we hear for ourselves the stories that were most important to Paul, we are not to import into our own mental landscape a concrete bunker of doctrines, rigid, known in advance, and alien to their new surroundings. We are to plant trees for ourselves and let them grow.

Some of these trees had already grown, long before Paul, from each other's roots. Adam was made in the image of God; the Wisdom of God was the image of God's goodness; the Law was the expression of Wisdom. Once Adam and Jesus were linked, Jesus was linked, as we shall see in the next few pages, with the whole root system from which these thoughts had sprung.

We will, of course, never recreate the mind of Paul in ourselves. Today we know that readers cannot step out of their own cultural setting, history, and character and into the shoes of an author to perceive the world exactly the way the author did. But we can try to imagine Paul's world and the way he saw it. We can dwell for ourselves on the hopes, concerns, and questions—and on the texts—that dominated his life. We just know that we must never claim too much for ourselves or our imaginings.

TALKING OF GOD

There is a danger, especially in churches, of invoking such texts and their terms and then explaining them by a pious paraphrase. We sink into the religious language of centuries past, a language that can speak coherently—and perhaps beautifully—of experiences that we can locate nowhere at all on the map of our own physical or conceptual world. A good sci-fi novelist can create a universe internally consistent, rich with detail, and apparently credible—but quite unlike our own. So too a historian of the New Order can use the language of its own time to speak of journeys to heaven, the glory of God, and shining faces. All of them, on their own terms, fit with each other and with the cosmology of that distant age. But we rarely confront these biblical stories with the understanding that we use, in our own everyday lives, of space, time, and their inhabitants. And until we do, we are doing the Bible no justice. We are insulating its stories from the world they were written to interpret and illumine—the world we live in day by day.

We are heirs of a long tradition that speaks of God in human terms. This is a God who speaks to his people and who acts with outstretched arm. We balk at such human features so often ascribed to God in the Old Order, for we ask our questions from the wrong angle. We wonder: How can God be like us? The Old Order sets up a quite different perspective. It insists, we are made in the likeness of God. *In the image of God God created him* (The Beginning [Genesis] 1:27). It is thanks to this likeness—and to this alone—that we have any hope of knowing anything of God. To speak of it we will need analogies and qualifications. But if we are to describe God at all, then it will be in terms of that image and likeness of God to which we have access and some hope of understanding, in terms, that is, of humankind.

We have heard of a supposed individual, *adam,* and of *adam,* humankind. The first Adam was created in the image of God. We are bound to link him with *the likeness as the appearance of adam* that Ezekiel saw upon the throne of God. At the Fall the one Adam—and so every *adam*—lost the glory he once enjoyed. But in heaven this remained the form in which God's glory took shape. It remained as well the form in which—and in which alone—a seer could hope to grasp anything of God.

The journey to heaven is a journey to the Holy of Holies and to Eden. This is no naïve travelogue. Before Paul ever wrote, the sectarians of Qumran, as we shall see, were clear that the Holy of Holies was the gathering of the community of the elect. Paul will take up the theme. The site of unveiling is not somewhere "out there"; it is in the assembly itself and its members. We will not learn about God by straining our eyes or minds toward the clouds, for we cannot find out first about God and then compare our discoveries with our knowledge of humankind. To find what can be found of God we should, Paul is sure, turn to God's own image, Jesus Anointed, and to those made in that image— humankind. To find what can be found about humankind we should turn to Adam. And so the spiral of this deepening knowledge wheels around. We turn to the old Adam, his glory gone, and so once more to the new Adam, God's own image on the throne.

It was, then, through human self-understanding that people might be brought to a knowledge of God, to a knowledge, first and foremost, that they were—they just *were*—in a relation to God. This could be denied or ignored as easily then as now. The Jewish philosopher Philo, Paul's contemporary, looked for ways to stir such recognition. He lamented the polytheism of the pagan world and its apparent craving for pleasure. The Old Order required a quite different standard. Philo expounds the insistence of Joseph's sons, *"We are all sons of one man, we are peaceful"* (The Beginning 42:11). They were, he says, lovers of peace inasmuch as they had enrolled themselves as children of one immortal father, the Man of God, who is the Word of the Eternal and so must be immortal himself. Philo returns later to the theme. He thinks of those who see gods and powers everywhere and who succumb to the philosophies of pleasure. What encouragement can he offer such pagans? They may not be ready to join those whom Moses calls the children of God. But there is an easier move they can make first: they can find in God's image instead the one father that they need to acknowledge. Philo lists some of the roles in which this image, the Word, can be known to them.

Philo is circling the mystery of God's Word, God's self-expression. He invokes all the categories within which pagans might catch a glimpse of the Word and of their own relation to it. Here will be the start of their journey into wisdom—when they recognize the Man according to the Image.

If there be any as yet unfit to be called children of God, let them be eager to take their ordered place according to the Word, his First-Born, the eldest of the angels, as it were their arch-angel [ruler of angels], being of many names. For he is called the Beginning and the Name of God and the Word and the Man according to the Image. . . . For if we are not yet ready to be thought of as children of God, yet we are of his invisible image, his most holy Word. For the Word is the eldest-born image of God.

ON THE CONFUSION OF TONGUES, 41, 145–46

If we are to understand Paul, we must follow this line of thought carefully. But in it there are palpable dangers. The glory of Adam seems to encourage a wild optimism, a proud confidence in human ability and stature that loses sight of God and our dependence on God for all that we are and have. Ezekiel's vision hints as well at particularities that we might now regret. *Adam* in The Beginning's first account of creation is a human being; in the second account—which includes the story of the Fall—Adam is specifically a man, over against Eve. Jesus in turn was male. How easy it was, in prayer houses and assemblies, to believe that men were made in the image of God and that women bore only a reflected glory, an image of the image. We might admire the richness and the care of Ezekiel's imagery, but they cannot disguise or counteract the dangers to which the imagery itself, ever since, has given rise.

WHEN PAUL WRITES TO THE CORINTHIANS of his journey to heaven he is not spinning a tale to give authority to teaching he claims to have learned there. On the contrary, he does not tell what the disclosures were at all; they were still, even in these last times, too secret to be divulged. He wants the Corinthians to know simply of the journey itself. It is time, then, to take such journeys more seriously and to discover, as best we can, how they came about. Time and again we will find in the seers a full and richly colored portrait of an experience just lightly sketched by Paul. Paul expected his assemblies to recognize his subject from a few deft strokes of the brush. The subject is strange to us now. Our eye must get used to Paul's style. We need to look back and forth from the seers' finished portraits to the sketch by Paul until the sketch makes sense, and with a completeness and unity we could never have expected to find.

This does not come naturally to us. We like to think of Paul as a modern man, as one of us. No wonder, then, that biblical scholarship in the twentieth century attempted to free the New Order from any dependence on a cosmology long since superseded by science. Some of these attempts were brilliant.

According to the most famous of all, Jesus himself and the New Order's authors had inherited a rich supply of poetry from the Old Order and had used it in the same way—as we ourselves use poetry. Jesus himself had stirred thunderous old texts into the darkest and most extravagant combinations: as threats, warnings, and scenarios that would urge the faithful on. But within decades this flood of hopes and fears was congealing into a diary of the last times. The metaphors of Jesus and his first followers, which had been fluid as a river and light as air, were already turning to concrete. What had been a rich universe of poetry became the rigid template for all cosmology and human history. Here, it now seemed, was a straightforward description of the past, present, and future world.

For centuries the description was credible, but science made great strides. To believe in the Bible's description of the world was to deny increasingly wide tracts of scientific thought. How could the churches remain both faithful to the Bible and open to the modern world? Scholars revisited the New Order. They found signs that Paul and John had already seen how easily misunderstood were those images that so enriched the very first assemblies. Paul and John, it emerged, had worked to counteract the danger. They had provided, with this poetry, its philosophical interpretation.

And clearly in the modern world we needed it. The fantasies of the New Order and of the seers were surely mere icing on the cake of any serious thought, scholars alleged. They were poetic, and in our world poetry is a luxury of the imagination, to be indulged in when the real business of life is done for the day. Paul must have reached all his serious insights in ways we could recognize as the ways of our own thinking. Paul, like other seers, might then have decorated his results and his route to them to make them more dramatic, compelling, attractive, or frightening. But such metaphors have nothing to tell us of the process of Paul's thought; they were simply the flourish with which he marked its grandest moments. At last, it seemed, thanks to modern scholarship, we could strip off the decoration and get back to the substance beneath.

Any such attempt is quite misguided. The metaphors most strange to us were the terms in which Paul thought his deepest thoughts. Paul made every move along this route within the terms and images of a heavenly vision. Within these terms he saw and recognized everything that was dangerous about the claim he finally came to, everything that a seer should know to resist. Within these terms the majesty of the claim and its consequences dawned upon him. Here is the language of Paul's thought, the images in which he makes his vital moves. We speak of images, for Paul is making his connections visually. These are not dispensable metaphors. Paul is not evading, with these images, serious thought or decorating it. They *are* his thought, thought just as subtle as any we can manage in our quite different style. And we cannot follow the moves in this thought unless we learn something of its language too.

The seers were not expected to offer themselves as blank sheets of paper on which disclosures could be written by God in any language or pattern. They were steeped in a tradition and followed it. Their journeys were the framework within which they could hope to receive divine disclosure. Without some such framework, the seers would have had no visual or verbal language in which to imagine or think or appropriate any supposed disclosures at all.

And in particular, the earliest assemblies and then Paul are seeing, thanks to this language, connections unimaginable before. Their insights reactivate the Old Order's images with a character they did not have before. Far from reducing his own dependence on the language of unveiling, Paul stretches that language to impart to his addressees an unveiling greater than any seen before. We must see fully what unveilings were offered to earlier seers in order to see the explosive connections Paul made between their elements and Jesus. We must hear the language used to describe those earlier unveilings in order to hear the contortions to which—quite deliberately—Paul subjected it.

Paul and the Beginning: "In Our Image and Likeness"

THE FIRST LIGHT

Most of this book (Chapters 13–27) will trace Paul's arguments, letter by letter. Only within their own setting can we do justice to their greatest passages, and only by an overview of each letter, from beginning to end, can we see the achievement, far greater still, of the letter as a whole. But in these first chapters we revisit the network of Paul's most important ideas. Once more we will look far back into the Old Order, for it is here, as have already seen, that we can find the strongest threads and the tightest knots that bind Paul's thought together. We need to tug at more such threads than we have yet touched on to see how far they reach into Paul's thought and how they are connected with its other strands.

We start where the Old Order starts, at the beginning of all things:

> *In the beginning God created the heavens and the earth. And the earth was wildness and waste; and darkness was over the deep. And an almighty wind moved over the waters. And God said, "Let there be light." And there was light.*
>
> THE BEGINNING 1:1–3

This light is not the light of sun or moon. Their light will follow on day four of creation. No, the light of day one was immeasurably brighter than the sun's. The light of day one, said later rabbis, was made from God's own splendor, from the light of his garment. God commanded, we hear from one seer, that a ray of light be brought forth from his treasuries, so that his works might then appear. This great light would have enabled humankind to see the world at a glance, from one end to the other. It was hidden from the world at the Fall. Will it ever shine again? Yes. God's Anointed, we hear, will have the prophet Elijah blow on a trumpet to inaugurate his reign on earth, and then at last that first light will reappear.

Paul knows the significance of different lights: the light of day four and the light of day one with its source in the light of God himself. To understand Paul's conversion we must understand which light he believed had blinded him at his conversion. *The God who said "Light shall shine out of darkness" is the one who shone in our hearts, to bring about enlightenment, the knowledge of the glory of God in the face of Jesus Anointed* (2 Cor. 4:6). This sentence sparkles with connections. Paul saw *the glory of God in the face of Jesus Anointed.* The sight is important for the insight it gives him: God is shining *in our hearts, to bring about enlightenment.* And Paul knows what it took to bring about that enlightenment—an act of God as dramatic as creation itself, when God said, *"Light shall shine out of darkness."*

Paul is making the most of light and darkness here, of God's act that makes all knowledge possible and of mental darkness broken by a flash of insight. To describe what he has undergone, he hints at the grandest of claims: he is part of a new creation. From darkness to light, from the old creation to the new—this was a route his converts too would follow. They will need no such dazzling vision as Paul himself enjoyed. But in writing of such light, Paul is not exaggerating. For the seer himself, within the setting of a vision and its brilliance, there could be no mistake. To speak together of light and creation was to speak of day one. He had been blinded by that first light that shone in answer to God's command *"Let there be light."* This is the light that God hid from the world when Adam fell, light that will shine out again only at the world's great restoration. To see this light shine on earth is to know that the restoration has begun. To see in that light the features of Jesus is to know that Jesus was active on day one of God's creation, before the elements were fixed or Adam was created. Jesus was active before humankind ever came to be born and is active once more as God's agent at work on his new creation, here and now.

THE GLORY OF ADAM

God's creation continues. On the second day he creates the vault that separates the waters on earth from the waters above; the vault is called "heaven." On the third he draws together the seas and has the dry land appear. On the fourth come sun and moon. And so on until the sixth day:

> *And God said, "Let us make* adam *in our image, after our likeness. . . ." So God created* adam *in his image, in the image of God he created him; male and female he created them.*
> THE BEGINNING 1:26–27

The word used for God, *Elohim,* is plural in form. The story evokes a scene of king and courtiers together. *Our image* is the form that king and courtiers can be said to share, the physical, bodily form of the gods in God's council. With good reason, then, the story's Greek version translates *image* with the word used for statues of kings and gods, *eikon.* (Our "icon" stems from this word.) The same word is used in Greek literature for the likeness caught by a statue. A pagan epigram praised

Pheidias's famous statue of Zeus, king of the gods: "Either god came to earth from heaven to show you his image, Pheidias, or you have been there to see the god." So pervasive were such statues that the rabbis borrowed this Greek word, *eikon,* to describe them and created Hebrew and Aramaic forms of it for themselves. In the earliest surviving use of such a borrowed word for "statue" we hear: "As the statue is the image of the king, so is man the image of God." The rabbis were not embarrassed to speak in such physical terms.

Says a psalmist:

> *You have made man little less than God,*
> *and you crown him with glory and honor.*
> PSALM 8:5

No wonder, then, that Adam was a glorious figure. When Adam and Eve fell, according to one version of the story, Adam turned on Eve: "What have I done to you," he asked, "that you have deprived me of the glory of God?" In the world to come Adam's glory will be restored. "Your sorrow," promises God, "shall be turned into joy; and I will transform you to your former glory, and set you on the throne of your deceiver." When Adam and Eve had eaten the fruit of the tree of the knowledge of good and evil, *Look,* said God in warning, *the man has become like one of us* (The Beginning 3:22). In the last days, claimed rabbis, he will be like God indeed.

We will be looking later at the beliefs fostered at Qumran, the community that produced the Dead Sea Scrolls. We will need to ask: What fruition did the sectarians believe they enjoyed already? And what were they still waiting for? In the *Community Rule* are the instructions that the master of the community is to give about the battle between good and evil fought out in every human. The struggle is unremitting.

> But in the mysteries of God's understanding and in his glorious wisdom, God has ordained an end for injustice, and at the time of the visitation will destroy it for ever. . . . God will then purify every deed of man with his truth; he will refine for himself the human frame.

The perspective shifts, and the master himself and his role in the instruction of others are now in mind:

> He shall be plunged into the breath of purification, that he may instruct the upright in the knowledge of the Most High. . . . For God has chosen them for an everlasting Order; and all the glory of adam shall be theirs.
>
> 1QS 4.22-23

Which *adam*'s glory is in mind here, the glory of the individual Adam or the glory for which all humankind was made? The two converge. The glory that was Adam's at the start shall be the glory of his children, of all *adam,* at the end. And is this end yet to come? Or does the community at Qumran bear the glory of Adam already? One of the hymns from Qumran draws freely on the imagery of Eden and of the cherubim who have guarded its entrance since the Fall. Against the unfaithful these cherubim bar the way; but the faithful are admitted, to live once more the life of Eden.

> The bud of the shoot of holiness of the plant of truth was hidden and was not esteemed. You hedged in its fruit, O God, with the mystery of mighty heroes and of breaths of holiness and of the whirling flame of fire. No one shall approach the wellspring of life or bear fruit with the plant of heaven who seeing has not discerned and considering has not believed in the fountain of life. . . . The fruitful plant by the everlasting spring shall be an Eden of glory bearing fruits of life.
>
> 1QH 16.10-14, 20

Eden, as we have seen, was represented in the design and decoration of the Temple. But the Qumranites were divorced from the Temple in Jerusalem and from its rituals. They needed, then, a sacred space—a Temple and an Eden—of their own.

Moses sang, at the Escape from Egypt, that God would plant his people in the mountain of his inheritance, in the sanctuary that the Lord would build, the sanctuary of God, *miqdash adonay* (The Escape

[Exodus] 15:17). To take the Temple's place the sectarians of Qumran need no sacred building. They have themselves, for God himself has planted them as his garden. God "commanded that a sanctuary of adam [*miqdash adam*] be built for himself, that there they may send up, like the smoke of incense, the works of the Law" (4Q174 1.6). The community itself is the sanctuary, a sanctuary of *adam* in its members, their hierarchy, their communal life and discipline.

The sectarians are keeping in their terms the balance that Paul must keep in his. So much is already fulfilled, but there is more to come. All that is done here and now—even God's instruction for the purified rituals of the Temple—is only an interim measure, "until the day of creation when I shall create my sanctuary, establishing it for myself for all time" (11QT^a 29.9–10).

The Adam of old, the Adam to come, and the *adam* that we are ourselves—Paul knows the theme well. But for his greatest hopes he does not just look backward, to the first Adam. Paul looks for far more than restoration. The glory of the second Adam, he insists, shall far outshine the glory of the first.

> *For since death came in through man, so through man the rising of the dead. For just as in Adam all die, just so in Anointed shall all be made alive. . . . The first man, adam, was made into a living soul—but the second man into a life-giving breath. . . . The first man was from the earth, made of dust; the second man is from heaven. As the one was who was of dust, so too are those who are of dust. And as the one is who is heavenly, so are those who are heavenly. And as we have borne the image of the man of dust, so shall we bear the image of the man of heaven.*

1 CORINTHIANS 15:21–22, 45–49

Humankind has meanwhile lost the glory of God. Do we, in any degree at all, still bear his image? God decided: *Let us make adam in our image, after our likeness.* Long after the expulsion from Eden, Adam and Eve had a son, Seth. *In the day*, we hear, *that God created Adam, in the likeness of God he made him. . . . And Adam lived a hundred and thirty years, and had a son in his likeness, after his image* (The Beginning 5:1, 3). Seth is made in the image of his father, Adam, but a genuine continuity is being stressed, from God through Adam to his descendants. No wonder God can later tell Noah why murder must still, in a generation that lived long after the Fall, be punished with death: *for in the image of God he made man* (The Beginning 9:6).

The image of God is sullied in us. But in the likeness that survives there lies a crucial possibility that would otherwise be closed to humankind. Here is the condition that makes it possible for *us* to know anything of God, and that makes it possible for anything of *God* to be known by us.

WISDOM: THE IMAGE OF GOD'S GOODNESS

Where else can God's work be seen? First, in his creation. The created order is the fruit of God's wisdom, of his care and carefulness, his plan and its execution. This order underlies both the natural and the human world—all that is in, among, and around us. If only we would recognize and grasp the work of this creative and ordering wisdom for what it is! Says Wisdom herself in the book of Proverbs:

> *The Lord created me for his works, the first of his ways,*
> *before the aeons he established me, in the beginning.*
> *When he was preparing the heavens, I was there with him,*
> *and when he was making strong the foundations of the earth.*
> PROVERBS 8:22–23, GREEK VERSION

"Wisdom is a reflection of eternal light," we read in the Wisdom of Solomon, from the first century B.C.E., "an unspotted mirror of the working of God and an image of his goodness" (7:26). But Paul is clear that Jesus is the image of God. He is the form in which God can be known. What can he be, then, except the wisdom through which God created the world? Paul insists to the Corinthians:

> *For us there is one God, the father,*
> *from whom are all things and we to him.*

Paul echoes the great Jewish prayer *Hear, O Israel, the Lord our God is one Lord.* Paul's motto would appeal to a good many Gentiles too who looked beyond the pagan pantheon to a single supreme god. But Paul's thought of creation leads him on:

> *and one Lord, Jesus Anointed,*
> *through whom are all things and through him—ourselves.*
>   1 CORINTHIANS 8:6

Here in the Anointed is the Wisdom of God, in and through which God ordered the light of creation to blaze.

WISDOM AND THE LAW

And how can God's work in creation be seen for what it is? Our insight is clouded by pride and wrongdoing and a delusion of independence from God. We need to cultivate our understanding. We too need care and carefulness, a plan and its disciplined execution. In a word, we need wisdom. And we can have it. We can grasp something of the wisdom of God because we have been offered a wisdom of our own. It is the wisdom that befits the creatures made in God's image, a wisdom imparted by the Wisdom of God. Here too we can see something of God; the medium of our understanding is itself informed by the object of our understanding.

This is not won by mere meditation. It is a practical, lived-out understanding. In the book of Proverbs Wisdom appeals to the readers:

> *It is you, all people, I am calling,*
> *and sending out my voice to all humanity.*
>   PROVERBS 8:4

Wisdom proclaims that she speaks the truth: there is nothing false or crooked here. She is more precious than jewels or the finest gold. She hates arrogance and lies. Hers are good counsel, safety, prudence, and strength. By her, kings rule the earth. She loves those who love her, and whoever searches for her will find her. Here is the source of the proverbs—the maxims for private and civic life—that make up the main part of the book.

But has God given us any guidance through which to win the wisdom that he wishes for us? To Israel, his own people, he has entrusted the Law. This is not just a set of commandments, but the basis on which all creation is sustained. In the Law God's Wisdom comes to expression; in their obedience to the Law the Jews live out the life to which that Wisdom summons them. In the book of Sirach, Wisdom says:

> "Come to me, you who desire me,
>   and eat your fill of my produce. . . .
> Those who eat me shall hunger for more,
>   and those who drink me will thirst for more."

Then comes the crucial explanation:

> All this is the book of the order of the Most High God,
>   the law which Moses commanded us
> as an inheritance for the prayer houses of Israel.
>
> WISDOM OF SIRA'S SON [SIRACH] 24:19-23

But it is the Anointed, Paul insists, who has unveiled the Wisdom of God. What role, then, did Paul see for the Jewish Law—among Jews or among Gentiles—in the new creation he proclaimed? If the Anointed in his death and rising had unveiled the Wisdom of God to all humanity, was there any longer a call for that Wisdom's earlier disclosure in the Law? Why was there any need to look beyond the Anointed himself? Was the Law now rendered redundant?

The vast majority of Jews still relied on the blessings offered by the Law. Jesus remained for them a criminal of no significance. How, then, would God bring to fruition the promises he had given his people the Jews? Here are questions that will agonize Paul throughout his missionary life. And his circuitous, tortured answers have agonized his readers ever since. We will hear of them again. At stake in the good news was God's loyalty to his own people—the justness of the God who had given the Law to his people, imposed its observance, and promised its blessings.

At stake was Paul's loyalty to that same people too, his own nation, the people who would not accept his good news. Says Paul, with sad intensity:

> *I tell the truth in Anointed, I do not lie, my conscience bears me witness in the holy breath, that my sorrow is great and my pain is unremitting in my heart. For I have prayed to be accursed, I myself, cast out from the Anointed on behalf of my brothers in the flesh. They are Israelites, theirs are the sonship and the glory and the Orders and the possession of the Law and the service of God and the promises, theirs are the fathers and from them is the Anointed, as far as mortal flesh is concerned.*
> ROMANS 9:1-5

So RICH AND VARIOUS and interconnected are the elements of Paul's blinding insight. How much this unveiling must portend. We have heard already of the primordial light that blazed at day one. If that light is once more blazing over the earth, then the promised time of Israel's deliverance has surely dawned. This is the time foreseen by Isaiah when all the Gentiles will acknowledge Israel's God and pay tribute to Jerusalem. They will acknowledge God's Anointed too—the image, Paul now sees, in which God can be known to all humankind. This second Adam, his glory far greater than the glory of the first, is the pattern for all humanity, Jews and Gentiles alike.

All parts of the jigsaw puzzle fit. Jesus far exceeds any hopes Paul had inherited for the Anointed. The light from the throne that blazed round Paul was the primordial light that launched all creation. The Wisdom at its heart was the wisdom that shaped all creation. All humanity, all creation is caught up in the movement. *Creation itself will be freed from the slavery of destruction into the freedom of the glory of the children of God* (Rom. 8:21).

Paul is a giant on the shoulders of giants—of the prophets Isaiah and Ezekiel and of the seers whose thought was shaped by these prophets' visions. We will understand Paul's movements when we have traced theirs. For a few pages, then, we follow where Isaiah and Ezekiel have led; they take us straight to the holiest place on earth, to the Temple in Jerusalem.

PART II

PAUL AND THE PROPHETS

CHAPTER 4

PAUL AND ISAIAH: "HERE AM I! SEND ME"

THE TEMPLE IN JERUSALEM

Paul writes to the Corinthians, *You are the sanctuary of God* (1 Cor. 3:16). What of the sanctuary in Jerusalem, the Holy of Holies that his converts replaced? Paul never forgets the Temple in Jerusalem. Its sanctity and rituals shape his good news from the foundations up. And in the Holy of Holies, the sanctuary itself, lay inspiration for all seers and their journeys, for the sanctuary was Paradise, at once in heaven and on earth. It was the house of God, the court of heaven.

"There are ten degrees of holiness," we hear in the Mishnah, the collection of Temple laws and lore compiled a hundred and fifty years or more after the Temple's destruction:

> The land of Israel is holier than any other land. . . . The walled cities of Israel are still more holy. . . . Within the wall of Jerusalem is still more holy. . . . The Temple Mount is still more holy. . . . The rampart is still more holy. . . . The Courtyard of the Women is still more holy. . . . The Courtyard of the Israelites is still more holy. . . . The Courtyard of the Priests is still more holy. . . . Between the porch and the altar is still more holy. . . . The sanctuary is still more holy. . . . The Holy of Holies is still more holy,

for none may enter therein except only the High Priest on the
Day of Atonement at the time of the Temple service.

KELIM [VESSELS] 1:6–9

In Paul's day the Temple's buildings covered thirty-five acres on a
vast plateau, largely constructed, at the eastern edge of Jerusalem.
"Whoever swears by the temple," said Jesus, *"swears by him who lives in it"*
(Matt. 23:21). The Temple was the house of God. To approach closer to
God's presence than was proper or permitted was to risk death.

The degrees of holiness recorded in the Mishnah were marked out
in the design of the Temple itself. To draw nearer to the Holy of Holies
was to draw nearer to the center of the world, the mountain of God,
the source of the power that suppresses chaos and sustains all creation.
Gentiles were allowed only in the Temple's great courtyard to the south
of the sanctuary. This was a vast open area in which birds were sold for
sacrifice, animals checked, and money changed. A balustrade, four feet
high, gave due warning: "No Gentile is to enter within the next courtyard and the balustrade around the sanctuary. Whoever is caught will
have himself to blame for his subsequent death."

Up twenty feet and two flights of steps, past a high wall, was the
next courtyard, for Jewish women. It was closed by another wall, whose
balconies gave the women a view of the sacrifices performed by the
priests beyond. Next was the courtyard whose borders were reserved
for Jewish males. The central area of this court, up two more steps and
beyond a parapet, was the area for the priests alone.

Here was a vast bowl of water and the great altar, built of stone,
forty-eight feet square at its base and rising nine feet from the courtyard
itself. The sacrificial animals were killed in this courtyard to the north
of the altar; a ramp on the altar's south side led up from the courtyard to
the altar's flat top. Here the fire was always lit and those parts of the animals were burned that were consigned to God.

At the west end of the priests' court, up twelve more steps, was the
sanctuary itself, consisting of the Anteroom and the Holy of Holies.
The façade of the sanctuary, a hundred and fifty feet high and wide, was
sheathed with gold. It faced east and was dazzling in the morning sun.
We hear from the Jewish historian Josephus, writing around 75 C.E., of
the entrance to the sanctuary:

Before the doors of the Anteroom there was a hanging, of Babylonian tapestry, with embroidery of blue and fine linen, of scarlet also and purple, wrought with marvelous skill. This mixture of materials had a significance of its own. The hanging contained them as an image of all things. For in the scarlet, it seemed, was an allusion to fire, in the linen to earth, in the blue to the air and in the purple to the sea. In two cases the comparison lay in the color. In the linen and purple it lay in the material's origin; for one is produced by the earth and the other by the sea. On this tapestry was portrayed a panorama of the heavens.

THE JEWISH WAR 5.212-13

The altar of incense was kept in the Anteroom, which was entered by the officiating priests twice daily, for the rites of the morning and evening sacrifice.

A second hanging or veil protected the Holy of Holies itself. The room was a perfect cube. It was entered just once a year, on the Day of Atonement, by the high priest alone, first with incense, then with the blood of a bull, then with the blood of a goat. The rituals atoned for the contamination of the priests and the people, the holy place, and the altar itself. In the time of Solomon the altar was a chest whose cover— or lid over the cover—was the "mercy seat" on which the blood was sprinkled. By the time of Paul, however, the mercy seat had long since been lost. The Holy of Holies was empty.

THE TEMPLE AS A WHOLE represented all of heaven and earth. It was remembered, centuries later, that the blue and white marble of the Temple walls resembled the sea. No wonder Rabbi Akiba, before the four rabbis' journey to Paradise, had warned his companions, "When you approach the stones of pure marble, do not say 'Water, water.'" The great bowl in the priests' courtyard was actually known as "the sea." And the Anteroom? The rabbis related that to the earth. And the Holy of Holies to heaven itself.

In The Escape [Exodus] 25–31, Moses is commanded by God to build a mobile Dwelling for God; it is to accompany the people as they trek toward the Promised Land. The specifications for this Dwelling are closely linked with those of the Temple that will later be built in

Jerusalem. God issues his instructions in seven speeches to Moses. The commands of each speech match, in order, the work of one day in the story of creation. On the third day of creation God divided the land from the sea; in the third speech God lays down instructions for the Dwelling's great bowl, which in the Temple will be called "the sea." On the seventh day God rests; in the seventh speech God speaks of the Sabbath rest and its importance for Israel, *for in six days God created heaven and earth, and on the seventh day he rested* (The Escape 31:17). The construction of the Dwelling—and so of the Temple—represented the creation of all things; the Dwelling itself—and so the Temple—represented all that was created. And at its heart was the sanctuary, the innermost dwelling, beyond the vault of heaven, of God the Creator himself.

The materials and colors of the Temple's outer veil united all the elements; its decoration represented the vault of heaven. And so to pass beyond the veil was to pass from earth to heaven. It was to enter the court of God himself. And conversely, to imagine a journey to heaven, the seers drew on the imagery offered by the Temple, the imagery of a journey to the Holy of Holies.

The Jewish philosopher Philo knew this symbolism well. It provided the language he needed to unite Jewish thought with the philosophy of the Greeks. "The highest, and in the truest sense the holy Temple of God is, as we must believe, the whole universe. Its sanctuary is the most sacred part of all existence: heaven itself. Its votive ornaments are the stars, its priests the angels." Philo dwells on the inner veil, dividing the Anteroom from the Holy of Holies:

> In the universe, heaven is a palace of the highest sanctity, and earth is the outer region. This region is estimable in itself; but when it comes into comparison with ether, it is as far inferior to it as darkness is to light, night to day and mortal man to God. The furnishings of the Anteroom represent the realities of heaven as far as they can be apprehended by the senses. Things in the Holy of Holies beyond the second veil, in heaven itself, are invisible; they are accessible to the mind alone.
>
> *LIFE OF MOSES 2.194*

To enter the Holy of Holies in the Temple was to enter the court of God. As we read rabbinic stories of the Temple and of heaven, we are not to envisage two distinct places. The Holy of Holies was not a portal between one world and another, like C. S. Lewis's wardrobe that opened into Narnia. To pass through the great blue hanging before the Holy of Holies was in itself to pass through the vault of the sky, to leave behind the world of our space and time, and to enter heaven.

All the seeds of Paul's thought germinate in the sanctuary and its role. There the rituals of the Day of Atonement were enacted with blood and with God's "mercy seat" at their heart. When the Temple itself was defiled, Israel sought that atonement in the blood of faithful martyrs. In a vision of God's throne in the Holy of Holies Isaiah was called to be a prophet, and in a vision of the figure on that throne Paul himself was summoned in his turn.

Paul and the Prophet Isaiah: "A Light to the Nations"

"HERE AM I! SEND ME."

The prophet Isaiah tells of his vision in the Temple in Jerusalem:

> In the year that King Uzziah died [740 B.C.E.] I saw the Lord sitting upon a throne, high and lifted up; and his train filled the Temple [or in the Greek version: the house was full of his glory]. Above him stood the seraphim; each had six wings: with two he covered his face, and with two he covered his feet, and with two he flew.
>
> ISAIAH 6:1–2

Seraphim are "burning ones"; the word is used elsewhere of dragons. The seraphim guarded the way to God's throne. A winged cobra, in Egyptian art, frequently protects the king. Isaiah continues:

> And one seraph called to another and said:

> *"Holy, holy, holy is the Lord God of hosts;*
> *The whole earth is full of his glory."*

> *And the foundations of the threshold shook at the voice of him who*
> *called, and the house was filled with smoke.*
>   ISAIAH 6:3–4

The altar of incense was in the Anteroom, outside the veil that kept the Holy of Holies hidden. When the offerings were taken through that inner veil on the Day of Atonement, the priest was to ensure that the cloud of incense hid the mercy seat, so that he did not see what human eyes should not see and incur death (The Laws of Ritual [Leviticus] 16:13). Isaiah is well aware of the penalty:

> *And I said, "Woe is me! For I am lost, for I am a man of unclean lips,*
> *and I dwell in the midst of a people of unclean lips; for my eyes have seen*
> *the king, the Lord God of armies!"*
>   ISAIAH 6:5

Isaiah has seen God. Later writings in the Old Order show deep suspicion of such claims. According to the Hebrew original of The Escape, *Moses, Aaron . . . and seventy of the elders of Israel went up* Mt. Sinai to confirm that Israel accepted God's Law, *and they saw the God of Israel. And under his feet there was a paved work of sapphires, as clear as heaven. And God laid not his hand upon them; they saw God, and ate and drank* (24:10–11). The Greek translators could not countenance this. *They saw the place,* reads the Greek version, *where stood the God of Israel . . . . And not one of the chosen ones of Israel perished; and they were seen in the place of God and ate and drank.*

What can be seen of God? What can be known? And who can see and know it? For the New Order these were the most central questions of all, for God had unveiled in Jesus what had never been seen or known of God before. How was it to be apprehended in principle— and in practice? God had not offered this unveiling with a roll of thunder or a national triumph, but in a life that stumbled to a shameful end. The disclosure could all too easily be missed.

Isaiah continues. Paul had good reason to dwell on what follows.

*Then one of the seraphim flew to me, having in his hand a burning coal
which he had taken with tongs from the altar* [in the Anteroom]. *And
he touched my mouth, and said, "Look, this has touched your lips; your
guilt is taken away, and your wrongdoing is forgiven." And I heard the
voice of the Lord saying, "Whom shall I send, and who will go for us?"
Then I said, "Here am I! Send me."*

ISAIAH 6:6–8

ISAIAH WAS WARNED that those to whom he preached would not
believe him. The prophet knew the sorrow that the early emissaries
would come to know in their turn. His message would be rejected, and
so would theirs. All four gospels invoke this vision of Isaiah. When
John comes to the end of his story of Jesus' public teaching and of the
signs he wrought, John steps in with an author's comment. The people
had seen so many signs but did not have faith in Jesus. John says:

For this reason they could not have faith, as Isaiah said:

> *"He has blinded their eyes, and hardened their heart,
> so they should not see with their eyes
> or understand with their heart and turn—
> and I will heal them."*

*Isaiah said this because he saw his glory and it was about him that he
spoke.*

JOHN 12:39–41, ADAPTING ISAIAH 6:10

John is quite clear. Isaiah, writing centuries before Jesus was born, saw
his glory, the glory, that is, of Jesus. Isaiah was speaking about *him,* that is,
about Jesus. For John, Isaiah's great vision of the Lord upon the throne
was a vision of the Anointed. Paul's great insight was not Paul's alone.

THE HOLY OF HOLIES: OLD AND NEW

Isaiah's call, as he describes it, was a sight of the Lord in the Holy of
Holies. The significance of the sanctuary was known in the first century:

"This vision," wrote the Jewish philosopher Philo, "raised and lifted up the prophet Isaiah"—to the court of heaven. Just as significant is the context evoked by the vision, for to be in the Holy of Holies was to be the high priest on the Day of Atonement. This is not to claim that Isaiah was ever high priest or that he was called to be a prophet during the ritual of Atonement. What mattered was the ritual setting that his account implied. No reader could ignore it. The followers of Jesus, before Paul ever joined them, already spoke of Jesus' role in atonement. How did this role relate to the great ritual of Atonement and to the access to God that the ritual made possible?

Paul's letters give hints of his heritage. We will be hearing of Stephen, active in Jerusalem among Jesus' followers, and of his circle of liberal Greek-speaking Jews. Stephen was martyred in Jerusalem. Some members of his circle, Luke tells us, then made for Antioch and began to preach to Gentiles there. It is to Antioch that Barnabas will take Paul after Paul's conversion; and Paul will first preach the good news under the leadership of Barnabas as an emissary of Antioch's assembly. Paul, then, would have come under the influence of the beliefs evolving there, and we can likely trace, behind some of Paul's grandest statements, formulas current in Antioch when he arrived.

In the good news, writes Paul at the start of his letter to the Romans, *the justness of God is being unveiled, from faith to faith* (1:17). But the anger of God is being unveiled too, for Jews and Gentiles deny themselves the knowledge of God that is available. They can even spin themselves an excuse—an excuse that some had ascribed to Paul himself—that God would be unjust to punish them for what they do. And the Law? It can do no more than reveal this delinquency. The letter to the Romans, in its first few pages, seems to be leading us toward despair.

Into this scene of dereliction breaks a fanfare of hope. All the plangent themes of Paul's letter so far are reprised in a major key. In the passage below, I have kept intact Paul's top-heavy prose. It has suggested to many scholars that Paul is quoting—and extending—a formula that he has inherited, probably from Antioch, and that he expects the Romans to know. I have put this supposed formula in quotation marks. It contains several words that we do not hear again from Paul, not least of which is a term translated "mercy seat." In the principal Greek version of the Old Order, this is most often used for the cover on the throne in the ancient Holy of Holies, but it can refer to other objects too. Four times in one passage of Ezekiel it designates part of the stone platform that would support the great altar in the new Temple's courtyard, in front of the Anteroom and Holy of Holies; twice in another Greek version it refers to Noah's ark. Did Paul or his predecessors have the throne itself in mind? Or a more general "means to secure God's favor and protection"?

A pagan inscription from the Greek island of Cos reminds us how much cultic language the early assemblies shared with their pagan neighbors. In it are terms the churches still know well today: "deliverance" or "salvation"; "son of God"; and our present term, a "means to secure God's favor." In this pagan context the word cannot suggest the Jerusalem Temple or its furniture. The inscription reads: "The people (dedicated a gift) to the gods as a means to secure their favor for the deliverance [salvation] of the emperor Caesar, son of god, Augustus." Paul certainly knew of the mercy seat in Jerusalem; so had Stephen and his allies there. What Paul's Roman addressees, most of them Gentiles, would have made of the grand formula Paul uses is hard to say.

Paul is moving us from despair to hope, from wrongdoing to deliverance. He writes:

> But now without the law the justness of God stands revealed, to which the Law and the prophets bear witness, the justness of God, that is, through Jesus Anointed's faith for all those who have faith. For there is no difference; for all have done wrong and fall short of the glory of God, being held just freely by his grace through the redemption that is in Anointed Jesus; whom
>
> > "God has set forth as the [or a] mercy seat"—through faith—"in his blood
> > for the manifestation of his justness
> > > on account of the remission of former wrongdoings
> > > > in the forbearance of God,"
> > toward the manifestation of his justness
> > > at the present vital moment,
> > > > for him to be just and to hold just those dependent on Jesus' faith.
>
> ROMANS 3:21-26

The high priest in Jerusalem conducted his ritual hidden from view in a Holy of Holies from which the mercy seat itself had long since disappeared. God has now presented Jesus himself as both the place of ritual and the blood of its sacrifice. (Paul will think of himself, when writing to the Philippians, as both an element in the sacrifice and its minister.) Perhaps the formula acknowledged that the Temple's sacrifices had been valid and the former wrongdoings remitted thanks to them; far more effective, then, had been the sacrifice of Jesus. Or perhaps it claimed God in his forbearance had been holding back from punishment, knowing that Jesus' sacrifice would effect the remission that the old sacrifices could not. Either way, the Temple is no longer the nodal point at which the relation between God and his people is solemnized.

THE MERCY SEAT: OLD AND NEW

God has set forth Jesus Anointed *as the* [or *a*] *mercy seat—through faith—in his blood*. This is the most striking claim of all in this formula taken over by Paul. The role of the mercy seat is now taken by Jesus himself. We learn most about the Day of Atonement from the Mishnah, in which the Temple's rituals were codified long after its destruction in 70 C.E. According to the Mishnah, the high priest entered the Holy of Holies on the Day of Atonement three times: first with incense, then with the blood of a bullock, and finally with the blood of a he-goat. The bullock was sacrificed for the wrongdoings of the high priest, his family, and the other priests. The goat, according to The Laws of Ritual, was sacrificed for the wrongdoings of the whole people. But the emphasis in this part of the ritual is not on the forgiveness of the people; it is on the purification of the Temple itself from contamination by their wrongdoing. The Temple itself must be cleansed. The forgiveness of the people is chiefly effected by the later part of the Day of Atonement ritual, in which a second he-goat, the scapegoat, is sent from the Temple into the desert with a foreigner who will push the goat over a cliff, well away from the holy place. This goat bears the wrongdoings of the people, which in this way are taken out of the city.

For the forgiveness of the people, then, the image of the mercy seat and the blood in the Holy of Holies is oddly inapt. The Anointed has in this pre-Pauline formula a different role—to be himself a new Holy of Holies purified from all contamination by wrongdoing. He is himself the Temple that he purifies by his blood. Here, then, is the sanctuary of the last times. No wonder Paul will speak of the Corinthians, the Body of the Anointed, as the temple of God. The sectarians of Qumran were not the only people to be seeking a new place for the holiness of God, independent of the Temple in Jerusalem. *You are the sanctuary of God and the Breath of God dwells in you. . . . The sanctuary of God is holy, which you are* (1 Cor. 3:16–17).

When Paul writes to the Romans he makes the formula his own, expanded and set within this passage of triumph. He builds a sentence about the present to match the formula's sentence about the past. The passage started with the justness of God and it will end there too, above all, with the disclosure of this justness. It is no longer hidden behind the veil, no longer liable to the casuistry of those who ascribe a scandalous message to Paul. Wrongdoing had contaminated the old Temple. It was a contagion that had to be wiped away. The justness now disclosed is a contagion too. The new Holy of Holies is the Anointed, is cleansed by his own death, and cleanses those who follow him and who form his Body. The justness of God spreads justness.

THE FAITH OF JESUS ANOINTED

Are these followers of Jesus, then, simply to have faith in the Anointed? The phrase *faith of Jesus* or *faith of Jesus Anointed,* frequent in Paul's letters to the Galatians and the Romans, has traditionally been understood as referring to humans' faith in him. This is certainly the direction of saving faith by the time Luke writes. But the old suspicion, raised once more in recent decades, is that, as a Greek phrase, the words most naturally refer to the faith of Jesus, that is, to the faith or faithfulness with which Jesus obeyed God's will and died. We heard above of *those dependent on the faith of Jesus.* Paul uses the same turn of phrase a page later when he speaks of *those dependent on the Law and those dependent on the faith of Abraham* (Rom. 4:16). His reference here is clearly to the faith that Abraham had, not to the faith of others in him. It may well be that

Paul's prime reference in *Jesus' faith* or *Jesus Anointed's faith* is not to his followers' faith at all. It is for them to develop such faithfulness in imitation of Jesus, but the faithfulness that won God's forgiveness for Jesus' followers is the faith held by Jesus himself.

We are gradually uncovering the mechanics, as Paul saw them, by which the death and rising of Jesus won deliverance for his followers. Paul is sure that the death of one person has secured the life of those around him. Such a notion was emerging in the Judaism of the first and second centuries B.C.E. Perhaps a nation's ransom could be paid by the death of an individual—a death undergone in faithful obedience to God's will. Central, then, to the death's effect was the faithfulness that led the martyr to it.

In the second century B.C.E. the Jews fought for freedom under the leadership of the Maccabees. We have two versions of their story. The later one was probably written in Antioch toward the end of the first century C.E. A high point in the drama is the ordeal to which the enemy, King Antiochus Epiphanes, subjects a priest, Eleazar, and a mother and her seven sons. He offers them their lives if they will break the Law. They refuse, one by one, and die horribly. Eleazar says these last words as he dies:

> "You know, O God, that though I could have saved myself, I am
> dying in these fiery torments for the sake of the Law. Be merciful
> to your people and let our punishment be a satisfaction on their
> behalf. Make my blood their purification and take my life as a
> ransom for theirs."
>
> 4 MACCABEES 6:27–29

Near the end of the book the author adds his own comment. His whole account is an expansion of the earlier version of the story, which had hardly a trace of the thoughts he now provides. We see the exploratory care with which he is defining the effect of these martyrs' deaths:

> Through them our enemies did not prevail against our nation,
> and the tyrant was punished and our land purified, since they
> became, as it were, a ransom for the wrongdoing of our nation.

> Through the blood of these righteous ones and through the
> means of securing God's favor and protection [or the mercy seat]
> in their death, the divine providence rescued Israel.
>
> 4 MACCABEES 17:20-22

The author knows full well that God must be appeased for the wrongdoings of his people. This had once been achieved by the Temple's rituals, by sacrifices during the year and by the scapegoat on the Day of Atonement. But the Temple was defiled in Antiochus's day and had been destroyed before this author wrote 4 Maccabees. The question was acute: How was reparation to be made for the nation's wrongdoings when the route laid down by God was closed? The answer was beginning to emerge: by the death of faithful martyrs.

After Antiochus's oppression of the Jews a hymn was inserted into the Greek version of the book of Daniel. (We cannot date more closely the composition of the hymn or its insertion.) It is sung by Azariah, one of four youths who have refused to worship false gods and are now to be burned to death. It refers to "our sacrifice" offered to God. If the hymn was in general use among the Jews, "our sacrifice" will have been the Jews' own prayers, of which the hymn was part. But in the setting of Azariah's torture, the sacrifice is the death facing him and his friends. The hymn hangs midway between the two meanings. In gestation is the belief that the death of martyrs might be as powerful as the sacrifice of fattened lambs.

Azariah speaks of the Temple, defiled by Antiochus and unusable:

> "There is not at this time any leader or prophet or prince,
>   no burnt sacrifice, no offering, no oblation, no incense,
>   no place for offering firstfruits before you or for finding mercy.
> But worn down as we are and knowing our own degradation,
>   may we be as acceptable to you
>   as in holocausts of rams and of bulls,
>   as in thousands of fattened lambs.
> So may our sacrifice be before you today,
>   to bring about reparation before you."
>
> DANIEL 3:38-40, GREEK VERSION

In the climax of Azariah's plea, the verb he uses, "to bring about reparation," is related to the noun for mercy seat, the means to secure God's favor and protection.

All such themes are raised to a new pitch by Paul. His inheritance from Stephen's followers in Antioch has not provided him with all that he will want to say, but it has given him the language in which he can describe the faithfulness and work of Jesus, for him a martyr far greater than Azariah.

Isaiah in his vision had seen God upon his throne. It was a throne seen, outside of visions, only by the high priest and only on the Day of Atonement. Paul has seen Jesus on that throne. Here is the image of God that has purified God's new temple—his own followers—and has secured atonement for their wrongs. The second climax in the letter to the Romans takes up the theme of the first:

> There is now no condemnation for those who are in Anointed Jesus. For the Law of the Breath of life in Anointed Jesus has freed you from the Law of wrongdoing and of death. For what was impossible for the Law in its weakness through the flesh, God has done, sending his own son in the likeness of the flesh of wrongdoing, and in atonement for wrongdoing he has condemned wrongdoing in the flesh.
>
> ROMANS 8:1–3

ISAIAH AND PAUL: CALL OR CONVERSION?

We speak of Isaiah's call, but of Paul's conversion. We can see why. Isaiah's understanding of Israel and of himself was not, as far as we know, turned upside down at his call. He was right to think of himself as a wrongdoer and in drastic need of forgiveness, right to fear for his life in the presence of God. What changed at his call was his own role. Even this change, as it is presented in the arrangement of his book that has reached us, was less dramatic than we might expect. We hear of his call after several pages. We have already heard his voice warning and threatening. When Isaiah or his pupils edited his prophecies, the call was not made the awesome start to his mission; it was used to confirm how stubborn the people would be.

When Paul seeks words with which to do his own commission justice, he heads for the great prophets of Israel's past. He could see in himself the hallmarks of a prophet. As the prophets of old had been selected by God before they were even born, so was he; he uses the same terms for his selection that the prophets had used long ago of theirs. *From my mother's womb,* said Isaiah or the Servant of God he evoked, *he called my name* (Isa. 49:1). The prophet Jeremiah was told by God, *Before I formed you in the womb I knew you, and before you came forth from your mother I made you holy; I appointed you a prophet to the nations* (Jer. 1:5). And Paul himself? God *had set me apart,* Paul tells us, *from my mother's womb and had called me through his grace to unveil his son in me, so that I might preach the good news of him among the nations* (Gal. 1:15–16).

Yet Paul never speaks of himself as a prophet. When writing to the Corinthians he reminds them that God has appointed *first emissaries, second prophets, third teachers* (1 Cor. 12:28). And he himself had the highest calling of all, that of an emissary. Why then did Paul link his being selected so closely with the calls of Isaiah and Jeremiah?

Isaiah was famous, above all, for the promise he relayed to God's people that God would deliver them. Isaiah 40:9 in the Hebrew text reads:

> *Get up to a high mountain,*
>> *O Jerusalem, herald of good news* [or, *herald of good news to*
>> *Jerusalem*] . . .
> *Say to the cities of Judah,*
> *"Look, your God!"*

In the Aramaic version, used in Paul's day, that one city or one person is rendered as "prophets":

> *Get up to a high mountain,*
>> *you prophets that bring good news to Jerusalem* . . .
> *Say to the cities of the house of Judah,*
> *"The kingdom of your God is revealed."*

The emissary called to declare God's final intervention was an Isaiah of the last times. Here indeed was Paul's mission. And eventually, he knew, it would take him back to Jerusalem, the Holy City itself.

• • •

WHEN WE SPEAK, THEN, ABOUT PAUL, should we talk of his conversion to a new faith or his call to be a prophet of the old? The distinction may be too crude. Let's look for a moment at the conversions around him. At first sight, the gentile members of Paul's assemblies were clearly converts. They changed religion; they moved from the worship of Greek and Roman gods to the worship of the Jews' one God. Converts from paganism had previously been a part, however lowly, of the dominant religious culture. They had taken part in the great festivals, frequented the city's temples, and welcomed and been welcomed in the regular social life that revolved around the local cults. Upon declaring allegiance to Jesus, however, they set themselves apart. For them, the pagan cults were now the cults of demons, their adherents were idolaters, their festal meat was infected with the error of the priests who prepared it.

We shall look in more detail, later on, at the difference—to social, economic, and ritual life—that such conversion made in practice. But meanwhile we need to be aware that even for pagans joining the assemblies, conversion may be too strong a word. We know of Gentiles who were attracted to Judaism but did not convert to it, of men who were not circumcised and families who did not observe the whole Law. Josephus refers to "Jews and those who revere God" as if they formed two categories. Luke has Paul, speaking in a prayer house, address "Israelites and those who fear God" and in the same speech "Children of the race of Abraham and those among you who fear God" (The Mission [Acts] 13:16, 26).

We have learned more, in recent decades, of such "God-fearers," sympathizers with Judaism whose allegiance was public and valued. An inscription has been discovered in Aphrodisias, a city of Asia Minor, that reveals that there, at least, such a group was clearly identified in the third century C.E. The inscription is little more than a list of names and abbreviations, but from such spare information we can conjure up the dignity and alliances of a whole community.

The marble block is inscribed on two sides, in different hands and perhaps from different times. One side commemorates those who had given to a Jewish charity, probably to a center for the distribution of food. The names of several donors are followed with additional details:

one was an elder and priest; another was a senior official; and the mother of this last man was the building's patroness. And in the same style, three of the names are followed by the description "convert," two by "God-fearer." The inscription's second side has been damaged at the top. It now starts in the middle of a list of names, of which fifty-four survive, many of them Jewish. Next comes a gap, then the heading "And such as are God-fearers." Beneath this is a second list, of fifty names. By each of the first nine is the word "town councilor." Only one name in this second list is even partly Jewish, "Eusabbathios," a hybrid that had featured several times in the list inscribed above.

This is a charity run by the Jewish community with which leading Gentiles—including town councilors—wanted publicly to be linked as God-fearers. The term is likely, then, to have been a one of honor within the Jewish community and, at the least, respectable in the city as a whole. Among these sympathizers we can be pretty sure that the town councilors continued to sacrifice to pagan gods; their civic life carried on as before. We cannot of course read back, with any assurance, the conditions of one city into the life of others almost two hundred years before, but we will keep in our mind's eye these God-fearers of the third century.

How might the Christians' claims and life and forms of worship have looked to any equivalent, in Paul's world, of those distinguished Gentiles of Aphrodisias? What did God-fearers give up—socially, economically, civilly—if they became full-fledged members of a Pauline assembly rather than figures on the fringes of a prayer house? We shall later be looking at the low-key rituals, daily and domestic, of paganism and will ask which of such converts might have maintained after their conversion to Paul's faith. It was a world full of gods. Their idols had to be renounced, but what compromise or accommodation might have been allowed in different assemblies? What did the grand Erastus, who is mentioned as a member of the assembly in Corinth and was likely the city's treasurer, do at the pagan civic sacrifices? The Corinthians—and not just Erastus—confronted Paul with such questions; others must have faced them too.

Call or conversion: how crude our few categories seem. What changes or ambiguities, if any, did Paul face for himself? He continued to worship the God of his ancestors, who had unveiled himself through the Law and the Prophets and now, as he came to believe, in Jesus Anointed. He had, as a Jew, stood throughout his life at a distance from the civic—and civil—life of paganism. He had always belonged in the Jewish communities, and in the aftermath of his conversion he belonged there still. Jesus had been Jewish; all his first followers were Jewish; all the movement's leaders in Jerusalem were Jewish; and so was Paul. Paul was, like Isaiah, called to preach to a recalcitrant people, not to abandon it.

But his relation to that people had to change. Holiness was no longer centered in the Temple or the Jews. Purity was not maintained by separation from Gentiles and their contamination. The boundaries of Paul's *Israel of God* were moved. Entry into that Israel and good standing within it were newly ritualized and defined. To Gentiles, Paul would now seem a Jew who had elevated liberalism to a principle.

Paul was not alone. As a consequence of his new insight he declared his loyalty to Jesus' followers, a small group, chiefly of Jews, that had members in various Jewish communities. Here he was among the liberals who already had in Stephen a martyr of their own. They were taking shape as a group with its own conditions for entry and membership, its own ethos, shared loyalties, and heroes. To this group, Paul would be a welcome new arrival with ideas that bolstered its own.

Some of his Jewish peers, from the start, would look askance at this new allegiance; others would come only later to see Paul as a danger to the life of their prayer houses. Paul had proved himself unstable, but not yet an apostate. In the early years, the local prayer houses and their leaders may well, as Luke suggests, have offered him a—wary—welcome. But they would soon suspect he has abandoned all principle for liberalism. He was a dangerous man.

And how did Paul's change look to himself? We know only from his letters, written many years later and with a polemical edge. By now he must denigrate the claims that rival preachers are making for circumcision. He must make the distinction as sharp as possible between his own past and present life. We hear the arguments he needs to make to his addressees at the time of writing. But how had things looked twenty-five years before? The chasm had not yet opened up, in those early days, that he purposely deepens as he writes to the Philippians:

Everything that was a gain to me, I thought it, on account of Anointed, to be a loss. No, more than that: I actually think everything to be a loss, on account of the higher standing of the knowledge of Anointed Jesus my Lord, on whose account I have suffered the loss of all things and count them as excrement, in order that I might gain Anointed and be found in him.
PHILIPPIANS 3:7–9

Things have moved fast. In Paul's circles—though not in all others—the Christian community has grown into a life of its own, autonomous and self-sustaining. Paul's relation has changed to both Jews and Gentiles. His call has become his conversion.

CHAPTER 5

PAUL AND EZEKIEL: "THE LIKENESS OF THE GLORY OF THE LORD"

THE CHARIOT-THRONE OF GOD

Of all the vision stories, the most famous was the vision of Ezekiel, priest and prophet, that opens his book of prophecies. Ezekiel's first sight of God's chariot-throne inspired seer after seer, and not least Paul himself.

When Ezekiel saw this first vision around 592 B.C.E., he heard his call to be a prophet: *"Son of man,"* said God, *"I send you to the people of Israel, to a nation of rebels"* (Ezek. 2:3). Ezekiel, like Isaiah before him, heard the summons to God's difficult, dangerous service. Whatever Paul himself hoped to see or undergo through his study of Ezekiel, he could not assume that he would just look on, watch a drama unfold, and then return to his former life unchanged.

Ezekiel's imagination was fired by the scene that fueled Isaiah's over a hundred years before—the sight of the throne of God. But Ezekiel wrote in exile from Jerusalem. The city had been captured. The Temple had been defiled and has been—or is about to be—destroyed. Ezekiel saw it only in visions. God's throne now resembled a chariot, with good reason. In one of his visions Ezekiel saw God's glory come out from the

Temple, God's home on earth, and leave it desolate and ready for destruction.

We can fail to see, as we skim through the Old Order, how important was Ezekiel's sight of the chariot-throne—and how perilous for later generations. We read in the Mishnah: "It is forbidden to discourse . . . on the chariot-throne in the presence of one [alone], unless he is wise and able to understand of himself" (*Hagigah [The Festal Offering]* 2:1). It was dangerous to draw too near to the Almighty, even in study and contemplation. A man who came from Galilee to Babylon, we hear in a later source, was asked by the people there to discourse on the chariot-throne. When he did so, he died.

Study of the passage was restricted, but still possible. According to a story about two rabbis of the third century C.E., Rabbi Yohanan son of Zakkai was one day traveling on a donkey. His pupil Rabbi Eleazar son of Arakh was walking behind him. Eleazar asked his master to "teach him a chapter" in the work of the Divine Chariot. Yohanan reminded his pupil of the ruling we have heard from the Mishnah: a master can "discourse" about the chariot-throne before a single student only if the student is wise and able to understand of himself. "Teaching," "chapter," and "discourse" are all terms used for the normal study of scripture. The study of Ezekiel's opening chapter called for standard procedures to be adapted, not abandoned. Eleazar wanted Yohanan to quote a phrase from the vision and to expound it by reference to other passages in scripture; the result would be a chapter of teaching. These seers were not outlandish figures avoiding the center of Jewish life. They were, first and foremost, scholars of scripture. In it their imagination found fuel and guidance, and in it too they found the material for their teaching on daily life.

We hear elsewhere that "many have discoursed on the chariot-throne and have not seen it in their lifetime." The rabbis were clear that to study the passage was not necessarily to have a vision. When we speak of Paul and the chariot-throne, we are speaking of the tireless study of a passage of scripture that opened the door, it was believed, to truths normally hidden. That door might open, on any one occasion, onto some form of a vision or, for those trained in a particular form of meditation, onto a journey and its vision of the throne. But it might not.

When Yohanan refused the request of his pupil, Eleazar saw what was needed. He had to show his master that he, Eleazar, was wise enough to hear what his master had to say. Eleazar asked permission to discourse on the passage himself. Yohanan got off his donkey and put on the shawl required for prayer and other rituals sanctioned by God. They both sat down under a tree. Eleazar spoke. At the end of his discourse, Yohanan stood up, kissed him on the head, and blessed him for knowing how to understand and to discourse on matters pertaining to the glory of his Father in heaven.

Two more versions of the story have reached us. As the rabbis sat down under the tree, says one version, fire came down from heaven and surrounded them, and the ministering angels were dancing before them as groomsmen rejoicing before the bridegroom. An angel's voice spoke from the fire: "It is as you say, Eleazar. This is what the chariot-throne is!" The other version tells of the fire's descent as Eleazar began to speak. The fire surrounded all the trees in the field and the trees themselves began to sing a song of praise (as in Ps. 148:7–9).

Paul too had a journey to undertake—to Damascus. He had no reason to waste his time. What was in his mind as he set out? Both Paul and Luke, in their different ways, have left clues behind that take us straight to the story of Ezekiel that Paul knew so well.

Paul dwelt on such visions and journeys to heaven far more often than he underwent them himself. Luke would have known of such journeys too from the Greco-Roman world, where they were respected. If he had any grounds to think that Paul had undergone such a journey to heaven on the road to Damascus itself, he would have said so with pride. But no, the road to Damascus was where Paul was and where he stayed. Yet what he saw belonged in heaven. To see it on earth was to know that ancient patterns of unveiling were undone. And so was bridged the great gulf between heaven and earth, between God and humankind. The glory of day one blazed once more on earth, and God's new creation was under way.

Paul set out for Damascus. He turned his mind to Ezekiel. And more than angels danced before him as he went.

"THE LIKENESS AS THE APPEARANCE OF A MAN"

The heavens were opened, declares Ezekiel at the start of his book, *and I saw visions of God* (1:1). We are about to hear a summary of the opening vision. Such a shortened form can do no justice to the sense of mystery and awe present in the full account.

Ezekiel sees a great cloud coming from the north, flashing with fire. From its midst emerges *the likeness of four living creatures: they had the form of men, but each had four faces, and each had four wings* (1:5–6). These creatures are drawn from the cherubim, winged animals with human heads, that were carved on the walls of the Anteroom and Holy of Holies. Most awesome of all were the two giant sculpted cherubim in the innermost sanctuary, who stood wing tip to wing tip and together spanned the whole width of the Holy of Holies.

Each figure in Ezekiel's vision faced four ways, so the group could move forward in any direction without turning. In the middle of this group was *something that looked like burning coals of fire* (1:13), and out of this fire came lightning. Beside each of the four figures was a wheel, and these wheels moved with the four creatures. Over the creatures' heads was *the likeness of a vault, shining like crystal* (1:22). Ezekiel now moves from sight to sound. *When they went, I heard the sound of their wings like the sound of many waters, like the thunder of the Almighty, a sound of tumult like the sound of an army; and when they stood still, they let down their wings* (1:24).

A view is open beyond the vault. Ezekiel writes with great care. He is seeing more than the human mind can hope to grasp. He uses, of course, the categories that he and his readers know. It is only in such terms that he himself can have the vision, and only in such terms that his readers can envisage it for themselves. Ezekiel doubts he is using appropriate language at all, the language of thrones and precious stones and the human form and bronze and fire. He claims only *likeness* after *likeness.*

> *And above the vault over their heads there was the likeness of a throne, as the appearance of a sapphire; and above the likeness of a throne was the likeness as the appearance of a man upon it.*
>
> EZEKIEL 1:26

The appearance of a man, or *of Adam*—the phrases in Hebrew are the same.

> *And upward from the appearance of his loins I saw as it were gleaming bronze, as the appearance of fire round about within it; and downward from the appearance of his loins I saw as it were the appearance of fire, and there was brightness round about him. Like the appearance of the bow that is in the cloud on the day of rain, so was the appearance of the brightness round about. Such was the appearance of the likeness of the glory of the Lord.*
>
> EZEKIEL 1:27–28

AND PAUL, ALL THOSE CENTURIES LATER? What did he see in any such visions? We know of the journey he would make to Paradise and of the unspeakable words awaiting him there, but that was long after his conversion, and he mentions only what he heard, not what he saw. What, then, of his experience on the road to Damascus? Luke and his Paul speak only of the light that blinded Paul, not of any figure there or of any further detail. How, then, do we identify any more specific object within that blinding light? We have more than once invoked a striking passage in 2 Corinthians. It is time to hear it at greater length.

> *If our gospel is veiled at all, it is veiled among those on their way to destruction, among whom the god of this aeon has blinded the thoughts of the faithless, to prevent them seeing the light of the good news of the glory of the Anointed, who is the image of God. For we do not preach ourselves but Jesus Anointed as Lord, and ourselves as your slaves on account of Jesus. Because the God who said "Light shall shine out of darkness" is the one who shone in our hearts, to bring about enlightenment, the knowledge of the glory of God in the face of Jesus Anointed.*
>
> 2 CORINTHIANS 4:3–6

Here is the glorious face of the Anointed, the image of God. We shall see later how carefully Paul is here deflecting any danger that the Corinthians will worship himself; he is almost too closely related to the

Anointed and must allow no misunderstanding of his status or role. The Corinthians have had Paul among them, and he re-presents the Anointed to them. But the final object of their gaze is not Paul; it is the Anointed whose face Paul has seen directly and now makes accessible indirectly, in his own person, to his converts.

And when had Paul seen the face of the Anointed? There is more than one possibility. When he journeyed to Paradise perhaps (2 Cor. 12:2–4). Or when *in ecstasy* he saw Jesus in the Temple, as we hear him tell in The Mission ([Acts] 22:17–18). Or on an occasion of which we are not otherwise told. Perhaps. But his letter to the Corinthians steers us to one moment and one only.

In 2 Corinthians 4:3–6 Paul has conversion in mind. He is drawing a sharp—and neatly balanced—contrast between those with faith and those without, between those on their way to destruction and those who accept Paul's proclamation. And so he thinks of the move from one group to the other. *"Let there be light,"* said God at the start of creation. Paul evokes the foundational moment of light and new life. From darkness into light: as the light of day one launched creation, so the light of day one launched Paul's re-creation. God, Paul says, *shone in our hearts*, not, the Greek verb is clear, with a steady blaze then or now, but as a single event. And thanks to that single event he now re-presents to his assemblies, day by day, *the image of God*. At that moment of re-creation he saw the image, face-to-face. Its glory now illumines his face. And so in turn he can bring glory to the faces of his converts.

Images from the Old Order are the fuel for Paul's thought; and when that thought breaks out into new and dazzling flames, the Old Order in turn makes possible its interpretation. We cannot separate Paul's experience from the images that shaped it. Paul had dwelt throughout his training on the glory around God's throne. And when, informed and encouraged by that training, he saw such light shine about him, its character was clear. Paul had dwelt too on the figure on the throne. And at the moment when he recognized that figure, he himself, in his own view, moved from darkness into the light of the new creation that was shining all around him. From the creation of the universe to the moment of disclosure—Paul draws for both on the same image of light. The figure that he recognized in the dazzling light of his own day one was the Wisdom of God, through whom that light had blazed at the dawn of all things. *Anyone who is in Anointed,* he will tell the Corinthians, *is a new creation* (2 Cor. 5:17).

We might still be tempted to think of Paul's experience on the road to Damascus as a terrifying surprise, an experience for which nothing had prepared him and for which he later sought precedents and explanations. Not at all. The vision came to Paul in the visual language he already knew like the back of his hand; it was well within the tradition and expectations of a seer. Paul was hard at work on his way to Damascus. He was dwelling on every detail in Ezekiel's vision of the throne.

EZEKIEL DID NOT HAVE HIS VISION of God's throne in the Temple itself, for God had left on his chariot-throne. His city of Jerusalem was ripe for destruction; so also was his home there, the Temple.

But Ezekiel had another vision, one of the Temple yet to come, to be built for God's return. The old Temple had palm trees, flowers, and cherubim carved on its walls. Ezekiel dreams of the new Temple, its courtyards decorated with palm trees, its interior with palm trees and cherubim. From this Temple flows a river that brings superabundant life. These motifs echo through the Old Order. The Beginning [Genesis] tells of the trees and rivers of Eden and of the cherubim that have barred its entrance since the Fall. The Temple of Ezekiel's vision represented creation, as God had created it to be, as Paradise.

Paul the Pharisee, before his conversion, had sought to maintain in his own daily life the rigorous purity that was required of anyone who approached the presence of God in the Temple. As the Temple was holy, so the whole people of Israel was called to be holy: chosen by God, blessed by him, and dedicated to his service. Therefore, Paul, the convert and emissary, had to discover afresh: Where in the light of the Anointed was the Temple now to be found that represented all creation? Where was its sanctuary, the Holy of Holies, that held the secrets of God's plan, will, and faithfulness? Where was the people now called to be holy as God was holy? Where was atonement wrought and peace with God restored? *The sanctuary of God is holy,* writes Paul to the Corinthians, *which you are* (1 Cor. 3:17).

This insight shaped all that he thought and wrote. At its heart was the fusion, in the Temple, of Paradise and the court of heaven. Paul does not, at his conversion, leave the Temple and its imagery behind. Far from it. They are the mirror in which he discovers and defines all that he will say about the role of the Anointed.

"ONE LIKE A SON OF MAN"

The relation between heaven and earth, their inhabitants and their truths, was subtle, poetic, and forever reimagined. Ezekiel's figure is on the throne at the center of light. The vision became the template from which variations could be developed without end. The book of Daniel, which reached its present form around 163 B.C.E., is famous for the seer's vision of *one like a son of man:*

> *In my vision at night, I, Daniel, looked. And there before me was one like a son of man, coming with the clouds of heaven. He approached the Ancient of Days and was led into his presence. He was given authority, glory and sovereign power; all people, nations and men of every language worshiped him. His dominion is an everlasting dominion that will not pass away.*
>
> DANIEL 7:13–14

Ezekiel's *appearance of the likeness of the glory of the Lord,* God's image, is taking on the form of an individual. The Lord's glory has split off from the Lord himself and is now strangely independent. We can almost watch the development in action within the translations of this very passage. According to one of the Greek versions, *on the clouds of heaven there came one as a son of man, and he was present as the Ancient of Days, and those around were present before him.* He does not come *to* the Ancient of Days, but *as* him; the incipient split between them seems still, to these translators, too drastic and too dangerous—too likely to suggest a second power, supreme in heaven, besides God's own.

Daniel's *one like a son of man* will evolve still further; in later unveilings the *son of man* is presented as a heavenly individual with a fully developed history. A similar division affects Wisdom in the centuries immediately before Paul's: God's Wisdom is imagined with increasing clarity as an agent working for or beside God. Paul could think what he did about Jesus thanks only to the thoughts about Wisdom by those who went before him.

But Daniel's figure is an individual within a dream, and the dream is interpreted to Daniel by an angel. The role of the *one like a son of man* in the dream will be filled in history, the seer is told, by the people of the saints of the Most High. They will be given on earth the dominion that the visionary figure is given in the heaven of Daniel's dream. The figure would have been less strange then than now. Each nation was imagined to have its own angel, in part the embodiment of the nation's life and character, in part its own protecting power. That figure seen by Daniel exists in heaven. It is accessible to sight in a dream, but nowhere else. And the dream unveils to Daniel what is—without any doubt—to come. God's plan is set in heaven, and no horrors or opposition on earth can prevent its final fulfillment.

By the time of Mark's gospel the *son of man* has become a figure who can walk out of the visions of heaven and appear on earth. Mark confounds all the familiar categories of such visions. The *one like a son of man* that represented the saints of the Most High in a dream now gathers the saints of the Most High around him in Galilee. The victory of Daniel's *one like a son of man* in heaven had portended and guaranteed for Daniel the eventual victory of the saints on earth. But for Mark the battle on earth has now been fought, by the *son of man* himself. And he has surely lost, shamefully and beyond recall. Mark knows how hard it will be for his readers to grasp what he must disclose to them. We will hear more of his attempts to make it possible, for the *son of man,* against all appearance, has won the victory that the followers he represents are still waiting and longing to see revealed.

Paul too writes, with a different arrangement, of the Anointed in heaven and of his Body on earth. For Paul too the traditions of disclosure must be overturned. The Anointed has won the battle and been glorified. But what of his followers on earth?

Luke's Paul, on the road to Damascus,

> *heard a voice saying to him, "Saul, Saul, why are you persecuting me?"*
> *He said, "Who are you, Lord?"*
> *"I am Jesus. You are persecuting me."*
> THE MISSION 9:4-5

Paul had been attacking the followers of Jesus. And in doing so he had been attacking Jesus himself, for these followers are the Body of the Anointed. The Anointed is in heaven, but his Body is on earth. And its members are still waiting and longing to see the victory of their Lord revealed.

PAUL THE EMISSARY

Ezekiel was so awed by the sight given him in that first vision that he fell to the ground:

And when I saw it, I fell upon my face, and I heard the voice of one speaking.

And he said to me, "Son of man, stand up on your feet, and I will speak to you.". . . And the Breath came upon me and set me up on my feet; and I heard him speaking to me. And he said to me, "Son of man, I send you to the people of Israel, to a nation of rebels, who have rebelled against me; they and their fathers have transgressed against me to this very day. . . . I send you to them. And you shall say to them, 'Thus says the Lord God.'. . . And they will know there has been a prophet among them. And you, son of man, do not be afraid of them, nor be afraid of their words, . . . for they are a rebellious house."

EZEKIEL 1:28–2:7

It was just such a mission that Paul had undertaken before he left Jerusalem for Damascus: to bring back to due obedience a small group of Jews who were in rebellion against God. But the rebellion was not where he had thought. It was in Paul himself. Paul too fell to the ground, he will tell the Roman authorities, and *heard a voice talking to me.* In Luke's rendering of the story, Jesus says to Paul:

"Stand up, stand up on your feet. For I have been seen by you for this end, to choose you as servant and witness of what you have seen of me and of what you shall yet see, delivering you from the people and from the Gentiles to whom I am sending you to open their eyes,

for them to turn from darkness to light
and from the power of Satan to God,
for them to receive forgiveness of wrongdoings
and an inheritance among those made holy by their faith in me."

THE MISSION 26:16–18

Where is this great drama to be played out? We are about to hear of seers, in Paul's own time, who saw in heaven the destiny of Israel and its enemies. Paul found that destiny fulfilled within his assemblies. He was not alone in such a view. We'll listen as well, in the next chapter, to the great hymns of Qumran; the sectarians believed themselves to be living already the life of heaven and preparing the way, in their own life, for God's great intervention in the world.

CHAPTER 6

"YOU ARE THE SANCTUARY OF GOD"

Paul and the Seer Enoch:
Approaching the Great Glory

From the priest-prophet Ezekiel to Paul, we have jumped six hundred years. Ezekiel saw his vision around 592 B.C.E. Paul was called in the 30s C.E. Can we really believe that he attended so deeply to one ancient text? We know a great deal about the value given in Paul's own day to that opening vision of Ezekiel. Paul was part of that tradition, the tradition of visionaries who journeyed to heaven and who saw there the cherubim and the throne and glory of God. The glory of God is the "weight" of his presence that showed itself as light, illumining, dazzling, blinding. God's glory is the source of his radiance.

> Shine, shine, Jerusalem, for your light has come,
> and the glory of the Lord has risen upon you.
> Look, darkness and gloom will cover the earth upon the nations.
> But upon you the Lord shall appear,
> and his glory shall be seen upon you.
> And kings shall come to your light and nations to your brightness.
> ISAIAH 60:1-3, GREEK VERSION

Light was an image, then as now, for goodness over against the darkness of evil. Pure light, freed from all darkness, was an image for perfection. And more important still, where there is light there is the possibility of knowledge. We see by light and we look—dazzled and veiled—at the source of the light. In the source we see what makes possible our sight of all other things and the distinctions we draw between them. As the world outside us is illumined by light, so we speak of a light that can illumine our minds too, a gift that appears to come from outside us to bring clarity to our muddles and assurance for our doubts. Thanks to it, we too can bring light to situations where there is ignorance or confusion. This is not, for the seers, a matter of mere thought. At issue is the life of individuals, communities, and the people of Israel. Without light is no life. And the source of all light and of all life—physical, moral, and intellectual—is God.

We are about to hear of two journeys. One is ascribed to Enoch, a primordial sage, and the other to the prophet Isaiah. The accounts were actually compiled in the centuries immediately before and after Paul's. The story of this Enoch gives us details of the journey to heaven such as Paul himself would have known. The story of this Isaiah gives us a glimpse of such seers in action in a group of master and pupils; the story reached its present form in the second century C.E. and opens a door for us upon the ways of Christian prophets just a few decades after Paul's death. From Enoch we hear of the Holy of Holies in heaven; Paul traveled to it rarely, dwelt on it often. From Isaiah we hear of transformation in the ascent to heaven and of words that cannot be repeated.

THE VISION OF ENOCH

Enoch walked with God, and then was no more; because God took him (The Beginning [Genesis] 5:24). Enoch lived, we are told, for 365 years, a perfect year of years. Legends gathered around his name, in particular, stories of his journeys to heaven and of what he saw there. The largest collection of such material is still part of the Bible of the Ethiopic church in Africa. We shall ask below how much such stories tell us about actual visions or journeys and how much of this written record is a pastiche of earlier accounts. For the moment we will just listen to the stories themselves. In the words ascribed to Enoch we hear a story much like the one Paul could have told the Corinthians about himself, for Paul had been to Paradise, heaven's Holy of Holies and the site of God's throne.

In Enoch's day, we hear, two hundred of the highest-ranking angels came to earth, seduced human women, and brought violence to human-kind. Enoch prepares to intercede for them before God. But in vain. He is given a vision that makes it clear that they are condemned. Enoch must relay God's verdict, and he does so by telling of his vision. Once more such a vision is inspired by the prospect of judgment and the hope of atonement. Enoch recalls:

> And it was shown to me thus in a vision. Behold, the clouds were calling me; and the dark clouds were crying out to me; and the course of the stars and the lightnings were rushing me on and driving me; and in the vision the winds were causing me to fly and rushing me high up into heaven. And I went on in until I approached a wall which was built of the crystal of hailstones and surrounded by tongues of fire and it began to frighten me.
>
> *1 ENOCH* 14:8-9

In one version of the narrative this is more than a wall; it is a house. Enoch is journeying to heaven; his route recalls in every detail a move-ment toward the Holy of Holies in the Temple. Two more houses still lie beyond him, the Anteroom to the heavenly Holy of Holies and the Holy of Holies itself. Enoch comes to the Anteroom:

> And I came into the tongues of fire and drew near to a great house which was built of the crystal of hail, and the inner walls were like paving stones in tessellation, made of crystal or snow, and the ground was of crystal. The ceiling was like lightnings and meteors on the path of the stars, and in the midst of them stood fiery cherubim, and their heaven was clear as water.
>
> *1 ENOCH* 14:10

We have met these cherubim before. They are inspired by the winged creatures engraved in the Temple on the Anteroom walls.

These creatures in turn embodied the winds and dwelt between heaven and earth.

Enoch has passed the protective wall built around heaven in the heavenly elements of ice and fire:

> And flaming fire surrounded the walls, and its gates were burning with fire. And I entered into the house, which was hot like fire and cold like ice, and there were no delights of life in it; fear covered me and trembling seized me.
>
> *1 ENOCH* 14:12–13

In fire and ice, Enoch's heavenly Temple matches the Temple on earth. "The exterior of the Temple," the historian Josephus tells us, "was covered on all sides with massive plates of gold. At the first rising of the sun it radiated an intense fiery flash and forced those who were straining to see it to turn away their sight as from the rays of the sun. To new visitors, as they approached, it looked like a snow-clad mountain; for all that was not overlaid with gold was the brightest white" (*Jewish War* 5.222–23).

Enoch has reached the threshold of God's presence in heaven. Enoch has more yet to see, but he cannot pass right into the throne room itself; not even the angels, we are told, can cross the threshold—let alone a man of flesh and blood.

Enoch continues:

> And as I shook and trembled, I fell upon my face and saw a vision. And behold there was a second house greater than the former, and its door was quite open before me, and everything was built with tongues of fire. And in every respect it excelled the other, in glory and great honor, to the extent that I cannot recount to you its glory and greatness. And as for the ground, it was of fire and above it were lightning and meteors on the path of the stars; and as for the ceiling, it was flaming fire.
>
> *1 ENOCH* 14:14–17

Enoch has beneath him now the elements at which we gaze when we look at the sky. He is approaching the heart of this visionary tradition: his sight of the throne itself. The Holy of Holies in Jerusalem and the throne room of heaven—all that our author knows of the one fuels his dream of the other.

> And I observed and saw inside it a lofty throne: its appearance was like the crystal of hailstones and its wheels like the shining sun, and there was a vision of cherubim.
>
> And from beneath the throne there issued burning streams of fire, and I could not look on it. And the Great Glory was sitting upon the throne. As for his clothing, which was shining more brightly than the sun, it was whiter than any snow.
>
> *1 ENOCH* 14:18-20

The Glory in the Holy of Holies is dressed in white. The high priest too, on the Day of Atonement, would remove his multicolored vestments and enter the Holy of Holies in white linen, for the high priest on that day represented both his people and the Glory enthroned.

> None of the angels was able to come in and see the face of the Glory, by reason of its splendor and glory; and no flesh could see him. The flaming fire was round about him, and a great fire stood before him, so that none who surrounded him could draw near to him. Ten thousand times ten thousand stood before him. He needed no council, but the most holy ones who are near to him neither go far away at night nor move away from him.
>
> *1 ENOCH* 14:21-23

Enoch is lifted up and brought to the door. He is privileged above the angels—and certainly above all but the holiest mortals of flesh and blood.

Enoch stands before a splendor far too bright to look upon. And such a splendor blazed on Paul: on the road to Damascus and in Paradise. To see that light in Paradise was to be a privileged seer. And to see such light on earth? When that light broke out of heaven and shone on earth, the time was at hand for God's final intervention in the world.

Paul and the Seer Isaiah:
From Glory to Glory

From Ezekiel, through the seer of the book of Enoch, to Paul—what striking, strangely privileged individuals these are. They seem to stand by themselves, each alone in his generation. But not so. A hundred years after Paul wrote, another seer, a Christian, described such an ascent to heaven. His account is likely influenced by Paul himself. He unfolds the blossom that Paul had left in bud.

This seer presents himself and his contemporaries in disguise. To give authority to his own disclosures, he writes as "Isaiah" and pretends to be the great prophet of the past predicting Jesus, his descent from heaven, and his return. This "Isaiah" is surrounded by pupils. Their description casts light not on the great Isaiah's school, but on the seer's own following nine hundred years after Isaiah's death. This is a fascinating glimpse of such a group at work.

The Paul who was taken up to the third heaven, visited Paradise, and heard words too holy for mortal ears; the Paul who was blinded by the light shining around the Anointed—this Paul was steeped in the language, techniques, and expectations of such seers. As we watch the pupils of "Isaiah" around their master, we should envisage the young Paul, a hundred years before, learning and watching and immersing himself, deeper and deeper, in such a world as this. The school of seers that evoked Isaiah took care with its choice of patron. As the Isaiah of old had been a prophet, so they were prophets too. And so was Paul.

THE VISION OF "ISAIAH"

As in Enoch's story, so also in this Isaiah's story we have that ascent and that dazzling light. More details are offered here. This Isaiah stands in the tradition that knows of seven heavens, not three. He travels through the seven heavens, individually described; he records the increase in brightness, heaven by heaven. And as the brightness around him intensifies, so does the brightness of his own person. Isaiah is being transformed: God's glory gives him glory. But our seer is still a mortal, with a life on earth to lead. He must return there.

Forty prophets had assembled when they knew Isaiah was going to prophesy. Isaiah did not work alone. They would hear him, and he would hear them in turn.

> They came that they might greet him, and that they might hear his words, and that he might lay his hand on them, and that they might prophesy, and that he might hear their prophecy; and they were all in the presence of Isaiah.
>
> ASCENSION OF ISAIAH 6:4-5

We hear elsewhere of pupils gathered around a seer to hear the seer describe his "journey" through heaven during that journey itself. One story tells of the visionary Rabbi Nehuniah. In the middle of just such a journey he began speaking of something his pupils could not understand. The pupils touched him with an impure object. It brought him out of his trance—and his pupils could ask him to explain more clearly.

Isaiah's story continues:

> And when Isaiah spoke with King Hezekiah the words of justness and faith, they all heard a door being opened and the voice of the Breath. And they gave glory to the one who had thus graciously given to a man a door in an alien world.

> And while Isaiah was speaking with the Holy Breath in the hearing of them all, he became silent, and his mind was taken up from him, and he did not see the men who were standing before him. His eyes indeed were open, but his mouth was silent, and the mind in his body was taken up from him. But his breath was still in him, for he was seeing a vision.
>
> ASCENSION OF ISAIAH 6:6, 8-12

Isaiah, then, is separated from his body for his vision. "The wisdom of this world," we will hear later, "was taken from Isaiah as if he were dead." We need not be surprised that Paul was uncertain whether his own journey to Paradise was undertaken in or out of his body (2 Cor. 12:2–4).

Isaiah is given an angel guide. He is to see further into the secrets of heaven than anyone else ever has who was due to return to earth. But some things he will not learn. Two names in heaven are so secret that not even the angels know them: the name of God and the name of his Chosen One. And Isaiah, destined to return to earth, cannot know the name even of his angelic guide. He is such an outsider here that his progress through the heavens is challenged. "How far," asks a voice, as Isaiah rises toward the seventh heaven, "is he to go up who dwells among aliens?" But his guide can reassure the guard that Isaiah has the permission of the Lord himself. We have heard of such a hindrance in Paul's way too. He had been given *a thorn in the flesh, an angel of Satan, so that he might not be overelevated* (2 Cor. 12:7). He may be speaking of such a restraint on his own ascent.

By the third heaven Isaiah realizes that "the glory of his face is being transformed" as he goes up from heaven to heaven. Other seers underwent such transformation too. We have encountered already the most famous of all the stories of Enoch. Such narratives abound. A second book about Enoch was edited over centuries; we can no longer be sure how old its components are. It tells of Enoch's ascent to the seventh heaven. The Lord orders the archangel Michael, "Go, and extract Enoch from his earthly clothing. And anoint him with my delightful oil, and put him into the clothes of my glory."

> And so Michael did. He anointed me and he clothed me. And the appearance of that oil is greater than the greatest light, and its ointment is like sweet dew and its fragrance [like] myrrh; and it is like the rays of the glittering sun. And I looked at myself, and I had become like one of his glorious ones, and there was no observable difference.
>
> 2 ENOCH 22:9–10, LONG VERSION

As Enoch reached the seventh heaven, so does our Isaiah. Finally he is brought before the Great Glory itself. "And I saw the Great Glory while the eyes of my breath were open, but after that I could not see, nor the messenger who was with me, nor any of the messengers whom I had seen worship my Lord." Can anyone, then, gaze on this glory? The righteous dead can: "I saw the righteous as they looked with great power on the glory of that one" (*Ascension of Isaiah* 9:37–38). But Isaiah is given just one glimpse. Thereafter he can only hear—and even see—the praise offered to the Great Glory, but cannot see the glory itself.

In these higher heavens Isaiah hears of the robe that is waiting for him after his death. "Then you will receive the robe that you are going to see, and other numbered robes placed there you are going to see, and then you will be equal to the angels who are in the seventh heaven." When Isaiah reaches the seventh heaven he sees the righteous dead, "stripped of their robes of the flesh and dressed in their robes of above" (*Ascension of Isaiah* 8:14–15; 9:9). Isaiah is being given a sight during his life of the glory that the righteous before the Anointed could only hope for after death. His face becomes glorious; their faces have the glory of angels. His robe is waiting for him; they are already clad in theirs. The seer is being given a foretaste of heaven. Just one thing is still beyond these saints. They are not yet on their thrones or invested with their crowns. For that, Isaiah is told, they must wait until the Anointed has descended, died, and risen once more to the seventh heaven—and by the time this Isaiah actually writes, he has.

In 2 Corinthians we find Paul surveying his converts' past, present, and future at three climactic moments in the letter with three rolls on a single drum. At the first Paul recalls their baptism: at which God *put his seal on us and gave us the down payment of the Breath in our hearts* (1:22). At the second he reminds them of their ongoing transformation: *all of us are being transformed . . . from glory to glory* (3:18). And at the third mention of the Breath, once more recalling its guarantee of things to come, Paul looks forward to the triumph ahead. The Corinthians' transformation shall be complete. They too shall put on their new garments of glory. Past, present, and future—Paul has in mind throughout the letter the transformation through which he is guiding his converts.

> *We who are in this* [mortal, earthly] *tent are groaning with the weight. Not that we want to put this off, but to put more on top, so that the mortal might be swallowed up in life. And he who has wrought us for this very thing is God, he who has given us the down payment of the Breath.*
> 2 CORINTHIANS 5:4-5

Our Isaiah's vision is over. Only the other prophets even knew what had happened:

And the people who were standing by, apart from the circle of
prophets, did not think that the holy Isaiah had been taken up.
And the vision which he saw was not from this world, but from
the world which is hidden from the flesh.

ASCENSION OF ISAIAH 6:14-15

To LIVE THE LIFE OF HEAVEN. Others before Paul or our supposed Isaiah
had raised such a possibility without any reference to Jesus at all. Might
that veil be thinner and lighter than it seems, that majestic embroidery
between the Anteroom and the Holy of Holies? Or that vault of heaven
above the world of the winds? Might God ever draw back the barrier
between his court in heaven and his people on earth?

In particular, if God is launching his final intervention in the history
of his world, if he is about to establish his court here as it has been
established from all eternity in heaven—might he not give his loyal,
beleaguered followers some hint of what is soon to come? A glimpse of
that court perhaps, a share of the life already lived there by his angels, or
a taste of the power that will bring about God's victory and of the joys
that will follow it?

Such hopes were lived out at Qumran and were celebrated in a series
of extraordinary hymns.

Qumran: The Worship of Heaven

The sectarians of Qumran believed themselves to be sharing some parts
of the life of heaven. A distinctive exegesis of scripture, at the hands of
their leaders, gave them a knowledge they prized highly. A manual of
instructions has survived, compiled for those leaders. It includes a song
for their own use:

My eyes have gazed on what is eternal, on wisdom concealed
    from men,
on knowledge and wise design hidden from the sons of adam;
on a spring of glory hidden from the assembly of flesh.
God has given them to his chosen ones as an everlasting
    possession,

and has caused them to inherit the lot of the holy ones.
He has joined their assembly to the sons of heaven
to be a council of the community.

1QS 11.5–8

The sectarians are already, here on earth, living the life of angels. We have caught a glimpse of the growing assurance, in Judaism, of a life beyond death. The belief took hold in the centuries immediately before Jesus. Documents surviving from Qumran do speak of rewards and punishment after death, but not in detail, for the sectarians need no instruction on the character of the life that awaits them. They are already, in this life, enjoying the fellowship of the angels and the life of heaven.

And I know there is hope for him
whom you have shaped from dust for the everlasting community.
You have cleansed a perverse breath of great wrongdoing
that it may stand with the host of the holy ones,
that it may enter into communion with the assembly of the sons
of heaven.

1QH 11.20–22

Is this just the imagery of leaders bolstering their role with a grandeur and authority beyond question? If so, they pursued it with extraordinary vigor. A set of thirteen songs (found in fragments at Qumran and at Masada) marks the first thirteen Sabbaths of the year. These hymns are deeply indebted to the visions of Ezekiel; in them are the throne-chariot of God and the unsullied Temple that Ezekiel saw in heaven. But the songs are not just *about* those visions. They summon the Sovereign Princes and the Breaths of the Temple to join in praise; they then describe the heavenly Temple through to the Holy of Holies, the cherubim, and throne itself; and the last song describes the high priest in the Holy of Holies.

The songs describe and orchestrate the praise to be offered by *elohim* and *elim*, "gods," who are heavenly figures, by a people of discernment, by teachers, and by a priesthood with territory and an inheritance. Who, then, is undertaking this worship? Angels and humans alike? *Elohim* and *elim* certainly suggest the creatures of heaven, but all the other terms are used elsewhere for the roles or titles of humans, not of angels or other heavenly powers. Far more likely, then, is that all these terms are addressing or describing the sectarians themselves. The sectarians themselves are *elohim* and *elim,* for they are living the life of heaven.

We never hear the words of the praises themselves. The sectarians, who would have known scripture like the back of their hand, would have followed the commands with words they already knew. The songs, then, functioned as a conductor's score, leading the praise of the community. And the community itself is approaching the throne in heaven. The sectarians themselves are the teachers, the priests—and the *elohim*.

The sectarians at Qumran were far from the Temple in Jerusalem, whose calendar and rites they decried. We cannot know what permanent or temporary structure, if any, served as their Holy of Holies. Perhaps they did not need one at all, for they were themselves the temple in which was the dwelling and presence of God. Heaven and earth were united in their worship around the throne.

First we hear of the priests.

For he has established supreme holiness among the everlastingly holy, to be for him the priests and ministers of the presence in his glorious Holy of Holies. In the assembly of all the gods of [knowledge], he engraved his precepts for all the works of the Breath, and his glorious judgments for all who lay the foundations of knowledge, the people endowed with his glorious understanding, the gods who are close to knowledge.

4Q400 1.2–6

The second song contrasts the praise of the singer with the far higher praise offered by the residents of heaven. Here alone in the songs we hear of a contrast between human and heavenly beings. These heavenly beings are not summoned to praise; their worship is just described.

They are glorified amid all the camps of the gods
and feared by companies of men. . . .

They recount his royal majesty according to their knowledge
and exalt his glory in all his royal heavens. . . .

What shall we be counted among them?
And what shall our priesthood be counted in their dwellings?
And how shall our holiness compare with their supreme holiness?
How does the offering of our tongue of dust compare
with the knowledge of the gods?

4Q400 2.2–8

There are thirteen songs; the seventh lies at their center. The sixth,
as a prelude, sets a new tone and launches the worship itself. It does not
include the words of praise, just descriptive lists of the powers that sing
them. Sevenfold praises are described in a rhythmic, repetitive incanta-
tion: seven Sovereign Princes sing psalms with seven words of praise,
thanksgiving, or exultation and offer seven blessings of seven words
upon the just. The descriptions are weighty, repetitive, hypnotic. Long
sentences pile up phrase after phrase. Formulas pound out a stately
rhythm. We are being drawn into the worship described. The sixth
song ends with a blessing of the laity by the community's priests. On
the imagined template of the Temple itself we are still in the Courtyard
of the Israelites, where priests and laity mingle.

Description gives way to summons. At the center of the cycle, in the
seventh song the psalmist calls on the powers of heaven to praise God:

O princes of the praises of all the gods, praise the God of
majestic praises.
Exalt his exaltation on high, O gods, above the gods on high,
and his glorious divinity above all the highest heights.

4Q403 1.1.31–33

The singer describes the whole Temple. We are still outside its holiest areas, but are now looking inward toward the Anteroom and the
Holy of Holies. In the eighth song we are hearing of the "seven mysteries of knowledge in the wonderful mystery of the seven domains of
the Holy of Holies." Seven "sanctuaries" are envisaged, to match the

seven heavens through which the sectarian must pass. This will be the direction of the next seven songs. The singer evokes the Anteroom of the Temple in the ninth song; in the tenth song the veil before the Holy of Holies; and in the eleventh song the architecture, living brick-work, and chariots of the Holy of Holies. The twelfth song takes us far-ther still to see the one great chariot-throne of God himself. We hear of the cherubim and their wings, the firmament, above it "the image of the chariot-throne," and the angels between and around its wheels. The songs have brought their audience to the Holy of Holies, to imagine the sight and sound of the worship—and so to be *part* of the worship—in which heaven and earth are one.

> The gods praise him when they take up their station, and all the Breaths of the clear vault rejoice in his glory. When the gods of knowledge enter by the doors of glory, and when the holy angels depart toward their realm, the entrance doors and the gates of glory proclaim the glory of the king, blessing and praising all the breaths of God when they depart and enter by the gates.
>
> 4Q405 23.1.6–10

But why is there no sign here of *likeness as the appearance of a man* that we have come to expect from all the heirs of Ezekiel? Why, instead, does the final and climactic thirteenth song turn to a description of the high priest? Because the high priest in the Holy of Holies re-presents the glory of God himself. Here for the sectarian, in the community's worship, is the vision of glory once given to Ezekiel and his heirs.

The sectarians are before the throne of heaven. This is where they belong—on earth and yet in heaven, mortal and yet angelic. Those who heard the songs were not mere spectators of the heavenly court, like the viewers of a spectacular movie. They were part of it themselves. Their vision of the Holy of Holies is evoked by elaborate songs and no doubt by ritual to match. Yet the vision is not intended to take them away from real life into a world of imagination; it unveils their real life by means of that imagination.

How did the songs function in practice? We are not dealing with the single vision of a seer. The songs were performed, no doubt as part of a communal ritual, over the Sabbaths of thirteen successive weeks. Participants in the ritual must have sustained a view of themselves, through the week, that enabled them to take up their progress toward the Holy of Holies where they had left it the week before. They did not return, in between, to a life divorced from heaven.

Who heard the songs and sang praise in obedience to their commands? The whole community was envisaged as a new temple, freed from the corruptions of Jerusalem.

The community was holy; the priesthood was the Holy of Holies. "Among those seven times refined and among the holy ones God shall sanctify for himself for an eternal sanctuary and for purity among the cleansed. And they will be priests, his just people, his army and servants" (4Q511, frag. 35, ll. 2–4). The council of priests was itself the sanctuary and fulfilled its functions:

> The Council of the Community shall be established in truth. It shall be an everlasting plantation, a house of holiness for Israel, an assembly of supreme holiness for Aaron the Priest. They shall be witnesses to the truth at the judgment, and shall be the elect of Israel who shall atone for the Land and pay to the wicked their reward. . . . It shall have everlasting knowledge of the covenant of justice, and shall offer up sweet fragrance. It shall be a house of perfection and truth in Israel . . . and they shall be an agreeable offering, atoning for the Land and determining the judgment of wickedness. And there shall be no more iniquity.
>
> 1QS 8.5–10

It may be, then, that the later—or even all—the songs were for performance among priests alone. The songs may have been sung at the initiation of new priests. Here was the confirmation they needed that their cult, cut off from the earthly Temple where it had belonged, was indeed the cult acceptable to heaven. The community and its members—and in particular its own priests—came most fully to their God-given life at their worship as and in the heavenly temple. There they could most clearly realize what and who they really were. So they could crystallize and confirm in worship the character of their entire lives as a community on earth.

• • •

THE WORSHIPERS AT QUMRAN were at one with the worship of heaven. The angels inhabited the court of God; so did the sectarians. So did Paul. And it is to the life of heaven that he brings his converts in turn.

For Paul, everything flows from his vision of the figure at the center of that heavenly worship. But this does not restrict the figure, in Paul's thought, to heaven. Far from it. That figure is present on earth in his Body, the Body of the Anointed. This is now the Holy of Holies, purified by the blood of the Anointed himself. And in turn his Body is on earth, but is living there the life of heaven. What, then, can the life of Paul's converts be, if not the life of angels? *Do you not know,* Paul asks the Corinthians, *that you*—as an assembly—*are the sanctuary of God and that the Breath of God dwells in you?* (1 Cor. 3:16).

Such convictions gave rise to confusion. Some of Paul's Corinthians denied that the dead will rise, for they were already standing on—even over—the threshold of the heavenly life. This is the course of their transformation—into heavenly beings here and now. The death that matters they have already undergone. As Paul himself would say to the Romans, *Do you not know that all of us who have been baptized into Anointed Jesus have been baptized into his death?* (6:3). In the Breath of God the baptized have already received the deposit or down payment of the blessings that are yet to come. They are already enjoying the first blessings of the dead, as the dead wait for the final resurrection.

From the Corinthians' confusion sprang divisions and ways of life never intended by Paul. He had to correct them. The Corinthians, he insists, are not just their own, to do with themselves as they wish. They are God's home. And *whoever destroys the sanctuary of God, God will destroy them. For the sanctuary of God is holy, which you are* (1 Cor. 3:17). This is their life as an assembly; and as individuals too. *Do you not know that your body is a sanctuary of the holy Breath that you have from God?* (1 Cor. 6:19). Some at least among the Corinthians are being immoral. They have failed to see what a heavy responsibility—as individuals and as an assembly—they bear: to be as holy, day by day, as the Holy of Holies in Jerusalem.

This is the transformation that Paul wishes for his converts. This—and no special gifts—will mark their growth into the heavenly beings they believe they already are.

PART III

THE ROAD TO DAMASCUS

CHAPTER 7

ANCIENT WORLDS MADE NEW

WE HAVE HAD THE SEED of Paul's thought under the microscope. We have decoded its DNA. It is nearly time to watch the seed take root and grow. As we leave the laboratory, however, we have good reason to raise two questions. First, do any of these stories give us an account of anything that we would call an authentic vision or a genuine journey? And if they do, what assurance does this give us that the vision was not just feeding off and fueling the fantastical hopes of the visionary? Time and again we check the knowledge a visionary claims about God's plan against the passage of history, and time and again the vision is found wanting.

We are about to survey these visions briefly from three viewpoints. Such visions had by their very nature authority in Paul's day; time has dented this authority, but has not thereby impugned all claims to visionary experience. The visions gave access to a realm to which, in the most famous of all theories from the ancient world, we need access if any knowledge is going to be possible at all; that theory is abandoned now, but we can readily rediscover its power. And the visions evoked a realm immune to the turmoil of the present age; the turmoil is still with us—and so is the sense of a threshold we can attain between this world and its perfection.

First, then, let's stand back from the disclosures and ask whether we are right to speak of visions at all. We acknowledge we would be hard-pressed to define what would constitute a vision, let alone what would constitute a journey to heaven such as Paul's, *whether in the body or out of the body, I do not know* (2 Cor. 12:2). But we may wish in principle to treat their claims with respect. Of course we would expect any seer to be steeped in the stories of those who had seen or traveled before him; and we would expect any new vision to grow from such old stories at work in the imagination and dreams of the seer. An example stands before us in the book of Unveiling [Revelation] in the dependence of John the Seer upon the visions of Jesus himself. To discover such dependence does not worry us in itself. (The mystical experiences of St. Thérèse of Lisieux in the nineteenth century were grounded in the experiences she knew had been undergone by her patron, St. Teresa of Avila, in the sixteenth.)

All this we may concede. But we can still ask: What distinguishes a vision of heaven from the work of an intense imagination? And how would we know, without some prior confidence in the text and its authority, that we are reading a record of the first and not a fantasy of the second?

There are perhaps too many claims to such visionary knowledge in the Bible and related literature. They do not inspire confidence. They are so clearly contaminated by the conditions—scientific or political— of the age that gave them birth. Daniel was assured in visions that Israel would be rescued and its enemies destroyed. Daniel, placed within the story around 600 B.C.E., foresees the course of Israel's history with impressive accuracy from 300 to 163 B.C.E. Then his predictions become vague. He imagines the final vindication of God's people and the rising of the righteous dead to join the angels as the stars of heaven.

Israel would indeed be rescued from the dark oppression of the 160s B.C.E., but not as Daniel foresaw, nor with the final vindication of God's heroes, living and dead. As an opponent of the church already saw in the third century C.E., the book of Daniel was compiled into its present form in 167–163 B.C.E. The author could concoct predictions of events already past when he wrote, and so could win for his text the respect of its readers. But at the crucial moment, as he surveys the crisis facing his own addressees, the author must hope and guess. Now, much in the book of Daniel is far older than its final compilation. But the more such debts we find, the stronger grows the suspicion that an editor has sewn a disparate mass of old stories into one unwieldy whole. Among those old stories might have been the records of visions seen long ago, stories that had been adapted and elaborated, perhaps, over centuries. But we cannot hope to identify that genuine visionary core. The seer Daniel and his visions fade from view like *Alice's Adventures in Wonderland*'s Cheshire cat.

Of course, a journey to heaven was useful for writers and compilers; it provided a narrative framework and an indisputable authority for the claimed disclosures. Writers could plunder familiar elements from earlier stories to give their own an authentic and authoritative air. All the better, if the journey could be ascribed to some visionary hero from the past.

The knowledge given by such a vision will remain exclusive to the seer and to the favored addressees with whom he shares it. Those who are the source of such knowledge or control it have power. Those allowed to share in the knowledge are confirmed in their sense of separation from the mass of men and women around them. They are more than separate; they are superior. They are the insiders who understand the real nature of the world and its traumatic history. Their shared knowledge gives them cohesion. And if it includes the promise of their final vindication, it gives them confidence to face what lies between the present and that glorious future. Texts that impart such knowledge are texts well suited to a sect and a boon to its leaders.

We can see, then, *why* writers used the device of such a journey. And that, we might think, is exactly what it was—a literary device, nothing more. Even fading from view is that modest picture of an intense imagination at work in an ancient tradition on an ancient story. We are left with just the quiet calculation of a community's leaders.

One famous passage shows well how powerful such visionary language could be. Mark's Jesus speaks at length as he overlooks Jerusalem just days before his death. The speech comprises, as it stands in Mark's gospel, a mixed bag of short passages neatly, but still discernibly, adapted and interwoven. (All the stories we have glanced at from the gospels have clearly been elaborated during the decades between Jesus' life and the gospels' completion.) Among these short passages there may well be some warnings issued by Jesus himself. But the climax of the speech is spun from prophecies of Isaiah and the vision of Daniel; it claims no new vision, and needed none. The tradition of such prophecies was so well known that an editor—or Jesus himself—could cut and paste to great effect. Let him add a few lines of his own in the same style, and even without laying claim to a vision he has a speech with all the gravity that a vision would give it.

Paul himself in his letters twice invokes the authority of a special unveiling without reference to his journeys to heaven or to any vision. Both times he is encouraging his addressees to trust in Jesus' imminent return. In the earlier letter he expects himself and his Thessalonians to be alive and waiting when the Anointed comes. *We tell you this in a word of the Lord*—perhaps a prophecy uttered by Jesus when on earth, perhaps a prophecy he has imparted to Paul from heaven—*that we who are living, who are being left for the coming of the Lord, will not be ahead of those who have gone to sleep* (1 Thess. 4:15). In the latter he assumes less: *Look, I tell you a mystery: We shall not all sleep, but we shall all be changed, in an instant, in the twinkling of an eye, in the sounding of the last trumpet* (1 Cor. 15:51–52). The last survivor of Paul's age fell asleep in death nearly two thousand years ago. The trumpet has not sounded yet. Paul too, it turns out, had to hope and guess.

Daniel foresaw a rescue that never came. Paul encouraged in his converts a hope for Jesus' quick return that still remains unmet. What credence should we give to such claims, dressed up to impress their audience with privileged access to God's hidden truths? We can sharpen the challenge with our particular question in mind. Why should we believe that any of these claims record a genuine vision or journey at all?

My own response to such an argument is in two parts. First, a historical judgment. And then a fuller account of the roles played by these visions.

First, then, for a careful but clear historical judgment. It will not surprise you. The argument I have just outlined must, I am sure, be turned on its head. We have heard from Paul's own account to the Corinthians that he believed himself to be a seer and to have journeyed to heaven. And we shall see throughout this book that he offered to his converts here on earth the blessings enjoyed by seers in heaven. What roles we ascribe in all this to literary debts or a trained imagination or a privilege granted by God—that will depend on far wider decisions we must make about the action of God in the world. But the claim Paul made for himself and his converts was no bluff. The most plausible account we can give of it is also the most straightforward: Paul encouraged those converts to believe of themselves what he believed of himself. Their experience came to fit his offer and description. They were, they believed, living the life of the heaven that their emissary had visited.

In such a light the unveiling of the gospels too makes sense. The evangelists drew upon the tradition because the tradition was alive and well. Ancient visions were of such value to the evangelists because new disclosures were growing out of them. These were experienced as visions in their turn. New life was drawing on old literature and, in the gospels, a new literature draws on the new life. Had Jesus himself seen that a new form of unveiling was under way in his life and that it would take a quite new form of apprehension? Or did the assemblies come later to see what strange truths must be disclosed about his life, and so come to develop stories of that life—and ways of telling those stories—that would meet the need? We cannot know now. We would like to distinguish clearly between the events, their understanding at the time, and the understanding that their literary record made possible in the following decades, but we are unlikely ever to untangle the skein. We need, for ourselves, simply to recognize such outstanding questions and not to expect an answer too quickly.

ANY CONVERSATION ABOUT SOCIETY, politics, or ethics will want to have words for a world in which justness dwells. For such a consummation to which the route is unclear we speak of looking forward through time. We less often think nowadays of such perfection already present, assured but elusive; for this we use the language of heaven and of looking upward though space. This second dimension offers, more obviously than the first, a sense of assurance. This offer is valuable, but dangerous. We need to believe that our fragmentary world offers more than just willful or fantastical grounds for hope. We can be tempted to speak of the ideal as a reality, already fixed, more real than the world around us. We are trading in hope, but we call it knowledge.

There was good reason, in Paul's day, for confusion between the two. We have lost sight of the tradition, central to the thought of ancient Greece and Rome, that all knowledge involves insight into a "world" more real than the world we see around us. This insight was claimed to be the condition under which alone any knowledge was possible at all: every immortal soul, embodied on earth, remembers from its previous existence the true, immaterial "forms" of which all objects and qualities in this world are faint, degraded copies. So—and only so—can knowledge be assured, shared, and imparted. So much for the knowledge involved in daily life. What, then, might be accessible to a soul that self-consciously sought the immaterial world of eternal truths? What escape might such a soul win from the illusions that the world of the senses weaves around us? Such escape would call for years of intellectual, moral, and spiritual formation. And that formation could lead to a knowledge far deeper than the sensory world encourages us even to look for.

The Jewish philosopher Philo was steeped in this Platonic thought. Much of Philo's work is an allegorical account of the books that open the Old Order. In one passage he tells of God's command to Abraham to leave his ancestral home, and of Abraham's later fear that he will die with no heir. Abraham, in Philo's interpretation, must leave his land, that is, his body; his relations, that is, his senses; and his father's house, that is, the speech that gives a home to his mind. God's house is the Word of God itself, and this is the home that Abraham must seek.

The Word of God divides and distinguishes; God's action as creator is presented as the active discrimination that constitutes knowledge. The true activity of the human mind, made in the image of God's, is to realize order in chaos. Here is a claim of the greatest importance: in our thought we catch in and for ourselves a glimpse of the work of creation. And the philosopher knows it. The upward spiral of self-consciousness leads to a consciousness of God and so to deeper self-consciousness in turn. We must see ourselves for what we are—made in the image of the Creator.

Such self-conscious thought, properly exercised and recognized for what it is, will take the individual far beyond the limits of normal understanding. And it will make that individual the heir of Abraham.

If any yearning comes upon you, my soul, to be an heir of the good things of God, then leave behind you not just your land, your relatives and your father's house; but be a fugitive from yourself and come forth out from yourself—just as those who are possessed and in the frenzy of the Corybantic mysteries—being inspired as those in the Bacchic rites and being carried by God, just as the prophets are inspired. For if the mind has divinity within it and is no longer in itself but is stirred to its depths and maddened by heavenly love, led by That Which Truly Is and drawn upward to it, with truth leading the way and removing all obstacles before its feet—that person is the heir.

WHO IS THE HEIR OF DIVINE THINGS, 69-70

Philo himself has undergone such "frenzy." He is uncertain exactly how to describe it. Was he in ecstasy, in which the reason was elevated to heights beyond the normal reach of the mind? Did divine inspiration fill his mind ? Or did it displace his mind and take him over itself? His own experiences shape his description of the mind's ultimate insights and its route to them. He too uses the language of ascent and of the sight of God's glory. The mind, he says, contemplates the air on soaring wing. It is swept up into the heavens and is whirled around with the dances of the planets and stars, following the love of wisdom that guides its steps. Higher and higher the mind goes, to the world of things understood by the mind alone. There it sees the patterns and originals—the Platonic forms—of the things discerned by the senses on earth. The mind is filled with a sober drunkenness, like that of those who celebrate the Corybantic mysteries, but possessed by a longing far nobler than theirs.

Lifted by this to the point of the arch of things the mind can grasp, the mind seems to be on the way to the great king himself. But while it longs to see him, pure and unmixed rays of concentrated light stream forth like a torrent, so that by its gleams the eye of the mind is dazzled.

ON THE CREATION OF THE WORLD, 71

Few enough enjoyed the insights of a Philo. They sound like the esoteric fantasies of a strange elite. But the tradition of such journeys, in widely varied forms, dominated the ancient world. At issue was an understanding of knowledge itself, its conditions and possibilities. The stories of these visions are not designed simply to tell us a truth, but to reveal the truth about truth and the conditions under which we can discern it.

We nowadays fail to see what these stories are about. They disappoint us. And so we shunt them into a siding and neglect them. It is our loss.

Even if we keep sight of them, these stories no longer tell us the truth about truth. We look at knowledge and its conditions differently now. It would be hard, in Paul's day, for a Greek-speaking seer to be free from the influence of Plato. Philo gladly reinforced his claims by the most famous theory of knowledge and the soul that Europe had then—and has still—ever known. But for most of us that theory is at best a distant memory, heard of in high school and long since left aside.

LET'S ADMIT IT, THE NEW ORDER has been too successful for its own good. Secret knowledge of God is, it seems, secret no longer. We have climbed the ladder Paul offered, and so we do not need it now—and have forgotten that we ever did. The authors of the New Order have surely rendered redundant those techniques of theirs that we hardly recognize. Paul may have thought himself indispensable to his converts, but his success has made his deepest insights accessible to everyone, and without reference to himself at all.

Paul believed within the terms and ways possible in his generation. He could have believed—and been believed by his audience—in no other way. The terms and images became sacred and have been preserved; we use them still. Over centuries, however, their significance has changed. And we wonder now, perhaps anxiously, whether we can use them honestly. They have an aura of sanctity that they earned in a quite different setting to serve quite different experiences and expectations.

The world of thought inhabited by Paul is not ours. He could speak without a qualm of Adam and Eve, of heaven and of Jesus' return. Many of us still hear these spoken of in church; they may well strengthen us at times of temptation, bereavement, or sorrow. But they are pale shadows of their former selves. They were once rich in content and association. Adam or "man" represented all humankind. His story was not just ancient history or naïve invention. Heaven held the secrets of this life and was not just a home for the next; to think of heaven was not to evade our humdrum world, but to see it as it really is. Jesus' return was the hope of every day and week, not the point on the horizon, ever receding, where the prairie's highway narrows to nothing and meets the sky.

Paul's imagination was crowded with the inhabitants of heaven. A meager few live on in ours. Our forebears could look up at the vault of heaven and see there a solid division between our world and God's heaven. Now we see a space whose limit we cannot conceive, with no place set aside for a court of angels. Our forebears could count the generations between the world's birth and their own. Archbishop Ussher of Armagh worked in the 1650s to establish from the Old Order the first moment of the world's creation. "Which beginning of time," he wrote, "according to our Chronologie, fell upon the entrance of the night preceding the twenty-third day of Octob. in the year of the Julian Calendar 710 [4004 B.C.E.]." Our telescopes now look out at night on stars whose light, we know, has taken tens of thousands of years to reach us. We can enjoy, then, the stories of heaven, Adam, and the throne of God. We can respect the tradition that spoke of them. But what can we learn from this world of fantasy?

That Adam matters, for Christian faith, more than we might have expected. The New Order is clear that the deliverance of all creation is a mirror image of its fall. The first Adam was in Eden. He fell, was expelled, and was subject to death. The second Adam was obedient all the way to death. And so he has restored humankind to a glory far beyond the glory of the first. The new Jerusalem that will descend to earth, according to the book of Unveiling, is modeled in part on Ezekiel's vision of a new temple and in part—like Ezekiel's vision itself—on the Garden of Eden. But a mirror can bear an image only if an original is put before it. If we discredit the original, the first Adam and his history, then their image in the Anointed disappears. The New Order rounds off the Old, in our Bibles, with this triumphant restoration of Eden. An Eden that for many Americans, brought up on modern science, is the setting for a quaint but incredible story.

Paul and the evangelists have left us records, in these terms, of experiences that without those terms were unimaginable. The churches have built, century by century, on these lowest courses of the first floor's walls. The skyscraper is still rising two millennia later. The bricks we lay rest their weight on all that has been put in place before them.

We study those earlier courses, assess them, criticize them—and depend on them. Among those earlier bricks are all the interpretations of Paul that have helped the churches over the centuries. These are a part of our building, no less than Paul's own thought.

From our distance we tend to recognize in our view of the world just fragments of Paul's own. But Paul's building is now part of our foundations; its footprint has become ours. If our own superstructure seems sometimes ill-designed, it is in part because its load-bearing walls, forever remodeled in detail, still follow the plan of a building raised two thousand years ago.

Can we, then, do any more than respect that footprint, follow it, and recognize, from our great distance, how it came to be laid the way it was?

Yes, we can do more. Paul sets up, in his sustained images and his aims, a poetic world for his converts to inhabit. He developed a style and form of letter that suited their life between heaven and earth, between the present and the future. He disentangles them from their relations with the world of their past and defines them instead by reference to their future. With their rich tapestry of images, the letters weave a home for the thought and imagination of converts who are no longer at home in this world and not yet at home in the next. He gives them a place to live. He defines the threshold between two worlds, sets his readers on it, and steers them toward its other side. And he charges their life with significance for the whole creation. He writes to small, fragile communities, but has them believe that they are the axis upon which the world is turning.

This is not the knowledge of a world apart, to be discovered by the detached philosopher of independent means and well-served tranquillity. In a great tradition in the Greek world, one sought escape from the cares and passions of the body so one could attain truths from which the body will endlessly blind and distract us. The body is a tomb, ran a motto known to Plato: *sōma sēma*. Philo knows this tradition well. But through Judaism runs a different urgency: the search for an ever deeper insight into God's will for his people and his faithfulness. And such insight will only ever be granted to those who themselves are faithful to that will. The body is not our tomb; the body is the vehicle of our life. And as the world is sustained in life by the active will and power of God alone, to be separated from that God and that will is death. The present,

then, is not a gateway to the mind's eternity. It is itself charged with significance. It matters, moment by moment. And because every moment
is in the hands of God, every moment is charged with hope.

Nothing reveals more clearly the relation—alert, engaged, and
uncowed—that Paul's converts bore to the world than the relation their
Lord bore to the emperor. We have lost sight of the power claimed by the
emperor and his empire; we can no longer sense how radical—and so
how potentially dangerous—the good news would sound. Churches
speak about the kingdom of God, historians about the Roman Empire.
But the Greek word used to call God or the Anointed "king" was the
word used as well for Rome's "emperor." In this book I will at times
speak of the empire of God, of a dominion that claimed a Lord unmistakably at odds with the lord of Rome. This Lord's dominion empowered
his subjects to face derision, danger, even death at the hands of Rome.

The emperor Jesus and the emperor of Rome could both demand
the obeisance of the whole world. As subjects of Rome, the followers
of Jesus were under the power of the emperor; but as citizens of heaven,
they were under the dominion of God and his Anointed alone. Jesus'
followers could be harassed and even killed, but his dominion itself was
impervious to the legions of Rome. In their halfway world the assemblies of Jesus had found the way to survive.

Jesus' followers were not alone in needing the hope offered by
poetry and its evocation of a better world. Successive generals had
seemed by 40 B.C.E. to end the decades of civil war. The Roman poet
Virgil wrote then the most famous of all poems on a new age. He
mixes images as richly as Paul will himself. The degenerate age of iron
is giving way to the ideal, golden age of the god Saturn. Virgil adapts
the Etruscan image of a city's ten ages; he has the comet that followed
Julius Caesar's death in 44 B.C.E. mark the start of Rome's tenth age. I
use the famous translation of John Dryden, published in 1697:

> The last great Age, foretold by sacred Rhymes,
> Renews its finish'd course, Saturnian times
> Rowl round again, and mighty years, begun
> From their first orb, in radiant Circles run.
> The base degenerate Iron off-spring ends;
> A golden progeny from Heav'n descends.

Virgil speaks of a child's birth. By the fourth century some Christian theologians saw in that prophecy a prediction of the Anointed himself.

> The jarring Nations he in peace shall bind
> And with paternal Virtues rule Mankind.
> See, lab'ring Nature calls thee to sustain
> The nodding Frame of Heav'n, and Earth and Main.
>
> *THE ECLOGUES* 4.4–7, 17, 50–51

Virgil wrote in hope. But nine more years of civil war were yet to come. The same motifs would be sounded again at the accession of Nero in 54 C.E.; but within fifteen years the empire was once more in turmoil and armies were on the streets of Rome. "Peace and safety" were offered by the Roman Empire—in between the convulsions, ever renewed, of dynastic war.

The assemblies of Jesus longed for peace and safety no less than their pagan neighbors. And in their poetic, halfway world these assemblies would find it. And so they managed not just to survive, but to spread, for here in their own assemblies a last great age was dawning that was subject to no warring generals or false dawns.

When they say "Peace and safety," writes Paul to the Thessalonians, *then sudden destruction comes upon them. But God has not appointed us for wrath but for the obtaining of deliverance through our Lord Jesus Anointed* (1 Thess. 5:3, 9).

CHAPTER 8

SLOW BURN?

The Damascus Experience

TELLING THE STORY—AND EXPLAINING IT

"The road to Damascus," "the Damascus experience": Paul's conversion is a byword for a sudden, dramatic change of heart and mind. Nothing in Luke's story has prepared Paul—or readers—for this total turnaround. We hear from Luke of the preceding weeks and months in the assembly. But of Paul we have just that one mention, as he watches Stephen die. Luke recalls no warning signs in Paul's own behavior or feelings and no signals from God of his coming intervention. Paul's conversion, it seems, was a bolt from the blue.

Or was it? Any vision such as Paul's is likely, we have seen, to have followed years of study and training. Were these years as well of deepening doubt and unease? We have been aware for centuries of the psychological pressures that can build up to conversion. St. Augustine in the fourth century and Martin Luther in the sixteenth were both heavily influenced by Paul. Each saw, in retrospect, how a long intellectual, moral, and spiritual search within himself had culminated in a moment of dramatic change. It has sometimes been possible to see such a moment coming—and even to encourage it.

The most famous and influential of modern conversions may well be that of John Wesley. His diary for May 24, 1738, is quite moving:

In the evening, I went very unwillingly to a society in Aldersgate Street [just to the north of the northern boundary of the ancient City of London], where one was reading Luther's preface to the Epistle to the Romans. About a quarter before nine, while he was describing the change which God works in the heart through faith in Christ, I felt my heart strangely warmed. I felt I did trust in Christ, Christ alone for salvation; and an assurance was given me that He has taken away *my* sins, even *mine,* and saved *me* from the law of sin and death.

We may think of this moment as a classic example of instantaneous conversion, and this is the way such events were described in Wesley's time. But it was nothing of the sort. Wesley had been under the influence of the Moravian Brethren since his journey to Georgia in 1735. He was in constant touch with them in London as his turmoil grew more intense in 1738. They had developed a model of evangelical conversion as the event of a single moment (however long its gestation). John Wesley was acutely self-conscious. He treasured the accounts of such experiences in others; and his own brother Charles underwent such a moment some days before he did himself. He was both immersed in his own torment and aware of the result to which it might be leading. And by April 1738 he was hoping it would. The moment of his own conversion came as he was hearing an exposition of Paul's letter to the Romans; as we shall see in a few pages' time, the letter's central chapters were for centuries believed to describe Paul's own agony before conversion and joyful triumph after it. It takes nothing from the extraordinary experience, character, and achievements of John Wesley— and nothing from his integrity—to say that through the early months of 1738 he was grooming himself for conversion.

How much we would like to know of Paul's life and thoughts in the months leading up to his conversion. Had he seen the change coming? Had he found hope in those months from the good news of these subversive followers of Jesus? Perhaps he came to ask himself if this Jesus might after all be the longed-for Anointed, to dream of sharing the assurance Jesus' followers enjoyed, and to wonder if the gifts of the Breath, on view in the new assembly, might ever be Paul's own.

TELLING PAUL'S STORY THEN AND NOW

We would like to know of Paul's life and thought—on our own terms. So far we have been hearing voices from a world far from our own. We have accepted that Luke's story of the conversion must be taken seriously. But it may well be high time we look behind the language of visions, journeys, and the re-presentation of the Anointed. We need to place Paul in some modern categories in which we can make sense of the man, his supposed experiences, and his self-understanding. It is enthralling to watch Paul weave his own visual and conceptual connections into a wonderful tapestry, but we may still feel cheated. We seem to be hearing a grand paraphrase of Paul's own self-descriptions; we hear all the same words sung to all the same tunes, just differently ordered with neat variations and jazzier rhythms. To repeat what Paul says does not explain what Paul says, nor does it bring to life the Paul outlandish enough to say it.

We are seeking neither to deny God a role nor, however, to bring on God as a supposed explanation for what happened, for God's activity does not provide an explanation for human affairs. Appeals to God's activity can only bring to an end the search for an explanation. And readers who are offered God as a substitute for explanation could feel cheated, as Paul fades from view behind the smokescreen of a modern author's piety.

In our search, then, for a drive and passion in Paul's life that we ourselves can understand, let's look at a widespread modern view of Paul. Many people, whether or not they go to church, may find that these next few paragraphs are fleshing out a long-standing suspicion and a good reason for holding it—the suspicion, that is, that they do not *like* the tense, male-chauvinist Paul. In this view, Paul was a man under severe psychological pressure. At his conversion one part of that pressure was released. Paul was at last able to acknowledge—and enabled to combat—parts of himself that had flooded him with guilt. He was not reconciled to them; he was armed against them. And so that pressure, its cause, and its release left their mark on all that he taught and wrote thereafter, particularly on his views of women and sex.

PAUL, THE LAW, AND SEXUAL SUPPRESSION: STATING THE CASE

Psychological pressure can build up in us, unbeknown to ourselves. We may feel unloved and unlovable, unvalued by our parents, perhaps, or outshone by our siblings. We may feel guilty or ashamed, that we have failed to meet our parents' expectations or our own, that we have betrayed someone we love or the standards we believe we share. We may feel out of kilter with the culture around us and required forever to act out an alien role: women may have to pretend, to their families and themselves, that they want only to be homemakers subservient to their husbands; gays may need to pretend, to their families and themselves, that they are straight. We may feel insecure and in need of the respect that we would like to have from others and for ourselves. Our education, job, income, lifestyle, neighborhood, friends, children—all can help give us the confidence that we are, in society, where we belong; and any, if they fail to meet the standards to which we aspire, can undermine our self-respect. We may feel powerless and may long to assert our will against a failing marriage, disruptive neighbors, our boss at work, redundancy, or the federal government.

The resulting pressure can simmer beneath the surface for months or even years, growing ever more intense. It can show itself in unsettled behavior and strong feelings; but even if a friend were to suggest a connection between this behavior and some deep pressure, we would in all honesty fail to see the link. The pressure grows. A single incident triggers its release, and suddenly we are overwhelmed with love or anger or tears. We can recognize at last what a weight of passion has been building up behind our mental dam and has at last broken through in a wave of emotion. And not just emotion. When such passion is released we have a chance to see ourselves—our deepest urges and all we have done to control or suppress them—more clearly than we have for years.

We do not just see ourselves more clearly. We come to see ourselves *differently*. We rewrite the story about ourselves and our past that we tell ourselves and others. Our priorities for the future change. We find different things in ourselves to praise and different things of which to be ashamed.

This is all, it seems, walled in within the mind of the individual. Surely there are effects from outside? In the buildup to such a crisis or during or after it we will often find ourselves more at ease in a newly found community. Thanks perhaps to the prior membership of our friends or family, we may well have been growing into the values of that community for months or years already. We may have found ourselves made welcome and valued. The more clearly old ties and allegiances are threatened by a public statement of a new allegiance, the more we rely on the security and friendship offered by the community that lies ahead.

How might this pattern apply to Paul? In his first appearances in The Mission [Acts], Paul is known by his Jewish name, Saul. *Saul*, Luke tells us, *was breathing threat and murder against the pupils of the Lord* (The Mission 9:1). Paul himself confirms as much to the Galatians:

> *You have heard of my former way of life within Judaism: I used to perse-cute the assembly of God to the utmost, and was destroying it, and out-stripped in Judaism many of my contemporaries within my own people, being far more zealous than they were for the traditions of my forefathers.*
> GALATIANS 1:13-14

Was there more to this furious attack than meets the eye? Sometimes we see people far more fervid for a cause than anyone else is, far more fervid, indeed, than we think that cause could possibly warrant. We wonder what else is driving them. And we wonder: Are they hiding some weakness right behind this abrasive show of strength? Are they proving to themselves and to others that they deserve every respect and praise—at the very point where, deep down, they are afraid of some shameful secret about themselves? Paul was the most ferocious opponent of Jesus' followers. Perhaps there was something in these followers or their message that struck a chord in Paul himself—a chord that he dare not listen to or even acknowledge he had heard. The good news of Jesus' followers made God's anger incomparably vivid—and his forgiveness incomparably close. Perhaps Paul was looking for a forgiveness that in all his life so far—and in all the depths of the Judaism he had known since birth—he had been quite unable to find.

Let's pursue this line of thought. Of himself, Paul says:

> If anyone has reason to have confidence in the flesh, I have more: circumcised on the eighth day, from the people of Israel, the tribe of Benjamin, a Hebrew born from Hebrews; as to the law, a Pharisee; as to zeal, a persecutor of the assembly [of the followers of the Anointed]; as to justness under the law, blameless.
>
> PHILIPPIANS 3:4–6

Readers have often wondered if Paul had been quite as secure in his former world as he claims here in retrospect. In his letter to the Romans Paul mounts a vast argument about God and all humanity. He draws a stark contrast between two conditions of human existence. On the one hand is the life and liveliness made possible by the Breath of God. On the other is the power within us that spurs us to do wrong, a power that lurks in the needs and appetites of the flesh. We will return to this famous passage and set it back where it belongs—at the heart of Paul's letter and of his plan to heal his readers of the desolation he describes. For the moment, however, let us hear it in isolation as the impassioned plea that at first it seems to be, a plea for Paul's own rescue from a conflict that is tearing him apart. He has been speaking of "we," "you," "they." Then he suddenly turns (at 7:7) with no warning or introduction to write of "I," "me"—and in the most anguished terms. Is this Paul's own confession of his torment under the Jewish Law, before he won release at his conversion?

Paul quotes the start of the tenth law in the Ten Commandments: *You shall not desire the wife of your neighbor* (The Escape [Exodus] 2:17). Writes Paul: *I would not have known wrongdoing except through the law. For I would not have known desire if the law did not say, You shall not desire. And wrongdoing, taking its opportunity through the commandment, effected in me every desire* (7:7–8). That desire is normally thought of as covetousness, the jealousy that wants to possess its object. But the word is also used specifically of sexual desire. Such desire lurks in the very first stories of the Old Order. The devil, says Eve in The Beginning [Genesis], *deceived* her; and one tradition claimed that the devil seduced her. It is surely no coincidence that Paul evokes in this paragraph the language of Adam and Eve and their temptation by the devil. *Wrongdoing,* writes Paul, *taking its opportunity through the commandment, deceived me utterly and through it—killed me* (7:11). Lurking, then, just beneath the surface of Paul's agonized "I" is a single torment: the guilt of a sexual urge condemned by the law and stirred by that very condemnation, an urge that was rampant in Paul's limbs and beyond his control.

> For we know that the law is filled with the Breath, but I am made of flesh, sold [like a slave] under wrongdoing. For what I am effecting, I do not know. For what I want—that's not what I do; but what I hate— that's what I do. And if what I don't want, that's what I do—then I say "Yes" to the Law, and agree that it is fine. And now it is no longer me effecting this, but the wrongdoing that lives in me. For I know that the good does not live in me, I mean in my flesh. For to want it, that is close to hand, but to effect what is fine—that is not. For I don't do what I want, the good; but what I don't want, the bad—that is what I do. And if what I don't want, that's what I do—then it is no longer me that is effecting it, but the wrongdoing that lives in me.
>
> So I find the Law, for me who wants to do what is fine—I find that for me what is bad is close to hand. For I share the delight in the law of God, in my inner person; but I see another law in my limbs, waging war against the Law of my mind and taking me prisoner in the law of wrongdoing which is in my limbs. What a wretch I am! Who will rescue me from the body of this death?—But thanks be to God through Jesus Anointed our Lord!—So then: I myself in my mind am a slave to the law of God, but in my flesh to the law of wrongdoing.
> ROMANS 7:14–25

This Paul had not been relaxed and confident in his observance of the Jewish Law. He had been tortured by his incapacity to fulfill its demands. The Law was not just ineffectual against the desires and practices that it forbade. Far worse than that. It had stirred just these desires in Paul; and for as long as he looked to the Law for support and for God's favor, his battle against these desires was in vain. And of all the assaults of evil, the most potent and most personal was sexual desire.

Until the good news brought rescue and reassurance. *There is therefore no condemnation to those that are in Anointed Jesus* (8:1). Paul does not say that the urges fade away, still less that he feels permitted to yield to them. But he has an ally in the fight against them: the Breath. He no longer feels himself a slave to the passions that attack him still. And in this new stage of the battle he is free from the agony of his former self-examination.

Many readers will so far have nodded in agreement. Such a portrayal would explain a lot. But in Judaism—ancient and modern alike—such an angry view of sex is almost unknown. *Go forth and multiply,* commanded God, so that is precisely what we should do. It is Christianity that has found in sex such a source of evil—a Christianity heavily influenced by Paul himself. But why should Paul, Jewish to the core, have looked so darkly on this God-given blessing?

Paul gives the Corinthians various instructions about ways of life and about worship. He quotes a slogan from the Corinthians' own letter to himself: *It is good for a man not to touch a woman* (1 Cor. 7:1). This is their recommendation, not his. But where did they get it from? Almost certainly from Paul himself. They may have misunderstood him. But although he refines the instruction (married couples should abstain from sex only by mutual agreement and for short periods, to promote prayer), he does not dismiss it. He is clear: *I want everyone to be like me* (7:7)—unmarried. He would prefer that the men among his converts keep women at a distance. Is he afraid of women's sexual appeal, its power to confuse him and the men among his converts? If so, we would expect this fear to inform all his instructions on the role and power of women.

And so indeed it does. The Corinthian assembly is divided over the role of women in worship. Women, Paul insists, must have their heads covered, men not. *A man is the image and glory of God; the woman is the glory of man. For man is not created from woman, but woman from man. For man was not created on woman's account, but woman on man's* (1 Cor. 11:7–9). He carries on, adducing ever more feeble arguments: *You, judge among yourselves: Is it right for a woman to pray to God with her head uncov-*

ered? Doesn't nature itself teach you that it's a dishonor for a man to wear long hair, and an honor for a woman? (11:13–15). At this distance, we are likely to answer no, this is not a matter of nature at all. Paul himself expected just such a cynical response from the Corinthians. He stumbles to a close: *And if anyone wants to be contentious—well, we do not follow such a custom, nor do the assemblies of God* (11:16). This is not the only time Paul appeals to the customs in other assemblies to close down an argument. It is sad to see him bluster.

At least in this section of the letter Paul accepts a role for women in public prayer and public prophecy. By the time he is rounding off his guidance on worship, he has hardened his line. *As in all the assemblies of the saints, let the women be silent in the assemblies.* Once more that resort to unnamed others. *For it is not fitting that they should speak, but let them be kept subordinate, just as the Law says too. . . . For it is a disgrace for a woman to speak in assembly* (1 Cor. 14:33–35). The assembly's local leaders are, it seems, welcoming the contribution of the women. Paul has no argument to mount. To face down any hint of women's leadership in worship, he can resort only to sarcasm. He must quell the Corinthians' independence: *Or has the word of God come out from you, or has it come to you alone?* (14:36).

It is good for a man not to touch a woman. We can see how the modern rumor takes wing that Paul was afraid of women and so did all he could to restrict their role in his assemblies. This Paul writes from a dark turbulence of sexual guilt and suppression. There may be good news embedded in his letters, but such news is forever distorted by the unacknowledged torment of his deepest desires.

Is *this* the man whose thought has shaped all Christendom?

CHAPTER 9

"POWER MADE PERFECT IN WEAKNESS"

WE HAVE SKETCHED A MAN IN AGONY. This is a man we can hardly revere—but a man, nonetheless, whose drives and turmoil we can understand. Paul may be alone in his mission, but in his torment he is one of thousands. The saint emerges from the shadows of the churches' ancient—and ever more defensive—piety and is at last seen in the clear light of day as a brilliant, tortured, driven man.

But having made these charges against Paul, I will be the first to say that they will not do. Here are some of the flaws in the last chapter's argument, which an advocate for Paul's defense will—quite rightly—point out to the jury.

The first and general point is about Paul and his observance of the Jewish Law. Paul writes of his life under the Law: *as to the law, a Pharisee; as to zeal, a persecutor of the assembly; as to justness under the law, blameless* (Phil. 3:5–6). He has a good reason to make the claim where he does. He is warning the Philippians against the blandishments of those who are urging them to be circumcised and to take on the Law's observance. If the Law had been such a curse to him before his conversion, he could have said so here to good effect. But he does not say that the Anointed is a gain over against the loss that the Law had been. Far from it. The Anointed was a gain so great that Paul counted all other gains (chief among them the Law) as loss. It was not a relief to give up his reliance on the Law; it was a sacrifice.

Second, and at a level more general still, all that Paul says about marriage to the Corinthians is shaped by a single thought: *The time is cut short. The form of this world is passing away* (1 Cor. 7:29, 31). Paul is waiting for the return of the Anointed, and if the Anointed is due anytime, marriage becomes a distraction, not a calling. Paul's viewpoint may raise for us two larger questions: Was he in error over the Anointed's return? And if he was, does it matter to those who value Paul's teaching today? But for the moment we adopt Paul's own viewpoint, and from here his position is clear. As long as the present order lasts, he insists, there is a balance to be kept in the rights of husband and wife. Far from subordinating the wife to the demands of her husband, Paul calls for a symmetry between them.

What then of worship? Here Paul has drawn on the story of Adam and Eve in The Beginning [Genesis]. Adam was made first; God saw that it was not good for him to be alone, and created Eve as his helper. Paul speaks of women's creation on men's account. He realizes instantly that his words might be misunderstood and be used to belittle women. Clearly refining what he has just said, he reasserts the relation between men and women with great care: *Nevertheless: there is neither woman without man nor man without woman in the Lord. For just as the woman is from the man, so the man is through the woman; and all are from God* (1 Cor. 11:11–12). When Paul draws on the tradition he has inherited from The Beginning, he is redressing the imbalance that the tradition has made possible. The Beginning has apparently offered a basis for the systematic subordination of women. Paul does not build on this foundation. On the contrary, he undermines it.

We might again ask, for our own sake, if Paul's reliance on the story of Adam and Eve is reliance upon a perniciously patriarchal myth; and if so, whether modern churches should decide to put less weight on Paul's words today than our forebears did. But such reliance on The Beginning, common to the Judaism of Paul's day, would not reveal, in itself, much to us of Paul's own thoughts or personality.

Why, then, is the whole passage on worship so weakly argued? Because Paul is prejudiced in favor of the old practices he has known since his Jewish childhood. The new ways in gentile Corinth are alien to him and are certainly not what he had in mind when he founded the assembly there. Paul, then, has a conservative streak. Where his good news has not called for change, he values the conventions he has known all his life. And so do most of us. We have so far found in Paul only examples of the kind of limitations we suffer from ourselves, not his personal drive toward a newly restricted role or diminished status for women.

And so we come to his closing command that women be silent in the assembly. We have an unexpected preliminary to settle here—the passage may not be part of Paul's letter at all. In some manuscripts it is found slightly later in the letter, rounding off the section on worship. It is as if the paragraph was once free-standing and has been inserted by different scribes in different places. We must then ask: Was the paragraph written by Paul himself at all? Might it have been issued by an aide who was more conservative than Paul was himself? We hear such a voice in a pupil's letter, 1 Timothy. The role of women in the assembly was clearly still debated. In this instruction, all Paul's care and acuity has been lost. *Let a woman learn in silence, in all subordination. I give no permission for a woman to teach nor to have authority over a man, but to be in peace and quiet. For Adam was made first, then Eve. And Adam was not deceived, but the woman was deceived and is fallen into transgression* (1 Tim. 2:11–14).

What, then, of our closing instruction in 1 Corinthians itself? *It is a disgrace for a woman to speak in assembly* (14:35). I suspect it is by Paul himself and belongs in 1 Corinthians. There are verbal links that tie it closely to the rest of the section. In a careful, sustained maneuver that we shall see him undertake twice in this letter, Paul has worked his way around to the position that he himself endorses. On his way he has brought into view the whole context within which his decision—and the Corinthians'—must be made. He is not simply imparting a decision; he is enabling the Corinthians to make such decisions for themselves. It is all the more striking to see him bluster at the critical moment. Does his final, brusque command for women's silence, then, reveal his own pathological need to keep women at a distance even when all arguments fail him? No. This is still the conservative Paul, unsettled by the one assembly that has misunderstood his teaching in this way and made it an excuse, as he sees the situation, for a dire disorder.

We set out some pages ago to test the widespread view that Paul was driven by the suppression of his sexual desires. I have done the best I can for this suspicion. But my case, I am the first to admit, is in disarray.

PAUL AND POWER

We have used modern tools to open an ancient lock. So far, without success. The tools we have used are nothing more than examples of the devices that modern readers have to hand. It is too soon to abandon the search among them for a suitable key. For a second attempt, let's draw back from Paul's conversion itself and ask instead what inner needs or urges in Paul were stirred or satisfied by his relation to his converts. He was called to a belief, and so to a community; and perhaps—there and then, on the road to Damascus—to a mission. Ahead of him, then, lay a new relation with Jesus, as Jesus' servant; and with Jesus' followers, as a brother to some and a father to others. And Paul needs these children just as much as they need him.

PAUL INVESTED EVERYTHING IN HIS MISSION. When he writes to the Philippians he parades the grounds for boasting he had from his very birth. He had been circumcised when eight days old; he was, then, the child either of Jews or of proselytes to Judaism. But he was from the people of Israel; no gentile blood here. Some Israelites could not prove their ancestry. He could; he was of the tribe of Benjamin. The tribe's territory included Jerusalem, which was heavily influenced by Greek culture. But Paul was the purest of the pure, a Hebrew speaker and a Pharisee (Phil. 3:5).

But by the time he writes to the Philippians he has come to blows with the prayer houses of the cities he has visited; he has given up the respect that was due to an educated and articulate Pharisee and to his resolute observance of the Law. He may well have foregone the family wealth that made possible his sophisticated education. He may have taught himself, in preparation for his mission, the menial skills of an artisan. At least for a while he had enjoyed the standing and value of an authorized missionary from the assembly in Antioch, but he has broken with that too. He is on his own. He has his past converts and his converts yet to come, or he has nothing.

I have become all things to all men (1 Cor. 9:22). This might win him the respect of all, or the respect of none. He is too easily distrusted. Does he tell Jews quite the same things as he tells Gentiles? Or does he trim his sails to please—and so to win over—the audience of the moment? *I have become to the Jews as a Jew, so that I might win Jews; to those under the law—* that could be Jews or proselytes—*as one under the law (not being under the law myself) so that I might win those under the law; to those not under the law as one not under the law (not being free from the law of God but under the law of Anointed) so that I might win those not under the law* (9:20–21). This might have shown the dexterity of an effective orator and appealed to the gentile Corinthians. But any Jew could be heartily offended by the suggestion Paul was free to put on or take off the Law like a coat, depending on the weather. And any of his addressees, hearing how differently he had preached elsewhere, would have wondered where, if at all, Paul had spoken without fear or favor. The flexibility that gave Paul his appeal was the greatest danger to that appeal. He had to rely ever more heavily on his converts' personal dependence upon him, on their trust in him, fondness for him, and reliance on his honesty.

The Thessalonians, Galatians, and Corinthians—Paul will urge all of them to recognize how important he is to them and they are to him. He reminds the Thessalonians how devoted he was to them when he was with them and tells them how much he longs for them now. He looked after them as a nurse looks after her own children; absent from them he is as one bereaved. The Galatians are listening to newly arrived teachers who are urging them to undertake the Law's observance. Paul responds angrily and describes himself as the Galatians' own mother, in whose womb they are still coming to the form in which they should be born. The community, he claims, is—only—as strong as its links with the parent on whom it depends.

How does he use the power these links give him? Paul's relations with Corinth were never stable. He rocks the boat himself, and not least in his own letters. We will watch him, in 1 Corinthians, tear down the confidence of his converts and then rebuild it. The first five chapters of the letter are mesmerizing. Paul disowns all reliance on worldly wisdom or worldly rhetoric—in a paragraph (1:18–31) as highly and finely wrought as we could find in the speech of any worldly orator. The paragraph is part of a long buildup to the letter's first climax

(5:1–5): a demand that the Corinthians obey Paul here and now, in his absence. To secure their compliance Paul softens them up: he lulls them, impresses them, humiliates them, berates them, mocks them, threatens them, and finally reemerges as their caring father who will either embrace them or punish them. It is a tour de force.

In 2 Corinthians similar questions are raised, but more subtly and on a larger scale. Right at the letter's start Paul sets up a balance between himself and his converts: *We are your boast just as you are ours in the day of the Lord Jesus* (1:14). He has been promising to revisit, but has repeatedly let down the Corinthians. They are disappointed, even distrustful. Has Paul, they wonder, been quite honest with them in his statements of purpose and protestations of care? Paul insists that he has been totally open with them. Such is his commission and his relation to the good news, that to be less than wholly transparent would be to betray the good news itself. So far so good. They can be reassured of Paul: *We are your boast on the day of the Lord Jesus.* Paul then moves to the other half of his equation: *Just as you are ours.* How are they to fulfill this role? A new theme enters: they are to give generously to the collection that Paul is gathering for the assemblies in Jerusalem—*that* is how they will enable him to boast in them. Paul has proclaimed his total transparency—in the very paragraphs he is covertly using to prepare a request for money.

When you have read Chapters 16–21 in this book and have watched the progress of Paul's strikingly elegant arguments, it will be for you to decide how you view his maneuvers in 1 and 2 Corinthians. I admit I find them unsettling.

Everything in every part of Paul's life is dedicated to and is part of his mission. He is forever intense, driven, serious. In his letters he rarely smiles. But then, why should he? We hear his voice chiefly in a handful of urgent letters written to counter clear and present danger. Any slight from an assembly that belittles him belittles his good news and vice versa. He is as sensitive to such slights as the membrane on a drum, responding to every brush and tap of the stick. And the slights he himself offers to his assemblies? The manipulation, sarcasm, and bullying? Paul was too defensive to see how badly he could hurt his assemblies and aggravate their difficulties. He was too vulnerable to admit where his own preaching had given rise to misunderstanding. So did he always gauge his response rightly? No. Did he anger his assemblies when he meant to soothe them?

Almost certainly. Did some of his teaching bemuse or misguide them? Yes. Did he ever exaggerate the truth or reshape it? Yes. Did he ever admit to being misleading, let alone mistaken? No.

You may wonder if we can draw the sting from such challenges by turning once more to the theology of the letters and leaving to one side Paul's relations with his addressees, but this is just the error we can no longer afford to make. Paul writes his letters to heal, support, and reinforce communities. It is the life of these communities that shapes what he says and the way he says it. *How* he hopes to achieve these aims is the theme of this book. We will watch his febrile, fragile relations with the assemblies from his viewpoint and from theirs. These relations were central to his understanding of himself and of his mission. They will be central to our understanding of Paul too. And from our viewpoint, unsympathetic as it may seem, we are bound to ask what needs of Paul's own were being met as he met the needs of his good news and its recipients.

Paul is a father who depends on the love of his adolescent children and dares not let them go.

PAUL CAME TO CITIES with more than just his message. The Lord told Paul: *Power is made perfect in weakness* (2 Cor. 12:9). Paul had extraordinary powers. He lists to the Corinthians some of the different roles given by God to different people: to be emissaries, prophets, teachers; to have miraculous powers, the gift of healing, or skill in support and administration; to have the gift of speaking in tongues or interpreting them (1 Cor. 12:9–11).

And Paul himself as an individual? He fulfills role after role. He is an emissary, he speaks as a prophet, he teaches. He can reveal God's plan for the dead *in a word of the Lord* (1 Thess. 4:15). He can disclose the effect of the Lord's return with the portentous introduction, *Look, I am telling you a mystery* (1 Cor. 15:51). He comes at last, with apparent reluctance, to tell the Corinthians of his *visions and unveilings;* but holds back from speaking too much of his *extraordinary unveilings* (2 Cor. 12:1, 7). We have heard already of his journey to heaven; we will hear more of his vision on the road to Damascus; and Luke has him recall another vision, when *I saw Jesus talking to me* in the Temple at Jerusalem (The Mission [Acts] 22:18).

He reminds the Corinthians of *the signs of the emissary* that he has wrought among them, *with signs and wonders and demonstrations of power* (2 Cor. 12:12); he tells the Romans what he has done *in the power of signs and wonders* (Rom. 15:19); and Luke tells of Paul's healing miracles and of the miracles wrought around him (e.g., The Mission 14:8–18). Paul knows how much the Corinthians value speaking in tongues; but *I give thanks to God,* he says, *I speak in tongues more than all of you* (1 Cor. 14:18). Paul himself is a one-man band of all the most precious spiritual gifts with which God endows his assemblies.

Sociologists have long realized that there are some social settings more susceptible than others to the apparent exercise of strange powers. Paul proclaims a setting as striking as any: he himself re-presents the Anointed whom he preaches and he offers his converts a first taste, here on earth, of the life of heaven he himself has seen. Such terms as these, of course, are not the terms of our explanation, but we need to recognize they are the terms to be explained.

How easily we airbrush such powers off our map of the early assemblies. We do not know where to place visions and miracles and speaking in tongues; we are embarrassed by the importance apparently attached to them. But they were evidence of the presence and activity of a god within the emissary and his community. In Corinth, at least, Paul had given his converts, on his visit, grounds enough to see themselves as endowed here and now with the life of heaven. Distrust and doubt might have soured the assemblies' relations with their founder, but he undoubtedly had powers. He identified clearly the god who had invested him and therefore his converts with these sensational gifts. It would be obtuse—and could be dangerous—for them to ignore this active and indefeasible god.

WITH REGARD TO PAUL'S POWER AND POWERS, perhaps we have been drawn too easily to the glittering surface of Paul's missionary life—the very surface that misled the Corinthians themselves. Paul speaks too of his weakness, for by the time he writes to the Galatians he is sure he re-presents the Jesus who suffered and died.

Paul lets us glimpse the signs of frailty—and of consequent courage— that even an outsider with no sense of Paul's mission would be hard put to deny. It would be difficult to imagine a person more resolute. All of his great gifts have won him no remission from suffering. *Five times I have been given the thirty-nine lashes by the Jews* [a punishment administered by local Jewish communities], *three times I have been beaten with rods* [a Roman punishment], *once I have been stoned, three times I have been shipwrecked, I have been in the open sea for a night and a day; continuously traveling, I have been in dangers from rivers, in dangers from robbers, in dangers from my own people, in dangers from Gentiles, in dangers in cities, in dangers in open country, in dangers at sea*—and so on (2 Cor. 11:24–26). But Paul's Corinthian converts could see nothing in such dangers except the degradation of their emissary.

Power and weakness, in all their different forms, will occupy a lot of our attention in the pages that follow. So will the value Paul finds in them both. We are looking for modern terms in which to unlock the secrets of Paul's missionary drive. Power and weakness, inseparably linked, are the keys to the first and outermost door.

We have dwelt on Paul's power; so do some of those confident modern churches whose leaders feel called to exercise such power themselves. Other churches dwell, rather, on Paul's weakness. These too are shaped by their setting in society and their own view of that setting as marginal, perhaps, and fragile. Neither emphasis does justice, by itself, to Paul. In the pages that follow, we will be watching not just what Paul says, but what he does. He can disclaim power, but still use it, for in his weakness and his strength alike he re-presents the Anointed.

Neither Paul's weakness nor his power is his own. Three times, Paul tells the Corinthians, he had asked the Lord to free him from the *thorn in the flesh* that tormented him. He relays the reply of the Anointed in the perfect tense, as a settled decision rather than as a single statement. But Paul relays it, nonetheless, as direct speech. This Paul spoke directly to the Anointed, and the Anointed spoke directly back to him.

And he has said to me: "My grace is sufficient for you. For this power is made perfect in weakness" (2 Cor. 12:9).

CHAPTER 10

FROM JESUS TO PAUL: FROM SEER TO SEER

SEERS SUCH AS PAUL were hardly a dime a dozen. Paul's gift and training set him apart from almost all his contemporaries, but he was not unique. We have caught glimpses of the seers and the communities that nurtured ideas and aspirations like his. These, though, are people deep in the shadows of history about whom we know almost nothing. We would feel far more comfortable with such a visionary Paul if we could find another visionary to set beside him from his own age and culture. And we can. To set beside him we have Jesus.

When Paul was resisting Jesus' followers, he was combating the claims of another visionary. The followers of Jesus found in Jesus far greater gifts than Paul would ever claim for himself. The gospels record words and actions of Jesus that make sense at last when we put him back where he belongs—among the rare, privileged seers of Israel.

Any account of Jesus must account for two later phenomena: the character of the beliefs about him that grew after his death and the character of the gospels that were written, in the 60s–80s, to encourage those beliefs. We will be keeping our eyes on the second one: Why did the stories of Jesus' life take the form they did? The force of this question will become clear only when we let the gospels themselves emerge in all their strangeness, for two of our gospels are not content just to hint at Jesus' own experiences. Mark and John believe the whole structure of visions to have been turned upside down by Jesus. What should have been taking place in heaven took place instead on earth. For the evangelists, Jesus the seer enables his followers to be seers as well, not by any ascent to heaven, but by properly understanding his own descent to earth.

What the seers saw in heaven was fixed in God's plan. They might well be shown, in allegorical visions, the twists and turns yet to come in the history of God's people. From such visions Israel could take heart that however dark its present, its ultimate rescue was sure. But Mark and John are not just unveiling what is to come. In his own person—in his life, death, and rising—Jesus himself, they believed, disclosed the plan and will of God. In defiance of all categories a heavenly figure has walked the earth and effected in his own person, here and now, the changes that a seer's sight of heaven can only promise for earth's future. Mark, John, and Paul share a purpose and an acute sense of its difficulty. How are they to enable their addressees to see what is there to be seen? The veil has been removed that kept God from the sight of humankind, but how is the veil to be removed from the human minds and hearts that cannot see what stands revealed before them?

Right at the start of Mark's gospel his Jesus sees into the mysteries of heaven. Mark's readers can be sure that this Jesus will speak from his own knowledge of the truths of heaven, and all that he says and does will be inspired and authorized by the Breath of God.

> Jesus was baptized in the Jordan by John. And immediately, coming out of the water, he saw the heavens torn and the Breath like a dove descending on him. And there was a voice from heaven, "You are my beloved son, in you have I taken delight."
>
> MARK 1:10–11

JESUS THE SEER

The very first words of the Bible's book of Unveiling [Revelation] are almost a "title": *The unveiling of Jesus Anointed which God gave him, to show to his slaves what must soon take place.* John the Seer is charged to *bear testimony to the word of God and to the testimony of Jesus Anointed, that is, all that he saw* (1:1–2). The most natural meaning is as clear as it is startling. The book records the unveiling that God gave to Jesus, all that Jesus saw. Jesus, then, was a visionary who relayed to his followers all the heavenly secrets that were imparted to him in his visions.

And the book of Unveiling is based on those visions, visions that themselves are steeped in the traditions we have already explored. Here Isaiah's vision in the Holy of Holies and Ezekiel's vision of God's throne are both reimagined and redescribed with newfound emphases and details. But John the Seer can work with one conviction quite unknown to Isaiah or Ezekiel: that God had intervened in history, as never before, in that same person of Jesus, whose visions underlie John's own. Here is a seer who has learned well from his master. And in Unveiling he records the visions of them both. The dragon in the book of Unveiling, the great enemy of the Anointed and his followers, knew exactly who to attack: *those who keep the commandments of God and who have the testimony of Jesus* (1:1–2; 12:17).

In the book of Unveiling, Satan, the dragon, is cast down to earth. And so too in Luke's gospel Jesus' pupils return excitedly to their master to report on their new powers: *"Lord, even the devils are subject to us in your name."* Jesus, however, sets their gifts into a larger context: *"I saw Satan like lightning, falling from heaven"* (10:17–18). In Unveiling the great angel casts fire on the earth; this is the task of Luke's Jesus too. Heaven and earth are interlocked. Again, in Unveiling the seer relays visions of cosmic chaos and God's final vindication of his saints. In Mark (and in Matthew and Luke) we have heard Jesus speak, as he overlooks Jerusalem, of the dire times yet to come and of the rescue by God of his chosen ones. Jesus talks of cosmic chaos and of the coming on clouds of the Son of Man. The speech, like the whole story of Jesus, has been heavily edited in the decades between Jesus' life and the completion of the gospels. But the links confirm that the book of Unveiling preserves the character and terms not just of John the Seer—but of Jesus himself (Luke 4:5; 10:17–18; 12:49; Unveiling 12:9; 8:5).

Additional evidence is more heavily disguised. Luke and Matthew share (from their source of sayings, "Q") the strange story of Jesus' threefold temptation by the devil. The devil whisks Jesus from place to place, from the desert to a pinnacle of the Temple (in Matthew's order) and onward to a mountaintop, where the devil *showed him all the kingdoms of the earth and their glory* (Matt. 4:8). By the time the story is told in the gospels, it has become a quasi-rabbinic dispute over scripture. Jesus and the devil swap quotations from the Old Order, from the story of Israel's time in the desert. Moses issued commands to the Israelites, which the Israelites, forty years long in the desert, repeatedly broke. Jesus, the new Israel in the desert for forty days, appeals to those commands and resists the temptation to break them. Here is a carefully constructed contrast. Underlying it, however, is likely a story more dramatic still—of the seer Jesus discovering his powers and committing them to God's service.

More telling still is the story of Jesus' transfiguration at the midpoint of Mark's story. It is among the most mysterious scenes in the gospels. Many scholars have asked whether Mark—and, following his lead, Matthew and Luke—have moved a story of Easter back into the center of Jesus' earthly ministry. We are more probably hearing a story of Jesus' privileged access to the inhabitants and secrets of heaven, and of the training he gave his pupils to win access to the same. Jesus himself appears in a garment of glory. As our seer Isaiah will record, such are the garments of heaven. This external change signals a transformation of the whole person. Is Jesus, then, seen as an angel? Or as greater still? Peter, James, and John see splendor like that seen by the seer Enoch when he looked upon the Great Glory on the throne: "As for his clothing, which was shining more brightly than the sun, it was whiter than any snow. None of the angels was able to come in and see his face, by reason of its splendor and glory; and no flesh could see him" (1 Enoch 14:20–21). Matthew has Jesus' pupils fall on their faces, just as Ezekiel had fallen at the climax of his vision.

Here is Luke's version of the story. He knows well how strange it is and adds touches to do justice to its mystery:

> *Taking Peter and John and James he went up to the mountain* [traditionally linked with Mt. Hermon, to the southwest of Damascus] *to pray. And it happened while he was praying that the form of his face was different and his clothing was blazing white. And look, two men were talking with him, who were Moses and Elijah, who—seen in glory—were talking of his departure* ["exodus" is Luke's word, to recall the Hebrews' escape from Egypt], *which he had to fulfill in Jerusalem.*
>
> LUKE 9:28–31

Moses had been granted a glimpse of God as his glory passed by on Mt. Sinai. Elijah on the same mountain had seen the awesome signs of God's presence and then—most awesome of all and far more intimate— had heard the still, small voice of God (The Escape [Exodus] 33:18– 34:9; 1 Kings 19:9–18).

> *And Peter and those with him were weighed down with sleep. And as they woke up they saw his glory and the two men standing with him. And it happened as these departed from him that Peter said to Jesus: "Master, it is good for us to be here. And let us make three dwellings, one for you and one for Moses and one for Elijah." And he did not know what he was saying. And as he was speaking there was a cloud and it overshadowed them. And they were afraid as they went into the cloud. And there was a voice from the cloud, saying: "This is my chosen son. Listen to him."*
>
> LUKE 9:32–35

We will hear Paul, when he writes to Corinth, fighting off the claims of rival missionaries. These rivals are closely linked with the emissaries based in Jerusalem. Among those emissaries, Peter himself, we know, had adherents in Corinth; it is almost certainly a group linked with Peter that is causing Paul such trouble. Its leaders are speaking up for Peter. No doubt they are authorized by Peter and have adopted his good news and ways of preaching it.

It is in this setting that Paul speaks so carefully of his own *visions and unveilings*. He has no wish to boast in them or rely on them. Unlike his rivals. They clearly have more to claim than he does, and do so proudly—visions, unveilings, signs, wonders, and acts of power—for their leaders are adherents of Peter. The Peter, that is, who saw Jesus on the mountaintop ablaze with glory and flanked by the two heroes of the Old Order who had been given fleeting access to the majesty of God.

Peter had learned his master's lessons well.

THIS JESUS IS A VISIONARY, but hardly in the mold that Paul will fill. He speaks in wilder, fiercer tones. And he acts as he speaks—with unsettling power. Jesus' family, Mark tells us, tried to take charge of him, *for they said he was out of his mind* (3:21). Mark tells of their fears and next of the suspicions of the scribes who had come down from Jerusalem to check on the antics of this strange figure. They said that Jesus *was possessed of Beelzebul and that he was throwing out devils in the name of the prince of devils* (3:22). Jesus does not merely speak from a knowledge of heaven; he acts with a power that confuses and frightens those that see it.

At the gospel's climax Mark places his Jesus squarely within the great visionary tradition of which we have heard. Only now does Mark make it clear with a fanfare that this is where Jesus belonged.

Jesus is arraigned before the council in Jerusalem:

> *The high priest questioned Jesus: "Are you the Anointed, the son of the Blessed?"*

> *"I am," said Jesus, "and you will see the son of man seated at the right hand of the Power and coming with the clouds of heaven."*

> *The high priest tore his clothes. "Why do we still need witnesses?" he said. "You have heard the blasphemy. What do you think?"*

> *They all condemned him: he deserved to die.*
> MARK 14:61-64

It is a strange moment. With *the Power* Jesus is clearly referring to God, but the Old Order never uses this phrase as such a circumlocution. The *son of man* is both seated and moving, and therefore hard to envisage. And the council instantly determines that Jesus has committed blasphemy, but he has not obviously transgressed any law or guideline on blasphemy that has reached us.

The difficulties dissolve when we link Jesus' saying with the great vision of Ezekiel. *The Power* is a term used for God in the visionary tradition. The son of man is seated in the chariot-throne of God that Ezekiel saw; the throne is imagined drawing near to earth. To locate any such figure so close to God was to suggest, as we shall see, that God might share his power with his throne, and that a second Power deserved the worship that Judaism reserved for the one God alone.

We hear in the Psalms: *The Lord said to my Lord, "Sit at my right hand, until I put your enemies beneath your feet"* (110:1). Mark's Jesus is clearly alluding to this enthronement. Time and again the New Order calls upon these lines; we shall be hearing of them again. Jesus is evoking too the famous vision of the prophet Daniel. Daniel saw *one like a son of man, coming with the clouds of heaven. He approached the Ancient of Days, and was led into his presence. He was given authority, glory, and sovereign power* (7:13–14). This account is itself indebted to the vision of Ezekiel; the rabbis would consistently connect the two. We are at the heart of the visionary tradition; Jesus was at the heart of it too.

Two figures, one chariot: to be at the right hand of God on his chariot-throne was to be linked in every way with his power. (Such a shared throne is an image familiar from the pagan world.) But who could possibly share the chariot with God? Even to imagine such a second figure would be a blasphemy indeed, belittling God. Ezekiel offered one solution. He had seen not a figure next to God, but the figure who was himself the image of God. It was a solution that became far more dangerous than the difficulty to which it was applied. To identify Ezekiel's figure with an individual son of man, a human being, would be grotesque. But this is just the claim toward which Jesus' followers found their way.

We will later be watching the strange convergence of God and Jesus as a single subject of worship in the closing pages of the book of Unveiling. Unveiling portrays Jesus as a subject of worship from the outset. He himself says (3:21) he sits with God on God's throne. But the main narrative only gradually, it seems, acknowledges his place there. Early in the worship of heaven the Lamb of God appears *in the middle of* [in between] *the throne and the four beasts* of heaven (5:6); the beasts sing the praise *of him who sits upon the throne and of the Lamb* (5:13). At the end of the book the seer will clarify his claim: the water of life goes forth *from the throne of God and of the Lamb;* this is the throne that will come down to earth in the New Jerusalem (22:1; 22:3). Over and over in *The Gospel According to Paul* we shall find in the New Order an author preparing addressees, during the course of the text, to accept a claim that could have been confusing or shocking at its start.

Who, then, is the *son of man* envisaged by Mark's Jesus at his trial? The council is quite right to be appalled. This Jesus has hinted throughout the story—hinted, never stated—that he is himself Daniel's *one like a son of man.* And now these hints are too strong to be ignored. Not that Mark's chief concern is with the council itself, sitting forty years before he wrote. His concern is for the readers, who have followed the story of Jesus and been bemused by it, enthralled, encouraged, and perhaps even scared by it. Such readers have heard Jesus speak, all along, of the mysterious Son of Man. And now they can watch unfold before their eyes the claim that has lurked half hidden in Jesus' earlier words—the claim that he, Jesus, the Son of Man, is the figure on God's throne.

Mark knew of such a claim in the 70s. Did it have its basis in the teachings of Jesus himself? In this highly developed form, no. But we will be keeping our eyes on the strange figure of Jesus the seer and on the difficult—even frightening—questions to which the combination of his visions, teachings, and miracles gave rise. The route from Jesus himself to the Jesus of Mark was long, contested, and hard to embrace, but the road from one to the other, over highs and lows and rugged terrain, ran straight as a die.

THE SANCTUARY UNVEILED

Jesus had reached Jerusalem in the days before Passover. His entry, as our gospels record it, was a triumph. Within a week his pupils deserted him, his supposed subjects bayed for his blood, and the Roman governor sentenced him to death.

We have some knowledge of crucifixion and can reconstruct the likely course of Jesus' last hours. Two other troublemakers, we are told, were also due to be killed; the three of them could be dealt with together. Whipped and beaten, already faint from loss of blood, condemned men were made to carry the wooden beams from which they would be hung. The victims were led to a bleak patch of rising ground outside the city's wall, the regular site for executions. A series of posts stood out against the sky, eight feet high; into the top of each was cut a notch.

The routine was familiar. Nothing marked out this set of crucifixions from the last. Sometimes rope was used to fix the prisoner to the cross, sometimes nails. There is an ancient tradition that Jesus was nailed.

The beam was laid on the ground. The soldiers put Jesus onto his back across the beam and along it stretched out his arms. First one hand, then the other: a soldier would press the back of Jesus' hand against the beam, hold a nail to the wrist, and drive it home, through pulse and bone, to the wood behind. The soldiers lifted the beam's ends onto two forked poles, hoisted the beam and Jesus into the air, and slotted the beam's center into the notch at the top of the post.

Now for the feet. Each of Jesus' ankles was sandwiched between a block of wood and the side of the upright post. From each side a nail was hammered in.

And there Jesus hung, for as long as it took him to die.

It was an infamously cruel form of execution, used for rebels and runaway slaves. The longer they lasted, the better. A stool might be attached to the post, on which the victim could rest; his circulation would revive, and his suffering would be prolonged. So much the better too that the mob could see what became of troublemakers, a warning to those who might dare oppose the might of Rome.

At the crossbeam's center, above this convict's head, was a placard, we are told, for all to read: *Jesus of Nazareth, the king of the Jews.*

AND AT THIS VERY MOMENT, in Mark's story, the "heavens" are parted again. Their mysteries are unveiled. All that divided the court of heaven from the mortal world is torn away. All the Temple's carefully graded holiness is undermined, for God's plan, faithfulness, and glory can now be seen by all in Jesus' death. Here is an unveiling, an "apocalypse," that confounds all categories and all expectation.

And at the sixth hour there was darkness over the whole earth until the ninth hour. And at the ninth hour Jesus cried with a loud voice, "Eli, eli, lama sabachthani," which means, "My God, my God, why have you abandoned me?". . . And Jesus gave a great cry and breathed out his spirit.

And the veil of the Temple was torn in two, from top to bottom.
MARK 15:33–34, 37–38

MARK'S JESUS: OPENING THE EYES OF THE BLIND

In their final form our gospels reflect the insights and self-understanding of some assemblies in the 70s. It would be wrong to assume in advance that Jesus himself spoke or acted with any such insights in mind at all. But we might still ask: Why did any assemblies develop these techniques rather than others? Why did they put such weight on disclosure and its difficulties? Because they knew that this had been at the heart of Jesus' own message: the opportunity, here and now, to see what had through all of history been hidden from human view. The assemblies remained loyal to this heart of Jesus' teaching. And in the decades after his death these assemblies perfected the use of the story of Jesus himself as a vehicle for disclosure. The gospels of Mark and John are "unveilings" of immense subtlety and power.

As odd as any element of Mark's gospel is the Son of Man. The phrase is used in Mark only by Jesus himself, who appears to use it only in reference to himself in connection with his activity on earth or his glorious return. This Son of Man, however, is always "he," never "I"; we might well ask if Mark's Jesus is keeping some distance between himself and this strange figure whose earthly career so exactly matches his own. This Son of Man holds a vital clue to the character of Mark's gospel. Let's draw the paths together along which he has already taken us.

For our purposes, we can set aside the meaning of such a phrase in Jesus' own time and Aramaic language. Mark and his readers were thinking in Greek. And the term would remind such readers of the prophecy in Daniel that fueled the hopes of prayer houses and assemblies alike: *There before me was one like a son of man, coming with the clouds of heaven. He approached the Ancient of Days, and was led into his presence. He was given authority, glory, and sovereign power* (7:13–14). In Daniel's vision Daniel himself is an actor. He asks an angel to explain what he has seen. The *one like a son of man,* he is told, is a heavenly figure who stands for God's heroes, harassed, suffering, and eventually appointed to an everlasting power. Daniel's indefinite phrase was been translated into the Greek Old Order literally and directly: "like a son of man." In the proclamation of Jesus, however, Mark's Greek-speaking assembly was seeking and offering more. Mark's Jesus speaks of a precise and definite figure, *the son of the man*—duly capitalized in English, the Son of Man.

The Jews had known for centuries of visions in which the cosmic battle between God and evil is fought out in strange and allusive forms and its final outcome—the victory of God—is enacted in heaven long before it is apparent on earth. This is a sight offered to the seers. The seer's task is then generally to reveal what he has seen, or part of it, to those around him.

To do justice to this tradition we must leave aside the categories with which we are familiar: the tidy distinctions between dreams, on the one hand, and reality, on the other; between the ethereal symbols that we might credit in the first and the conflicts and dangers that confront us in the second. Once we suspend such distinctions, Daniel's angel does more than just decode the vision's various figures into their real counterparts on earth. To decode the figures is not to dispense with them. Daniel leaves in place both the figure in heaven and the figure on earth. They are as real as each other. The *one like a son of man* has really been seen receiving power in heaven; precisely this assures us that the heroes of God will finally be given power on earth.

Daniel's *one like a son of man* belongs in visions, in the battle imagined as fought out in God's own realm beyond the skies, far from our normal sight or understanding. Mark's Greek narrative, however, has far more to reveal. His Son of Man is both Daniel's visionary figure *and Jesus,* alive on earth as Peter's friend, healing, forgiving, and suffering. This is not where Daniel's *one like a son of man* should be at all. There is a strange and deliberate confusion here. Our familiar categories and distinctions are breaking down. A warrior has walked out of a heavenly vision and is striding the earth. This would be strange enough, if Mark's readers thought Daniel's figure had been just a figment of his divinely ordered dream. It is far more uncanny, if Daniel's vision disclosed, as his readers would have believed, a real battle waged in heaven, for its chief agent was now revealed for all to see, mustering his—frail, human— forces for its equivalent on earth.

If those around Jesus longed to see what a seer sees, to share that vision into the secrets of God's plan, they needed no dreams, no rare privilege. They needed only to open their eyes and to see what was taking place before their very eyes. The sight was easily missed.

> When Jesus was alone, those around him with his closest pupils asked him about the riddles he used. "To you," he said, "the secret of the Kingdom of God has been given. But to those outside, everything happens in riddles, so that [as Isaiah says]
>
> > 'Looking with all their might they may not see,
> > and listening with all their might they may not understand;
> > otherwise they might change their ways and God forgive them.'"
>
> MARK 4:10-12, QUOTING ISAIAH 6:9-10

No wonder Jesus' followers, in Mark's story, found Jesus so difficult to understand. No wonder Mark works so hard to help his readers, those in their turn who are around Jesus with his closest pupils, to open their eyes and *see*. To read the story as a straightforward story is to be among those on the outside, straining to see and hear and understanding nothing.

ON EASTER MORNING Mark has the women come to Jesus' tomb. Jesus' body is not there. A young man is in the tomb, dressed in white.

> "Don't be amazed," said the young man. "You are looking for Jesus the Nazarene, who was crucified. He has been roused. He is not here. Look, there is the place where they laid him. But go and tell his pupils and Peter, 'He is going ahead of you into Galilee. There you will see him, just as he told you.'"
>
> Trembling and bewildered, the women went out and fled from the tomb. They said nothing to anyone, because they were afraid.
>
> MARK 16:6-8

And with that, it seems, Mark has finished. What a strange way to end. Why do we not hear of the meeting between Jesus and his followers? Why does the story not follow them to Galilee and their reunion and his pupils' comprehension at last?

At our distance we look for some familiar and reassuring distinctions: between the earthly and the risen Jesus; between his power when on earth and his power after Easter; between his presence with his pupils and any "presence" his followers may claim for him since. But the Jesus of Mark's story was already in his own person and in his days on earth the Son of Man.

Jesus' pupils could not understand him before his death; Mark knew that the gospel's readers would still need help to understand him after it. It is time to start the story again, to go *back to Galilee,* where the story started. *Jesus came into Galilee preaching the gospel of God* (Mark 1:14). There the readers will hear of Jesus at the start of his work, long before his death and rising. But is this the Jesus that the readers want to encounter? Aren't they looking for the "risen" Jesus? Mark flouts the distinction on which any standard history of Jesus must rely. To look for the earthly Jesus in Mark's story as a figure distinct from the risen Jesus of his church is already to miss his story's point and so to be among *those outside.*

Jesus tells riddling stories in Mark's gospel. Their point does not lie "on the surface" and open for all to see. Gradually we get clear the riddling story that is the gospel as a whole. We can come at last to grasp who is really speaking in this narrative of the "earthly" Jesus—and who he is really speaking to.

ARE THE ACTIONS OF JESUS, for Mark and his readers, still signs in code? Such a sign, revealed here on earth, would seem to do the very thing it points to, to win the victory that it portends. We must wonder, then: Do these events disclose things to the reader, the new seer? Or do they achieve them? Do they anticipate a final battle or wage it? Jesus had fought his battle as standing for God's heroes, and despite all appearance he had been victorious. Mark wrote in the aftermath of terrible persecution. God's heroes were suffering still. Their victory was far from obvious and far from obviously assured. Mark keeps the most careful balance between the appearance of this war and its reality, its present and its future. His gospel is a poignant lesson in unveiling and its enigmatic ways.

JOHN'S JESUS: THE MAN FROM HEAVEN

We hear in John's gospel:

> *He who comes from above, what he has seen and heard, this is what he*
> *bears testimony to; and his testimony—no one accepts it.*
>
> JOHN 3:31-32

John's gospel is shaped by unveiling no less than Mark's. How much of his material can be traced back to Jesus and how much has evolved over the intervening years, we cannot hope to know for sure, but successive editors have clearly been at work. John's whole gospel is constructed as an unveiling, an apocalypse, turned upside down. It is on earth that the unveiling of God's own self and purpose has taken place.

Near the start of John's gospel the Jewish leader Nicodemus comes to Jesus by night. Jesus tells him bluntly: *"Anyone who is not born again from above cannot see the kingdom of God"* (3:3). Nicodemus is (unsurprisingly!) bemused and asks how this can be. Jesus steps back from this dialogue of cryptic statement and baffled question. He carries on:

> *"In God's truth I tell you, that what we know—that is what we speak*
> *of, and what we have seen—that is what we bear testimony to, and you*
> *do not accept our testimony."*
>
> JOHN 3:11

Here in the words of John's Jesus we are hearing the "us" of John's community. They bear witness to what they have seen; and what they have seen is the power of the Jesus who came down from heaven. And so back to Jesus.

> *"If I have told you of earthly things and you do not believe,*
> *how shall you believe if I tell you of heavenly things?*
> *And no one has gone up to heaven except he who came down from*
>   *heaven,*
> *the Son of Man."*
>
> JOHN 3:12-13

Here is no visitor to heaven from earth, but a visitor to earth from heaven. John declares this as his starting point and challenges his addressees to share it. Mark never makes the claim; he wants his addressees to reach its recognition for themselves, prompted, cajoled, and teased by every device at his command. John's readers are offered this insight as the road on which to travel. For Mark's, this insight is the destination.

Mark and John, time and again, offer parallels in their narratives to the methods Paul is deploying in his letters. We often hear nowadays of "apocalypse" as a term for the final cataclysm that will end earth's history and our own. By the end of this book, readers will, I hope, have come to relish its real significance—the "unveiling" of truths hidden from our normal view. The tradition of such unveiling was already sophisticated before Jesus lived. The gospels aim further still. They use the narrative of a life on earth to fulfill the function of a visit to heaven.

Jesus himself, as the assemblies believed, subverted in his life and person all the conventions of divine disclosure. And so in turn their writers subvert the conventions that have governed the record of such disclosure. They draw a new map that is effective only when its users see how drastically they have reworked the old. And to see that, the users must set out on the journey, maps in hand, for themselves.

These texts would be heard and read over and over. Readers, then as now, could get to know the journey well on which the texts were taking them. This terrain, that once had been explored with bafflement and awe, could become the reader's homeland, better known and valued on every walk through its extraordinary landscape.

To understand the claims of the New Order we must first be at home with the expectations that its authors turned upside down. The truthfulness of the Jews' God lies in his fidelity to his people through all time. The future ordained by God is secure. To see a vision of what is yet to be on earth is no more—and no less—than to see the plan that God has established, a plan to which he will inescapably be true. Now the authors of the New Order systematically disrupted the relations between heaven and earth, present and future. They brought the visions of heaven down to earth and so introduced the life of earth to heaven. They took the present life of earth into the postmortem life of heaven and so brought that future into the present. Through the Holy of

Holies—through the blood of the Anointed—earth and its perfection, the present and its consummation are permeable one to another.

Thirty years had passed since Jesus' death. At last his followers would perfect the use of his story to overturn those familiar expectations. But it was Jesus himself who worked those expectations loose from their ancient and venerable foundations.

CHAPTER 11

THE FIRST FOLLOWERS: JERUSALEM AND THE TEMPLE

THE HOLY CITY

Jerusalem in the early 30s C.E. was home to Jews from every country and background. Their outlooks, standards, and hopes were as varied as their origins. Different prayer houses served different constituencies in different languages. Among established congregations there were perhaps just a handful whose leaders valued or tolerated an allegiance to Jesus. Jesus' first pupils were, according to Luke, actively spreading the word; chief among them was Peter. Under their leadership, did some followers of Jesus meet in groups of their own for the Sabbath and during the week? Perhaps.

We have to dig for clues to discover exactly what Jesus' followers claimed about him in those very first years. It was two decades or more before Paul wrote his letters, in the 50s. Another twenty years would pass before our gospels reached the final form they have now. Time enough for hopes, claims, and insights to be developed out of all recognition. As we have seen, we can pick up a scent in Paul's letters, here and there, of quotations that Paul has drawn into his argument: formulas of the faith that will achieve Paul's aim precisely and only if they are already known to his addressees. We shall hear more of them below.

Here is Luke's Peter addressing the crowd in Jerusalem. The crowd is bemused by the effects of the Breath upon Jesus' pupils. How "earthly," in Peter's presentation, this man Jesus had been:

> "*Jesus of Nazareth, a man marked out for you by acts of power and wonders and signs which God did through him in your midst, as you know—this Jesus, handed over by God's determinate counsel and fore-knowledge, you, through the hands of men outside the law, nailed up and killed. . . . This Jesus, God has raised him up, and all of us are his witnesses. So he has been exalted by the right hand of God and has received from the father the promise of the holy Breath; and he has poured this out, which you see and hear. For the patriarch David* [traditionally identified as the author of the Old Order's psalms] *did not ascend to heaven, but he himself says,*
>
> '*The Lord said to my Lord; "Sit at my right hand,*
> *until I put your enemies beneath your feet."'"*
> THE MISSION [ACTS] 2:22-23, 32-35, QUOTING PSALM 110:1

Sit at my right hand: over and over in the New Order this psalm is cited as testimony to Jesus' exaltation. In those first years after Jesus' death, his followers came to be certain that in these lines the Lord God was speaking to the Lord Jesus. The Anointed was in glory, seated at God's right hand. We watch this image with care. We have envisaged a deputy who sits on a throne next to the king's and a figure who shares with the king the king's own throne. Where does Jesus sit? His follow-ers had the question forever before them. Their answer evolved. They discovered in their Jesus a glory greater than any psalm could offer them. At stake was not fantastical topography. At stake was the claim that would create the church.

SOME JEWS, WE MAY SUSPECT, moved to Jerusalem precisely out of rev-erence for this holiest of cities and its Temple. Some also likely came in expectation that God's climactic intervention in the world's history was due. They had good reason to be in Jerusalem. In the Holy City and the still holier Temple was the focus of their expectation.

> In the last days the mountain of the Lord and the house of God
> shall appear over the tops of the mountains
> and shall be seen above the hills.
> And all the nations shall come to it,
> and many nations shall come and shall say,
> Come, let us go up to the house of the God of Israel,
> and he will announce his way to us and we shall walk in it.
> For the Law shall go out from Sion and the word of the Lord from
>   Jerusalem.
> ISAIAH 2:2–3

Among those enthusiasts were the pupils of Jesus and the first of their adherents. Peter was a Galilean, from the northern limits of Israel. He had come south with Jesus. Had he stayed there at Jesus' death or returned to Galilee? Our gospels tell different stories for their own different reasons. If Luke is right, Peter stayed in Jerusalem. No wonder he attracted other Jews who shared his hope and were heartened by his assurance: the Day of the Lord was at hand.

But reverence for Jesus was likely, sooner or later, to disrupt reverence for the ways and ideals of Jerusalem, for the question would be asked: What had Jesus achieved? As long as the emphasis was on his example and teaching, the patterns of Jewish life within which he himself had lived were unchallenged. But what had his death and rising done, and how? The moment this was answered in terms of sacrifice, the seeds were sown for a bitter disagreement. Where did his achievement leave the Temple and its sacrifices? How did it affect them in principle or in the relations—from day to day, from festival to festival—between the Temple's hierarchy in the south and the followers of this hothead from the northern fringes of the Holy Land? The question was clearly vexed in Jesus' lifetime. After his death, it became more contentious still. And such a challenge to sacrifices, raised in Jerusalem itself, posed a challenge to the Law that ordained them.

We hear of these early days from Luke at the start of The Mission, the sequel to his gospel. Luke tells a story, wherever possible, of the assemblies' harmonious development. He has no incentive to recall old arguments. But he tells, near his story's beginning, of one dispute within the assembly in Jerusalem. The Aramaic- and the Greek-speaking followers of Jesus argued over the distribution of alms to widows. The pupils of Jesus, still in authority, appointed seven Greek speakers to ensure that the Greek-speaking constituency was not neglected.

Two of these helpers reemerge in critical roles. Far more, we can tell, was at stake in this dispute than the alms of which Luke speaks. The first helper, Stephen, is about to be accused by Jews with no allegiance to Jesus: *"We have heard this man talking blasphemy against Moses and against God. . . . This man does not stop speaking against this holy place and the Law"* (6:11, 13). Stephen will be condemned and killed, and so will become the sect's first martyr. The second helper, Philip, will baptize the first Gentile, a eunuch, into the community of Jesus' followers, and so will be the first to welcome into Jesus' fellowship a person who could not be member of a Jewish assembly.

Stephen was a dangerous man. But what had he been claiming? And how had it been received within the assembly of Jesus' followers itself?

For a clue, we turn again to the Jewish philosopher Philo. He was a contemporary of Paul's, and we can listen in Philo for the common intellectual property of Greek-speaking Judaism. Philo read much of the Law allegorically, and so, we may suspect, did Stephen. Scripture had an inner meaning that appealed to the mind and spoke of the mind. The great journeys of Abraham, Moses, and the people of Israel are truly understood when they are understood as the journey of the soul toward God; and essential to that journey is the deepening recognition, in itself, that the stories of the Old Order bear this hidden sense.

As with the stories of the Old Order, so also with its Law; the intention indicated by the Law mattered as much to Philo as the actual observance of the Law's ritual commands. Philo himself was adamant that the Law itself still had to be obeyed, but he clearly knew of those who had taken a still more radical turn away from the observance of the Law's stated commands. "There are some who regard the stated laws as symbols of things belonging to the mind. About the things symbolized they are overpunctilious; but the laws as stated they neglect in a carefree way." Philo demands a higher regard for a good reputation and for the customs laid down by men who were greater in their time than are those who neglect reputation now. "Yes, circumcision does signify the excision of pleasure and all passions . . . but let's not for that reason repeal the law laid down for circumcision. For we shall be ignoring the sanctity of the Temple and of a thousand other things, if we attend only to what is shown through inner meanings" (*The Migration of Abraham,* 89–92).

"To ignore the sanctity of the Temple and of a thousand other things": Philo knew that danger among the Jews of Alexandria. Here is likely the danger that Stephen posed to his fellow Jews in Jerusalem, when he spoke against the holy place and the Law.

Alexandria was a famous center for Greek culture, and Philo was influenced far more heavily than most Jews by the great tradition of Greek thought. For well-educated Greek speakers there was nothing strange in an allegorical reading of great texts; the poems of Homer, for instance, had been allegorized for centuries. We cannot assume, of course, that the philosophical movements that Philo knew in Egypt had reached Judea, but allegorical readings of scripture were known there as well as in Alexandria. The new assembly was inheriting, not creating, such ideas.

Jesus' death and rising posed a question: What had this death and rising achieved? Stephen and his allies found a radical answer. We would like, of course, to know more. Did Stephen's allies allegorize sporadically, just when a passage seemed amenable? Or consistently, as Philo did? Or drastically, as those thinkers whom Philo so angrily resists? We will never know. We can trace just enough of the arguments to diagnose the different viewpoints that inspired them.

We can trace the results too of such extreme allegorical readings. Once the physical observance of circumcision, the Sabbath, and festivals had been set aside, then Gentiles could respect the inner meaning of such rituals as readily as Jews. Stephen and his group in Jerusalem sowed the seeds of Paul's mission—the mission to Gentiles, who would on conversion remain free from observance of the Law.

Stephen and the other six Greek-speaking officials represented more than a language. They had a theology and a mission of their own, which was developing fast and was fiercely contested. To some of those who valued Jesus, Stephen would have been a hero. To the majority, he was likely an unwelcome disruption, antagonizing the many Jews in Jerusalem who sought no argument with their strange new group. For such Jerusalemites as these, Stephen's free-thinkers were a dangerous minority within a minority and on the verge of apostasy.

We set the scene: Some followers of Jesus, based in Jerusalem, were devoted to the Law and the Temple; their Jesus, restoring the purity of God's people, would restore with it the people's reverence for the Law and its ritual commands. Others saw in the achievement of Jesus a challenge to the Temple and its rituals ordained by the Law. Such disparate groups, each claiming to speak for Jesus, made for a volatile mix. It took just one charismatic speaker, according to Luke, to put a match to the tinder—Stephen, *filled with grace and power* (6:8). The drama is about to begin.

STEPHEN, THE FIRST MARTYR

Stephen is introduced by Luke only a few paragraphs before we hear of his arrest. Who are his antagonists? Immigrants or visitors, Luke tells us, from Cyrene and Alexandria (two harbors in North Africa), from Cilicia (the mainland area immediately north of Cyprus), and from Asia Minor. These will have been Greek-speaking Jews who put a high value on Jerusalem and its Temple. The Alexandrians among them will have recognized Stephen's allegories with disgust.

The radicals among Jesus' followers are about to have their views paraded around Jerusalem. Stephen and his allies represent just one view, within the assembly itself, about the Law and the Temple. But how much of the assembly is about to be tarred with the same brush? Stephen's preaching is about to imperil almost all of Jesus' followers.

Stephen's opponents suborned people to say, "We have heard this man talking blasphemy against Moses and against God." And they stirred up the people and the elders and the scribes and came upon Stephen and seized him and led him to the Council, and they set up false witnesses to say, "This man does not stop speaking against this holy place and the Law. For we have heard him saying that this Jesus of Nazareth will destroy this place and will change the ways that Moses has handed down

to us." And as they looked at him all those sitting there in the Council
saw his face, looking like the face of an angel.
THE MISSION 6:11-15

Stephen, runs the complaint, threatened the Temple's destruction.
The tradition was clearly well known that Jesus had made such a prediction. Mark records such a charge against Jesus himself at the time of
Jesus' own trial (Mark 14:57–59). Mark, oddly enough, both plays it
up—and plays it down. He insists twice that those who testified against
Jesus contradicted themselves. Mark protests too hard. John, by contrast, records such a prediction with relish. With it he sets up, right at
the start of his story, a relation that will inform his whole gospel and
bemuse its protagonists: between the old Temple ripe for destruction
and the new Temple that is the body of Jesus (John 2:19–21). And Luke
himself? In his story of Jesus' trial Luke had omitted all mention of this
threat against the Temple. His Jesus had warned the city and bewailed
its fate, but Luke did not even give space to a false suggestion that Jesus
threatened the Temple and the Law. Such a charge could only harm
Luke's cause. It is mentioned only at two removes, as a claim falsely
ascribed later to Stephen by bribed witnesses.

Luke is careful in the story of Stephen to acknowledge and rebut
one dangerous charge, but he has more in mind than this. He knows
that he can vindicate the assemblies only if he can prize the promises of
God from Judaism and its leaders. A pattern is under way that shapes
The Mission from beginning to end: the assemblies are the heir to
promises whose fulfillment, Luke maintains, almost all the Jews have
failed to see. Such Jews, in Stephen's day and in Luke's, were deaf to
God's word; so, according to Stephen, had their forebears been—for
generation after generation. Those ancestors had rejected Moses, who
had relayed to *the assembly* of the Jews (in the words of Luke's Stephen)
the words of life on Sinai; now they themselves have rejected his successor, Jesus, and oppose the assembly of his followers.

Luke has Stephen's words endorsed at the beginning of his speech
and again at its end. At its start Stephen's face is like the face of an
angel, and at its end he is given a sight of the Son of Man in glory. This
first martyr to die in Jesus' cause is given before his death the martyr's
reward. There could be no more compelling vindication of his words.

Stephen ends his speech:

"You stiff-necked people, uncircumcised in heart and ears, you always resist the Breath of God; as your ancestors did, so do you. Which of the prophets did your ancestors not persecute? And they killed those who announced in advance the coming of the Just One—whose betrayers and murderers you have now become, you who received the Law as delivered by angels and did not keep it."

When they heard this they were enraged and ground their teeth at him. But he, filled with the Breath of God, gazed into heaven and saw the glory of God and Jesus standing at the right hand of God, and he said, "Look, I see the heavens opened and the Son of Man standing at the right hand of God." But they cried out in a loud voice and stopped their ears and rushed together upon him. And throwing him out of the city, they stoned him to death. And the witnesses put down their garments at the feet of a young man named Saul. And they stoned Stephen as he called out and said, "Lord Jesus, receive my life." And he knelt down and cried out with a great voice, "Lord, do not hold this crime against them." And when he had said this, he fell asleep.

THE MISSION 7:51-60

Stephen dies as his master had, with trust in God and forgiveness for his enemies. This is Luke's model for martyrdom. In the first three gospels and in The Mission Stephen is the only person other than Jesus himself who speaks of the Son of Man; and his speech is the only text in these books that identifies the Son of Man unambiguously with Jesus. To follow Jesus as Stephen has followed is to be privileged with the direct unveiling of truths that most Jews denied and most Christians, whether Jewish or gentile, learned only through texts and teaching.

Luke is writing his account several decades after the events themselves. As he tells of Stephen's death, he is drawing on the story of Jesus that he has already told in his gospel, and he is anticipating, as we shall see, the story of Paul that will dominate The Mission. Luke, then, has likely edited his story to point up Stephen's transformation and vision, for Luke recognized—and likely strengthened—the link that Stephen provided in the chain from Luke's one great visionary to the other, from Jesus at one end to Paul at the other.

This moment seems complete in itself. But in one of his quietest and most compelling notes Luke introduces here the hero of his story's second half: Saul, to be known soon after his conversion and ever since as Paul. Nothing is said, then or later, of this Saul's feelings at the sight of Stephen's death. When his conversion comes, it will be sudden, complete, and controlled directly by God. For the moment he is wholly implicated but on the sidelines, a silent and sinister figure. The witnesses against Stephen strip off their outer clothes. They put them down at the feet of a young man called Saul. And they stone Stephen. *And Saul was consenting to his death* (8:1).

"THE WORD WILL REST UPON DAMASCUS"

A couple of pages later we hear of this Saul once more. He is on his way to Damascus, authorized, according to Luke, to arrest any followers of Jesus he finds there and to take them to Jerusalem.

The death of Stephen, Luke tells us, unleashed a persecution of Jesus' followers in Jerusalem. *Everyone was scattered except the emissaries* (The Mission 8:1). Luke of course has good reason to insist that the community's leaders stay at their post in Jerusalem. And he may have known that the more conservative followers of Jesus were left untroubled. Only those were in danger who—like Stephen—belittled the Temple and its cult, for as long as this group was in Jerusalem and among other Jews, its members attracted few or no Gentiles to their cause. The farther into gentile territory, however, these liberals were forced to go, the higher into view that lurking question rose: Might gentile converts be offered membership in the community without taking on obedience to the Law? Paul becomes the most famous emissary to ask this question, but he is not the first. He does not establish the mission to Gentiles, free from the Law. He joins it.

Paul was in pursuit of Jesus' followers, to bring them bound back to Jerusalem to face the discipline of the high priest or of the Jewish council. (So Luke tells us, but his account has been distrusted. Neither the high priest nor the council had any power to order extradition from

Damascus.) Paul headed up to Damascus. Why did he go so far north, right to the edge of Israel's ancient land? Luke, at least, suggests that there were closer targets within Judea and Samaria.

From Jerusalem, the 130-mile route to Damascus leads north through Judea, through or around Samaria, and into Galilee, the land of the ancient Jewish tribes of Zebulon and Naphtali, which is bordered on its west by the Mediterranean and on its east by the Sea of Galilee. Paul is nearing the borders of Israel's Promised Land, with the gentile world beyond. How far did the Holy Land extend? In Paul's day Damascus itself was in the Roman province of Syria, and it may have come briefly under the control of the Arabian kings from farther east. But according to the Jewish historian Josephus, the territory of the tribe Naphtali reached to Damascus; King David recovered it by conquest and imposed tribute.

The theme can be traced through later generations. Texts from the Old Order may appear to contradict each other, but the rabbis had to reconcile them. On the one hand, a psalm makes clear that Jerusalem is the Lord's resting place forever (132:14); on the other, the prophet Zechariah promises that Damascus will be the resting place for the word of the Lord (9:1). The rabbis drew the conclusion that in the last days Jerusalem itself would reach as far as Damascus.

A major scroll from Qumran mentions "the converts of Israel who went out of the land of Judah to dwell in the land of Damascus"; these are "the members of the New Order in the land of Damascus." We hear in the Old Order, *A star shall come forth out of Jacob and a scepter shall rise out of Israel* (The Census [Numbers] 24:17); according to the same document from Qumran, the star is "the interpreter of the Law who shall come to Damascus" (CD 6.5; 6.19; 7.18–22). Damascus may be a code name here for Qumran itself, but the code would have had a significance. Qumran itself was a place pregnant with the hope of God's intervention. If the sectarians used a code, they would have picked the name of another place as richly endowed with expectation. In speaking of Damascus the Qumranites may have been looking back to the patriarch Abraham. He had pursued his enemies north of Damascus; the sectarians may have taken this ancient victory as a model for the victory (whether in Damascus or at Qumran) yet to come.

And within the New Order? Peter made his great statement of belief in Jesus as the Anointed at Caesarea Philippi, which lay beneath the southern end of Mt. Hermon and its range, southwest of Damascus. No wonder the next story in Mark's narrative came to be linked with Mt. Hermon: the sight of Jesus, transformed into glory and flanked by Moses and Elijah, which dazzled Peter, James, and John on a mountain. The area around Damascus was rich in associations; it was within the promised territory of Israel, yet on the borders of the gentile world, the world of darkness and distance from God. When Paul looks back to his experience on the road to Damascus, he thinks of the God who said, *"Light shall shine out of darkness."* He is recalling the great command of God at the start of creation; he is recalling too God's promise to the people of Galilee and beyond:

> *He is doing this first, he is doing it soon, country of Zebulon, land of Naphtali, those living in the way of the sea and the rest living in the land beside the sea, Galilee of the nations, the districts of Judea:*
>
> > *You people that walk in darkness,*
> >   *look, a great light!*
> > *You who live in the region and shadow of death,*
> >   *upon you shall light shine.*
> >   ISAIAH 9:1-3, GREEK VERSION

Why had Jesus' followers fled to Damascus? Not just for its supposed safety. Damascus was a special place, a place where God might well reveal himself, his Anointed, and his great intervention in the world.

And why did Paul pursue these troublemakers so far? Perhaps because Damascus was a place precious in his own mind too. The adherents of this false Anointed were claiming a holy site for their pernicious error. It was a good reason to pursue them. It was a good reason too to be thinking, while on the journey, about the different hopes for the Anointed and for Damascus that Paul knew well. They were hopes he may well have shared: hopes offered by the Old Order, hopes known to be fostered at Qumran. Paul headed north through Galilee, the land of Zebulon and Naphtali, the land of Jesus himself, and on north toward the gentile darkness. What hopes, we might wonder, was he nurturing as he went, for Damascus, the Anointed, and the deliverance of Israel?

Paul pursued the Christians to Damascus, I suspect, because their hopes for Damascus were so close to his own. He too was waiting for the Anointed to be revealed. And he wondered too: Would the unveiling be offered in Damascus?

SETTING OUT FOR DAMASCUS

Paul sets out from Jerusalem, steeped in the traditions of visionary journeys of heaven. He is dwelling on the first vision of Ezekiel, the most dramatic of all the stories that fueled imaginations such as his. The Paul who sets out for Damascus is a visionary poised for a vision.

The first time we hear the story from Luke of Paul's conversion, he tells it as a straightforward narrative that an observer might relay. He claims no more knowledge than an observer could have had. Paul's companions hear what Paul hears, but see nothing but a dazzling light. We are told no details of what Paul saw, for no one else could see it. The story is presented ingenuously as an account untainted by anyone's agenda; it is a story that can be trusted. We will hear the story twice more from the mouth of Luke's Paul. Once Paul is speaking to the Jews in Jerusalem. According to this version of the story, Paul's companions saw the light, but did not hear the voice speaking. There was, then, no one present at the time who could later vouch for the instruction given to Paul; no wonder, then, he had been rejected by anyone who looked for such legitimation. Finally Paul tells the story again, to the Roman Festus and the quisling King Herod Agrippa. This time he abandons the tone and references that were suited to a Jewish audience; he even has Jesus quote a Greek proverb (which Paul heard, he remarks, in Aramaic). In Luke we are watching a skillful storyteller at work.

Here is that second version of the three. Paul is in Jerusalem, addressing the crowd that has tried to lynch him. No wonder he starts by talking of his Jewish pedigree. Says Paul:

> *"I am a Jew, born at Tarsus in Cilicia, but brought up in this city of Jerusalem, educated at the feet of Gamaliel according to the strict manner of the Law of our fathers, being zealous for God as you all are this day."*
>
> THE MISSION 22:3

Tarsus was a flourishing harbor well to the north, just where the coast of the Levant turns sharply westward. Tarsus was known for the eagerness with which its people sought education abroad. Paul too wanted better than he could get in Tarsus. He could have had no higher aspiration than to study with the Pharisee Gamaliel. Gamaliel would have fostered in Paul a zealous commitment to the Law and its interpretations, collated and refined from generation to generation. "When Gamaliel died," we read in the Mishnah, the great compilation of Jewish regulations from the third century C.E., "the glory of the Law ceased, and purity and abstinence died" (*Sotah [The Suspected Adulteress]* 9:15).

Paul continues:

"I persecuted this Way to the death. . . . I received letters from the high priest and the whole council of elders, and I journeyed to Damascus to take those who were there and bring them in bonds to Jerusalem to be punished.

"As I made my journey and drew near to Damascus, about noon a great light from heaven suddenly shone about me. And I fell to the ground and heard a voice saying to me, 'Saul, Saul, why are you persecuting me?'

"And I answered, 'Who are you, Lord?'

"And he said to me, 'I am Jesus of Nazareth, whom you are persecuting.'

"Now those who were with me saw the light but did not hear the voice of the one who was speaking to me. And I said, 'What shall I do, Lord?'

"And the Lord said to me, 'Stand up, and go into Damascus, and there you will be told all that is appointed for you to do.'"
THE MISSION 22:4-10

Luke's Paul is speaking to Jews. He plays up, therefore, the role of the Jewish Ananias, who came to find the blinded Paul in Damascus. Paul reminds his hearers, Ananias was *a devout man according to the Law, well spoken of by all the Jews living there* (22:12). No wonder he addresses

Paul as *brother Saul* (22:13). Here is a reliable witness informed by God of what has happened.

How carefully Luke has composed this speech in the mouth of Paul. Way back at the start of The Mission, Peter had spoken in Jerusalem of Jesus as *the Just One, set apart in advance* (3:14, 20). For the benefit of the crowd listening to Paul in Jerusalem, Luke has Ananias validate the vision of Paul in terms that they and Luke's readers know well. Says Ananias:

> *"The God of our fathers set you apart in advance to know his will and to see the Just One and to hear a voice from his mouth."*
> THE MISSION 22:14

The Just One: the crowd in Jerusalem, in Luke's story, is hearing again a claim made for Jesus that it had heard from Peter all those years before. *Set apart in advance:* as Jesus had been, so is Paul. From Jesus to Paul, from one chosen vehicle to another, and so to a mission that would change the world.

PART IV

PAUL AND ANTIOCH

CHAPTER 12

"AT ANTIOCH THEY WERE FIRST CALLED CHRISTIANS"

STEPHEN HAD DIED, ACCORDING TO LUKE, for his teaching on the Temple and the Law. His death triggered a general attack upon the followers of Jesus who shared his views. They fled up the coast. With them went their message, which they preached, as we would expect, to Jews. Some went as far north as Antioch. For Nicolaus, a convert to Judaism whom Luke lists among the seven Greek-speaking leaders, it was a return home. Among the fugitives, Luke tells us, were some Cypriots who brought to Antioch a dramatic claim: the good news, they maintained, should be preached to Gentiles too.

If, as Stephen's allies maintained, the Law was to be read allegorically, the Gentiles could obey it as readily as the Jews. What, then, should these Gentiles be encouraged or made to do? Were any of the Law's commands to be imposed literally? Or was it only the spirit of the Law that must be observed? Luke does not mention what conditions—if any—these preachers laid upon such Gentiles who wished to join Jesus' followers.

Whatever instruction Jesus had given about the place of Gentiles within God's empire, the instruction had not been clear enough to prevent dispute among his followers. Jesus' own emphasis was likely on the people and land of Israel, on their renewed or transformed holiness. And so God's blessing would come upon the Gentiles too, as this holiness expanded through all creation. Here, then, is the prospect of God's dominion, disclosed and fulfilled over all his earth. (We would nowadays distinguish, within this holiness, its political, social, religious, and spiritual constituents. The distinctions would have seemed quite artificial to Jesus and his pupils.)

Such hope was centered on the Holy Land; from there it would look outward upon the darkness of the gentile world. But how did this hope look from that gentile world, looking inward to the Holy Land and Jerusalem? And again, how did it look to Jews who lived and worked with Gentiles, Jews who spoke Greek as their first language and had come to respect Greek life, culture, and ways of thought? Enough such Jews had immigrated to Jerusalem, brought there just by family connections or business in the city; far more lived in the gentile world. Such Jews had good reason to wonder when God would embrace within his empire the gentile world they knew well and valued highly.

For such Jews as these, the Gentiles' future could become more important than the Temple's past. They accepted, of course, that Jerusalem was indeed the Holy City, its Temple the one true Temple of the one true God. But they owed no allegiance to the Temple's priests. If they joined Jesus' followers they could without qualm blame those priests for Jesus' death. If they made great claims for Jesus and had to shun Jerusalem, they would not miss its sanctity or rituals.

A new mission was taking shape in Antioch. Exactly what its missionaries offered to Gentiles and demanded from them, we cannot be sure. Nor, perhaps, could the leaders of the assembly in Jerusalem. There were certainly questions to answer and practices to justify. The leaders sent Barnabas to investigate. He was a good choice. Barnabas was from Cyprus, the large island that lies off the coast halfway between Jerusalem and Antioch. He would have known Antioch well, and no doubt have known the preachers too who had brought their new proclamation from Cyprus. If any envoy from Jerusalem could be valuable at such a delicate moment, it was Barnabas. As Luke tells the story, Barnabas is quickly convinced that the development should be encouraged. The mission to the Gentiles is under way.

Barnabas heads south again, to Damascus. He has heard the news that Paul, vehement opponent of the assemblies, is a changed man. Barnabas brings him up to Antioch. It is a brave move by Barnabas.

Paul had been no friend to any of Jesus' adherents. But fiercest of all had been his opposition to the liberal, allegorizing group that had surrounded Stephen—and was now prominent in Antioch. So prominent that their teaching and cohesion first gave Jesus' followers an identity and a name. In Antioch, Luke tells us, *the pupils were for the first time called "Christians"* (The Mission [Acts] 11:26).

IT WAS NOT ONLY JESUS' OWN TEACHING that left the final place of Gentiles unclear. The ancient prophets had declared that at God's final intervention God would regather his own people to Jerusalem from all the corners of the earth. He would gather the Gentiles to the Holy City too, to bring tribute and acknowledge its God. There will still, then, in this new order be those who rule and those who serve. In a stark inversion of all recent history, the foreigners will be the servants, the Jews their masters.

> *Lift up your eyes, Jerusalem, and look around and see your children*
> *gathered to you;*
> *look, all your sons have come to you from far away,*
> *and your daughters shall be carried on your arms.*
> *Then you shall see and shall be afraid and amazed,*
> *because the wealth of the sea, of nations and of peoples shall come to you.*
> *Foreigners shall rebuild your walls and their kings shall stand beside*
> *you. . . .*
> *And your gates shall be open throughout, day and night they shall not*
> *be closed,*
> *to bring the power of nations to you and for their kings to be let in.*
> *For the nations and the kings who do not serve you shall be destroyed,*
> *and the nations shall be utterly destroyed.*
>
> ISAIAH 60:4–5, 10–12, GREEK VERSION

To bring the power of nations to you and for their kings to be let in. But on what conditions will God accept these Gentiles' reverence? There was clearly scope for dispute. Must they be circumcised and undertake loyalty to the Law—and so become converts to Judaism and cease to be Gentiles at all? Or do they remain Gentiles, flocking to Jerusalem in obeisance? The God-fearers who attended the prayer houses, after all, already offered a faint sketch of the possibilities to come; they were Gentiles who came reverently to prayer houses and were welcome there, but were not circumcised.

At times Isaiah is clear: *No more shall the uncircumcised or impure pass through Jerusalem* (52:1). But even his grandest statements left room for differing views. Let's look at one of the most famous of his prophecies. In 56:3–8, Isaiah is pairing foreigners with eunuchs. According to The Second Law [Deuteronomy] 23:1 eunuchs were barred from the public worship of the people of Israel. But Isaiah's God promises that they will have in his house a monument better than that for children. Now, eunuchs could do nothing to change their state. If, therefore, they were to be admitted to worship in his house, it can be only when God changes the conditions of entry.

In the same passage Isaiah next makes a promise that foreigners too will be gathered in. Is he thinking of those Gentiles who would have converted to Judaism already, before this final ingathering? Does Isaiah even anticipate, before God's final deliverance dawns, a large-scale mission by Jews for the conversion of Gentiles? Or are the Gentiles to remain as Gentiles, observing only some parts of the Law such as the Sabbath?

Here is the introduction to the whole passage and then the promise to Gentiles:

> *Preserve proper judgment, do justness;*
> *for my deliverance has drawn near to be done and my mercy to be*
>   *unveiled.*
> *Blessed is the man who does these things and holds to them,*
> *who preserves the sabbath without defiling it*
> *and who keeps back his hands from doing injustice. . . .*
>
> *Thus says the Lord to the foreigners who adhere to the Lord*
> *to serve him and to love the name of the Lord, to be his slaves, men*
>   *and women,*
> *and to all who preserve the sabbath without defiling it and who hold*
>   *to my Order:*
> *"I shall lead them to my holy mountain and make them joyful in my*
>   *house of prayer.*

Their sacrifices will be acceptable on my altar.
For my house shall be called a house of prayer for all the nations."
ISAIAH 56:1-2, 6-7, GREEK VERSION

"My house shall be called a house of prayer," quotes Jesus when he over-turns the tables of the money-changers and dove sellers in the Temple (Mark 11:17). In the outermost courtyard, the Court of the Gentiles, Jewish worshipers changed their money into the coinage required for Temple offerings. Birds and animals were checked here, to ensure they were ritually acceptable, and were then sold to Jewish worshipers for sacrifice in the inner courtyards beyond. This outermost courtyard was the nearest that Gentiles could come to the Holy of Holies without risking arrest and death.

Mark alone of the evangelists has Jesus say those last words of Isaiah too, *for all the nations.* Jesus had likely been acting out, in old prophetic style, the destruction of the Temple that he saw ahead. But Mark has turned the emphasis from destruction to openness. His Jesus is inter-rupting the rituals that distinguish the Jews in the Temple from the Gentiles. This Jesus brings the time when God will lead all the Gen-tiles—as Gentiles—to his holy mountain and make them joyful in his house of prayer. This is the Jesus whose death is marked by the tearing of the great veil in the Temple. The Holy of Holies is open for all to see, Gentile and Jew alike.

Isaiah gives us a lavish picture of God's ingathering. This is the image before Paul. It raises deep questions about the Gentiles and their obser-vance of the Law, questions that all the earliest assemblies—and not just Paul himself—will have to answer. In their resolution the early assemblies will go through the bitterest disputes. And Paul will end up, among the great emissaries, in a minority of one.

"AT ANTIOCH THEY WERE FIRST CALLED CHRISTIANS"

Antioch was one of the great cities of the Roman East. "As large as Antioch" became a Jewish proverb; as many as 250,000 people may have been crammed within its walls. Antioch looked in all directions at once. Within fifteen miles its river reached the Mediterranean. The city lay in the crook of an elbow; Asia Minor was to the northwest, Arabia to the east, and the sea to the south and west. All the markets of the empire lay open to its ships.

There may have been a Jewish presence in Antioch since its foundation in 300 B.C.E. Josephus tells of Jewish mercenaries who had fought for its founder, Seleucus I. In his new capital they had been given space and special rights, proclaimed on bronze tablets. Such privilege was precious and easily threatened; it had to be declared as publicly as possible. The great prayer house in Antioch attracted royal patronage. King Antiochus Epiphanes, scourge of Israel, had plundered the Temple in Jerusalem in 170 B.C.E., but his successors gave the bronze from the booty to the Jews of Antioch, who used it to adorn their prayer house. The bronze was far from the spoils' most valuable part, but this was an unrivaled dignity for the building and its people. Josephus tells how the Jews of Antioch "adorned the temple with great splendor by the design and expense of their offerings."

By using the term "temple" Josephus is giving us, perhaps by mistake, a glimpse of the status that Antioch's prayer house had assumed in its people's life. The Temple in Jerusalem, after all, had been sacked by the time Josephus wrote; here in Antioch were the remnants of its ancient and precious contents. Here too, according to some stories, were the tombs of the martyrs killed by Epiphanes in their faith's defense; this was a venerable site.

The Jews of Antioch, Josephus tells us, "were constantly attracting to their ceremonies a large crowd of Greeks, and had made these in some measure a part of themselves." Here are the God-fearers of whom we have already heard. They had good reason to be attracted to the good news about Jesus offered by Barnabas and now by Paul. Such close encounters with Gentiles would transform the young community.

It is time for Paul himself to move on to the gentile stage. He has been known so far as Saul, his Jewish name; it was by that name that Jesus addressed him at his conversion. For his first mission, Barnabas and he are commissioned by the assembly at Antioch. They set out westward by sea to Cyprus, the island of Paul's senior partner, Barnabas. There they encounter a Jewish magician named Bar-Jesus, which means "son of Jesus." He served in the court of the island's Roman commander (proconsul), whose own name was Paul. Barnabas and Saul appear before the commander. Bar-Jesus is afraid that his commander will be converted to the faith that these missionaries proclaim, so he opposes them. And in the commander's presence *Saul whose other name is Paul* struck Bar-Jesus blind. On the one hand are the emissaries of Jesus; on the other, a Jewish magician bearing Jesus' name; and in between them the representative of imperial power. *The commander became a believer and he was astonished at this teaching of the Lord.* From now on Saul will be known in The Mission only by the gentile name that he shared with his first gentile convert, Paul (13:4–12).

At the start Barnabas and Paul were no doubt a good team. Barnabas was the delegate of the Jerusalem assembly, sent from there to Antioch and now authorized by this assembly too. He covered all the bases from the reverence in Jerusalem for Law and Temple to Antioch's new ideas for a welcome to the Gentiles. Here was a valued intermediary between these two centers, and so a valued teacher too for those outside. He and Paul wanted to speak in the prayer houses as they traveled. The name and standing of Barnabas would have won them a hearing. And with him was his assistant Paul, known, if at all, for his change of heart. Barnabas and Paul were from Antioch, known for its new ideas, but they were not obviously subversive. Paul himself did not allegorize the Law; and we have no reason to believe that Barnabas did. The allegorists were clearly contentious. A prayer house could think Barnabas and Paul, by contrast, a welcome pair of visitors.

Barnabas and Paul were not seeking converts from Judaism to Christianity. They were looking for a new recognition within the prayer houses that Jesus Anointed had disclosed God's will for Gentiles as it had never been seen before. God-fearers need no longer be on the fringes of Judaism, barred as it were from all but the outermost courtyard of Jewish life and worship. Jews and Gentiles alike should now recognize that through the Anointed God had lowered the parapet and leveled the steps that separated Jew and Gentile. The Law was, as it had always been, God's great gift to the Jews. The Gentiles as Gentiles— uncircumcised and without the Law—were now invited too into the holiness of the people of God.

Paul's namesake, the Roman commander of Cyprus, had family in Galatia, deep in the mainland of Asia Minor. It is no surprise that Barnabas and Paul next sail north, land, and head inland toward the estates of this new patron's relatives. With them they would have had valuable letters of introduction. Travel in the region was relatively straightforward. A cluster of Roman colonies was linked, at the southern end of Galatia, by the Romans' Augustan Road (Via Sebaste). Among them were the cities visited by Barnabas and Paul: Antioch-in-Pisidia (a second city with the name Antioch), Iconium, and Lystra.

Barnabas and Paul return to Antioch. Paul has come of age as an emissary. It may be some years before he sets out again, but next time he will be the leader, with Silas, an assistant of his own. We know less about Silas than we would like. Luke knows of him as a representative of Jerusalem (The Mission 15:22, 32); he will reappear as Peter's assistant in a letter ascribed to Peter and written to the assemblies in Galatia, Asia, and elsewhere. The letter is written to former pagans who can now be addressed as part of the Jewish "Dispersion" (Diaspora) throughout the world. How striking, that Silas is now allied to Peter; perhaps he had never been as committed to Paul's good news as Paul had hoped. Might he even have been relaying news to Jerusalem while on this journey with Paul? If so, he was in the longer term an ally Paul could do without.

Paul and Silas set out from Antioch in the spring of 46. They travel overland; the Cilician Gates, the vital pass over the Taurus Mountains from the coast into the heartland of Asia Minor, become passable in April. Ever farther to the north and west they go, through the cities of Paul's earlier mission and up to the farthest angle of Asia Minor.

There would have been areas where Paul could preach almost exclusively to Gentiles. The issue of the Law need not arise. But if it did? Luke tells of Paul's visit to Lystra, in southern Galatia. He encountered Timothy, a half-Jew whose mother was a Jewish convert to the assembly and whose his father had been gentile. Paul took Timothy as a traveling companion, and so had him circumcised *on account of the Jews in those parts; for everyone knew his father had been Greek* (The Mission 16:3). It is a striking—and often discredited—story. But if it is true? The action was easily misunderstood. Perhaps this half-Jew Timothy had attended the prayer house all his life with his mother; perhaps he had lived as a pagan; perhaps he had mixed the two ways of life. Whatever his history, he had never been circumcised. But this was not good enough, if he was to be Paul's assistant.

Timothy will become Paul's most loyal and valued lieutenant, but he is an ambiguous figure. What will others make of his circumcision? Of course Paul can say that Timothy, uncircumcised, could not have been his companion, for no prayer house would have accepted such a Timothy as an emissary's assistant. And of course this excuse would be ignored, whenever Paul's converts or his opponents, in the battles of later years, asked if God was really reserving his highest favor for those who observed the Law.

FOR PAUL, SILAS, AND TIMOTHY, Asia Minor was behind them; ahead, to the west, was Greece. In the autumn of 48 they take ship westward along the coast of Thrace and disembark at the port of Philippi in Macedonia. Paul is on the network of the great Roman roads. Philippi, Thessalonica, and all of Greece lie open before him.

Paul and his team move westward to Thessalonica. Luke tells of their visit; it ended, we hear, in accordance with Luke's favored schema, when the city's Jews tried to have them lynched. Paul heads south through Greece. By the spring of 50 he is in Corinth and from there writes to his converts in Thessalonica. Nothing in the letter suggests that Paul had Jews in mind among his addressees. In Thessalonica he had founded a gentile assembly. He had been looking for a fresh start. And in Macedonia he had found one.

Paul Among his Peers

In the next chapter we will read Paul's letter to the Thessalonians section by section. In this way we will find its shape emerging into view. Few of us will ever devote so much attention to the letters, speeches, and sermons of his contemporaries, but Paul and his addressees were quite at home with the fashions, tropes, and tricks of public speaking. Paul writes in styles he and his converts knew well. Within seconds of turning to a TV channel, we know if we are watching a talk show, documentary, or the news. We know if the person talking—whom we may never have seen before—is a celebrity, politician, or newscaster. The speaker's style of speech and self-presentation are giveaways, before we even know the subject of the program. Paul's audience was as fluent in its culture's codes as we are in ours.

Paul's converts in Thessalonica were not his most sophisticated audience. He will move south through Greece to Athens and to Corinth. Athens had been for centuries the most famous of all university towns. Its great days were long past when Paul was there, but its residents were nothing if not proud of its intellectual history. The Athenians and the foreigners living there, says Luke wryly, *took pleasure in nothing except saying or hearing something novel* (The Mission 17:21).

Corinth was a hectic, cosmopolitan city in which anything and everything was on offer. Wherever Paul went, the moment he began to teach—in a prayer house, in a shop, on the street, in a house—he would be compared with the speakers and teachers who could be heard every week. We read him as one of a kind, and perhaps he was, but his hearers would come to that conclusion only after they had compared him with others they had heard before him.

As a public speaker Paul was, at best, a minor player in a large league. He had no political cachet. He had no obvious social stature or ready access to the powers that be. He was not employed by those powers to address their public assemblies on state policy or public morals. Luke occasionally puts him in front of gentile crowds, but an artisan such as Paul would most likely have had little access to such public meetings—except when a crowd was stirred up to lynch him.

Nonetheless, he and his converts knew the conventions of public speaking. It befitted his dignity and theirs to use them, to give his letters the ring of authority and public standing. Such conventions were also—and very simply—*useful*. Points could be made concisely, clearly, and with real verve. No wonder Paul mastered the art. He knew all the tricks of the rhetorical trade. He uses them on every page.

We have, from the end of the first century, a glittering sketch of the teachers and speakers available in a great city. It comes at the beginning of a speech given in Alexandria by the orator Dio Chrysostom ("Golden Mouth"). Dio was a professional orator, hired by cities to deliver important speeches to their citizens. (He delivered two speeches in Tarsus, where Paul had been brought up.) Dio is a man with all the skills that an audience in Rome's eastern empire would admire.

In a vivid (and biased) sketch of public teachers in Alexandria, Dio shows us how readily such teachers were mocked. If Paul stood out at all, it was for the chameleon message that he could fit to any audience. But this did not make him unique. If Paul's converts once distrusted him, they had quite enough categories—all of them damning—into which to fit him.

Here, then, from Dio's summary are some of the types with which Paul could be compared; and Dio himself makes yet another, as he sets himself apart from the rivals he is so determined to despise. Dio concedes that the Alexandrians may never have been exposed to a stern but benevolent critic such as himself. It may well not be themselves but "the so-called philosophers" who are to blame, for there are those who never speak in public. Others speak only to a controlled audience in their lecture rooms. Others again, "the ones called cynics," are present in the city en masse; they make a living at street corners, cracking acid jokes and mocking pretension. They have the worst effect of all—they accustom their audience to laugh at philosophers. Then there are the masters of public declamation who give speeches—and even recite their own poetry—for display. Fine, if they were poets or orators, but not if they do it "for gain and for their own glory" under the guise of philosophy. A few advisers have spoken frankly, but they say only a couple of words in insult and then make off in case there is "uproar." But in Dio the Alexandrians have a quite different speaker.

> To find a man who will speak with frankness, honestly and without trickery, and taking advantage of no one for the sake of glory or money, but who is ready, if need be, out of goodwill and concern for others to be laughed at and to submit to disorder in the crowd and uproar—to find such a man is the fortune of a very lucky city. . . . For myself, I feel that I have chosen this role not of my own volition, but by the will of some deity. For when the gods take thought for people's future, they provide for them both good counselors who need no urging and words that are appropriate and profitable to hear.
>
> *DISCOURSE* 32.11

We will hear of such claims again. Paul will tell the Thessalonians that he had *spoken with frankness*. Nothing he said *emerged from error, from immorality or in trickery*. He had never been found *in a word of flattery* or looked for a way *to take advantage of another* or *sought glory from humankind* (1 Thess. 2:2–6).

Dio and Paul both knew the suspicion to which all such speakers were exposed: that they were doing it for power, esteem, money; that they were flattering, wheedling, lying. Both knew the convention by which such suspicions could be deflected: face them head-on, deny them, and point out all the contrasting evidence of probity, honesty, and genuine care.

Paul was famously courageous. But even—or especially—such a public figure as Dio had to take care. He is addressing his speech to the Alexandrians, but his patron the emperor (who is likely to visit the city) will no doubt hear of its contents. The published form had to keep the emperor as vividly in mind as the first rowdy audience. The emperor involved was probably Vespasian (who ruled 69–79 C.E.). Vespasian certainly had strong opinions about troublesome thinkers; he banned first all Cynics from Rome, then all philosophers except the favored Musonius. When two Cynics slipped back into Rome, one was flogged, the other beheaded. Dio himself is said by a fourth-century historian to have urged the emperor to expel philosophers from land and sea. Among those known to have belittled the emperor one may well have come from Alexandria itself.

Where did Dio himself stand among the factions who had every reason to fear imperial displeasure? He had strong reason to distance himself from the yapping, aggressive Cynics; all the stronger, if he really wore the cheap cloak that was the Cynics' hallmark and had, as he says, been taken for one. He is, he insists, rather, the true philosopher, the physician of the body politic, who speaks out boldly against and despite intimidation by his audience. He returns to the theme later in the speech. Here we see quite clearly that he has had particular local teachers—well known, no doubt, to his audience—in mind all along. His earlier summary was carefully matched to Alexandria and its dangers. Dio is not going to avoid the assembly's anger, as the local philosopher Theophilus had, by a superior silence. There are certainly those who flatter, "sophists and deceivers." There are those too who sing in their lectures or before the assembly, "orators and sophists." To be as forthright as Dio, by contrast, is to face the charge of seeking glory—or of madness. Now we can see what had motivated Dio's opening comments. He must insist that he is no flatterer, no Cynic, no singer, no coward. He treads carefully as he distinguishes true philosophers from false. The Alexandrians are lucky to have a visit from a man such as himself, "in the glut of flatterers and deceivers and orators."

Alexandria was volatile. The city had acclaimed Vespasian emperor with enthusiasm. It expected privileges in return. Vespasian did not grant them. Crowds rioted at the disappointment; bitter lampoons circulated freely. This is the emperor whose plans, so Dio hints, are known to Dio himself. The emperor is likely to visit. Surely this was an incentive to the calm dignity that the Alexandrian crowd famously lacked. Dio has, we may guess, been invited to give the speech by the city's authorities. They have an eye to possible disturbances during the emperor's visit. The authorities have good reason to be worried; either at recent games or at a musical competition the rivalry between different claques had led to a riot that involved the imperial garrison. To placate the emperor and to prepare the crowd, they invite Dio, a thinker favored by the emperor, to speak. Dio has come to upbraid the crowd. He knows what he is up against. He had been in the city with Vespasian at the emperor's acclamation. There is no reason for the crowds to value Dio's speech; and, it seems, they do not.

It is fascinating to have a speech that still bears the marks of its original delivery. Paul was not the only speaker to be heckled. We might have expected such an orator as Dio to polish his text before its "publication," to have woven an elegant introduction and rousing peroration. But, instead, we have Dio starting with a call for silence; his arrival, it seems, had been met with raucous laughter. He wins the people's attention halfway through, but is clearly in trouble again by the end. He closes his speech abruptly. In his criticism of the Alexandrians, he says, he is like the musician who accused a tone-deaf tyrant of having an ass's ears. The musician was flogged for his pains and a war was the result. And so Dio issues the speech. The emperor can be clear when he hears of it that his favored speaker has done all that could be done, but the Alexandrians will not be curbed. If we imagine Paul in front of a great crowd at all, we should imagine as well the catcalls and interruptions, the laughter and insults.

Dio asks whether he is out to please himself or his audience. Quite obviously not, he says, for he has a fractious and disrespectful crowd in front of him, and here he is to berate them—for being forever fractious and disrespectful. But how about Paul? Is he out to please himself or his converts? The evidence in his favor is more ambiguous. If things go wrong, the kindness of a new and solicitous friend can come to look like the slithering of a snake in the grass. To reestablish his integrity Paul will have to appeal with ever greater intensity to his converts' own memory and to God.

From the grandest of public orators to a traveling artisan, from the crowded arenas of the empire to discussions carried on cross-legged on a workshop floor—a great gulf separated Dio's world from Paul's. But they shared a language and a culture and its conventions. Dio works his conventions hard. So does Paul.

Dio is a worried man. He has failed to smooth the emperor's path. When Paul writes to the Thessalonians, he is a worried man too. The Thessalonians were once confident of Paul's insight, honesty, and love. They are starting to see him as one of those hucksters whom Dio derides. Paul will use every device available to him to defuse the crisis looming in his converts.

Dio's mind is on the return of the emperor to Alexandria; Paul's is on the return of the Lord Jesus. For all his public standing and large crowd, Dio is fretting on a stage far smaller than Paul's. Dio saw trouble in store for the unruly Alexandrian crowd; Paul saw trouble beyond all conception in store for the world. We already hear Paul speak of it in the earliest of his letters to survive, when he writes to Thessalonica.

The Coming of the Lord

You turned to God from idols to serve the living and true God and to await his son from the heavens, whom he roused from the dead, Jesus, the one rescuing us from the coming wrath.

1 THESSALONIANS 1:9–10

This is a fanfare, a stirring summary of the good news that Paul had brought to Thessalonica, perhaps in the very words he had used at the time. These lines launch the first letter we have from Paul. In them we have too the starting point for all Paul's preaching—the imminent return of the Anointed.

It is hard for us now to sense the excitement with which Jesus' first followers looked forward to his return. He was coming, and coming soon. God's anger was lowering over the world like a storm cloud rolling over the hills. As the landscape darkens, a chill wind rises, and the earth is splattered with the first great drops of water—so had God given due warning: his anger was about to be rained down on the world. Was there any escape from the fury to come? It was the life and death and rising of Jesus that gave due warning of the storm; it was the same Jesus, died and risen, who offered his followers escape from its wrath. It would not be long now. *We who are living, who are being left, shall be seized up together with the dead in the clouds to meet the Lord in the air* (1 Thess. 4:17).

The New Order is alive with this expectation. There is nothing bland in it. The hope offers recompense for present suffering, but that suffering itself is real and calls for explanation. A long-standing tradition expected "tribulations" before the Day of the Lord; there may even have been those who were excited to recognize the arrival of these troubles as a sign of the impending end. But there are limits to endurance. It was hard to bear isolation from the security, friends, and natural place the converts had once had within the city. And it was all the harder, if pagan hotheads added verbal, physical, or economic attack. When would God bring an end to these troubles?

The Lord could be present in more ways than one. As the converts moved from the old creation onto the threshold of the new, so the Anointed stepped from the realm beyond and inhabited the threshold too. The present was shot through with the future, earth with heaven. And never more vividly than when the assembly met for worship.

When Paul writes 1 Corinthians, he rounds off his letter with a series of short greetings and blessings. They will have been formulas familiar to his addressees. He takes over from the scribe to write this conclusion himself:

The kiss of greeting—in my own hand, Paul's handwriting.
If anyone does not love the Lord, let them be cursed.

Maranatha.
The grace of the Lord Jesus be with you.
My love with you all in Anointed Jesus.
1 CORINTHIANS 16:21–24

Maranatha is a term in Aramaic, the language of Jesus himself and of his earliest followers. It may be read with various meanings: "Our Lord, come," "Our Lord has come (in earthly humility)," "Our Lord is come (and is here now)," or "Our Lord will surely come (in his longed-for return as judge)." The followers of Jesus had here taken over an older expectation and its expression. The letter of Jude explicitly quotes the book of Enoch, on which we drew in Chapter 6. *Enoch, the seventh from Adam, prophesied, saying: "Look, the Lord will surely come among his tens of thousands of holy ones, to execute judgment on all humanity and to accuse all its impious ones for all their deeds of impiety"* (Jude 14–15). This prophecy ascribed to Enoch predates Jesus, let alone his followers. When Jesus' followers spoke of their Lord's return, they were adapting for themselves an already ancient warning of God's judgment on the world. As for Enoch, so for Jude: Our Lord will surely come—*Maranatha.*

Why does Paul use the term untranslated in his closing lines to the Corinthians? *Maranatha* was almost certainly used in the worship of the earliest assemblies as a prayer or acclamation that summed up their great hope. It was used in the assemblies that spoke Aramaic, among the very first followers of the risen Jesus, in Palestine itself, within years or even months of Jesus' death. By the time of Paul it is well known to the Greek-speaking assembly of Corinth. Where the mission has gone, *Maranatha* has gone too, with the mystery and the authority of a term in Jesus' own language used by Jesus' own pupils.

We will hear it again. At the end of the book of Unveiling [Revelation] is a series—or perhaps more accurately, a jumble—of short prophecies and commands. They round off the whole book. Our seer "Isaiah," we remember, had been told that his vision had to be kept secret until the last generation. There is no need for John the Seer to be so reticent now.

And he said to me: "These words are trustworthy and true, and the lord God of the breaths of the prophets has sent his messenger to show his slaves what must happen soon. And look, I am coming soon. Blessed is the one who keeps the words of the prophecy of this book."

And he said to me: "Do not seal up the words of the prophecy of this book. For the due time is near.

> *The unjust—let them be unjust still;*
> *and the unclean—let them be unclean still;*
> *and the just—let them do justice still;*
> *and the holy—let them be holy still.*

"Look, I am coming quickly, and my reward is with me, to give to each as their deeds deserve. I am the A and the Z, the first and the last, the beginning and the end."

UNVEILING 22:6-7, 10-13

As Unveiling comes to an end, the threads of the book are drawn together. Earlier hints and allusions are brought out into the open. At the start of Unveiling God had spoken: *"I am the A and the Z, the being and the was and the coming, the almighty"* (1:8). Shortly afterward, a person spoke who was derived from Ezekiel's image of God and from Daniel's *one like a son of man.* We learnt his history (it was Jesus' history) and his status: *"I am the first and the last"* (1:17). As Unveiling reaches its climax we are shown, seated on the throne of the New Jerusalem in heaven, *the A and the Z, the beginning and the end* (21:6). And at the end of the book Jesus declares openly that all these titles are his. The role and standing of Jesus—and their fusion with the role and standing of God—are being unveiled, carefully and progressively, in the Seer's portrayal of worship in heaven and on earth.

A final antiphon begins. Jesus has promised his coming. The Breath that enlivens the assembly replies. The New Jerusalem in heaven replies as well, *prepared like a bride for her husband* (21:2). And so, we read, let all the members of John's assembly, hearing this book recited—let them reply too in this crescendo of prayer. The one seated on the throne of the New Jerusalem had promised earlier, *To those who are thirsty I will give the water of life freely* (21:6). And here at last the promise is fulfilled. The members of the assembly know such antiphons well. Here these members are part of an antiphon that fills heaven and earth:

And the Breath and the bride say: "Come!"

And let those who hear say: "Come!"

And let those who are thirsty come,
let those who want take the water of life freely.
UNVEILING 22:17

And so back to Jesus. On his visions these visions of Unveiling are based. He himself now answers the answer of his people. The Jesus who saw these visions is their protagonist:

He who bears witness to these things says: "Yes, I am coming quickly."

And so the antiphon draws to its close. The worship of heaven and the worship of earth are one, for the book of Unveiling would have been recited at the assembly's service, at the Lord's Supper itself, when Jesus is as vividly present to his people as at any time on earth. The reader—perhaps the whole assembly—responds to Jesus' promise with a final plea:

"Amen. Come, Lord Jesus."
UNVEILING 22:20

Come, Lord Jesus. The Lord is so close, he and his followers can speak with each other. He is so close to his worshipers, and so close to his return as judge. The two times can hardly be distinguished. The Day of the Lord, the long-awaited day when God would judge the world and wreak destruction on God's enemies, is for the assemblies the Day of the Lord, the day when the Anointed rose from the dead, on which his followers now meet in worship. Those who eat and drink the Lord's Supper unworthily, warns Paul, are liable for the Lord's body and blood; they are eating and drinking judgment here and now upon themselves. The followers of Jesus have, throughout Unveiling, heard from the Seer of the worship of heaven. The figure on God's own throne, in these last lines, is now addressing them.

Come, Lord Jesus. Once more, in the last words of Unveiling and of the whole New Order, we hear in reply that call from the earliest years of Jesus' followers: *"Maranatha."*

PART V

PAUL AND THESSALONICA

CHAPTER 13

RESCUE FROM THE COMING WRATH

PAUL REACHED THESSALONICA between 48 and 50. Luke has him in the city for just three weeks before the authorities are persuaded by the Jews that he and Silas are a danger to public order, for they are proclaiming a king apart from the emperor (The Mission [Acts] 17:1–9). The circumstances in Thessalonica likely stirred particular support for Paul—and particular opposition. The business elite in Thessalonica had closer relations with Rome than the governing class in most comparable cities. The manual and other laborers, meanwhile, had a distinctive cult, that of Cabirus, a young man killed, according to legend, by his brothers and due to return to Thessalonica to aid the powerless and support the city. Under Emperor Augustus the city's elite had appropriated the Cabirus cult and made it part of the city's official regime. Cabirus, once the champion of the indigenous poor, had become another vehicle for the elite, which so conspicuously looked to Rome for its status and advantage.

Enter Paul, with the good news of Jesus killed, risen, and offering his blessings here and now. No wonder the laboring classes found his message attractive—and the authorities found it subversive. *"These are the men,"* complained the Jews in Luke's story, *"who are turning the inhabited world upside down"* (17:6). It was a well-placed charge.

We look to Paul nowadays for doctrine. And so we should. We will turn in a couple of pages to his *word of the Lord* to the Thessalonians about Jesus' return and the "rapture" of his followers to heaven; we will be joining the legion of readers who have wondered at this promise, lived by it, doubted it, or scoffed at it. But before Paul speaks to the Thessalonians of the future, he speaks at length of the past, he past that he shares with his converts. This is the landscape in which Paul has built his house. Here alone the materials, style, and outlook of the house make sense to an observer.

Why must he dwell so long and so intimately on the evidence he showed the Thessalonians, when he was among them, of his love for them? Because, behind his confidence and praise, he is deeply worried. The hope that he fired in the Thessalonians is cooling. Without his help, it will be extinguished altogether.

We need not be surprised. Paul's converts have abandoned the long-cherished rites of their fellow Thessalonians. Their change of allegiance has been inescapably public. They have had confidence in their new cause. Some of them have given up work altogether to await the coming of the Anointed. They have responded to their opponents defiantly and have antagonized their pagan neighbors. They will have thought—and spoken—of those neighbors as Paul had taught them to, as subject to the looming wrath of God. All and only those who trusted in Jesus would be delivered at his return. And that return was portended by the very opposition that the Thessalonians had suffered from their neighbors. Paul describes their suffering as *tribulation,* the word linked with the final suffering that God's chosen ones must undergo before God reveals his glory and dominion at last. It should have brought God's judgment in its train. All eyes in the assembly are on Jesus' return—any day now.

But he does not come. Has he failed them? Or have they failed him? Was their suffering or their endurance not enough? And now, worse still, members of the assembly have died. Paul had probably said nothing when he was in Thessalonica about such deaths at all. Why should he, when Jesus' return was so close? But if Paul had been mistaken or disingenuous over this, what weight can the Thessalonians place on anything he has said? The challenge to their faith is not intellectual or theoretical; it is stirred by the death of loved ones and the fear that—far from being rescued—these loved ones are lost forever.

We should not assume that all the assembly's members responded in the same way to the initial hope raised by Paul, or to its disappointment. But under pressure differences become divisions. As the converts' confidence weakened, so did their cohesion as an assembly. Paul's preaching had glued together into a single assembly a number of households, each with its own background, loyalties, and ideas. In Paul's absence, the assembly has been violently shaken. Cracks are appearing, ever wider and deeper, where the glue cannot hold.

PAUL: FATHER, MOTHER, FRIEND

How does Paul respond to this threat? He knows that he needs far more than an argument that will convince his converts. The Thessalonians have come to question the prospect that Paul had held out to them. The keystone of their hope is loosened, and with it the whole structure of their faith. They need Paul's reassurance. But it is Paul who raised that hope in the first place. What, then, is his reassurance worth? During his visit they had been convinced by him—so powerfully that Paul can describe his impact as the work of the Breath of God. He writes of *power:* miracles had been involved. *Our good news did not come to you in word alone, but in power too and in the holy Breath and in full conviction* (1 Thess. 1:5). But how do they see him now? He may have been deluded. He may have been seeking power for himself. He may have claimed a love for them that was a love only of their respect for him.

If Paul's converts once doubt what he says because it is Paul saying it, he must make one move before all others: he must reestablish their trust. How can he prove he was not deluded? He cannot. He can repeat or elaborate what he has said before; he can introduce a saying they had not heard before; he can appeal to the highest authority and the most direct disclosures from God. (When he comes to address their deepest fear, he introduces a new teaching in a *word of the Lord*.) But just such claims as this are the object of the assembly's suspicion.

He takes, then, a different tack. He revives their sense of his love and care for them. Here is the voice they remember, of their father in the faith who urged them to be worthy of the empire of their heavenly father God. Here is the voice of their brother too. (He calls them "brothers" in this letter fourteen times.) Here too, he tells them, is the voice of their mother and nurse, of their dearest friend bereaved by his own separation from them.

This, claims Paul, is the Paul that they suspect. How can they? He took no material benefit from their conversion. His own reward is the reward he is offering them at the coming of the Anointed. He has invested his life in this faith and invited them to do so too. It is his love for them that will overcome their doubts and discouragement. And how can he show that love? What they want, above all, is for him to visit. They need his presence, his return. The return of Paul and the return of the Anointed are tightly connected. As Paul "re-presents" the Anointed to his assemblies, so his coming—in power and knowledge and love—hints at the greater coming of the Lord.

Paul could not go back to Thessalonica, so he sent his lieutenant Timothy, well known to the Thessalonians from the visit of Paul's team. In the letter Paul gives Timothy as high a status as he can: *our brother and a fellow worker of God in the good news of the Anointed* (3:2). *A fellow worker of God:* scribes and scholars alike have balked at such a grand claim. (In some manuscripts the description was changed to "servant of God"; in others, to "servant of God and fellow worker with ourselves.") But Paul has an apology to make. It was not Timothy whom the assembly wanted; it was Paul. He must insist that in Timothy they were not shortchanged. Paul knows as well as they do that it is his own visit that will assure the Thessalonians of his love and reestablish their confidence in him, in themselves, and in all that he has told them. The letter is his substitute for such a visit. Paul does the best he can. He writes about his converts in rich, evocative language, for the Thessalonians need an emissary who loves and needs them. And here in the person of Paul, as he himself insists, is that emissary.

Paul is their focal point, the creative and sustaining center of their life as a community set apart, united, and holy. Their conversion had marked them out from those who worshiped idols—from their own neighbors, that is, and colleagues and extended family. Paul speaks specifically of his tireless work *among you, the ones who believed.* It is within this group alone that the word of God is at work in Thessalonica: *among you, the ones who believe.* But what of the other Thessalonians? Paul does not want to worsen the antagonism between his assembly and the rest of the city. According to Luke, there has been quite enough trouble already. So Paul draws his contrasts carefully. His converts are *to behave graciously toward those outside*. The unconverted in general are just called *the rest*. If anything, they deserve pity. They are sleepers; the day of the Lord is about to catch them unawares (2:10; 2:13; 4:13; 5:6; 4:12).

So far, so mild. But there has been opposition. Paul's converts have been unsettled. Paul must acknowledge their concerns. It's worth remembering the praise Paul gave the Thessalonians in the letter's introduction: they had imitated Paul and the Lord himself. Imitating the Lord—it was a striking claim. Only now, several pages later, can we see clearly why Paul made it. He sets out a comparison between the Thessalonian and the Judean assemblies, between, on the one hand, the gentile opposition to his mission in Thessalonica and, on the other, the Jewish opposition in Judea to Jesus, to the prophets, and to Paul. He must reassure his assembly that its opponents are condemned. But he will avoid raising the temperature by outright attack. So he targets the opponents in Judea of Jesus himself and the Judean assemblies; they have taken every chance for wrongdoing they have had, *and the wrath [of God] has come upon them—utterly.* As upon them, so upon the Thessalonians' opponents. The local opposition stands condemned by association (2:10–16).

IT IS TIME FOR A RAIN CHECK. If Paul seems so immediate and so personal, it is surely because he wanted to. In all that follows, we must be aware that he was working hard, in letter after letter, to bind his assemblies to him in loyalty and love. It was as well known to public speakers in the ancient world as it is to politicians today that a speaker must win the trust of the audience. The hearers must feel that the speaker cares quite especially about *them*. If they feel the speaker is their friend, they may be receptive; if they feel the speaker is distant, superior, personally ambitious, or using them for his or her own ends—they almost certainly will not. It was standard practice to belittle one's opponents for just such dishonesty and to contrast it with one's own care, concern, and openness. The rule then, as now, was "Be personal." And Paul is.

Is there, then, any way to distinguish, in the public speakers of Paul's day and in Paul himself, between the truly personal and the façade?

Perhaps we can put the question less abrasively. Can we distinguish between those feelings, on the one hand, that Paul would gladly have expressed to the individual members of his assemblies, people he knew and liked, if he was with them, was relaxed, and had no need to resolve any crisis, and those feelings, on the other, that he thinks they need to hear him express in the face of a crisis triggered precisely by his absence and their suspicion that he does not care about them?

We are right to be wary. And we can never get behind the text to see for ourselves what Paul was thinking. As this book continues, however, I hope readers will find a coherence and completeness in the portrait that emerges, a portrait that finds in Paul an extraordinary sense of his own status and role, a passionate care for his converts—and a dependence on them that is both human and theological at the same time. These converts need Paul. Paul needs them. And he attempts to meet those needs—theirs and his—with every means at his disposal.

Paul Writes to Thessalonica

LAUNCHING THE LETTER

We have looked over the terrain in which Paul's letter is set. Now we can do justice to the mansion at the heart of the landscape, the letter itself.

Paul sets out the letter's themes right at its start. We shall see him do the same in letter after letter. His addressees have a lot to take in as they hear it. They do not have the options that we enjoy as readers. We can turn back to reread a difficult passage, check an earlier point, pick up the thread after a long aside. We can simply pause in the middle to take stock or have some coffee. Our Bibles have chapter divisions; many have paragraph headings, notes, and cross-references. None of this was available to the audience when a letter from Paul was first read out loud in the assembly. The reader, as far as we can tell, would simply read on and on. And if the whole letter to the Romans, for instance, was read aloud at a single session, the assembly would still be listening—to an unremittingly complex letter—an hour later.

We will be looking at Paul's letters one by one. In each case we will concentrate on the letter itself, on the clues it gives us to its own structure, tone, emphases, function, and purpose. These are all clues that readers could pick up and follow for themselves. I do not mean to be disingenuous (or to declare my own book redundant!). The particular trails we will be following are not those that might first catch the eye; scholars with other presuppositions have tended not to see these clues or their importance at all. But they are there to be found. And I hope that by the end of this book its readers will want to pick up Paul's letters and read them—perhaps for the first time, perhaps for the tenth—for themselves.

Some readers may expect me to describe the many accounts of effective rhetoric and manuals for public speakers that have reached us from the ancient world. They have been intensively studied in recent decades. It can be shown that Paul follows a good many of the practices they recommend. But I am concerned with rhetoric not as a technique, but as a purpose—to effect changes in the audience. Paul's technique serves his purpose, and the letters themselves give us, for both, the clues we need.

As readers now, so listeners then: they needed all the guidance that Paul could give them. And so he would start with a summary of his letter's themes. In the first ten verses of 1 Thessalonians he lays out all the concerns, informally but carefully ordered, that have prompted the letter. Let's hear this introduction sentence by sentence:

> *We give thanks to God for all of you at all times, making mention of you in our prayers, remembering you for the work of your faith, the labor of your love and the endurance of your hope in our Lord Jesus Anointed before our God and Father.*
>
> 1 THESSALONIANS 1:2-3

Paul will deal with the faith, love, and hope of the Thessalonians each in turn. He has this triplet in mind from beginning to end. Not that he admits as much. Their faith in God is so well known that, Paul says, *I have no need to tell you anything.* About their brotherly love of each other *you have no need that I write you.* And about the time and trigger for the Anointed's return—and all that these imply for hope—*you have no need for anything to be written you* (1:8; 4:9; 5:1). He will, he says, not write on these themes at all; however, these are just the three themes about which he writes half his letter. His aim is encouragement, and the first way to encourage those who doubt themselves is to tell them they need no encouragement. At issue here, as ever, is not what Paul says he will do, but what he does—and what he is trying to achieve by doing it.

How alert Paul is to the assembly's situation. The Thessalonians need to be reassured that they are still in good standing before God. Paul will both reaffirm that good standing and pray for it. The Thessalonians need the strength that he gives them by his confidence in them, his love and hope for them. If Paul believes in their good standing, then they can believe in it themselves. They look to him for assurance and will justify that assurance by their response to it. Paul is praising in the Thessalonians what his praise will create.

But this is a dangerously fragile ground for the assembly's confidence. After all, its members must once more trust Paul, both the honesty of what he says and the insight—into themselves and into God's purpose and will—on which he bases what he says. No wonder Paul works so hard to remind them of his love specifically for them, his converts. If they doubt him again, if they doubt his commitment to them, his honesty, or his privileged knowledge of God's will, then isn't their existence as a community surely threatened? Yes, indeed it is.

FAITH, LOVE, AND HOPE—Paul heralds them right at the letter's start, but he addresses them only in its second half. Before then, he speaks at length of the relationship between the Thessalonians and himself. It becomes an important section. So important, that he almost starts the letter again when he comes back at last to that opening triplet. He needs first to embrace the assembly, to remind and reassure his converts how deeply he loves them and how closely they have modeled themselves on him. He is opening the eyes of the Thessalonians to a relationship closer than they have yet recognized. Once more he alerts them to the theme in advance, so his introduction continues:

> Brothers beloved by God, we know that you have been chosen. Our good news did not come to you in word alone, but in power too and in the holy Breath and in full conviction; just as you know how we were among you for your sake. And you yourselves became imitators of us and of the Lord, receiving the word in great tribulation with the joy of the holy Breath.

1 THESSALONIANS 1:4–6

Each sentence of the introduction alerts the listener to a theme or symphony of themes that will shape the letter as a whole. We are reaching the last sentence of that introduction, which is a ringing reminder of the good news that the Thessalonians heard from Paul when he was with them. Here is the subject of all their hope. It is reported, worldwide,

> *how you turned to God from idols to serve the living and true God and to await his son from the heavens, whom he roused from the dead, Jesus, the one rescuing us from the coming wrath.*
> 1 THESSALONIANS 1:8–9

Paul is now ready to go on to the main body of his letter. He addresses first the Thessalonians' own relation with himself, then faith, then love, and then hope. And as he rounds off the last movement of his symphony, Paul will offer a reprise. He brings the letter, at its end, right back to its start: *But us, let us be sober, putting on a breastplate of faith and of love and as a helmet the hope of deliverance, because God has not appointed us for wrath but for the obtaining of deliverance through our lord Jesus Anointed* (5:8–9).

PAUL AND THE THESSALONIANS

Paul has finished his introduction with that most important point of all: his converts are waiting for Jesus' return. To be sure in this expectation is to have at hand the answer to all present questions and worries. But just this hope is threatened, and with it the converts' trust in the Paul, who raised it. Paul turns back to the past, to his time in Thessalonica and the love for his converts, which he showed in all he did and said. How can they doubt that love now?

This recollection of the past (2:1–16) is carefully composed. We should imagine it being read out loud. It has a clear rhythm—and a whole series of triplets—to drum home its point. Paul cannot afford to have this paragraph ignored. He appeals to the Thessalonians' memory of him; they would know if he had flattered them. He appeals to God as his witness; only God will know if Paul was trying to take advantage of his converts. Then a few verses later he rounds off the theme with ever greater insistence: *You remember . . . you are my witness and so is God . . . as you know . . .* (2:9–11). Paul is on the defensive. And he can vindicate himself against suspicion only by appeal to the very objects of that suspicion—his motivation and behavior when he was with them.

He reminds the Thessalonians how badly treated he had been in Philippi, and how he faced trouble just as severe in Thessalonica itself:

We had the confidence to speak out in our God, to tell you the good news of God amid great opposition. For our encouragement does not emerge from error or from impurity or in trickery. But just as we have been reckoned by God a person to be entrusted with the good news, so we speak: not pleasing humans but God, who makes the reckoning of our hearts.

For we were never to be found using a word of flattery, as you know; nor using any excuse for taking advantage of another, God is our witness; nor seeking glory from humankind, either from yourselves or from others, although we could have made demands as emissaries of Anointed.

But we were gentle [or like infants] in the midst of you, just as a nurse might cherish her own children, that is how we longed for you. And so we decide to share with you not only the good news of God but also our own lives, because you became dear to us.

1 THESSALONIANS 2:3–8

There had been nothing *impure,* he insists, in his behavior; he had not *taken advantage* of anyone; he had, he reminds them, been *faultless* toward them (2:10). As the letter unfolds the assembly is encouraged to imitate Paul in detail. And so Paul's themes reemerge. The converts' hearts too are to be *faultless;* they must not *take advantage* of one another; they were *not called to live in impurity but in holiness* (3:13; 4:6–7).

More than mere detail is at issue. Paul looks forward to Jesus' return and imagines his converts and himself standing together before their judge. Paul and his converts stand in the closest possible relation. Here in this earliest surviving letter Paul is already reaching toward the insights that will govern his later masterpiece, 2 Corinthians. In Paul is their father, brother, nursing mother. And as he draws to the end of the section he sums up in a fanfare of vivid, emotional language:

> *We ourselves, brothers, have been bereft of you, orphaned, although only for the time being, in person and not in affection. We have had an especially strong desire to see you, person to person, a great longing. So we have wanted to come to you, that is Paul myself, and not just once but twice, and Satan thwarted us. For what is our hope or joy or crown to boast in—what if it is not you, you yourselves—before our Lord Jesus at his coming? For you are our glory and our joy.*
> 1 THESSALONIANS 2:17-20

FAITH, LOVE, AND HOPE

We have heard of faith, love, and hope in the introduction; Paul is now ready to address them in turn (3:1–5:11). He starts with faith, where he can find most to praise. He moves on to love, where he has deeper concern. And last of all he confronts hope and its imminent collapse. Best, he knows, to steer his way through the lesser problems first and only then, propelled by their resolution, to move on to the greater ones.

The assembly in Thessalonica has met with opposition and simply with the isolation and unease, no doubt, that converts had to expect when they publicly abandoned the rites that united their city, their crafts, their trades, and their neighbors. Paul has been concerned that his converts' faith might falter. He has sent his assistant Timothy to encourage them. Timothy has reported back that the Thessalonians' faith, we hear, is holding steady. It is a report of which they will be pleased to hear.

But Paul believes there is more to be done. He builds on the theme, and with reference always to himself. It is the ties between his converts and himself that are to hearten them, the care he has for them, the joy they give to him. It is a heartwarming passage. But why is it needed? Its last line lets a shaft of light onto the needs Paul knows he must meet. For all his confidence and praise, he wants to see them face-to-face *to put in order what is missing in your faith* (3:10).

So much for faith. Paul is ready to round off this short section, and with a second fanfare. Here are just the same motifs that we heard in the first, but now he has the addressees' own triumph in mind. The first time around Paul looked forward to his own role at the judgment, pleading his converts as his pride and joy. Now we are to envisage these converts themselves, delivered thanks to Paul's preaching from the looming wrath of God. He is weaving a beautifully balanced web of mutual love and reliance. At the moment at which it really matters, he is dependent on them and they on him. They must be brought to see that the emissary and his converts are inseparable.

Here is this ringing conclusion. Throughout the letter Paul keeps in view the coming of Jesus. Its delay lies at the heart of the Thessalonians' fear. Eventually he must formally address this delay, but by the time he does so, he has over and over assumed Jesus' return as the basis of his converts' life. He helps them take for granted what they wanted him to prove. Here are lines as stirring as any Paul ever wrote; no wonder some scribes added "Amen":

> *May God our father himself and our Lord Jesus guide our path straight to you. And for you, may the Lord increase and enrich you in love for each other and for all just as we have love for you, so that he may set your hearts firmly to be faultless in holiness before our God and father at the coming of our Lord Jesus with all his holy ones.*
>
> 1 THESSALONIANS 3:11–13

FROM FAITH, THEN, TO LOVE. There has been some sexual immorality in the assembly. As Paul sees it, some have succumbed to the *passion of desire* in a way that *offends against* and *takes advantage* of others (4:5–6). If some members of the assembly had committed themselves and their families to sexual abstinence, others could have seen and taken there the opportunity for flirtation or adultery. Paul warns that such wrongdoing does not belittle just the other people involved, but God.

This leads Paul to a broader theme: *brotherly love.* In a technique that we shall see him use over and over, he praises his addressees before entering a warning. First the praise: *About brotherly love you have no need for me to write you, for you are yourselves taught by God to love one another, and you do so, in your love for all the brothers in the whole of Macedonia* (4:9–10). The Thessalonians have been able to support Jesus' followers throughout the area. Paul praises the steady work and uncontentious life that have made this possible. Then a warning; and Paul shows, by returning to the theme at the letter's end, why it was needed. Some members of the assembly have abandoned the disciplines of daily life. They have stopped working. Paul presents the problem as a breakdown of brotherly love, a problem for brotherly love to resolve. But without success; a second letter, our 2 Thessalonians, suggests that his mellow words went unregarded. Paul cannot be sure of judging his intervention aright; and often enough he doesn't. Here in 1 Thessalonians he has played down this problem of indiscipline, but it will reemerge later, more damaging than ever.

AND SO FROM LOVE, FINALLY, TO HOPE. Here is the Thessalonians' most dangerous weakness. Paul has wisely left it until last. Some members of the assembly have died. The Thessalonians had not expected this. Surely Jesus was due, any day now, to return to earth to rescue and reward his own? Paul responds in two stages. First he must reassure the Thessalonians that their loved ones are not lost. He offers *a word of the Lord.* He may well have heard this as an inspired prophetic saying, given him by the risen Jesus and imparted (as he would have had no doubt) by the Breath of God. *For we tell you this in a word of the Lord, that we who are alive, who are being left here until the coming of the Lord—we shall not have any priority over those who have gone to sleep. For the Lord himself at the word of command, at the voice of the archangel and at the trumpet of God will come down from heaven and the dead in Anointed shall rise* (4:15–16). So much for the particular worry. But the larger question still looms: When is Jesus going to return? Hope can so easily falter. Paul must keep up the sense of expectation and urgency. But he must raise no hopes that might again be dashed or foster the dangerous enthusiasm of those who are stopping work. It is, after all, almost certainly Paul's own teaching, given on his visit, that has triggered their febrile hope—and so its disappointment.

Paul turns to a formula he had used, it seems, when he was in Thessalonica: *The day of the Lord, like a thief in the night—that is how it is coming* (5:2). This time he needs no word of inspiration. He can draw on a teaching ascribed to Jesus on earth. It may be in the middle of the night, says Luke's Jesus, that the master comes back from the feast, and blessed are his servants if he finds them awake. *"And you may be sure of this,"* Jesus continues, *"if the householder had known what time the thief was coming, he would not have let the wall of his house be broken through"* (Luke 12:38–39).

Suddenly, unexpectedly, says Paul, the Day will be upon us. But he gives some sense of a likely time scale. He continues: *When they say "Peace and safety," then sudden destruction comes upon them, as the pain of childbirth comes upon a pregnant woman* (5:3). A woman cannot know in advance exactly when she will come to term, but she knows when the nine months will have passed. Time, Paul insists, is short, but exactly how short? Paul keeps a nice balance between imminence and uncertainty. And he juggles on, keeping image after image in the air. Next comes an elaborate set of contrasts, their literal and moral senses brought neatly together: day and night, light and darkness, wakefulness and sleep. The Thessalonians are children of light. They are to stay wide awake. Then the Day of the Lord will not catch them unawares.

Paul rounds off this third section with the stirring return to his opening triplet: faith, love, and hope. Its introduction here is not as tidy as we might expect. Paul has to work hard to introduce it. As he made clear the letter's shape at its start, so he reminds his listeners of its themes at the end.

> *Those who sleep sleep of a night, those who get drunk get drunk of a night. But us, we are people of the day. So let us be sober, putting on a breastplate of faith and of love and as a helmet the hope of deliverance.*
>
> 1 THESSALONIANS 5:7–8

"To Await God's Son from the Heavens"

The coming of our Lord Jesus with all his holy ones (3:13)—this theme dominates 1 Thessalonians. Did Paul steady the situation in Thessalonica by his balance between encouragement and warning? Almost certainly not. The first letter to the Thessalonians could be read in different ways by different people. *The day of the Lord,* Paul said, *like a thief in the night—that is how it is coming.* So, ask some Thessalonians, has the day started already? Still hidden like the thief, but clear to those in the know? And again: *God has not appointed us for wrath,* says Paul, *but for the obtaining of deliverance through our Lord Jesus Anointed* (5:9). Are the Thessalonians then safe in their election and freed from any need for discipline? They might be "wakeful" in work and restraint or "asleep" in laxity. No matter, according to their (mis)understanding of what Paul had said. Either way, they are safe. *So that whether we wake or sleep, we may live with him* (5:10).

We have a second letter written to the Thessalonians in Paul's name. The second letter repeats, in a more or less revised form, much of the argument presented in our first letter to the same assembly. It would not be surprising if Paul sent such a second letter when he heard that his first had not had the required effect. Perhaps he just moved quickly to defuse a situation that is clearly getting worse. More Thessalonians, it seems, had abandoned the normal restraints of daily life. Why bother to work, why worry about the future, why respect the tired morality of the normal world, if God's agent is appearing and has chosen us as his own?

> *We ask you, brothers, concerning the coming of our Lord Jesus Anointed and our being gathered to him: Do not be easily shaken from your understanding nor be disturbed, neither through an inspiration of the Breath, nor through a report nor through a letter purporting to be from us that seems to say that the day of the Lord is here.*
>
> 2 THESSALONIANS 2:1–2

It sounds as if the Thessalonians had received just such a letter. We could even imagine that Paul's own 1 Thessalonians was the letter in question. Our author certainly sounds defensive. He is likely discrediting a belief that he knows is widespread—and might be well founded.

Here is a striking scenario. Nowadays we think of the Day of the Lord, if at all, as due to dawn with awe-inspiring, unmistakable signs. No one would need an insight from heaven or a letter from Paul to know that the Day had come. Peter, after all, had reminded the crowd in Jerusalem of the prophecy of Joel:

> *I will give wonders in the heaven above*
>   *and signs on the earth below,*
> *blood and fire and a mist of smoke.*

> *The sun shall be turned to darkness*
> *and the moon to blood*
> *before the coming of the Day of the Lord,*
> *the great and open day.*
>
> THE MISSION 2:19-20, QUOTING JOEL 2:30-31

We do well, however, to stand back from portrayals of such cosmic horror and to think locally instead. The Thessalonian assembly comprised a small number of Macedonians in a city three hundred miles from Athens or Corinth and a thousand miles from Jerusalem. Most of its members are likely to have been indigenous and far removed from the city's cosmopolitan elite. They got news, yes, along the great Egnatian Road linking Asia Minor with the western coast of Greece and so, across the Adriatic Sea, with Rome. The assembly at Philippi was only a few days' walk away. They heard news too from seafarers; the harbor linked Thessalonica with the great cities—and the assemblies of Jesus' followers—of southern Greece and the seaboard of Asia Minor. But these converts knew they were not at the center of the world. For a few months in the 40s B.C.E. Thessalonica had been home to the most powerful men in the Roman Republic, but they had come and gone. Battles could be fought between the greatest armies in the world, Rome's Republic could fall, one emperor and another could die, but the news of such changes took time to reach the working classes of Thessalonica, their effects far longer still.

Paul had written:

> *The Lord himself at the word of command, at the voice of the archangel*
> *and at the trumpet of God will come down from heaven and the dead in*
> *Anointed shall rise first, and then we who are living, who are being left,*
> *shall be seized up together with them in the clouds to meet the Lord in*
> *the air. And so we shall always be with the Lord.*
>
> 1 THESSALONIANS 4:15-16

But where will the Anointed come? Surely to Jerusalem, scene of God's great assize. As we nowadays dwell on the Day of the Lord, we give weight to images of universal change; we should give weight to the

Day's vivid details too. To converts waiting for deliverance, such details *mattered*. If Jesus was to return to Jerusalem, the news would have to spread—by land and by sea, by letter and by word of mouth—or by divine inspiration given to some privileged figure within the assembly. Modern readers may find this just too pedestrian, too dully literal. On the contrary, here was an expectation, coherently thought through, that could fuel a hope to live by and to suffer for. The news would spread soon enough, and God's wrath would rise like a wave across the world and sweep away God's enemies.

THE QUESTION OF THE THESSALONIANS echoes through the New Order. At times we hear embarrassment because a fervent expectation is giving way to doubt within the assemblies and cynical mockery from without. Remember, we are told, *that in the last days there will come sarcastic scoffers, saying, "Where is the promise of his coming? From the time the fathers died* [the first generation of Jesus' followers] *everything is carrying on as it has since the start of creation"* (2 Pet. 3:3–4).

At other times we hear a call to courage. The seer of Unveiling [Revelation] sees martyrs' souls under the great altar of heaven:

> *"How long will it be," asked the souls of those killed on account of God's word and of the testimony to it which they had borne, "how long, O master holy and true, before you pass judgment and avenge our blood on the inhabitants of the earth?"*
>
> UNVEILING 6:9-10

The answer is given to those souls in heaven, but will be heard in the book of Unveiling by the assemblies on earth. Here is no easy encouragement. There is more suffering to come; and the book's readers can expect to undergo it.

> *Just a short while now, until the numbers are completed of their fellow servants and of their brothers who were to be killed just as they too had been killed.*
>
> UNVEILING 6:11

A Second Letter

Imagine Paul dictating a letter to an assembly and an assistant of Paul's going off to deliver it. The letter is read aloud in the assembly—and then? In every case we are bound to wonder what happened next. Did the letter work? Did it lay anxieties to rest and reassert Paul's position? Or did it lead to further misunderstanding and dispute? Our 2 Thessalonians gives the basis for an answer, but exactly what that answer is is not as clear as it may seem so far. Scholars have long wondered if 2 Thessalonians is really by Paul at all. It seems out of character; some of the language and style—and thought—does not match what we know of Paul's. It is all the more striking, then, that 2 Thessalonians ends with an emphatic reassurance: *This greeting is in my own hand, Paul's hand, which is the sign in every letter. This is how I write. The grace of our Lord Jesus Anointed be with you all* (3:17–18). The writer is determined to prevent any doubt: here is Paul's handwriting, the letter is from him.

Perhaps Paul heard of the deepening problem in Thessalonica and commissioned an assistant to dictate a corrective. Second Thessalonians, then, could have been dictated by someone in Paul's circle without a full grasp of Paul's thought and style. Paul himself might just have reminded this assistant of the familiar position that he must reiterate. The writer will not concede that anything Paul had said or written could be thought to *say that the day of the Lord is here.* Any such claim must be ascribing to Paul some spurious letter or teaching; it is, therefore, disowned. (The dismissal is oddly roundabout; the author is clearly unsettled.) Then Paul himself might have given this new letter his own seal of approval with the closing signature.

Or perhaps Paul was writing to two different assemblies in Thessalonica, which he knew to be facing slightly different problems, in slightly different terms. Second Thessalonians, for instance, might have been better suited than its partner to an assembly in which most members were Jewish. Paul might have dictated 1 Thessalonians himself and left its adaptation to an assistant. No wonder, then, 2 Thessalonians has a different feel to it.

Or perhaps our 2 Thessalonians really was, to put it bluntly, a fake, written and issued without Paul's authority at all. Its writer knew

1 Thessalonians well. He likely had a copy of it in front of him, and he set out to correct the errors that he sees there. (They may have been "errors" only because they misled a few febrile members of the assembly. Perhaps that was enough to prompt the new letter.) The writer wanted to displace 1 Thessalonians with a new version. Here is a strange scenario: a letter (2 Thessalonians) claiming—spuriously—to be by Paul warns its readers that another letter (1 Thessalonians) is spurious that in fact really was by Paul.

This prompts some intriguing questions. If such a fake was more or less contemporary with 1 Thessalonians, and not a far later confection, who had the power, within this or any other assembly, to suppress Paul's letter and to "issue" its replacement? Only an assembly's leaders, appointed, we may expect, by Paul himself. Such a group may have had the best of intentions. Paul's own letter was causing turmoil they are sure he never intended; he has been misunderstood, and they were taking it upon themselves to correct the misunderstanding. Was it the Thessalonians' own leaders who saw this policy through? There is already a strange hint of their independence at the end of 1 Thessalonians. *I call you to swear by the Lord,* writes Paul, *that this letter be read to all the brothers* (1 Thess. 5:27). Did he already wonder if the leaders themselves might be infected with error and be reluctant to have it publicly corrected?

What muddy waters these are. It may never be possible to see clearly what happened. All the care Paul put into 1 Thessalonians, focusing his converts over and over on the Lord's return, has poured fuel on an error whose flames it was written to douse. We have watched 1 Thessalonians unfold, its structure clearly marked by Paul. Everything looks toward the Lord's return, and right at the end Paul concludes with a final roll on the same drum. He will hear its echo back from his converts, all too loud and clear.

> *May the God of peace himself make you holy all through, and may you be kept unblemished all through, your breath and soul and body, without fault at the coming of our Lord Jesus Anointed. Faithful is the one who is calling you, who will also effect it.*
>
> 1 THESSALONIANS 5:23–24

"Our Lord, Come!"

Let us leave the Thessalonians with their fragile hope and their letter from Paul, a sorry substitute for the return of their father and friend. The letter was no doubt read first to the assembly's leaders; in it they hear Paul insist that the letter be read to the whole assembly. That public reading would have been at a service, probably a Service of Thanksgiving on the Lord's Day.

We know more about such services than we have yet heard. A manual of instruction has reached us from the end of the first century C.E. for an assembly's life and worship, called *The Teaching of the Lord to the Gentiles Through the Twelve Emissaries.* It contains instructions for the "Eucharist" or "Thanksgiving," apparently the name as well as the principal activity of a service that included the Lord's Supper. We certainly cannot be sure that this teaching was current in Paul's day, fifty years before, or that a text likely to have been compiled in Syria reflected any missionary practice in Macedonia, or that the service outlined in it had the significance of any modern Eucharist. And we must add yet another warning. As laid down in *The Teaching,* the order of events in the service seems odd. Its components may be muddled. Or the manual may represent a tradition that was still evolving as the years went by; it may preserve first a later and next an earlier version of the formulas used at a Service of Thanksgiving. Or these formulas may have featured in two distinct services. Or it may even be that neither is discussing the services on the Lord's Day itself—a very brief instruction about the Lord's Day is given later in the manual.

But let's capture, as best we can, the tone and structure of the service that is likely outlined in the main body of *The Teaching.* Here, then, is the instruction for the thanksgivings themselves. The first are said, it seems, before a meal, probably the Lord's Supper. Thanks are given first over the cup:

> We give you thanks, our father, for the holy vine of your son
>   David,
> which you have made known to us through your son Jesus.
>   To you be glory for all ages.

The order is striking. We might have expected the thanksgiving over the bread to come first. But Paul himself at one point (1 Cor. 10:16) draws on a tradition that focused first on the wine. And the manuscripts of Luke's gospel are divided over the details of Jesus' last supper with his pupils. The longer version has Jesus give thanks for both wine and bread before the meal, and then again for wine after it (Luke 22:17–20).

Then *The Teaching* gives the thanksgiving to be prayed over the bread. Again knowledge is central, the disclosure that Jesus brought:

> We give you thanks, our father, for the life and knowledge
> which you have made known to us through your son Jesus.
>   To you be glory for all ages.

The instruction then follows: "And after you are full, give thanks as follows." If the whole passage refers to the same occasion, then a full-scale meal has taken place at its center. That need not surprise us. Paul appears in 1 Corinthians to be opposing the divisions that arise when the Lord's Supper is combined with a large-scale meal: the rich gather in the dining room and eat and drink luxuriously, as a group of friends together; their dependents and the other poorer members of the assembly eat their leftovers in the courtyard.

Three thanksgivings are now laid down for use after the meal, fuller and more solemn than the prayers said before it. Here is the first:

> We give you thanks, holy father,
> for your holy name which you have made to dwell in our hearts
> and for the knowledge and faith and immortality
> that you have made known to us through your son Jesus.
>   To you be glory for all ages.

If Paul's letters were read at such a service as this, we do best to envisage their recital during or right after the meal. The compilers of *The Teaching* make no provision for any instruction from beyond the local assembly to be read. They just recognize that prophets should be allowed to give thanks for as long as they want. In almost all of Paul's letters his opening greeting is followed by a thanksgiving; perhaps a letter's recitation took the place of the ordained or prophetic thanks after the meal.

Paul certainly thinks of his letters as part of a liturgy. *Kiss each other,* he says at the end of both letters to the Corinthians, *in a holy kiss.* In 1 Corinthians he then reminds the Corinthians of his own spiritual presence, despite his distance, at this service of the assembly: *Here is the kiss in my own handwriting: "Paul."* He continues with a curse on unbelievers and seals it with that familiar term: *If anyone does not love the Lord, let them be cursed. Maranatha.*

The holy kiss, the curse, and *Maranatha*—when Paul writes to the Corinthians he has in mind the service at which the letter will be read aloud. He is leading with his last words into the liturgy's next section. We know of this section from *The Teaching.* In it the meal, as we have heard, is followed by three rich, fulsome thanksgivings. At their end *The Teaching* lays down a prayer in a strikingly new tone, a staccato of energetic pleas and imprecations:

> May grace come
> and may this world pass away.
> Hosanna to the God of David.

The world as we know it is on the verge of dissolution. As Unveiling describes it, the bride is ready for her groom: *Come, Lord Jesus,* pleads the assembly of the seer. As Paul insists, the living, those who are being left, are ready to be swept away to join the Lord. The hope of the Thessalonians is surely soon to be fulfilled, for they have *turned to God from idols to serve the living and true God and to await his son from the heavens, whom he roused from the dead, Jesus, the one rescuing us from the coming wrath* (1 Thess. 1:9–10).

Paul had marked the division sharply between those who share in the holy kiss and those who do not love the Lord. *The Teaching* knows just such a distinction too:

> If anyone is holy, let them come;
> if anyone is not, let them change their heart and mind. . . .

And so the prayer of *The Teaching* ends:

> *Maranatha.* Amen.

> Our Lord, come.

PART VI

PAUL AND GALATIA

CHAPTER 14

THE LINEAGE OF FAITH

JESUS HIMSELF HAD LAUNCHED the restoration of Israel, and on that basis—and that alone—the new movement of his followers would be a blessing to Gentiles too. Within the Holy Land, of course, this was a natural emphasis. Almost all of those coming across the new movement, whether in Jerusalem or Galilee, would be Jewish. But in gentile territory? The holiness of Israel was not shared by the lands beyond Israel's boundaries. But those boundaries were themselves fluid. We have seen how Damascus was on the borderline, in history and theology alike. It was even arguable that Antioch, far to the north, was within God's plan for his own land. Jesus' followers had good reason to ask how far, in the newly dawning age, God's Holy Land extended.

Here was the chief concern of James, brother of Jesus and leader of the mother assembly in Jerusalem. We hear of him from The Mission [Acts]; from the Jewish historian Josephus, writing in the 70s; and in far greater but less trustworthy detail from Christian historians of the second and later centuries. In the little we can glean one thing is clear: James sought the holiness of Israel in the terms and observances laid down by the Law.

As God's land must be kept holy, so must his people. The Jews were called by God to be his own people, separate from the nations, and in that separation holy to God. Jesus had not dissolved the conditions under which the Jews would live up to their calling. He had stressed and even tightened these conditions. And now there were Gentiles pressing for admission to Jesus' fellowship. There were emissaries encouraging them.

What effect would these Gentiles have on the restoration of the Jews themselves? The holiness of God's people rested on their observance of the Law. Might the welcome to Gentiles, without any insistence that they observe that Law, endanger the very restoration of Israel that alone could lead in the end to God's blessing on those Gentiles? The leaders in Jerusalem felt entitled to be consulted—and even to decide—on the conditions on which Gentiles could be admitted as full members of Jesus' fellowship.

PAUL LEAVES THESSALONICA HURRIEDLY, probably early in 50. He heads southwest for Beroea to evade his opponents, the Jews of Thessalonica, according to Luke, but more probably the civil authorities. He is still not beyond their reach. He must make a quick escape. He takes a ship south to Athens; Silas and Timothy are to follow as soon as possible. Paul is in the province of Greece now, and out of Macedonia.

He reaches Corinth in the spring of 50. Silas and Timothy catch up with him there. He is in the city for eighteen months. They are eventful enough: in the summer of 51 he is arraigned before Gallio, the Roman commander (proconsul) of Greece. We will hear much of Paul and Corinth in the chapters to come. For the moment we need only follow him as he leaves, late in the summer of 51. He sails east, for Ephesus and onward to the Holy Land, and so, with Titus, to a critical meeting in Jerusalem.

LUKE TAKES HIS STORY FORWARD SLOWLY. Every leader must be seen to have approved the stages of the move toward Gentiles, in particular to have confirmed that gentile converts need not observe the whole Law. Luke's Theophilus knew well, in the 80s, that the assemblies had left behind their Jewish home and its defining Law. Such impiety was at first sight clearly culpable and probably subversive. Luke, therefore, must make it clear that every step of this way was ordained by God and approved by the leaders in Jerusalem.

Right at the center of The Mission (chap. 15) Luke sets a climactic scene. A council is held in Jerusalem. It was summoned, Luke says, to decide whether circumcision was necessary for the salvation of male converts. In attendance are James and Peter, Barnabas and Paul. Peter speaks up for the gentile mission. James, the most conservative leader of all and natural head of the mother assembly, confirms a new ruling in the Gentiles' favor. At the end of the council, Luke tells us, its leaders sent a letter to the assemblies in Antioch and elsewhere. Four conditions are laid down for gentile membership of the assembly. Circumcision is not among them. Three relate to food: the Gentiles must abstain from food sacrificed to idols and from food improperly killed in either of two ways. The fourth forbids improper sexual relations. Everything is at last in place for Luke's Paul. He is free to undertake his independent mission, and its conditions are clear.

We cannot know what sources Luke used for his story of the council. He has written up a single dramatic scene and may for his story's sake have introduced elements from various meetings and from decisions issued at various times. It is at least odd that circumcision disappears from view. Odder still, that Paul nowhere shows any knowledge of this letter from the council or its contents. (There were teachers claiming that gentile converts had to be circumcised. In his fierce responses to them, why does Paul never simply say, "James himself denies the need for circumcision"?)

Scholars have wondered if Luke has codified into one story, the centerpiece of The Mission, the resolution of arguments that lasted, rumbling or raging, for years. With this possibility comes another. Luke has made an extended dramatic scene of this council, midway through his story. He tells of the mission of Paul, Silas, and Timothy as its aftermath (16:1–18:21). A good many scholars have argued that this mission took place before the principal meeting or council—such as it was—in Jerusalem. I have followed this view here.

Let's take it for now that some such agreement, as outlined in that letter Luke writes of, was gaining acceptance in the early years of Paul's mission. These four conditions that Luke lists are important for one feature they have in common. They are closely related to the four commands that are laid down in the Old Order's Laws of Ritual [Leviticus] as binding on both Jews and on the Gentiles who live among them (17:8–13; 18:6–30). The council's letter views the assemblies as an extension of the people of Israel. The Gentiles are the alien residents in a Jewish realm.

It is telling that three similar commands gained currency within Judaism as the ones no Jews should break even under the fiercest persecution; rather than compromise on these, Jews should give up their lives. The Jewish leaders of Jesus' followers in Jerusalem had to determine the minimum conditions whose observance would confirm a Gentile's identity as a member of their fledgling community. And where did the leaders look for guidance? To the minimum conditions that anyone must observe to be identified as a Jew within the Jewish community. Here was a Jewish community, the followers of Jesus, adapting to admit Gentiles into the bare minimum of Jewishness.

James emerges from this story as a figure of great stature. He had found a compromise. The assemblies, wherever they were, would have a Jewish "feel." Their gentile members would be showing a clear respect for the prayer houses in which they met. But these members could avoid circumcision, the condition that some radicals in the Holy Land had hoped to impose. They would still be Gentiles, taking their place as Gentiles in God's plan.

It was a promising compromise. It did not last. What went wrong?

LIVING ON THE BORDERS

Luke lists in James's letter, which follows the council, three conditions to clarify what members of the assemblies could or could not eat. The Jewish Law itself lays down clear rules on food that must not be eaten. Certain meats and fish have to be avoided, as well as the meat of all animals that have not been killed in well-specified ways. Some—not all—of these conditions would have been met by those who observed the conditions of James's letter.

Food supplied from gentile markets brought dangers with it. Pagans did not observe the Jewish laws on butchering. Meat might well come from animals slaughtered in pagan sacrifices, wine from supplies that had been used in pagan libations. Their consumption carried the taint of idolatry. To be safe, then, James's Gentiles would have gone to the Jewish markets and been confident of obeying James's conditions.

There is the food itself; this is the concern of James's letter in Luke's narrative. And then there is the company in which it is eaten; and here

THE LINEAGE OF FAITH   217

the gulf opened between the senior emissaries and their new radical, Paul. An assembly, Paul insisted, could hardly be an assembly if its members could not eat together. And the weekly ritual meal at the Service of Thanksgiving raised the stakes. A meal together gave encouragement and pleasure; it made clear too who were members of the group, within its boundaries, and who were outsiders. But more important still, Jesus' followers gathered at the Thanksgiving to eat, in obedience to Jesus' command, the meal that linked them most closely with their Lord and his promise for their future. An assembly's members, Paul was clear, needed to meet and eat together.

And why shouldn't they? "Separate yourself from the Gentiles," had commanded one Jewish text of the second century B.C.E., "and do not eat with them . . . for their works are impure and all their ways are a pollution and abomination" (*Jubilees* 22:16). Any meat provided by Gentiles from a gentile market might well come from animals slaughtered in sacrifice. But such danger was readily overcome by generosity and trust. Gentile hosts could again go to Jewish suppliers and bear the extra cost, and as long as their Jewish guests trusted them, all would be well. We are talking here of a meal shared by fellow members of a single assembly. If there was ever a setting for trust on such things, this was it.

(We should not assume such trust in general. The Mishnah has lengthy rules for a Jew's consumption of wine that has been left unattended among Gentiles, and not least at shared meals. If the Jew had been absent long enough for the jar of wine to be opened and reclosed and for a new clay seal around the stopper to dry, then the Jew must not drink it. Some of its contents could have been poured out, in the Jew's absence, for a pagan libation [*Abodah Zarah [Idolatry]* 5:5].)

Idolatry defied everything that set the people of God apart from their pagan neighbors. Let's assume for the moment—and it is a large assumption—that Gentiles who converted to the assembly of Jesus' followers would abandon all idolatry. Let's assume these Gentiles were known to respect, in their shopping, the scruples of any Jewish guests. There remained the question still, less dramatic but affecting every area of life, of the day-to-day rituals that maintained the Jewish people's purity. Normal human events like sexual intercourse, menstruation, and childbirth all called for simple rituals of washing and for time to pass before any return to the Temple. Contact (even indirect contact) with a corpse called for more, for a washing with ashes from a heifer killed in the Temple itself.

These and other laws of ritual purity were designed for life in Jerusalem itself. What should those millions of Jews do who lived hundreds of miles from the Temple? They had no access to the Temple to get those ashes or to pay a visit. Old rituals were adapted, new rules devised. Outside Jerusalem—and outside the Holy Land—people got by and remained confident that they were still faithful to the terms laid down by God for continued favor.

Sexual intercourse, menstruation, and childbirth are regular and natural functions. Was there anything to threaten purity for which the Law itself had not made provision? There were Gentiles, of course. They would not, for example, have observed any rules on washing. Now any Jew who systematically failed to follow such rules would have made any other Jew impure with whom he or she came in contact. But the Gentiles were not Jews. They were not subject to the Law. A Jewish scholar has recently observed that only in subsequent centuries did rabbis—in rulings that they themselves stated to be new—declare that Gentiles in themselves were ritually impure. We may have expected any Gentile to carry contamination, for example, from contact with corpses, which he or she would never have washed away. But perhaps not. In the first century C.E. a Jew had every reason to shun the moral pollution carried by idolaters. But a ritual pollution? No. A Gentile would not transmit such ritual contamination to a Jew.

(This makes one scenario easier to envisage. A good many Jews, we know, maintained some ritual of washing before attending the prayer house. They would then themselves be pure. And when the God-fearers came to join them? All was well. These Gentiles, even if they had not washed as the prayer house leaders recommended to the Jews themselves, did not contaminate the gathering.)

So far, so good—until the leaders of the assembly in Antioch regarded those Gentiles as full members of the Christian community. A serious question now arises. These converts are now members of the people of God. Are they still just Gentiles? Or have they now, in some way, taken on the Jewishness of Jesus himself, his first followers, and God's ancestral people? They have crossed a line, but which line? If they are now part of the people of God, then they are surely subject to the

THE LINEAGE OF FAITH

rules of purity laid upon that people. They can be impure and spread impurity. And so they will, unless they observe the rituals of their Jewish peers.

We have seen how carefully James's letter places the gentile converts on the borders of Jewishness, but borders are hard places to occupy. The rules are uncertain; they will likely be disputed from both sides. The Gentiles' standing and obligations were bound to be vexed. And James himself raised the stakes. He called Jews in Jerusalem to a greater purity, a higher level of holiness—both in their morals and in daily readiness to enter the Temple that he himself prized so highly.

The story of James recorded by the second-century Christian Hegesippus is clearly confused in details, but it gives unexpected clues to James's life and belief. James lived the life of a "Nazirite," under conditions laid down in the Old Order for special ritual purity. We are told, implausibly, that "he alone was allowed to enter the sanctuary"; he was to be found kneeling in the Temple praying for forgiveness for the people. He spoke of the "gate of Jesus," clearly a phrase as unclear in Hegesippus's day as in ours. The authorities appealed to him to reassure the people that Jesus was *not* the Anointed. They expected him, it seems, to confirm that the Anointed was yet to come. Here Hegesippus turns to the gospels and draws on material about Jesus; perhaps he did not know how James responded or was embarrassed by what he had inherited. James, he says, disappointed the authorities. He declared the son of man to be on the right hand of the power. The crowd responded, "Hosanna to the son of David!" This is a James whose priority was the holy people, the Holy Land, and its holiest of all places, the Temple (Hegesippus, quoted by Eusebius, *History of the Church* 2.23.4–18).

JAMES AND THE DREAM OF ISRAEL'S PURITY

What might such a James have sought in practice, in his own life? Here is a later example of the grades of purity sought by or required for different people in different roles. It is taken from the Mishnah. Throughout the Mishnah the particular distinctions between the priests involved in different rites and between the objects in their care are coherently maintained:

A Pharisee: if he is in contact with the clothes of an ordinary Jewish layperson who has suffered a discharge [of semen or menstrual blood], the Pharisee becomes impure. A priest: if he is in contact with such clothes of a Pharisee, the priest becomes impure. A priest who is given the holier offerings to eat that are brought to the Temple: if he is in contact with such clothes of an ordinary priest, he becomes impure. A priest who is dealing with the water that is itself used to purify the impure: if he is in contact with such clothes of a priest eating the holier offerings, he becomes impure . . .

The Mishnah rounds off this paragraph with reference to food. Jews who cared for their own purity would avoid eating with Jews who they could expect to be less pure, for their own purity would be affected. Pharisees set out to maintain a level of purity in their daily lives higher than that stipulated for laity. They would not expect, in general, to eat with other laity who made no such efforts. But this did nothing to overcome the norms themselves as listed above. And so we hear of the Pharisaic Johanan:

One Johanan always ate his common food in accordance with the rules for eating the holier gifts; but if a priest dealing with the water of purification came into contact with such clothes of Johanan, that priest became impure.

HAGIGAH [THE FESTAL OFFERING] 2:7

NOW LET'S ASK THE QUESTIONS that James must have asked, faced as he was with gentile converts on this strange border between the Jewish and the gentile worlds. James's first priority was to raise the level of purity in which the Jewish followers of Jesus lived their lives. This was one step in the restoration of Israel. This restoration would open the doors of God's blessing to Gentiles. So where on the scale of purity did gentile converts stand? Where could they be brought to stand, if the right rules were found for their observance? And who else could they eat with, among the assembly's members, without rendering those others impure?

James's answer was stark. Jews and Gentiles formed a single assembly, but they should not eat together. The Gentiles would corrupt the very purity that gave the assembly its value.

James's position did not prevail. It may seem oddly crabbed and narrow now, but he knew the Old Order well. He knew of the great prophecies that had to be fulfilled, of the day when the purity of the Temple would be spread throughout the land. Says the prophet Zechariah:

> On that day, there shall be inscribed on the bells of the horses, "Holy to the Lord." Then the pots throughout the house of the Lord shall be as holy as the bowls before the altar itself. And every pot in Jerusalem and Judah shall be sacred to the Lord.
>
> ZECHARIAH 14:20-21

Jesus' followers in Jerusalem had good reason to dwell on this prophecy, for they remembered the story of Jesus himself clearing the dove sellers and money-changers from the Temple's Courtyard of the Gentiles. Here, come to life, was the prophecy of the prophet's final words. The days of this purity, James was sure, had come; and nothing and no one could be allowed to contaminate the Holy City, the Holy Land, or the holy people of God:

> There shall no longer be a trader in the house of the Lord on that day.
>
> ZECHARIAH 14:21

ONCE MORE, ANTIOCH

Luke tells of consensus in Jerusalem, a consequent letter, and ongoing expansion under its terms, but all was not as calm as Luke would have us believe. Antioch, we know from Paul, was the scene of a bitter dispute. On the one side was Paul; on the other were Peter, Barnabas, and the representatives of James.

For the winter of 51–52, Paul returns with Barnabas to Antioch. They are pleased with the council's result. They apply its rulings as they have understood them. The Jews and Gentiles of the assembly

eat together. Peter arrives and eats with the Gentiles too. Enter, however, the representatives of James, who are appalled. They insist on a
division between Jews and Gentiles. Peter and Barnabas give way.
Paul, determined that all members of the assembly should eat together, is on his own.

The dispute at Antioch started as the crackle of some loose kindling
catching fire. Far more was soon in flames. Peter and Barnabas saw the
force of James's argument, but Paul saw a threat in it to all the Gentiles
in the assemblies founded from Antioch. A decision to separate the two
parts of the assembly undermined the central insight of the faith:

> There exists no Jew nor Greek,
> There exists no slave nor free,
> There exists no male and female.
> For you are all one person in Anointed Jesus.
> GALATIANS 3:28

Paul is sure the last times have dawned. The great restoration of
Adam and of all creation is under way, taking humanity back behind all
divisions and forward beyond them. Once Jews and Gentiles are divided
at table, the questions will quickly arise: Which group has precedence?
Which is more blessed before God? Eyes will turn back to Isaiah's great
prophecies. Every scope for division will be found. Born Jews and converts to Judaism, after all, will be at home in Jerusalem; God-fearers and
other Gentiles will be the foreigners bringing their wealth in tribute
and themselves in obeisance. If the mother assemblies in Antioch and
Jerusalem divide Jews and Gentiles, it will not be long before their
daughter assemblies are made to follow. What is important for Jews
within the Holy Land will undermine all Paul's efforts among Gentiles
beyond its borders.

We have looked so far at the religious rulings on such purity. There
was likely, as well, political pressure on James from the Temple hierarchy in Jerusalem. In 40 C.E. the emperor Caligula had threatened to
desecrate the Temple. The greater the threat from the Roman authorities, the greater the need among the Jews for clear boundaries and disciplined cohesion within them. Nothing could be permitted that could
be seen, by Romans or by Jews, as deviant, subversive, or in any way

threatening to good order or the Temple. The assembly in Jerusalem was Jewish and had no mission to endanger the Jews of the city at large.

Jews in Antioch itself were exposed to fears too. An anti-Jewish riot is reported there by a late historian in 39–40 C.E. In 41 the emperor Claudius issued an edict confirming the religious and civic rights of the Jews. It is part of a pattern. Just such an edict for Alexandria in Egypt was issued in the same year. The Jews had long enjoyed special rights in Alexandria, rights that were deeply resented by the other Egyptians. Fatal riots had broken out there against the Jews in 38, and in response the Romans reaffirmed their privileges.

Such resentment simmered on in Antioch. In 67 an apostate Jew named Antiochus accused his own father and the other Jews of plotting to set fire to the city. The story may have been confused in the telling. After the great fire of Rome in 64, the Christians had been accused of arson. Antiochus's target, three years later, was likely the Christian Jews in Antioch, a deviant sect of a distrusted minority.

The assemblies were small and vulnerable. As long as they were regarded as Jewish prayer houses, by their neighbors and by the Roman authorities, they were in danger of attack as Jewish, but at least they gained the Romans' protection. But how would an assembly be regarded that stood apart from its city's prayer houses and insisted it was in fundamental ways simply different? No one had yet needed—or perhaps even been able—to contemplate such a breach. Until Paul's position threatened to impose it.

The leaders in Antioch would have been appalled. We have our eyes, at the moment, on the politics of Jewish life in Antioch. Let's glance, then, at just the political implications of the change that Paul could bring about. What could be the benefits—and what the dangers? First, for the assembly's Jewish members, every day, in every street, they would still be known—and in dangerous times, endangered—as Jewish. Its Gentiles, meanwhile, would lose even the respect a God-fearer might look for from his or her neighbors. And all of them might still expect the official protection on which the prayer houses could hope to rely. They might even all seek the privileges granted to Jews, but without the obligations that went with them (exemption from military service, for instance, and from the imperial cult; but without being required to pay the Temple tax due from all Jews). None of their non-Christian neighbors, however—least of all the leaders of the prayer houses and of civic administration—would have any reason to let these converts have their cake and eat it.

Go it alone? This was a sure-fire way to inflame other Gentiles, alienate other Jews, and arouse the suspicion of the authorities. It was a recipe for resentment and danger. The assembly's leaders in Antioch had good reason to follow the guidance from Jerusalem—for the sake of the assembly itself and of the Jewish nation as a whole. In unity lay the safety of all.

AT ANTIOCH PAUL FOUGHT. And lost. He thought he was defending the good news for which Antioch stood, but if any of Antioch's leaders sided with him, we do not hear of them. In the spring of 52 Paul went west to Ephesus. It was a good choice, a major city within reach of the east by land (and so of Asia and Galatia) and of the west by sea (and so of Greece and Macedonia). But he left a lot behind. He would never visit Antioch again.

GATHERING THE GENTILES

> You mindless Galatians! Who has bewitched you! Jesus Anointed was paraded before your eyes, crucified. I want to know just this from you: Did you receive the Breath from doing the works of the law or from believing what you heard? Are you so mindless, that you started in the breath and now finish off in the flesh?
>
> GALATIANS 3:1–3

Bad news from Galatia. The dispute at Antioch left Paul out on a limb. The mother assemblies in Jerusalem and Antioch mount a countermission to minimize the damage that Paul's teaching can cause. They hold all the trumps—their established authority and a teaching on which, it seems, they have all agreed.

From the Cilician Gates to Ephesus, between Paul's assemblies is a long thin line of communication, easily ambushed. Paul, now in Ephesus, hears that new teachers have reached his assemblies way back in Galatia. These teachers are telling his converts that their conversion will be complete only if they undertake to observe the Law. Paul's whole mission is under threat.

It is unclear where in Galatia the assemblies to which Paul is writing are. He writes as one to whom the assemblies could—and should—be looking as the sole source of their instruction, for that is exactly the impression he wants them to have. If in fact he is writing to southern Galatia, Paul's addressees would have started his letter with a quite different outlook. This is the area once visited by Barnabas and Paul together, then by Paul and Silas. They had been emissaries of Antioch; on the first visit Barnabas had been the senior partner. The Galatians have clearly heard of the subsequent dispute between Paul and the leaders of longer and higher standing than his own. Barnabas had sided with Paul's opponents. If the southern Galatians have to make a decision for Paul or for Barnabas, it is Barnabas they will turn to. No wonder Paul plays down Barnabas's role as he reminds the Galatians of that visit. The Galatians' eyes must now be on Paul and on Paul alone.

Galatia: Paul and the Teachers

STARTING IN THE BREATH

Glance through the letter to the Galatians and the impression is clear that Paul is resisting opponents who are—and know they are—undermining the very foundations of his good news. He stands for God's grace and rescue by faith; they stand by contrast for the rigid observance of the Law. The battle lines are clear, and the fighting is fierce. That is clearly what Paul wanted the Galatians to think. Thanks to his letter, they may well have done so; so have almost all subsequent readers.

The new teachers had come from Jerusalem itself or from Antioch. They asserted the rights and leadership of the Galatians' mother assembly in Antioch. They came, almost certainly, with the authority of Barnabas himself. Paul, then, has been proved right: more and more of the Law is being demanded from more and more assemblies. At Antioch the argument had been: Could Jewish members of the assembly eat together with its Gentiles? In Galatia it has become: Must the assemblies' gentile males be circumcised?

Paul of course presents the new teachers as forcing his converts to be circumcised (6:12). Here is the explanation for their success. But how much coercion was there? In the very next verse Paul hints that those getting themselves circumcised are actually encouraging others to follow suit. Those taking such a "final" step would certainly be glad to have others join them. But there need be nothing reluctant or resentful here. Paul wants to see coercion, of course, but he is putting his own slant on a spreading enthusiasm among his converts for a further, apparently fuller conversion—and the fuller, surer rewards it will bring.

The new teachers have told the Galatians of the argument in Antioch. Paul must give his own version of the story, which is that Peter and Barnabas had been too weak to stand up for the good news. Paul quotes his own speech. He had been speaking with Peter about "us," the Jews. It had been easy to lay the charge against Peter and Barnabas of playacting or hypocrisy. They would have exposed themselves to an admission of wrongdoing if they reverted to old rules. Such slippage back to old ways effectively denied the power of the new.

All this is clear. But Paul's speech, as he relays it in the letter, moves across to the first-person singular, to speak of "me." He seems to leave Antioch behind and to speak to the Galatians themselves. He deepens the argument. Far more, he insists, is at stake than his opponents at Antioch had seen.

> *I myself through the law have died to the law, so that I might live to God. I have been crucified with Anointed. And now I live no longer, but Anointed lives in me. As for my now living in the flesh, I live in faith, in the faith of the son of God who loved me and handed himself over for me. I do not nullify the grace of God. For if justness is through the law, then Anointed died in vain.*
>
> GALATIANS 2:19–21

All those who are in the Anointed have died. They have been taken by and with the Anointed to the life beyond, to the life of Adam's former glory, under the dominion of God and at peace with him in the new, unfading Paradise. They live out this life of hidden glory here and now, in confidence that the Anointed's glory will soon be revealed—and then theirs will be too. Paul's assemblies are part of the new creation. But

Paul insists that they are threatened. It was not the Law's observance that brought them to this life in the Anointed. Nor will it keep them there.

Had Paul really said all this in Antioch? We cannot know. Just one thing is clear—his arguments were to no avail. He was a minor figure, railing against the leaders who had known Jesus himself and led his followers ever since. Paul records the argument in Antioch, but the Galatians know what he does not tell them: he lost the argument. And with that defeat he lost his links to the Antioch assembly and the authority that they gave him. He is no longer an emissary from a major center of the faith; he is a maverick and on his own. He no longer has the endorsement of any human agency. To claim any authority at all, he must claim it from God himself. And so he does.

FINISHING OFF IN THE FLESH?

Paul had promised so much. In the death and rising of Jesus God had triggered the final act in the current history of the world and its powers. The protection and blessing with which God sustained his own people, the Jews, were now offered to Gentiles too, in particular their protection from guilt and punishment when God unleashed his anger on a disobedient world. The Gentiles too could inherit the kingdom of God.

But Paul engendered in his converts more than fear and relief from fear. He offered an intimacy with God, and the life of his assemblies bore witness here and now to the power, the character, and the action of the God he spoke of. Converts gained the right and the confidence to address this God by the name that Jesus himself had used to speak with him: *Abba,* "Father." This is the Jesus who, Paul will remind the Galatians, *loved me and handed himself over for me.* Paul's converts no longer enjoy the unthinking assurance with which they had belonged within their tribes' or cities' social and civic lives. They now belong first and foremost in the assemblies of Jesus' followers. And there they are united in the love of the Anointed for each of them and in the protection that their father God offers them all.

Enter the new teachers. They are appalled by what they find among Paul's converts. Or more simply, perhaps, they are bemused. Of course, they say, Gentiles have a place now within God's blessing. They have it on just the same basis as the Jews themselves, on the basis of grateful obedience to God's own Law, imparted to the Jews as their greatest privilege.

These new teachers had a clear and coherent message: Abraham, father of the nation, was circumcised into the Order that God made with him, and he became the model for all male converts. The Anointed now summons gentile converts into an "adoptive" membership of the Jewish people, and so into the lineage of Abraham, and so into the blessings that God promised to Abraham and his seed. God promised that Abraham would be the father of many nations (The Beginning [Genesis] 17:5); and now, in these last days, that prophecy is coming to fulfillment. *Come, let us go up to the house of the God of Israel,* say the nations, *and he will announce his way to us and we shall walk in it. For the Law shall go out from Sion and the word of the Lord from Jerusalem* (Isa. 2:3).

God ordered Abraham to circumcise the males of his whole household, and he did so. Males from other nations who had now been chosen by God to join that household, to become the children of father Abraham, must of course be circumcised in their turn. And so they will acknowledge their part in the nation to which God has given both the Law at Sinai and Jesus, his Anointed. Upon descent from Abraham— natural or adoptive—everything depends. Says the prophet Isaiah:

> *Hear me, you who pursue justice and seek the Lord: . . .*
> *Look at Abraham your father and Sarah who gives you birth.*
> ISAIAH 51:1–2

We readily think of these teachers as Paul's opponents. And so indeed he presented them, for they were attacking his good news and his credentials to preach it. But these visitors may have seen themselves quite differently. Let us explore for a moment a surprising possibility that can still be seen beneath Paul's angry attacks.

First, a look at Paul's own teaching. We imagine Paul as the fierce and consistent opponent of any demand that gentile converts should observe the Law. He may not have given that impression himself. Paul asks indignantly: *If I still preach circumcision, why am I still being persecuted?*

(Gal. 5:11). It is a teasing question. He is clearly picking up a description of his teaching that the Galatians know—probably from the newly arrived teachers. Paul, they say, has elsewhere preached in a way that Paul himself can here sum up as "preaching circumcision." And Paul does not respond, "How absurd. Of course I never have." At one stage, then, he had. So has he, over the course of time, changed his tune? He would never admit as much, without reserve. But if the charge had been made he would have to do something to rebut it. And he doesn't.

Most likely, then, the teachers can plausibly claim that Paul is still doing what he always has done, preaching circumcision. We cannot be sure what this summarizes; Paul had no incentive to give a detailed or unbiased airing of the teachers' views. But they know of his visits to Jerusalem. They think, naturally enough, that he was heavily influenced there by Peter and James. They may even have heard that he was seen in public in the assemblies in Judea, conforming to their practices and endorsing their good news. How much room for misunderstanding there was here. Paul might well have seemed, in assemblies within Judea made up largely of Jesus' Jewish followers, to have had just the same priorities and principles as James himself, the brother of Jesus. Paul himself, after all, will later say that he has *become to the Jews as a Jew, so that I might win Jews* (1 Cor. 9:20).

The teachers can point to Paul's own earlier practice within Galatia. We have heard from Luke of Paul's journey with Barnabas, of their preaching in the prayer houses. No prayer house would have invited the visitors to speak, if they had been known to tell Jews and God-fearers that the latter should actually avoid the Law's observance. There may well have been a time, then, when Paul simply did not dwell on the Law. Unless he had to. And on such an occasion, on his journey with Silas, he had Timothy circumcised.

We may even hear an echo, within his letter to Galatia, of Paul's "preaching circumcision." He responded fiercely, he says, to Peter's withdrawal from the shared table fellowship of Jews and Gentiles in Antioch. *"Knowing that no human is held just from works of the law unless through Jesus Anointed's faith, we too have had faith in Anointed Jesus"* (Gal. 2:16). *Unless:* Do such works, then, function for Jews as additional to faith? Or should we abandon the most common meaning of the term and instead translate it *but instead*? In that *unless* we are likely picking up just a hint of the good news that Paul—as these teachers knew—had accepted in Jerusalem: Jews should combine the works of the Law with the Anointed's faith.

And this is the message of the new teachers for Gentiles too. They have not come to oppose Paul, but to complete what he has started. Paul will ask the Galatians, *Are you so mindless, that you started in the spirit and now finish off in the flesh?* (3:3). *Finish off:* the terms may well have been used by the new teachers, insisting that this is just what the Galatians needed to do. And they expected Paul to agree.

As for Paul's teaching, so for his commission to teach it. The teachers were not being combative; they took for granted what they expected Paul to take for granted too. They were sure that any teacher—whether Paul or themselves—should stand loyally in the line of "traditional" teaching and of the scholars who taught it. These new teachers would themselves have acknowledged the authority of the mother assembly in Jerusalem or in Antioch. And Paul's angry argument in the first chapters of Galatians best makes sense if they had gone further and said that Paul himself, a teacher just like them, was like them under the authority of Antioch or Jerusalem.

By describing Paul as they have, the teachers have declared him to be an emissary duly commissioned. By the leaders in Jerusalem in 37 C.E. on his first visit after conversion, by the leaders in Antioch when Barnabas took him there, and by the leaders in Jerusalem again at the recent council. For the new teachers, to be authorized from men or through men is not a charge against Paul; it is the basis upon which he is an emissary at all.

The teachers claim to be completing Paul's good news, and with an authority like his. They are messengers who do not speak on their own authority, but on the authority of those who have commissioned them. And that means the leaders in Antioch or Jerusalem. Paul claims an extraordinary authority for his teaching. The teachers do not dispute it. They have such authority themselves. Theirs is not self-sufficient. Nor is his. They are still subject to the mother assemblies and their good news. So is he.

The picture offered by the new teachers had convinced at least some Galatians. And we can still see its force. Paul had certainly been instructed by someone, somewhere, in Jesus' teaching. He knows far more than he quotes openly of the traditions about Jesus that have reached us in the gospels. He is likely to have learned them from Peter. When he writes to the Galatians, however, he will admit no such influence. He resorts to a calculated ambiguity: speaking of his first visit to Jerusalem after his conversion, he uses a word that might mean *to get information from Peter*—or might mean simply *to meet Peter*. And did he meet with any other emissary? Certainly not, he says. When Paul insists he spoke only with Peter and James, he does so with an oath: *What I am writing you, look, I tell you before God, I am not lying* (Gal. 1:20). Clearly there were rumors that he had consulted more widely.

The new teachers believe they are helping the Galatians to finish off what they have started. Paul believes they are drawing the assemblies into errors that deny any effect to the Anointed at all. These teachers have not seen what Paul has seen. They have no notion of Jesus' standing or role.

And as the assemblies are drawn away from Paul's teaching, so they are drawn away from Paul himself. Paul is isolated. He is badly stung, and he writes a stinging response.

A Letter from Heaven

The faith of ancestors and the ancestry of faith are the twin themes of Paul's letter to the Galatians. Paul is a craftsman at work, unpicking the silk of an old and precious tapestry and reusing its threads to weave a new and previously unimagined picture. To modern eyes, some of this new tapestry is compelling, some of it is quite moving, and some of it strangely far-fetched. All of it is driven by the pressure Paul feels to vindicate his good news and his own independence, and to belittle the alternative to his good news and the authority claimed for it. At stake is the nature of his assemblies. At stake too is his own role in the assemblies' life. He must make it unmistakably clear to the Galatians that he is their mother and they need him. It would be just as true to say he is their mother and he needs them.

In most of his letters Paul follows his opening greeting with gracious thanks to God for his addressees. He dwells in other letters on the faith, love, and hope of the Thessalonians, on the acuity and knowledge of the Corinthians, on the faith of the Romans. In each case he praises what he is about to criticize. But he does not give the Galatians even a hint of such praise. Paul is furious, in good measure because he is frightened, frightened that his assemblies are being led astray from his teaching and from himself. Galatians is a personal, passionate letter. Paul is fighting at close quarters and hits out with every weapon he can find. His sentences tumble out:

> *I am amazed that you are so quickly being diverted from the one who called you in grace, to another good news—not that there is another— except there are some people who are unsettling you and want to pervert the good news of Anointed. But even if we or an angel from heaven were to preach to you good news other than the good news we preached you— let him be accursed. As I have said before, I say again now too: if anyone preaches good news other than the good news you received—let him be accursed.*
>
> GALATIANS 1:6–9

At issue is the good news itself: God's offer to the Gentiles, as the new teachers claim, to adopt those Gentiles into the ancient lineage of Abraham. Paul trumps their claim. The genuine good news, which he has brought, has offered the Galatians adoption as the direct, unmediated children of God. The Anointed himself is the seed of Abraham, the one singular "seed" to whom God had promised his blessings. Those blessings are won by his co-heirs. As he is the son of God, so they too become the children of God.

Paul does not deny that "ancestry" matters, but the important lineage is not the family tree of Judaism, traced back to Abraham, Isaac, and Jacob. It is the link of a single generation from God the father to Jesus Anointed, his son, and to those who are declared God's sons and daughters with him. Indispensable to this link is Paul himself. He develops the theme—and his role in this family—with a Shakespearean grandeur. He will bind the Galatians and himself together in an extraordinary knot of connections, poetically conceived and beautifully expressed.

At issue too is authority, of the new teachers and of Paul himself. The teachers ground their authority in a lineage of Law and its instruction that stretches back for generations. Where, then, shall Paul base his own authority? His position is not strong; he has no allies now among the leaders in Jerusalem or Antioch. He is the leader of an independent mission. If he is to sustain a network of his own assemblies at all, they must owe allegiance to just one leader on earth—to Paul himself. And in the present letter he must show the Galatian assemblies why. His commission is from God, direct and unmediated, just as the adoption of his converts is their direct and unmediated adoption by God. From the very first words of the letter he insists he is Paul, emissary on no mission through human command, but through Jesus Anointed and God the father.

As I have said before, I say again now too: if anyone preaches good news other than the good news you received—let him be accursed. A curse at the letter's start; and at its end, a blessing: *And for all those who will follow this elemental rule, Peace upon them and mercy, and upon the Israel of God!* (6:16). This Paul speaks with all the authority of the act of worship in which the letter will be heard. Its contents are framed between threat and promise. This is no ordinary letter advising, instructing, encouraging. Paul asserts his authority from the start: he can invoke—and effect—the blessing and curse of God.

What the Galatians *do* on receipt of the letter will determine their own future in God's plan. If they collude with the new teachers, they will be subject to God's curse no less than the teachers themselves. The curse is closer to them than they realize: *All those who base themselves on works of the law, they are under a curse* (3:10). The letter comes with the power it speaks of: it brings blessing and curse, here and now, as it is received. And Paul stands back to watch that power. Immediately after the opening curse, he asks, *Am I persuading humans, right now, or God? Or am I seeking to please humans? If I were still pleasing humans, I would not be the slave of Anointed* (1:10). The teachers claim that Paul is, of course, authorized by human leaders more prestigious than he is himself. Paul interprets that as a claim he is out to please humans, not God. And here in his very opening lines he shows—in action—how wrong they are. The teachers, so valued by the Galatians, are the targets of his curse; and the Galatians themselves, unless they move, will be dangerously close to its explosion. Are these the words of a man currying favor? Paul's addressees do not just receive the letter. They are to watch themselves receive it, and so to see what sort of person with what sort of mission is writing it—and where they stand in relation to its curse and blessing.

The Galatians had received Paul on his arrival *as an angel of God, as Anointed Jesus* (4:14). As Paul spoke then, so he writes now—with the authority of heaven. He was not the only author to claim such authority. At the start of the Bible's own book of Unveiling [Revelation] the Seer is *in the breath on the Lord's Day* (1:10). He is ordered by the *one like a son of man* to write a book of what he sees and to send it to seven assemblies. This *son of man* himself dictates a set of seven introductory letters, one to each assembly. They share a carefully wrought structure:

> *To the angel of the assembly in Ephesus* [or Smyrna, or Pergamum, and so on], *write* . . . [then follows the letter]. *Let those who have ears hear what the Breath is saying to the assemblies* [then follows a conclusion].

The scene then moves to heaven, and the rest of the book is the seer's report of what was seen and heard there. The book ends with a stark warning: *I bear witness to all those who hear the words of the prophecy of this book: If anyone adds to it, God will add to him the plagues described in this book; and if anyone removes any of the words of the book of this prophecy, God will remove his portion from the tree of life* (22:18–19). The whole of Unveiling is presented as a letter from heaven; parts of it were dictated there and parts of it report what had been seen there. And this is just the authority that Paul claims for his letter to the Galatians. Here is a letter from heaven written about the secrets of heaven by a seer who has seen them.

Paul: Taught by God Alone

FROM GENERATION TO GENERATION: TRADITION AND THE LAW

I would have you know of the good news that I preach, that it is not a good news defined by human standards: for I did not receive it from any human nor

was I taught it—but through the unveiling of Jesus Anointed (Gal. 1:11–12).
We may think of inspired teaching entrusted to the individual as the
highest form of "religious" instruction. We have accepted Paul's own
presentation of himself, forced from him in a time of dire isolation. Not
so for the new teachers in Galatia. As we have seen, they expect Paul to
base his claims on just such a foundation as they claim for their own:
loyalty to and endorsement from a self-legitimating tradition. Such a
missionary should not be relying on a direct disclosure from God, but
on his training and validation by the guardians of ancestral knowledge
and wisdom. The human instruction undergone by Paul is, for his
opponents, the condition upon which his preaching is legitimated or
authorized at all.

Paul is not defending himself as the new teachers would have
expected. He is changing the paradigm. His opponents are challenging
his institutional standing; he is denying that he has one. They want to
know his place in a familiar and tested structure of legitimation; he
grounds his good news in an unveiling directly from God. And where
Paul leads, his converts follow. As he is in immediate relation to God
and is independent of human authority, so the Galatians shall be in
immediate relation to God too. Paul was made an emissary directly by
God; they in turn shall inherit the promise made to Abraham's offspring—directly from God. They shall then be under no human
authority but Paul's own; no other teacher will have any hold over
them.

It is worth our seeing, for a striking contrast, how the Jews' ancient
heritage of teaching was legitimated in the Mishnah. One tractate
stands out by its form and content from all the rest, *Aboth, Sayings of the
Fathers.* Its first chapter lists a succession of teachers, most presented in
pairs. Each name is accompanied by one or more short sayings:

> Moses received the Law from Sinai and delivered it to Joshua, and
> Joshua delivered it to the elders, and the elders to the prophets,
> and the prophets delivered it to the men of the Great Prayer
> House [the council believed in later tradition to have been
> founded in Jerusalem in the fifth century B.C.E.]. They said three
> things: Be deliberate in judgment; and raise up many pupils; and
> make a fence for the Law.

Simeon the Just was of the remnants of the Great Prayer House. He used to say: On three things the world stands: on the Law; and on the service [of the Temple]; and on the doing of kindnesses.

Antigonos of Socho received from Simeon the Just . . .

Jose son of Joezer and Jose son of Johanan of Jerusalem received from them . . . [and so, through three more pairs to two great leaders of the first century C.E. whose teaching Paul himself will have known:]

Hillel and Shammai received from them . . .

ABOTH [SAYINGS OF THE FATHERS] 1

Here are no claims to inspiration or an unveiling from God. The teachers' task was to interpret the Law for the day-to-day life of those around them. The sayings ascribed to each are straightforward ethical instructions: "Let your house be opened wide," for instance, "and let the poor be your household." (Since the ninth century C.E. at the latest, the six chapters of the *Sayings of the Fathers* have been read as part of the Jewish liturgy, most frequently, in current practice, on the six Sabbaths after Passover.)

The Law's teachers had been entrusted with the Law and had all the authority they needed to interpret it. This is the point of a famous story of a dispute between rabbis. It's worth hearing in full.

Rabbi Eliezer is said to have made a decision on the ritual uncleanness of a certain category of clay oven. He said that by the nature of their construction such ovens could not contract uncleanness. His peers disagreed with him. "If the Law accords with my position," said Eliezer, "this tree will prove it." And the tree was removed 150 feet from its place. There was no doubt, then, of Eliezer's sanctity or gifts. But his colleagues were unimpressed: "There is no proof," they said, "from a tree." Eliezer again: "If the Law accords with my position, let the stream of water prove it." The stream reversed its flow. But they said again: "There is no proof from a stream of water." Once more, Eliezer: "If the Law accords with my position, let the walls of the schoolhouse prove it." The walls began to tilt and were about to fall. But Rabbi Joshua interrupted and addressed the walls: "If the pupils of sages are disputing in matters of the Law, what business do you have getting involved?" Out of the honor due to Joshua, the walls did not fall; but out of the honor due to Eliezer, they did not straighten up. And so, says the story, they are tilted to this day.

Eliezer then appealed for higher support: "If the Law accords with my position, let heaven prove it." An echo came forth (the "echo" of God's voice, all that can be heard on earth of his voice, in an age unworthy of the Breath itself): "What business have you [disagreeing] with Eliezer? For the Law accords with his position under all circumstances." But up got Rabbi Joshua. "It is not in heaven," he said, quoting a passage about the Law that we will hear again (The Second Law [Deuteronomy] 30:12). What did he mean? "The Law," explained a third rabbi, "has already been given from Mt. Sinai, so we do not pay attention to echoes from heaven, for you [in heaven] have already written in the Law at Mt. Sinai, 'You are to agree with the majority'" (The Escape [Exodus] 23:2).

At this point the story is interrupted. Rabbi Nathan came upon Elijah, the great prophet from Israel's ancient past, and asked him what God had done at that moment. "He laughed aloud," replied Elijah, "and said, 'My children have overcome me, my children have overcome me!'" (The story is told in the Talmud, the great commentary on the Mishnah, in *Baba Metzia [The Middle Gate]* 59a–b.)

This story was told at a time far later than Paul's, but it enables us to gauge the question to which Paul's good news would give rise: What does this Paul think he is—what must he think he is—to have the authority he claims, direct from heaven, to interpret and apply in quite revolutionary ways the revealed and unbreakable word of God? Eliezer had sought improperly to win a dispute over one question of the Law. The story about him continues. On that day the other rabbis brought together all of the objects that Eliezer had said could not contract uncleanness and burned them; they were so unclean that they were beyond all purification. The rabbis also took a vote against Eliezer and cursed him.

What, then, would have been punishment severe enough for Paul, if he claimed, on God's authority, his Jesus brought the blessings of Israel to Gentiles, who knew and observed nothing specific to the Law at all?

THE SUCCESSORS OF JESUS

From Moses to Joshua, as we have heard, to the elders and so through the generations to Hillel and Shammai—the Great Prayer House needed a succession of leaders. The early followers of Jesus needed a succession too, the successors to Jesus himself who would guide, sustain, and legitimate the community's affairs. There are signs of competition. Here we can only glance at the hints we have of disagreement. They reach us from later decades, even later centuries. They are relayed within traditions that have their own axes to grind and interests to serve. And they do not quite answer the question we would most like to ask: What sort of authority was sought and invested in these first leaders?

On the one hand was Peter, a leader during Jesus' earthly life who (in Luke's story) wrought miracles after it. On the other hand was James, the brother of Jesus. He had not, it seems, been one of Jesus' followers during Jesus' lifetime. Far from it. But the Bible contains one letter attributed to James and one attributed to a second brother, Jude. Where were these various leaders based? Peter and James, it seems, had their base in Jerusalem. But there were still followers of Jesus in Galilee, with leaders of their own; they too could claim succession from Jesus himself. Different leaders in different areas fostered different versions of the good news.

Mark puts at the center of his gospel Jesus' question to his pupils, *"Who do you say I am?"* Peter answers, *"You are the Anointed."* (8:29). When Matthew reaches the story, he follows suit, but his Peter gives a fuller answer: *"You are the Anointed, the son of the living God."* This is the cue for Matthew's Jesus to praise and commission Peter in words unrecorded by Mark: *"On this rock I will build my assembly, and the gates of hell shall not stand out against it. I will give you the keys of heaven . . ."* (16:18–19).

The Coptic *Gospel of Thomas* revisits this theme. This gospel claims to record the words of the risen Jesus, written down by Didymus Judas Thomas. Thomas (in Aramaic) and Didymus (in Greek) both mean "Twin." Other texts in the Thomas tradition make clear that Thomas was the twin brother of Jesus. The *Gospel of Thomas* is more discreet. Thomas is already like Jesus; and his text is designed to help his readers become like Jesus in their turn. It is in this sense, if at all, that he is Jesus' twin.

Jesus' pupils ask in the *Gospel of Thomas* who "shall be great over them" when Jesus has gone. Jesus replies: "Wherever you come, you will go to James the Just, for whose sake heaven and earth came into being." Jesus himself then poses just such a challenge as he had in Matthew's gospel: "Make a comparison to me and tell me who I am like." The gospel is setting out to redress the balance so heavily tilted by Matthew in Peter's favor. Peter answers first: "You are like a just angel." Then Matthew himself: "You are like a wise philosopher." But it is Thomas who does justice to Jesus' standing: "Master, my mouth will not be at all capable of saying who you are like." For this reply Thomas wins Jesus' highest praise. He is entrusted with three words so secret that they cannot be relayed to the other pupils. James, then, is the leader, and Thomas is the privileged recipient of divine truths. Between them they have all the authority the assemblies need. Other texts from the third century have James himself entrusted with secret unveilings from Jesus. The brothers of Jesus were not valuable to later generations just for the family connection, but for the access this gave them to Jesus' innermost knowledge.

We cannot now know when the relevant sayings reached their present form, nor, therefore, which generation wanted to reassert the claims of James and Thomas in this way. In the *Gospel of Thomas* they are heroes of the past; we do not know if these sayings were already known when they—and their rivals—were powers in the present.

As there are two pillars in the *Gospel of Thomas,* there are two in the gospel of John: Peter and the beloved pupil. Our text of John threads its way carefully through such rivalries. *The pupil whom Jesus loved,* mentioned in the gospel, is arguably the evangelist himself, that is, an eyewitness who compiled a first edition of the gospel (John 19:35 and 21:24); he or his followers will have been responsible for its development through to completion in the 80s or 90s. On the last evening Jesus spent with his pupils, it was this pupil who sat beside the master and leaned on Jesus' breast. And at Jesus' death, the gospel makes clear, it was not the brothers of Jesus who stood by him. At the foot of the cross were the Lord's mother and his beloved pupil. A new family is being created. In this gospel the dying Jesus commends his mother and this pupil to each other's care (John 19:25–27).

What, then, is the relation in power and authority between Peter and this pupil whom Jesus loved? According to John 21, almost an appendix to the gospel as a whole, Jesus had promised, *"I want him* [the beloved pupil] *to remain until I come"* (21:22), and this had been understood to mean that the pupil would not die. The pupil's years would become a clock for his community, trickling away like the sand in an hourglass. Before the grains all passed through the neck, Jesus would return. This would in itself have given the pupil, in his lifetime, a stature enjoyed by no one else.

And Peter? That last chapter of John's gospel ascribes to Peter too a particular authority. Three times Peter had denied Jesus, and three times in John 21 Jesus commands him to feed Jesus' sheep. Peter is restored to intimacy with Jesus and is commissioned for the future.

John's chapter 21 was completed after both Peter and the beloved pupil had died. A careful balance had to be kept between the two figures. Peter is the shepherd who feeds the flock of Jesus, the true Shepherd. *The pupil whom Jesus loved* is the one to know all that is to be known of Jesus and to compile the gospel. The gospel of John knows of Peter's leadership and the knowledge belonging to *the pupil whom Jesus loved,* just as the gospel of Thomas knows of James's leadership and of Thomas's knowledge.

James and Thomas, Peter and John the evangelist are different leaders who gained different allegiance in different places, each drawing on different criteria and loyalties. After the dispute at Antioch, another leader stakes his claim: Paul. He insists he himself is in his own way a "successor" to Jesus. He has been commissioned directly by the Lord and represents the Lord. No family member, no adopted son of Mary, and no friend of Jesus could have a higher claim over his assemblies than Paul has himself, for he is the father, mother, and brother to the members of the family of God.

Paul: Authorized by God Alone

We can see better now what was at stake in Galatia. The new teachers insist that Paul is subject to the same conditions they are. The leaders in Jerusalem and Antioch are the source of Paul's good news and of his authority to preach it. But Paul responds that neither he nor his assembly is bound by the conditions of transmission and allegiance on which these new teachers rely. Paul is not introducing his church into a clear ancestral community, defined for generations; nor is he himself an authorized teacher of that community. He is clear in his own mind that his relation to Jerusalem and to Antioch is transformed; so in turn is his relation to his assemblies. He stands in the tradition of Isaiah and Jeremiah as a prophet of God's new disclosure, not as a teacher of the old. Let any assembly, then, acknowledge itself as his own, and the relation of that assembly to Jerusalem and Antioch is transformed in its turn.

The Law was given by Moses, handed down to him by angels. He had been the mediator of the Old Order, at one remove from its source. Paul will not accept even such a role as Moses'. Paul is no postman delivering the mail. In his own person the mail arrives to be read and seen and acknowledged for what it is.

Paul is redefining the lineage of proclamation, and in just the same way he rewrites the lineage of God's people too. He now claims that his assemblies' members are the "direct" children of God, adopted by God himself, unmediated by tradition or Law or human agency. He does not, with this claim, foreclose the claim that they are Abraham's children as well; his converts' new status interprets that old claim and fulfills it. The parallelism between Paul and his assemblies is crucial. If he is bound to the authorized tradition, then he cannot preach freedom from it to them; and if they are bound to it, how can he be free?

Family lineage, then, dominates the letter, the lineage of Paul as an emissary and the lineage of the Galatians as children of God. The two strands in this thread are interwoven. In the next chapter we will follow them through Paul's argument. His own commission from God is the model for the Galatians' relation with God. As he was chosen from the womb of his mother for his task, so they are still—as he will say in the most striking passage of all—in gestation within his own womb. They need him. Without him they will never be born as the children of God they are called to be.

Readers might well wonder as they hear of this tour de force what sort of argument Paul was mounting. He finds lineage in every argument. To construct his position he takes words and lines from the Old

Order in ways unseen before. He reads a whole story in a sense un-imaginable to any conventional reader. He knows the result that he needs from every part of his discussion and will stop at nothing to secure it. Whatever in the Old Order the new teachers have used to make their point he must take over—and turn over—to make with it his own opposing point. A good many readers have found more to value in his conclusion than in the ways he gets there.

If the new teachers are still present in the assemblies when his letter arrives, it is hard to imagine them admitting defeat. With these strange arguments Paul has radicalized his position. He has deepened into a chasm what had seemed at worst a fordable stream between the teachers and himself. He has insulted the teachers viciously: *Those who are unset-tling you*—with their demand for circumcision—*I wish they would cut off something more substantial from themselves!* (Gal. 5:12) He has claimed a good news and an authority to preach it that no one loyal to the assemblies in Jerusalem could countenance.

We do not hear what the result of his letter was, but he has raised the stakes. The new teachers may not have been his opponents before, but they are certainly his opponents now. And every one of his arguments is vulnerable. Paul is riding for a fall.

CHAPTER 15

UNVEILING THE SON

IN HIS LETTER TO THE GALATIANS, Paul has an uncompromising point to make, and he makes it right from the opening words. We can most clearly see the shape and emphasis of this remarkable opening if we divide it into "lines." In the letter's very first words we hear the source of Paul's good news, hammered home; this will be the theme of the letter's first two chapters. Then sounds a fanfare of the faith; Paul elaborates his standard greeting to remind the Galatians what they know Jesus has done for them. Paul is at one point probably quoting from a statement of faith already familiar to the Galatians; we will put these words in quotation marks.

> Paul, emissary on no mission from men nor through man's command
>> but through Jesus Anointed and God the father
>>> who raised him from the dead,
> and all the brothers who are with me, to the assemblies of Galatia:
> Grace to you and peace
>> from God the father of ourselves and Lord Jesus Anointed,
>>> who "gave himself on behalf of our wrongdoings,
>>>> as the way to remove us from this age, this present wicked age,
>>>> according to the will of our God and father,
>>>>> to whom be glory for aeons upon aeons. Amen."

GALATIANS 1:1–5

Jesus Anointed and the father, the father and Jesus Anointed; Jesus *raised from the dead,* Jesus who *gave himself* for us—and all in relation to the father. Paul's Galatians are emphatically the children of God the father; this will be the burden of Paul's whole argument. And who is the link between father and children? Jesus Anointed. In Paul's letter to the Romans he will put weight on the father's love, not the son's (Rom. 5:8; 8:32), but to the Galatians he will stress the love of the Anointed.

And how is Jesus' love to be unveiled to his fellow children of God? It *pleased God,* Paul says, *to unveil his son in me.* Paul, *set apart from his mother's womb,* discloses in his own person the son of God *born from a woman.* The links between the Anointed, the assemblies, and Paul himself are already shaping all that Paul says.

PAUL INSISTS HE HAD BEEN DEVOTED to the traditions of his forefathers.

> *But when it pleased God, who had set me apart from my mother's womb and had called me through his grace, to unveil his son in me, so that I might proclaim the good news about him among the gentiles, straight away I did not consult with flesh and blood.*
> GALATIANS 1:15–16

From his forefathers' traditions to his mother's womb—Paul the emissary is not the accidental latecomer to mission that his biography might suggest. He was marked out before his birth. But there was a due time for Jesus' own birth, and a due time too for Paul to unveil God's son. Paul had been formed in the womb to be his mother's son, and formed there to re-present the son of God.

And now, we will hear, the Galatians are being formed in Paul's own womb, to be the sons and daughters of God they are called to be. Paul and the Galatians have all been called by God's grace, and in his formation into an emissary Paul sets the pattern for their formation into children of God. Paul is the nodal point of these connections, related without any mediation to the Anointed and to the Galatians alike.

We heard in Chapter 4 how Paul, in speaking of his own commission, recalls God's summons to his prophets in the Old Order. *"Before I formed you in the womb I knew you,"* God told Jeremiah, *"and before you came forth from your mother's womb I made you holy, I appointed you a prophet* to the nations" (Jer. 1:5). In particular we heard of the four passages in which Isaiah tells enigmatically of a Servant of God. It is too easy for us to isolate these four songs from their context. We should rather see them as part of the promises among which they are set, relayed by Isaiah for the deliverance of Jerusalem. Isaiah breaks suddenly into the first-person singular, "I":

> Listen to me, coastlands, pay attention, you nations.
>> From my mother's womb God called my name.
> And he said to me, "You are my slave, Israel,
>> and in you will I be glorified."
> And I said, "Vainly have I worked and to no avail,
>> and for nothing have I used up my strength. . . ."
> And now says God, who formed me from the womb to be his slave,
>> to bring Israel back to him: . . .
> "It is a great task for you, to be called my servant,
>> to set up the tribes of Jacob and to bring back the scattered people
>> of Israel.
> But look, I have made you to be an Order for the people, to be a light to the nations,
>> so that you might work for deliverance to the end of the earth."
>> ISAIAH 49:1, 3-6, GREEK VERSION

Isaiah's Servant feels he has worked vainly. Paul had spoken to the leaders in Jerusalem to ensure he was not running in vain and now admits his fear that for the Galatians he had worked in vain among them (Gal. 2:2; 4:11). The Servant is called to be God's slave. Paul is the slave of the Anointed (Gal. 1:10). The Servant will be said in the last song to have been without beauty or glory, to have been in trouble, calamity, and distress (Isa. 53:2–4). Paul, it seems, stayed in Galatia only because he was taken seriously ill—so seriously that the Galatians could have rejected him entirely (Gal. 4:13–14).

Paul is presenting himself as a prophet called directly by God, as a prophet should be. As he writes to the Galatians, this is just the role he can and wants to claim for himself—independent of human authority, without fear or favor, inspired and instructed by God alone. Paul is writing for himself the past that his present and his future need.

But the Servant is more than the prophet whose role is now fulfilled by Paul. The Servant is called as an individual to be *a light to the nations*. The Servant can also be addressed as "Israel," the embodiment of the communities to whom he brings good news and through whom he brings it to the nations at large. The Servant suffers for others. In all this the Servant anticipates the role of the Anointed. We shall see in Paul's later letters how heavily he draws on this image to do justice to Jesus.

Just as it does justice to Paul himself. Precisely in this role of the Servant Paul can stand midway between the Anointed and his own assemblies. Paul re-presents the Anointed, the great Servant, to his converts; and through his converts, who are the Body of the Anointed and *the Israel of God,* Paul brings the light of the Anointed to all nations. Here is the *slave Israel* in whom God will be glorified.

When Paul is ready, then, to round off in this letter his arguments over lineage, it is no surprise that he will return to Isaiah, to the lines immediately following the last song of the Servant. The Servant's task is done. He has not worked in vain.

> *Rejoice, you childless one, you who bear no children,*
> *burst into song and shout, you who suffer no pangs of birth.*
> GALATIANS 4:27, QUOTING ISAIAH 54:1, GREEK VERSION

"To Unveil His Son in Me"

It pleased God to unveil his son in me is purposefully phrased. Within these few words two features stand out. First, scholars have long wondered why Paul emphasizes that God unveiled *his son*—rather than, say, the Anointed. It is rare for Paul to speak of Jesus without further adornment as God's son. Scholars suspect Paul is adopting a formula already used in worship. But the answer lies within the letter. Paul is setting up the pattern of relationships he needs between all the "sons" involved, between the Anointed, the Galatians, and himself.

And second, the latter portion of the phrase is frequently altered in translation to read: *to unveil his son to me*. Parallels can be found for such a sense of the Greek phrase, but the phrase is easy and uncomplicated. No reader would be in any doubt when hearing it that Paul said and meant *in me*. (If we were looking for any other sense of the *in*, we should head for the Greek word's use to mean *by means of, with the help of*, but the search itself is misguided!) That shift to *to* cuts out the heart of Paul's thought. He is not the mediator of a New Order as Moses had been of the Old. Later in the letter he will disparage the Law, *imparted through angels by the hand of an intermediary* (3:19). Paul's good news is inseparable from Paul himself. The words of a letter are a substitute for the emissary himself, and they come with all his authority. But they steer the hearer back to the sender. That is where the true unveiling takes place.

We will be hearing more of Paul's re-presentation of the Anointed. We need to take care with the terms we use. So strange to us is Paul's self-understanding that we are in danger of forcing it into a pigeonhole familiar to us. And it will fit in none of them. We do well to remind ourselves of some questions we asked in Chapter 2. We have more material before us now with which to answer them. Paul re-presents the Anointed. Is he then "identical" with the Anointed? No. Does he "look like" the Anointed? Only to those who can see in his weakness what needs to be seen. Is his "personality" submerged in that of the Anointed? The question is too vague, but in any sense we might expect to answer it, no, Paul remains inescapably himself. But he is intrinsic to his good news and to the life of his assemblies. He has "identified" himself with his mission, for his good news' sake and for his own. He needs his converts' loyalty and friendship, for his good news' sake and for his own. He is exhilarated when they embrace him, deeply pained when they reject him—once more for his good news' sake and for his own.

Paul's relations developed with the assemblies and their other leaders. His self-understanding developed too. But how quickly? We cannot tell. Paul came to see himself as re-presenting the Anointed. Perhaps this became clear at his conversion, perhaps in the months immediately following, or perhaps only when he found himself in conflict with the emissaries of Antioch and Jerusalem and in need of a legitimacy they no longer afforded him. No wonder, then, he wrote of his extraordinary standing in a letter that was fired by that conflict.

We are not belittling Paul if we find in his behavior all the signs of normal human needs, tensions, and joys. We are discovering how he had the energy and determination to do all that he did—in the total convergence of his personal and missionary lives. He was hardly even a chariot drawn by two horses in harness. The horses became one and drew him onward, single-minded and with irrepressible power.

They did not always draw Paul's converts with them, however. There was room for this Paul to be disappointed and bitter. To bully and manipulate. To keep his converts for his own. To claim ever more for himself and his intimacy with them. And in the case of the Galatians, to subvert all the arguments of the new and dangerous teachers by rewriting these arguments—in quite extraordinary ways—to serve his own.

The Seed of Abraham

Paul unveils the son to the Galatians; the Galatians are themselves children of the same father. What, then, about Abraham and his descendants who observe the Law? Said God to Abraham:

> This whole land which you see, I will give it to you and to your seed for ever. And I will make your seed as the sand on the ground. If anyone can count the sand on the ground, then your seed will be counted.
> THE BEGINNING [GENESIS] 13:15-16

The newcomers to Galatia claim that all depends on the Galatians' being the heirs of Abraham. They have struck a chord. How, they can ask, does the arrival of the Anointed change the conditions of the distinction between Jews and Gentiles? The ancient promises will be fulfilled by the Gentiles' entering God's Order or Covenant with Israel, not by the Order's dilution to suit the Gentiles. God's command to Abraham had been quite clear: *This is the Order that you will keep, the Order between me and you and your seed after you for all their generations: Every male of you shall be circumcised* (The Beginning 17:10).

It is Paul himself who changes the perspective. The Anointed himself, he insists, is the single *seed of Abraham* for whom the promises were given. The Galatians are indeed part of this seed, because they are baptized into the Anointed. They are heirs of the promise. And once the promise is correctly understood, its results can be understood too. Seeking to be heirs under the Law, the Galatians seek to be no better than slaves, like children under the control of their father's staff. But free from the Law, like children come of age and like Paul himself, they have all the blessings of their lineage. They are sons and daughters of God, as the Anointed himself is. As sons, they are heirs not just of Abraham, but of God. The Galatians have let themselves be distracted from God's real offer.

Paul evokes that baptismal formula we have heard already and shall hear again:

You are sons of God through the faith in Anointed Jesus. For all of you that were baptized into Anointed have put on Anointed as a garment.

> *There exists no Jew nor Greek,*
> *There exists no slave nor free,*
> *There exists no male and female.*
> *For you are all one person in Anointed Jesus.*
> GALATIANS 3:26-28

And so Paul can turn the new teachers' argument to his own ends: *And if you are Anointed's, then you are the seed of Abraham*—as the Anointed was and as the teachers claim the converts need to be—*heirs by the promise* (3:29).

We are at the center of the letter with the passage at the beginning of chapter 4, and we shall find again later that Paul has a sure sense of the climax appropriate at a letter's heart. Slaves and free, children and heirs—Paul is ready to sound the theme of gestation and birth again. Last time it was his own gestation; this time it is the birth of the Anointed—and so the adoption of Paul's own converts. The passage is best divided into lines, to see how carefully Paul has constructed it. I have added the lettering on the right to point out the symmetry of its clauses.

Paul moves swiftly from "them" to "us" to "you" in general, and back to "us" and so to "you there" in the singular. Who, then, has been in mind? Paul lets the ambiguity hang in the air. When we were "infants," he says, we were enslaved to the elemental powers of the world (4:3). No Jew would accept such a charge, but would certainly hold it true of pagans. In this "us" Paul has linked himself, a Jew, with the paganism of which the Galatians had been part before their conversion. And so in the following verses he can, vice versa, link the Jewish observances sought by the new teachers with that old paganism of the Galatians: *How can you be turning,* he asks, *to the weak and poor elemental powers that you want to serve again?* (4:9). When the Galatians listen to the new teachers, he claims, the Galatians are not completing their new faith; they are reverting to errors as serious as the pagan errors they have left behind.

From "us" (including Jews such as Paul, who had been under the Law) Paul moves to "you," the Galatians (who had not): the Galatians need to recognize what has been done for them. "You there," in the singular, you are a child, not a slave; you are the "son" called to be a co-heir with the Son.

> *When there came the fullness of time, God sent out his son,*   A
> > *born from a woman,*   B
> > > *born under the Law,*   C
> > > > *so that he might buy the freedom*
> > > > *of those under the Law,*   C
> > > *so that we might receive adoption as his sons;*   B
> > *for inasmuch as you are sons,*
> > *God sent out the Breath of his son into our hearts,*   A
> > > *crying "Abba, Father."*
> > *So that you there are no longer a slave but a son;*
> > *and if a son, then an heir through God.*
> > GALATIANS 4:4–6

FIRST WE HEARD OF THE UNVEILING OF GOD'S SON, prepared in the womb that was carrying Paul. Now we hear of the birth from a woman of that son himself and hear of the Galatians' father God. And finally, in the most striking image of all, Paul will speak of himself as the Galatians' own mother. He knows that his letter will be offending them. He mollifies them. *Become like me,* he says at the start of this next paragraph, *because I have become like you, brothers* (4:12). Paul reminds them of his arrival among them, how they would have torn out their eyes and given them to him, if that would have helped him in his illness. Here, in those early days, was just the reciprocal relation that brothers should have.

How things will have changed by the time the Galatians get this far in the letter. Once more he invites them to stand back from its progress. *Am I become your enemy by telling you the truth?* (4:16). Paul needs to invoke a link with the assemblies far closer than the relation of brothers. He finds one, so physical that it outranks every possible claim or longing of the teachers. *My children, whom I am bearing still until the Anointed is formed in you* (4:19).

As the Galatians' father is God, their mother is Paul, still suffering the pangs of their birth. This is the sharpest paradox of the letter. Paul suffers the pangs of rebearing those, already born into their Christian life, whose gestation is not yet complete.

Paul was molded in his mother's womb to disclose the Anointed; and so in turn the Galatians are formed in his "womb" into the likeness of the Anointed. The Galatians' adoption as children of God is as direct as Jesus' physical sonship of his mother. This gestation allows no room for tradition or its teachers. It admits only the shortest lineage: God's promise for the offspring of Abraham is fulfilled in the person of Jesus and in those who are in the Anointed.

There is, then, no mediating tradition to which Paul or the Galatians are accountable. Their call was as unmediated as Paul's own. Paul himself is not the mediator of a faith brought to the Galatians from without; he is the mother of their new life.

And so Paul comes back at last to the new teachers' claims for Abraham. It is time to look more closely at Paul's extraordinary arguments about Abraham, circumcision, and the Jewish Law.

Paul, Abraham, and the Law

"THE JUST PERSON SHALL LIVE FROM FAITH"

Here is Paul's first argument from Abraham, in which he quotes four times from the Old Order in quick succession:

> All those who define themselves by works of the law are under a curse.
> For it is written: "Cursed is everyone who does not abide by everything

written in the book of the Law, to do it" [The Second Law (Deuter-
onomy) 27:26].

*The fact that in the law no one is held just in the sight of God is clear
from this: "The just person shall live from faith"* [Habakkuk 2:4].
But the Law does not stem from faith. Instead: "Those who do them
[the commandments] *shall live in them"* [The Laws of Ritual
(Leviticus) 18:5].

*Anointed has bought us out of the curse of the Law by becoming for us a
curse. For it is written: "Cursed is everyone that is hanged on a tree"*
[The Second Law 21:23].

*So that the promise made to Abraham might be for the Gentiles in
Anointed Jesus, so that we might receive the promise of the Breath
through the faith.*

GALATIANS 3:10–14

That opening passage from The Second Law, within its own context, does nothing at all to support Paul's case. The Second Law emphasizes over and over that if the people of Israel keep the Law, they will be
blessed. And here, in this quotation, is the other side of the coin: if they
do not, they will be cursed.

Many scholars have argued that Paul is here advancing—without
fully stating—his own view of the Law's fulfillment. For Paul the Law's
demands cannot be met. No one can observe the whole Law, so everyone, by the terms of the Law itself, is cursed. To undertake to observe
the Law—and necessarily to fail—is to put oneself under the curse of
God. There is no value, then, in the blessings promised by the new
teachers to the Galatians if they must be adopted by circumcision and
the Law's observance into the seed of Abraham.

Might this be right? Just as many scholars have argued, by contrast,
how odd this position would be. It is a parody of Judaism. At the heart
of Judaism is the recognition that we falter, do wrong, and need to be
forgiven. The Law itself makes provision for our failure to observe the
Law and for our restoration to good standing within God's favor.

We know something of the practices observed by some at least of those Jews who revered Jesus and observed the Law. The letter of James, which clearly claims the authority of the brother of Jesus (1:1), insists that the Law cannot be broken down into commandments to observe and commandments to ignore. James warns his addressees: *Whoever keeps the whole Law but trips up on one point, they are guilty of breaking it all. For the one who said, "You must not commit adultery" said as well, "You must not kill." And if you do not commit adultery but you do kill, you have become a breaker of the law* (2:10–11). Now James was no antagonist of the Law. Does he then believe that every breach of the Law—let us leave aside the extreme examples he has chosen—puts the offender beyond the pale of God's forgiveness? No. In this passage he is warning those who pay court to the rich that they are doing wrong. They cannot excuse themselves by pointing to the other laws they have not broken. Of course they may be tempted to pick and choose, but that will not fool God. They do need to be forgiven for the wrongdoing, and they can be. They need to change their ways, and they can.

It is odder still, if we take this view of Paul's argument, that Paul never says in this letter that the Law cannot be fulfilled. If he had believed it, surely he would have said it. But far from it. He will even describe himself to the Philippians as having been faultless in the Law's eyes. Can his argument, then, really be that the Law is beyond fulfillment?

No. His argument is shaped by the message of the newly arrived teachers. We can well imagine them invoking the first and third of these four texts. Together they make a neat and compelling statement. *Cursed is everyone who does not abide by everything written in the book of the Law, to do it.* But on the other hand, *Those who do them* [the commandments] *shall live in them.* The good news, they say, that the Galatians have so far taken on board from Paul is only fool's gold; here is the real good news, the good news of circumcision. Whether by misunderstanding or simply by error, Paul's converts are only halfway to the membership of Abraham's seed and to its inheritance.

Paul has responded with a deft move. He has inserted his own quotation from Habakkuk, a prophecy he will use again: *The just person shall live from faith.* This does not yet formulate his own position, but it puts a spanner in the works of any other. He has established his contrast between faith and works, a contrast that drastically divides what had clearly belonged together in every Judaism that believed God's promise and so undertook, as a blessing, the obligations that went with it. Yes, Paul has made a deft move, but one that has caused confusion for his readers ever since.

"The Jerusalem Above"

That first of Paul's arguments from Abraham was cryptic but neatly made; the second is almost bizarre. He is again turning an argument of the new teachers against themselves. Once more he draws his argument from the Old Order, this time by giving the Old Order's text a quite baffling twist. Was he working within parameters that were acknowledged and respected at the time for the exegesis and application of the text? Those parameters were certainly quite different from our own. (Here is a minor example. We heard earlier, in the dispute over clay ovens, how a rabbi dismissed the support that Eliezer won from the sound of an echo from heaven. The Law says, "You are to agree with the majority" [The Escape (Exodus) 23:2]. Eliezer was in a minority. The heavenly echo, therefore, intervening on Eliezer's behalf, was an improper intrusion. But at first sight the passage from The Escape does not support the rabbi's case at all. It reads: *You will not be led into wrongdoing by the majority nor . . . side with the majority to pervert justice.* The rabbi has to assume the justice of the majority view before he can adduce the passage to prove it.)

Or was Paul claiming access to a higher knowledge of the Old Order's meaning, based on an authority that the Galatians could not hope to share? It was, after all, as an angel, a messenger from God, that they had received him on his visit. And when he warns against any preacher whose teaching contradicts his own, it is an angel he warns against (Gal. 4:14; 1:8). The only "opponents" of Paul even worth consideration would be angels. As Paul dictates this letter he draws himself up to the full height of his authority. He writes as an emissary they dare not disobey. Within this letter he can himself lay down and apply, on his own authority and beyond all contradiction, the due forms and limits of interpretation.

It can also be asked, of course, whether any of his addressees would have known how he was manipulating the Old Order. Here as elsewhere Paul's argument depends on a close reading of several passages widely separated in the Old Order itself and brought by Paul into a tight connection with each other. The technique was well known; as we shall see in a moment, the newly arrived teachers were almost certainly doing the same. Whether the members of gentile assemblies, perhaps as little versed in the Old Order as most readers are today, would have picked up Paul's allusions, it is hard to know. In the present case the Galatians were more likely just to recognize those passages that the new teachers were using, to know that they were quotations, and to hear how differently Paul read them.

The teachers have drawn the contrast between Abraham's two sons, Isaac, born to Sarah as God had promised and the forebear of the Jews, and Ishmael, born to Abraham's slave girl Hagar and expelled from his household (The Beginning 15–17, 21). The teachers have traced for the Galatians the lineage of Abraham from Abraham to Isaac to Jacob and so on until the present day. These are the ancestors into whose family the Galatians need to be adopted.

Paul returns to the two sons of Abraham. Yes, one stands for those who observe the Law, and one for those who do not. But which child stands for which? Paul turns the historical picture inside out. The Order or Covenant made with Moses at Sinai ensnares its adherents in the slavery of the Law. This, then, is the Order for the descendants of the slave girl Hagar. And so on down to Paul's own day. The classic course of Judaism led from Sinai to Jerusalem. And look, there was the Jerusalem of Paul's time, duly enslaved along with its children, the Jews, under Roman rule.

And the child of Sarah, Isaac, born as God promised? He stands for Paul's converts. Now Ishmael could not inherit with Isaac, so God commanded that Ishmael be cast out. Once more we are hearing echoes of the teachers' words. They will have warned that Paul's converts are in danger of Ishmael's fate, cast out from the household. Paul turns the allegory around 180 degrees. It is not his converts who are in danger. It is those who are preaching the need for the Law's observance and those who follow their commands. Those in danger of expulsion are the very teachers who are threatening it.

Jerusalem at the start of the letter is seen as the center of the mission led by Peter and James; Jerusalem at the letter's end is seen as a city enslaved on earth. Paul's great symphony is drawing to its close. He evokes the last of the parents with which he ties his converts to the Anointed and to himself. It is a bold and beautiful move; here writes Paul the poet. He contrasts the earthly enslaved Jerusalem with its free counterpart in heaven, where Paul's converts belong: *the Jerusalem above which is free, which is our mother* (4:26).

The Jerusalem above . . . is our mother. Paul once more turns the teachers' promises to his own account. This is a theme, after all, close to Paul's heart. In the Jerusalem above is the sight of God and the life of angels to which the Galatians aspire. There is the new creation, fully realized, into which the Galatians are being born. Paul was not the only seer to dwell on it. John the Seer says:

> *And I saw a new heaven and new earth. For the first heaven and the first earth had passed away, and the sea* [the realm of chaos] *existed no more. And I saw the holy city, Jerusalem, new, coming down out of heaven prepared like a bride for her husband.*
>
> *And the one seated on the throne said, "Look, I am making all things new."*
>
> UNVEILING [REVELATION] 21:1-2, 5

"LOVE YOUR NEIGHBOR AS YOURSELF"

> *The whole Law is fulfilled in one word: "You must love your neighbor as yourself."*
>
> GALATIANS 5:14

What, then, is the status in God's own plan of God's own Law? Paul addresses the question in two letters, here for the Galatians and again when writing to the Romans. When he writes to Galatia he is fighting an immediate danger to his own good news, his converts, and his position among them. The tone of his letter and its content coincide.

He admits nothing that could give the teachers a toehold on his territory. Of course the Law cannot be actually contrary to the promises of God, for then God would not be true to himself and his own undertakings. But *if a law had been given that was able to make alive, then justness would indeed come from the law. But scripture has locked up everything beneath the power of wrongdoing, so that the promise, by the faith of Jesus Anointed, might be given to those who have faith* (Gal. 3:21–22). The Law was like a child's guide, walking him or her to school. Such children, however grand their future, are at the time no better than slaves themselves. And the Law is now a dangerous trap whose advocates seek to enslave the Galatians once more.

But what happens when Paul writes to Rome? Then Paul will write to a community in which some members already observe the Law. Its role is under dispute. Division is brewing. Paul must settle an argument and restore unity; to attack the Law's observance as he does to the Galatians will only worsen what he is setting out to overcome. He writes again with a personal passion. He has not been to Rome and the assemblies there owe him no allegiance. But it is his own version of the good news—misrepresented as wildly libertine—that has polarized the converts. So he confirms that the Law is holy, just, and good. He speaks of the promises made to the Jews and of all that God has given them: the status of children, the glory, the Orders, the endowment with law, and the service it brings.

In writing to the Romans Paul carefully restores the balance of the ship by resituating all the passengers around its decks; in writing to the Galatians he takes one part of the crew, crewmen who are tipping the boat dangerously to one side, and angrily throws them overboard. Can we then discover, from these two letters, how Paul really viewed the Law and its observance? To do the question justice we will review it again when we have looked more closely at the letter to the Romans. There we will see as well just what fierce opposition Paul stirred up—opposition to his version of the good news, yes, and to the Paul who spread it.

For the moment, then, let's make do with the insights offered by Paul's letter to the Galatians. We hear of developments in the early church through the polemic of Paul. We think, therefore, of "Christian" and "Jewish" belief and observance as separated by a rift as deep as that portrayed by Paul. He offers himself, very successfully, as a paradigm of this rift and of the need for it. His own conversion, as it is presented to the Galatians, offers a vivid psychological model for the individual convert. It offers too a model for the social independence that defines a new community and a focal figure around whose experience this new community can gather.

Paul defines the assemblies' identity by reference to his own, and his own by reference to his assemblies. Paul is drawn into two sets of parallel and ever more radical claims: for his own independence from Jerusalem and for his assemblies' independence from the Law. He needs a model for Christian life and community more strikingly and coherently separate from Judaism than a drawn-out, contested, and still partial breach from Law-observant assemblies can easily afford him. He finds it in a model of his own calling and authorization—as a prophet answerable to God alone. This emissary is ordained directly by God. He is indebted and answerable to no one on earth. His community comprises the children of God, born of the emissary in whom the Anointed himself is re-presented. It is a community descended from and answerable to no other power on earth. Here is clear blue water between Paul and the new teachers in Galatia. It will separate all who acknowledge from all who deny Paul's understanding of their own life and the life of their assembly.

This Paul who re-presents the Anointed and this Paul who fights for his own and his assemblies' independence—the theologian sees the one, the historian sees the other. But the two Pauls are one, the Paul who has invested in his mission everything that he has and is.

The Marks of Jesus

Paul takes the reed pen from his scribe and rounds off the letter himself in the middle of chapter 6. As we might use capitals or underlining for emphasis, Paul stresses what he has to say by the use of large letters. Theme after theme reemerges from the main body of the letter in these last lines. Opening curse gives way to closing blessing. If the Galatians heed his words, they have moved from the threat of God's curse to the promise of his blessing. They are members of the true Israel of God, adopted as God's children in the Anointed.

Paul speaks of bearing the marks of Jesus on his own body. Are these the "stigmata," the signs of Jesus' passion that have appeared on later saints? No. Paul is making a claim more striking still. These are the marks Paul bears of his own suffering, for Paul's whole life and person re-present the Anointed. What, then, are his wounds if they are not the re-presentation of Jesus' own? Paul writes here in a weary tone, as if the trouble with which the Galatians threaten him is adding to the wounds of the Anointed himself. Paul does not see his sufferings as his alone. It was no great distance from Paul's own understanding to the startling account of Paul's work given by a pupil in his name. *Now I rejoice in these sufferings on your behalf and I fill up what is lacking in the tribulations of the Anointed in my flesh on behalf of his body, which is the assembly* (Col. 1:24).

We may well wonder how much of the letter had Paul dictated word for word and how much his scribe had worked up from Paul's more general instruction or notes. We can never be sure. But if we want to hear the voice of Paul himself, we can turn to these closing lines. Here is the extended "signature," familiar in ancient letters, that brought Paul's own words to his converts and bring them, two thousand years later, to us.

See with what large letters I am writing you with my own hand. It is those who want to look well in the flesh who are forcing you to be circumcised, just so they might not be persecuted because of the cross of Anointed. For not even those getting circumcised themselves keep the law, but they want you to be circumcised, so that they might boast in your flesh.

But for me, far be it from me to boast—except in the cross of our Lord Jesus Anointed, through whom the world has been crucified to me and I to the world. For neither circumcision is anything nor uncircumcision—but a new creation. And for all those who will follow this elemental rule, peace upon them and mercy, and upon the Israel of God!

From now on let no one cause me trouble. For I bear the marks of Jesus branded on my body.

The grace of our Lord Jesus Anointed be with your breath, brothers.
Amen.

GALATIANS 6:11–18

"LEAST IN THE KINGDOM OF HEAVEN"

Paul describes himself as the least of the emissaries (1 Cor. 15:9). Some would have denied him even that. The letter of James may well be combating quite directly Paul's teaching on the role of faith. Paul invokes Abraham as a model of faith. *Abraham,* he writes to the Romans, *had faith in God,* who had promised him a child, *and it was accounted to him for justness. Now for those who effect things by actions, the payment is not accounted them as a generous gift but as their due* (Rom. 4:3–4, quoting The Beginning 15:6).

The letter of James, by contrast, lambasts reliance on faith alone. He too appeals to the story of Abraham and Isaac (The Beginning 22), but to quite different effect: *Wasn't Abraham our father held just by actions, having offered up Isaac his son upon the altar? You see that faith was working together with actions and by actions faith was brought to completion. And the scripture was fulfilled which says, "Abraham had faith in God, and it was accounted to him for justness"* (James 2:21–23).

Such anger with Paul's good news has likely shaped parts of our book of Unveiling. It continues to color texts that reached their final form in the third or fourth centuries; Paul is demonized, for instance, in a letter written as if from Peter to James, and again in a fictional dispute in which Peter trounces him. Within the New Order, meanwhile, just one text handles the questions of the Law and of Gentiles with the care and sophistication of Paul: the gospel of Matthew. Matthew works as hard as Paul to develop the views of his addressees while they hear or read his narrative. His viewpoint is quite different from Paul's. He probably wrote in Antioch, scene in Paul's day of such turmoil, and in the 70s. Matthew still had to respond to that movement away from loyalty to the Law that had infected the city forty years before.

Matthew's Jesus issues his greatest instruction in the Sermon on the Mount, at the start of his ministry. Matthew has organized the sermon's material with great care. He frames the bulk of it with two attacks on those who could so easily mislead his readers. As a preface to his instruction on the Law, he turns as well to a person or type who is the "least." It has long been wondered if he has Paul's self-description in mind. Matthew's Jesus says:

> *"In truth I tell you, until heaven and earth pass away, neither the dot on an i nor the cross on a t shall pass away from the Law, not until all things come to be. All who relax one of the least of these commandments and teach others to do the same shall be called least in the kingdom of heaven. And all who teach them and do them, they shall be called great in the kingdom of heaven."*
> MATTHEW 5:18-19

And as the sermon draws to its close, Matthew's Jesus turns to the attack again. Once more he lambasts those who abandon the Law. And who in Antioch has been a greater force for lawlessness than Paul?

> *"Beware of the false prophets, who come to you in shepherds' clothes, but within they are rapacious wolves.*
>
> *"Not everyone who says to me, 'Lord, Lord' shall enter the kingdom of heaven, but those who do the will of my father who is in heaven. Many shall say to me on that day [the Day of the Lord], 'Lord, Lord, did we not prophesy in your name and throw out devils in your name and do many acts of power in your name?' And then I shall tell them, 'I never knew you. Depart from me, you who work lawlessness!'"*
> MATTHEW 7:15, 21-23

Paul promised the Corinthians that he himself was the master builder of the sanctuary that they themselves were, and he had laid the foundations well. Or had he?

Matthew's Jesus ends his great sermon with a warning. It is as well Matthew's own warning to the assembly of Antioch: Shun the teaching of Paul—or beware the consequences.

> *"All those who hear my words and observe them shall be compared to wise people who built their house upon a rock. . . .*

"And all those who hear my words and do not observe them shall be com-
pared to fools who built their house upon sand. And the rain came down
and the floods rose and the winds blew and struck that house and it fell—
and what a fall it had!"

MATTHEW 7:24, 26–27

AT THE COUNCIL IN JERUSALEM, as its decision is recorded by Luke, James yielded an inch. Paul then took a mile. And so followed the furious dispute in Antioch. We readily think of it as a victory for Paul, partly because we have, from Paul himself, an account of his own words, defiant and brave, and partly because we have records of no one else's. James, after all, has faded from history; Paul has become a hero of the faith.

But at Antioch no other leader followed Paul. He was thereafter a maverick, distrusted by the assemblies of Antioch and Jerusalem and by all their dependents and allies. James was outflanked and, from then on, had to watch out for subversion in assemblies that had so far acknowledged allegiance, however informal, to himself and the other emissaries working out of Jerusalem.

Not that these implications were clear straightaway. The new teachers in Galatia expected Paul still to preach what they believed him to have preached all along. They expected him still to acknowledge the leaders who had authorized him all along. It was Paul who raised the temperature of the debate. From then on his mission had to be his own, or it would fail.

For all his independence, Paul would try to rebuild the bridge between himself and the leaders in Jerusalem. In his later letters, we shall see, he is drumming up support for the collection he plans to take to Jerusalem for the benefit of the assembly there. This was, perhaps, the substitute, from his gentile adherents, for the tax paid by all Jews to the Temple. Or it was the tribute that the Gentiles are due, in the last days, to bring to Jerusalem. As ever, old expectations were being revised and old rules redrawn. Paul had to define the relationship of himself and his assemblies to those around them, and he looked naturally enough to the relationships already in place, to adopt or adapt them where he could.

The collection was not a success. Paul was offering tribute, but not allegiance. The needs of the assembly had a call on him; the authority of its leaders, he insisted, did not. He brought the collection on his own terms, and the leaders in Jerusalem would accept it only on theirs. Did he bring the money with him on the visit to Jerusalem that Luke records toward the end of The Mission [Acts]? Almost certainly. But we have no record, from Paul himself or from Luke, of its delivery. We hear from Luke only of conspiracy, danger, and Paul's arrest. Did the assembly's leaders try to protect or rescue Paul? Apparently not. Only Paul's own nephew, in Luke's account, raised a finger to help him.

And the good news according to James? Within a decade of James's death Jerusalem had been besieged and sacked by the Romans, and the Temple had been destroyed. The form of faith for which James lived and died had lost its base. The future lay with the gentile assemblies. But not yet, by any means, with Paul. His good news was as radical in one direction as James's was in the other. His vision was too unsettling, the assemblies that pursued it too unstable. Paul's pupils and their successors would have to harness and direct the energy and the hopes that Paul himself had stirred to life.

Paul and James were both killed in the 60s. It would take a generation (and a deep struggle within the assemblies of the second century C.E.) to bring his good news back into the bloodstream of the church. And by then both the vision that had dazzled Paul and his call to represent its content here on earth were long since lost from view.

PART VII

PAUL AND CORINTH

CHAPTER 16

THE NEW CREATION

Baptism: "Take Off the Old Humanity, Put on the New"

In one breath we have all been baptized into one body,
whether Jews or Greeks,
whether slaves or free,
and we have all been given one breath to drink.

· 1 CORINTHIANS 12:13

WHEN WE READ PAUL'S LETTERS we are like airplane passengers in the window seats gazing down at the view as the shuttle circles the city and prepares to land. We see the layout of the streets, the landmark buildings, the diminutive cars. We get a good sense of the city's shape, areas, and age. But the view from two thousand feet is no substitute for an hour spent down there on the sidewalk or in a cab.

We are trying in this book to walk through Paul's letters at ground level. We have heard him alluding over and over to the teachings he relayed and the rituals he introduced in his time among his addressees. We will keep our eyes open for such allusions to ritual, for rituals matter. They solemnize and represent the community's sense of itself, its internal structure, and its relation to the world outside and to God. (Rituals often do so in a clumsy and outdated form, dominated by a small controlling caste or faction that uses them to validate and perpetuate its own prestige. Such a faction may well have created or controlled all the major records—in particular, all the texts and monuments—to reach us from a community. And we can then be hardpressed to hear how that community's other members saw its life and their part in it.)

No ritual was more important than baptism. Paul, as we saw in Chapter 15, could invoke one of its great formulas when writing to the Galatians. A close follower of Paul will later write to the Colossians in Paul's name. The letter is steeped in baptismal language.

> If you have been raised with the Anointed, look for the things above, where the Anointed is, seated at the right hand of God. Think of the things above, not of the things on earth. For you have died, and your life is hidden with the Anointed in God. When the Anointed is made known, who is your life, then will you too be made known with him in glory.
>
> COLOSSIANS 3:1-4

The Colossians have died, and yet still have parts of their earthly life to put to death. Our author is drawing heavily on the thought of his master, Paul. How easily the ritual becomes just that and no more, actions and words that fire a first flush of enthusiasm and then leave the lifestyle, standards, and outlook of the baptized just as they were before.

The Colossians hear:

> So put to death the limbs that are on the earth: unlawful sex, uncleanness, passion, evil desire, and greed, which is idolatry—on account of these the wrath of God is coming, and in these you once walked, when you lived in them.
>
> COLOSSIANS 3:5-7

The echoes of baptism grow clearer. Candidates would take off their old garments and after their baptism be clothed with new. From nakedness to new clothes—the newly baptized were born again.

> But now you too, put them aside, all of them: wrath, anger . . . having taken off the old humanity with its practices and having put on the new,

the humanity that is being renewed into knowledge according to the image
of its creator.

COLOSSIANS 3:8–10

Jesus' pupils in the *Gospel of Thomas* ask when Jesus will be revealed to them. "When you take off your clothing," he replies, "without being ashamed [or, when you take off your shame], and take your clothes and put them under your feet" (*Gos. Thom.* 37).These are clothes of Adam and Eve, given them after the Fall when they knew they were naked and were ashamed. God gave them *robes of skin* to wear (The Beginning [Genesis] 3:21). This, some thought, was their flesh. Now for the first time they were flesh and blood, as their descendants would be, for they had lost the glory of God, which had been, before the Fall, their robe of light.

Such imagery is fluid: the nakedness of infants, their innocence and their first clothing; the clothing of our skin, perhaps to be taken off, and its glorious counterpart, certainly to be put on. Paul will make good use of these images when he writes to the Corinthians. To be naked, even symbolically, and unashamed was to be once more as Adam and Eve had been before the Fall. The image of God was restored. No wonder the newly baptized would be clothed in the white of purity and glory, a new clothing that was both a new skin and a covering for their old wrongdoings. "When we are ready for the garment of the Anointed," writes Jerome toward the end of the fourth century, "and we have taken off the tunics of skin, then we shall be clothed with a garment of linen which has nothing of death in it, but is wholly white, so that, rising from baptism, we may gird our loins in truth and the entire shame of our past wrongdoings may be covered" (*Letter to Fabiola* 19).

To take off such clothes of flesh was to be returned to the innocence of Eden. But to take off the flesh was also to die, to leave behind the flesh and blood of human life. Described in these terms, the return to Eden was inseparable from death. *Do you not know that all of us who have been baptized into Anointed Jesus have been baptized into his death?* (Rom. 6:3).

At baptism the candidate is on the threshold between two states. Such rites of passage are well known. Baptism, however, is a rite stranger than most. Once across this threshold itself, the person baptized is on a threshold still, on a vast plateau between two worlds on which he or she remains until death or Jesus' return. And however high the rhetoric of a new creation may be, the world outside us and within us is intractably as it was before. Here is the halfway house of a community that enjoys the first—but only the first—of the blessings that will be showered upon its members at their Lord's return.

In the return to the state of Eden all those divisions that followed the Fall are undone. To bring his passage to a climax, our author reminds the Colossians of the acclamation they will have heard at their baptism:

> Here there exists no Greek and Jew,
> circumcision and uncircumcision,
> barbarian, Scythian,
> slave, free,
> but as all things and in all—is Anointed.
>
> COLOSSIANS 3:11

We have heard Paul himself, writing to the Galatians, invoke such a formula; writing to the Corinthians, he does so again.

All those distinctions are undone. And what in the life of the assembly and its members did this change? Were all such distinctions erased? Could women, slaves and unhellenized "natives" readily and on their own account become full members of the assembly, lead worship, and wield social, economic, and political power? Then the assembly was new indeed. Or did these old distinctions still define, in practice, the assembly's social and political life?

No Jew nor Greek, Paul himself told the Galatians, invoking just such a formula as our author to the Colossians uses. This was a fundamental change. Paul carried on: *no slave nor free* either, and *no male and female* (3:28). Two more changes, no less radical than the first. How much difference to the social order did these additional alterations make?

When Paul writes to the Corinthians about marriage, in 1 Corinthians 7, he sets up—with great care—an equality of regard between men and women. Its scope is important, but limited: any restraint from sex is to be undertaken as a shared decision. His principle in these last times is clear: the Corinthians do best to stay as they are, to undertake no divorce and no new marriage. To reinforce his point, he broadens his discussion. First he moves to circumcision, then to slavery. From male and female to Jew and Gentile, slave and free—Paul clearly has an eye once more on that same baptismal formula. If you were circumcised, he says, when you were called, make no attempt to reverse or disguise it; if you were not, remain uncircumcised (7:18). And then for slavery: *You were called as a slave? Make it no concern of yours. But if you are actually able to become free, choose rather to make use of your slavery. For those called in the Lord when they are slaves are freedmen of the Lord; similarly those called when they are free are slaves of Anointed* (7:21–22).

How different Paul's perspective is from ours. He sees before his assemblies a short interval before the Lord's return. A few years may pass, perhaps a couple of decades, no more. Paul himself expects to witness the coming of the Anointed. And his task, meanwhile, is to ensure that his converts keep their attention on the Lord until the Lord comes and so stand blameless before him when he does. Paul calls only for those changes that will help the converts do so. Between Jew and Gentile, the ritual and social distinctions are to be erased. Between husband and wife, relations are to become more nearly reciprocal. Between slave and master, the boundaries are to be left unchanged.

Paul's viewpoint was not the Corinthians'. Some at least were dissatisfied with his ambiguous conservatism. Paul heard a summons to radical social change in that favored slogan *No Jew nor Greek.* There were women in Corinth who heard just such a call in the slogan *No male and female,* for here as well was a change integral to God's action in the Anointed. But what old activities and relations were to be given up? What new things in their daily lives were to be done? Once more we find the early assemblies finding their way toward, into, and through new life. The exact forms of this life and their significance are not laid down in advance. Paul is thinking hard and fast, but he is not alone. His converts are thinking too. They too are part of this new life. They are seeking to understand it with Paul's terms and to symbolize it in his rituals. In their hands the terms and symbols take on new meaning and open new possibilities.

The results are not what Paul had intended at all.

IT WAS NOT JUST PAUL'S ASSEMBLIES, on the ground, that refined and developed his good news. As Paul and his pupils themselves sent instructions to different assemblies, they saw different needs and met them with different emphases. The pupil who wrote to Colossae had learned well from his master, Paul, well enough to tweak that master's teaching and so make it safe and effective for the letter's addressees. Let's hear from Paul on baptism, and then from the letter to the Colossians.

Paul writes to the Romans, *We were buried together with him through baptism into death* [almost with the force of *that baptism, that death*], *so that just as Anointed was raised from the dead through the glory of the father— so we too might walk in newness of life* (6:4). A new life that is ours already, in part. We are on the threshold between the earthly life of our past and the full newness of life that awaits us. Some Romans, enthused by confidence in God's grace, had thrown off all restraint; others were all too aware of the persecution here and now that threatened them. Paul must show himself, to both groups, alert to the gap between their present life and its promised fulfillment at the Lord's return. The light of day one has shone again, but the darkness is still around us.

How dark that darkness could still seem. Paul's assembly in Colossae finds it quite threatening. The Colossians are in danger of lapsing because they cannot see or credit at all the triumph of the Anointed spoken of by Paul. A pupil of Paul writes to reassure the converts that the powers they had formerly revered or feared had been wholly overcome by the Anointed. Jesus' victory really was complete already, and so was the victory of his followers.

The author turns baptism into a new circumcision that renders quite redundant the old. Skin is cut off in circumcision; the skin of corrupt flesh is stripped off in baptism. The Anointed put off the body of flesh at his burial; his followers put it off at their burial with him in baptism. And so in the rising of the Anointed his followers have been already brought to life. The author almost smothers his images in each other.

> *In him you were also circumcised with a circumcision not wrought by*
>   *hands*
> *in the putting off of the body of flesh,*
> *in the circumcision of the Anointed,*
> *having been buried together with him in baptism,*
> *in whom you have also been roused together with him*
> *through faith in the working of God*
> *who roused him from the dead.*

And you, being dead in your transgressions and uncircumcision of the
   flesh—
he has made you alive together with him,
having forgiven us all our transgressions.

COLOSSIANS 2:11-13

But what constitutes, here on earth, this new life with the Anointed, perfectly attained? The author cannot claim for his addressees what their own experience in this messy, imperfect world so starkly denies, so he talks of hiddenness. *You have died,* he says, *and your life is hidden with the Anointed in God* (3:3). They have the life they long for. Those around them, of course, cannot yet see it. But can even the converts see it themselves? Or must they themselves find confidence for the present in the great promise for their future? *When the Anointed is made known, who is your life, then will you too be revealed with him in glory* (3:4). The Colossians' new life is hidden even from each other and themselves.

Life in Corinth

RICH AND POOR

Time was when scholars of Paul wrote only about his thought and, in particular, about his theology. This was imagined as a solar system of insights revolving in a complex pattern around a single brilliant star. Two tasks were clear: to see more closely into that star itself and to understand its influence on the orbits of its planets and their moons. We know now that thought such as Paul's—and in Paul's case, such strange experience—should be set within the context in which it has grown. Almost all thought is more heavily influenced by the world around the thinkers than the thinkers themselves can see; it is observers, often long after the event, whose viewpoint takes in more of the landscape as a whole. And so on down the centuries. As we look back on the scholarship of the past, we can see such influence from the surrounding world at work on the theologians who have studied Paul. It was at work on Paul himself as well.

And not just influence from other philosophies or schools of thought. Over the last thirty years scholars have been looking with ever greater care at the social and economic factors of Paul's mission, at the part these factors played in his own life, in his converts' lives, and in the converts' needs and hopes that were met by membership in an assembly. If we can once envisage life in a Greco-Roman city, we can see what made Paul's good news attractive to different people—what needs or aspirations he satisfied, what fears he allayed, what hopes he offered. We can find, on page after page, aspects of such life illumined in 1 Corinthians.

Paul probably reached Corinth in the spring of 50. He was still in good standing with Antioch and Jerusalem, an energetic and valued emissary. (The Jerusalem council did not take place until the autumn of 51.) Corinth was a city in a hurry. It drew migrants as San Francisco drew prospectors during the Gold Rush. Corinth lay at the eastern end of the isthmus that nearly divides Greece in two. It was far quicker and safer to trade through Corinth (and even to haul a boat over the isthmus) than to sail round the Peloponnese. With the ships from east and west and land trade from north and south, there was money to be made in Corinth—and money to be lost. Corinth was a hub of trade; it would become a hub of Paul's mission too. A large transient population of travelers and migrants was hugely expanded every other year by the crowds that came to the Isthmian Games. (Paul himself was probably in the city for the games of 51.) New arrivals to the city could look for the familiar cults they knew from home, or they could find security in a cult as strange to them as they were themselves to Corinth. And those who had lived there for decades or generations? They knew as well as any in the ancient world the possible ups and downs of economic and social standing.

In Thessalonica Paul attracted the poor. In Corinth he found—and had likely looked for—a core of richer and more powerful followers. He will frame his closing greetings in the letter to the Romans with references to the assembly from which he is writing in Corinth (Rom. 16:1, 23). Here are valuable clues to the patronage upon which his assembly relied. Paul's letter reaches Rome with Phoebe. She is one of the first church officials of whom we ever hear, a *deacon* in the assembly of Corinth's harbor town of Cenchreae. She has been a patron to Paul *and many others;* she may well have been responsible for hospitality to Christians passing through the busy, cosmopolitan Corinth. She is clearly a woman of some wealth, with the reasons and wherewithal to visit Rome.

Gaius is another key figure; he is described as *host to the whole Corinthian assembly*. It is a telling description. When the whole congregation gathered (perhaps only occasionally) it was in the house of a single prosperous member. Numbers were still small; the home of a rich family could accommodate thirty to fifty people for a meal. Paul recalled at the letter's start that he had baptized hardly anyone in Corinth himself—except Crispus and Gaius (1 Cor. 1:14). It may be no coincidence that Paul himself had baptized such a prominent figure.

And who was Crispus? According to Luke, Paul started by preaching in the prayer house. The Jews there turned against him. So he moved from the prayer house to a house next door belonging to a God-fearer named Titius Justus. And *Crispus, leader of the prayer house, became a believer in the Lord with his whole household* (The Mission [Acts] 18:8). Here is the Crispus that sent his greetings from Paul to Rome. This was an important conversion, of a man of stature. And once more Paul did the baptizing. (A small prayer house would have only one "leader" to organize the worship. The prayer house in Corinth may well, in the course of time, have needed more.) While our eyes are on this short passage, we might well be struck by the Latin name Titius Justus. Titius was likely a genuine Roman, from the dominant class descended from the colonists established in the city when Julius Caesar refounded it in 44 B.C.E. He could open a good many doors for Paul. How striking that he lived next to the prayer house. (Which came first, we might wonder, his house there or his reverence for the Jews' God?)

We are not at the end yet of Paul's wealthy associates. Greetings came to Rome too from Erastus, *the city treasurer*. This Erastus may well be the subject of a famous inscription from Corinth: a certain Erastus, the city's aedile or financial officer, paved a central square in the city at his own expense.

These were people with influence. They would be expected to use it. Within the assemblies themselves we have already glimpsed the need for organization. Who took control? Who, in Paul's absence, was steering the progress of this community? How did Paul keep—or attempt to keep—his converts true to the faith and life they had embraced? We must wonder how many reins were gathered—and how tightly—into the hands of the wealthiest and most articulate members of the assembly. Paul assumes that 1 Thessalonians will be heard privately by some of its leaders; he urges them to have it read aloud to all the members. We may well wonder if it was a cabal of leaders, representing just one group in Corinth, who sent Paul the letter to which 1 Corinthians is the reply.

To be in charge of the simplest arrangements is to have the opportunity of control. The time and place of any gathering must be organized. Who will have the honor of being its host next week? The stature of a visiting teacher must be assessed and acknowledged. Will he or she be allowed to address the assembly? Discipline must be imposed or relaxed. Does the belief or lifestyle of a member call for his or her public rebuke and humiliation? Money must be guarded and accounted for, a serious responsibility if local leaders put their energy—and resources—behind Paul's collection. A letter will reach Paul only if a slave has been paid to write it and a messenger been given the means to deliver it—and only if those who are paying have endorsed its questions, information, and tone.

The rich had influence inside the assembly and beyond it too. There were codes governing the generosity of rich to rich and of rich to poor. To be generous was to be honorable, and such generosity had to be returned in kind (by those who could afford it) or by forms of service or loyalty (by those who could not). Humility about such links, on either side, was not a virtue. We know how much respect we seek from others and how badly a disgrace or insult hurts. Such dignity was even more important then than now. The rich were the patrons of the poor, who honored them for it and who brought them dignity in the eyes of their peers. The poor were dependents of the rich and won honor from the connection. A patron of high standing had access to patrons of a standing higher still. Through the help of their patron, clients could win access to a figure way beyond their own rung on the ladder of wealth and power.

Paul cut a strange figure here. He knew his need of rich converts, for the use of their homes and their contacts in other cities. But he would take no payment from them; he must be the protégé of no single household. He would rather work for a living; and in Corinth, hub of all the maritime trade in Greece and home to the Isthmian Games, there was work enough and more for a maker of sails and tents. Paul, then, worked as an artisan. According to Luke, he could devote all his time to preaching only when Silas and Timothy reached Corinth from Macedonia. They likely brought money with them, so that Paul could give up his manual labor. Here, then, was none of the dignity that a professional orator or paid philosopher could command for himself and offer to his entourage. And Paul's speaking matched his standing. Paul himself insists he relied on none of the eloquence that could captivate listeners and attract them to his school.

Paul does himself too little justice—and too much. We must look more closely at his assembly, at him, and at the power he wields among his converts.

Raising Hopes, Meeting Needs

The new cult of the Anointed offered security by offering a life, here and now, that was at its heart the life to come. Paul hoped by such good news to insulate his assembly from the search for standing in which its members lived their daily lives. He would soon be disappointed. His converts should be taking the ideals of the assembly into their daily life. They brought, instead, the expectations of their daily life into the gatherings of the assembly.

We can still see, all these years later, why Paul's good news attracted some Corinthians. Some at least of Paul's initiates were given extraordinary powers: to heal, to prophesy, to speak—as it seemed—in the language of angels. And none of these gifts, as far as we know, was graded to match the social or economic prestige of its recipients. Such gifts brought high standing in the assembly. This standing did not depend on Paul's say-so to the poor or his influence on the rich. It was apparent to all, at any meeting where the gifts were in use. A rich patron might still try to treat the assembly as his private entourage, but prophets, there in action, had an authority of their own.

Were all gradations in status at an end, then, between different members of the assembly? No. The old ladder had been thrown away; but a new ladder was soon propped up against the wall. We shall hear more of the tensions aroused by these new criteria of dignity and value. Paul speaks of the Corinthian assembly as a body, an articulated unity, for he must warn against the independence that some gifted members clearly feel. These men and women are not seeking power within the assembly. They simply think of themselves as free from any officers or control that the assembly might try to impose on them. First, then, Paul must reintegrate these free spirits into the assembly. He turns next to consider those members who are held in least honor by their peers, for the more gifted, once reestablished within the assembly, will look down on their less obviously gifted fellows (1 Cor. 12:12–31).

These new criteria of dignity and value caused trouble enough. And they would soon clash with the old. We do not know what power was exercised, in Paul's absence, by the recipients of what gifts. Once more the question arises: Who was running the administration? Letters were being written, messengers were traveling to and fro. Authority was being exercised and delegated. We would expect the best educated— and so, in general, the wealthiest—members of the assembly to have risen to a high proportion of positions of executive power. When looking back at his time in Corinth, Paul recalled one other household that he had baptized himself, which we have not yet mentioned, the household of Stephanas. Stephanas was one of those who brought to Ephesus the Corinthians' own letter, to which (in part) 1 Corinthians is Paul's reply. The correspondence itself is a small part in the exchange between Paul and his converts of information, advice, instruction, and encouragement. To be on the delegation to Paul is to have significant power, interpreting the assembly to Paul and Paul to the assembly.

At the letter's end Paul writes defensively in praise of Stephanas's household: *It is the firstfruits of Greece and they have set themselves to the service of the saints. You too be subject to such people and to everyone who shares in the work and who labors* (16:15–16). No great gift is ascribed to Stephanas. What has he brought to the assembly that its members should be subordinate to him? We are likely looking at a wealthy family. (Once more, Paul himself had baptized this prestigious figure.) Stephanas's leadership, however, is clearly not secure. The Corinthians have a higher regard for the gifts that Paul himself has encouraged them to value. Paul must speak up for his allies who have brought to the assembly nothing but their wealth.

The rich Stephanas may have hindered his own cause. Like Phoebe,

Gaius, Crispus, and Erastus, he lived a privileged life. The rich had ready access to the city's courts of law and to the ear of the magistrates; their high standing, when they appeared, was at least as important as the strength of their case. In the homes of the rich, spacious then as now, the hosts and their own friends could eat in the dining room, while their dependents ate in the more public areas of the house.

Scholars have seen whole sections of 1 Corinthians come to life in such a setting. Some of Paul's addressees had been going to the city's courts—an expensive business—for decisions against other members of the assembly. Surely it was the rich, of high standing and many resources, who had been taking the poor to court. Again, there had been a scandalous division at the assembly's meetings: some went hungry, while others actually got drunk. Surely the rich hosts had been entertaining their friends royally in the dining room and sending out to their poorer dependents such food as was left. This was no way to win the love or loyalty of charismatics who gauged themselves and those around them by quite different standards.

Members of the assembly had converted from paganism, yes. They had taken on standards and aspirations quite alien to the pagan world, but they were still enmeshed in a lifetime's allegiance to their former values. Some converts maintained these values and their conventions unchanged. Others applied them in new ways, grading new gifts for their rank and dignity. It was easier to declare an allegiance to the new faith than to recognize and satisfy all its implications.

We should not be surprised. Social and economic pressures affect us all in ways we hardly recognize. And did they affect Paul? He is normally spared the analysis to which his converts are subjected. He is presented as a keen-eyed analyst of the economic and social tensions that his converts face, as the one person who spots, confronts, and overcomes the dangers of patronage, status, and competition. He is seen as being always one step ahead of the game. He knows how to use patronage within an assembly without being bound to its few wealthy patrons and how to make or raise the money to survive without being dependent on one congregation or, worse still, its factions.

But Paul too had his needs. We have met Gaius and Crispus, Stephanas, Erastus, and Phoebe and have seen how Paul picked them out for special treatment. He is glad to call Phoebe his patron. She will deliver his letter to the Romans. It includes a request that they help her; at last he can offer her help in return for the support she has given him. Paul needed benefactors, and he could be a benefactor himself. A benefactor to individuals such as Phoebe, yes, but, more fundamentally, to all his converts.

We will look more closely at Paul's claims and denials. He renounces oratory, but does so in a tour de force of rhetorical skill. He has none of the dignity that the Corinthians would have hoped for, but he has powers himself—and has imparted powers to some of them—that almost beggar belief. He brushes aside the competing claims of worldly power and wealth, but he ranks the Corinthians' different endowments from heaven and is himself invested with them all. And above all, he has immediate access to the patron above all patrons—the Anointed, and through him to God himself.

WE HAVE WATCHED PAUL refine the apparent claims of the great baptismal formula. How little in his assemblies seems to have changed in the relations between the slaves and the free, between men and women. Perhaps these social relations seemed too superficial to matter; God was creating anew the inner person, not the assembly—let alone the society as a whole—of which the individual was a member. Or perhaps such relations were to be changed precisely from within, through the reformation of individuals. It was not the structures that needed to be changed, but the individuals who lived within them. And in this way would God transform the world.

Or perhaps—by contrast—with all such explanations we are simply making excuses for Paul. To satisfy the claims and the demands of the baptismal formula would cause trouble—trouble with the assembly's wealthy members, trouble with the heads of families, trouble in married life, trouble at worship. And to what end? There were higher priorities in the climactic crisis of the world than any unlikely benefit such disruption could bring. Few of us can sustain for long any wish or work to transform the structures of power that in their present form make possible our daily lives. Not many of us can even see the need to do so. And so Paul himself did not see—as at our distance we can—how his work for the new order was made possible by his collusion with the old.

Paul, Father of His Converts

One ladder of dignity and standing that needs our attention is the ladder that runs up through the generations of a family. At its top is the father of the family, and in the assembly's life that father is Paul.

We have heard of Paul as a father, but not of the power that image evoked in his time. Fatherhood speaks today of a relation far cosier and less hierarchical than it did then. To understand Paul's claims we must see his converts' father as a father was seen then—as a figure of untrammeled authority within his family.

Before looking briefly at the laws governing such authority, a couple of caveats are in order. First, the next few paragraphs do not do justice to the love of fathers for their children in Paul's day. And second, no such comparison between jurisdictions so far apart should be too closely drawn. The distribution of authority was quite differently weighted then; we have state and federal agencies to fill and police the roles that were then within the control of the family—and so of its head. These next paragraphs, then, can be only a corrective to the gentler fatherhood we admire today.

Aristotle in the fourth century B.C.E. spoke of the "household monarchy" and called parental power "kingly rule." "To be a son," wrote Epictetus, "is to regard all of one's possessions as the property of the father, to obey the father in all things, never to blame him before anyone, to support him with all one's power." Greek has two words for "domination." At the risk of drawing the distinction too sharply, a "lord," *kurios,* exercises lawful authority over his subjects; this is the title that the Old Order's Greek version uses for God when speaking of "the Lord." A "master," by contrast, owns his slaves as objects. From this second word, *despotes,* stems our "despot." The head of a Greek family is normally "lord," but the Jewish philosopher Philo can insist that parents are even "masters" to their children as well as instructors, benefactors, and rulers.

With the spread of Roman power, Roman law spread too. Paul's Corinthian children knew well of the overriding authority that Roman law gave to the "family father." The Roman family included husband and wife, children and adopted children, and the household's present

and former slaves. (A slave who was set free by the family father continued to owe him well-defined forms of obedience.) The family was the
property of the family father. When slaves were freed or children
adopted, the formalities were those for conveying or claiming property.
The family father decided whether an infant within the household
would be reared or exposed to die; the exposure of sick or unwanted
children was finally declared illegal under the emperor Valentinian in
374 C.E., but continued nonetheless. According to law, a father could
sell, imprison, or even kill his children. In 62 B.C.E., in the conspiracy
of Catiline, a son was put to death by the simple command of his father.

Children could get married only with the permission of the family
father, and a married daughter remained under her father's authority
until he died or formally passed her to her husband's domain. As the
members of the family were seen as the family father's property, so was
all the family's wealth. Children could not own property in their own
right or make a will. The device of a personal fund for sons allowed
them the management of property; but that property remained the
father's. If a son or slave committed a crime, the action was brought
against the family father; he had the choice of either paying the penalty
or handing over the offender to the complainant.

"Among bolder spirits," says Philo, "some who want to glorify the
name of 'parents' say that a father and a mother are in fact gods made
visible, copying as they do the Uncreated in his framing of life. Is it
objected that he is the God of the universe, while they only of those
they have begotten? Well, it would be absurd for the invisible God to
be revered by those who are irreverent to those who are visible and near
at hand" (*On the Ten Commandments* 120).

When we hear Paul address his children, we should certainly hear
the voice of love. But just as clearly we should also hear the voice of
command.

A WORLD FULL OF GODS

Paul is guiding his Corinthian converts in the ways of their new faith in
a hard-nosed commercial city that knew little and cared less about this
new assembly and its strange ideals. Not that the city was, in our terms,

secular. Far from it. The ancient world was full of gods. They protected the home and all who lived there, the workplace and the prosperity of all who worked there. They united all the members of a single trade, neighborhood, city, or race. Their images were everywhere, visible reminders of the powers enlivening, sustaining, providing, and controlling all there was. These were the great powers that had watched over the nation for generations, the city since its foundation, the land from the dawn of time. Around these hovered the lesser powers: the family's own forebears; the city's own heroes; the local powers of hearth or larder, of river, trees, or healthy crops.

Domestic, social, professional, civic, and political life all had their representatives within the network of divine powers. And all were closely linked. Paganism was not by its nature childish or naïve. In some minds it was sophisticated and nuanced; in others, simplistic and crude. But at both extremes and at all points in between, its adherents had the opportunity to recognize how many were the powers around and within us and how complex were the relations between them.

Paganism was also public, displayed in statues, shrines, and temples, in the sacrifices and processions of civic celebrations. Even the most secret cults had their public face. We will be hearing more of the cult of the goddess Isis, one among many "mystery" religions whose chief rites were kept secret from all but its initiates, members of the goddess's cult. Just outside Corinth each spring the cult held a grand and public procession. It was more than a show; the rite solemnized the start of the sailing season on which all Corinth depended. An author, Apuleius, whom we shall meet again, describes the pageant in glorious detail: the main characters in gleaming white and festooned with flowers, others in costumes and fancy dress; statues, images, and symbols of the gods; music from instruments and a choir; scents sprinkled on the streets. This was a celebration for initiates and a carnival for the crowds.

Scholars have long sought in Paul's thought a direct dependence on the "rebirth" apparently offered to devotees of the mystery gods, and among them to the devotees of Isis, at their initiation. More important than any debt, however, was mere similarity. According to Apuleius, membership in Isis's cult was expensive, beyond the means—and probably the social standing—of most of those who heard Paul speak. But here was Paul, offering to just such people, without crippling cost or the restraints of snobbery, a "mystery" that offered to initiates a new life in a new creation. And Paul was offering it to men and women, to the free-born, to past and to present slaves—to all alike. If Apuleius is not misleading, the cult of Isis was the preserve of their patrons and local grandees. The city's tradesmen, artisans, and laborers knew as much. But here was Paul offering no less—and perhaps far more—to them.

Isis was known and revered throughout the empire. Surrounding Corinth were also local, long-established powers, familiar to everyone in the city; some residents would have experienced their effects for themselves. Across the Gulf of Corinth lay Mt. Parnassus, home of the winter rituals of the "maenads." These followers of the god Dionysus celebrated his coming with wild rites and ecstasy. They used the same word for the god's "coming" that Christian emissaries used to speak of Jesus' coming in power.

Dionysus did not have Parnassus to himself. On its slopes was Delphi, famous throughout the ancient world for its prophetic oracle of Apollo. The oracle's sanctity could be ascribed to the presence there of a breath or breaths. According to Luke, this breath could be active elsewhere too. He tells how Paul met a girl, way north in Macedonia, who had powers of divination or ventriloquy (The Mission 16:16). Luke says she had a *breath, Python,* a breath, that is, linked with Delphi, where Apollo killed the snake Python and where his priestess was known as "the Pythian." No wonder Paul's converts in Corinth—more vividly, it seems, than in any other city—saw the life that Paul offered as life inspired by a god.

This was a world well used to describing, in myriad ways, the presence or activity of a godly power. Paul was not coming to a city that had no ways to understand his good news, but to one that had too many.

PAUL, LUKE TELLS US, spent eighteen months in Corinth on his first visit. It was the start of a tumultuous relationship. He left in the late summer of 51. We will hear, in the pages to come, of the preacher and philosopher Apollos, who reached the city by summer 52 with an endorsement from Paul's own allies in Ephesus, chief among them the Aquila and Prisca, who were well known to the Corinthians. Preachers from Peter in Jerusalem came too who were far less sympathetic to Paul and suspicious of his good news. *There must be divisions among you,* Paul tells the Corinthians, *so that those who reckon aright may be clear among you* (1 Cor. 11:19). But divisions became factions, and a single assembly became a cauldron of ill temper, suspicion, and malice.

Paul kept in touch by means of a letter, now lost, that he likely wrote in 52. But apart from that he left them and their local leaders alone, it seems, for over two years. It was a mistake. By the time he was once more involved, disputes were deeply set over authority and the good news itself. In spring 54 the staff of a businesswoman, Chloe, returned from Corinth to Ephesus. They brought bad news. Paul sent Timothy to investigate and report back. In his absence a delegation arrived from Corinth itself, with a letter from the assembly. How interesting. In the turmoil of division the local leaders secured agreement on this at least, that the assembly would ask the advice of Paul himself on the practical questions that were under dispute. Who made that decision? A gathering in which Paul's supporters could muster a majority? The assembly's leaders, still his own appointees? Or just those leaders and members—perhaps a minority by now—who took it upon themselves to ask their father in the faith? If Paul himself could not visit, at least they could get a letter from him, a counterweight to Peter's allies and the growing influence of their supporters.

In the two letters that we have from Paul to the Corinthians we are eavesdropping on a long and topsy-turvy correspondence. Paul replies to the Corinthians' letter in our 1 Corinthians. After that Paul likely paid another brief visit before writing another—and highly fraught— letter, which is again lost. Then followed two more letters; one of them is our 2 Corinthians 1–9 and the other, our 2 Corinthians 10–13. We have, then, just three letters out of six, all from Paul, and none from the Corinthians. And we have none of the interim news that reached him verbally from allies, assistants, and other preachers.

But three letters are better than one. And they are part of a sequence. In 1 Corinthians Paul is clearly taking up questions or claims from the Corinthians' own letter; they in turn were picking up, in that letter, on points that Paul himself had made when he first wrote; and further back still, in that opening letter Paul had been explaining or refining parts of the teaching he himself had offered when with them in Corinth. How indirect this all is; how easily we might misread, in our 1 Corinthians, the reflection of a reflection of a reflection. But we are bound to ask: What can we recapture of that first fervent preaching? What did Paul demand? And what did he offer?

CHAPTER 17

THE LIFE OF ANGELS

"THE TONGUES OF HUMANS AND OF ANGELS"

> *If I speak with the tongues of humans and of angels,*
>   *but have not love—I am become a sounding bronze or ululating*
>   *cymbal.*
> *And if I have prophecy and know all those mysteries and all that*
>   *knowledge*
> *and if I have all that faith so that I move mountains,*
>   *but have not love—I am nothing.*
>   1 CORINTHIANS 13:1-2

SPEAKING WITH *the tongues of angels* is, as the Corinthians themselves believed, exactly what they did. And we know why. Paul promised his converts they would experience in their way what he had experienced in his. Paul the seer had been seized as far as the third heaven. He had seen what the angels see: the court of heaven, the throne itself, and on that throne *the likeness as the appearance of adam.* He had recognized the figure—it was Jesus. Paul had joined the worship of heaven, had heard the mysteries of heaven, and now had knowledge that only heaven could give.

And so would his converts. The good news opened the way to share on earth the worship of heaven and to hear the mysteries of heaven.

Paul's converts, here and now, would be living the life of angels, and never more vividly or completely than when they were at worship.

What, then, are we to make of *the tongues of angels?* In the first century B.C.E. or C.E., probably in Egypt, a new version was composed of the Old Order's book of Job. In it Job himself tells of the causes and consequences of the troubles he underwent with such conspicuous patience. Toward the book's end, perhaps in an addition of the late second century C.E., we hear of Job giving his three daughters their legacy. To each of them he gives a cord or sash, shimmering with fire, for her to wear round her breast. Each puts hers on in turn. The first "took on another heart, no longer minded toward earthly things; but she spoke ecstatically in the angelic dialect, sending up a hymn to God in accord with the hymnic style of the angels." The heart of the second, Kasia, was changed too, and she sang in the dialect of the heavenly rulers and praised God for the creation of the heights. And then the third sang too, this time in the dialect of the cherubim, glorifying the Master of Virtues. The song of the second, we hear, was recorded in "The Hymns of Kasia"; the song of the third in "The Prayers of Cornucopia," clearly an anthology.

Then Job's brother breaks in, in the first-person "I": "After the three had stopped singing, while the Lord was present as was I, the brother of Job, and while the holy angel was also present, I sat near Job. And I heard the magnificent things, while each daughter made explanation to the other. And I wrote out a complete book of most of the content of the hymns." It is an intriguing scene. The inspiration of the daughters was evidence of the Lord's presence. To hear them was to be awed. Their angelic hymns were sung, it seems, extempore; it is not clear what were the "explanations" or notes each daughter was making for the others. Despite their angelic dialects, the songs could still be written down by a listener, even if we are promised only a "trace" of the last, perhaps the poetic rhythm (*Testament of Job* 46–51).

This section of the *Testament of Job* likely reflects practices of the late second century. The Christian sect of Montanists (named after its founder, Montanus) was encouraging ecstatic prophecy. Its opponents asked what precedent could be given from biblical history for such performances. An editor has probably expanded the *Testament* to provide just the precedent required. This is no record of Israel's ancient history, but the vivid self-defense of a sect that valued its own version of the tongues of angels. Now the Montanists drew on the writings of Paul; what they read there helped shape and foster their own experience. We cannot project back from the Montanists into Corinth what the Montanists attained and believed with the help of Paul's Corinthian letters. But the Montanists do give us some clues to what could, under the indirect influence of Paul, be credited and valued as the speech of angels.

And so they help us shine a shaft of light right back to Corinth in the 50s. To speak there with the speech of angels was to have immense prestige. Too much prestige, thought Paul. By the time he writes 1 Corinthians he is talking up the importance of prophecy and playing down the value of tongues.

Angels surrounded the throne of God. So too, as they awaited the final resurrection, did the righteous dead. But mortals, prior to death? Only the seers, a well-trained few, had ever enjoyed such a privilege. Until, that is, Paul the seer invited his converts to share these blessings straightaway. The question soon arose: What effect had death upon converts such as these? They were already, it seemed, emerging from the confines of human life into a new and previously unimaginable knowledge of God. Their worship was already inseparable from the worship enacted in heaven. They were surely "on course" for their final liberation from flesh and its frailty, for a continuous growth into the full enjoyment of a heavenly life that was half theirs already.

PRESENT KINGDOM, FUTURE THRONES

What an extraordinary set of ideas this is for the Corinthians to have held about themselves. We might well ask how they came to it. The answer, in outline, is clear: Paul, shaped through and through by his own experience, had offered a blessing to his converts like the blessing he had received himself. And there was confirmation before their very eyes: Paul had the gifts of healing, prophecy, and tongues. And now members of the assembly had them too.

But surely not for much longer. Not in their present setting. For Paul anticipates once more the return of Jesus. On every page this expectation shapes his teaching. If Jesus is about to appear, for instance, and the judgment to fall, what should the Corinthians do about marriage and its commitments? Paul uses condensed, dramatic terms in his answer. *In view of the imminent* [or even, *of the present*] *distress*, it is best for the Corinthians to stay in their present state (1 Cor. 7:26). *The time is cut short,* says Paul, with a word for "time" or "trigger" that speaks of looming change—the long-awaited moment for God's action (7:29). Paul sums up his recommendations: *Those who are making use of the world, let them be as though they were making no use of it. For the form of this world is passing away* (7:31).

All of history has been building up to this climax. Looking back on Israel's past, Paul can see warnings and examples laid down there precisely to help those who were going to face the dangers and fears of his own time. The Israelites in the desert had been immoral, put God to the test, and grumbled against him; in each case the guilty were killed. *These things happened to them by way of example, and were written down to be a warning to us, on whom the ends of the aeons have come* (10:6, 11). What a status those converts could imagine for themselves who were seeing the world's whole history culminating in their daily lives.

In such a context we can ask again, as we asked about Paul's preaching to the Thessalonians: What had Paul said to his audience, when he was in Corinth, about the rising of the dead? The answer may well be nothing at all. Jesus was on the point of return; his followers would all be alive; he would rescue them from the evils of this present order, protect them from condemnation at God's great assize, and give them their due reward in his kingdom. Jesus had risen from the dead precisely so that they would not need to. They had been brought into the life of angels now; and they would, once Jesus came back to claim his own, enjoy a higher status still. Paul berates them for using outsiders to arbitrate in a dispute between members: *Do you not know that the saints will judge the world? And if in you the world is judged, are you unfit to form the most everyday courts? Do you not know that we shall judge angels—let alone everyday matters?* (6:2–3). To be such judges is to share in Jesus' rule. This still lies ahead. But some of the Corinthians, in this as in so much else, have heard Paul's promises and seen them as fulfilled already. Paul mocks such pretensions: *Oh, you Corinthians are already filled to satiety, you have already become rich, without us you have become kings! How I wish you had become kings, so that we ourselves, as well, might become kings beside you!* (4:8).

Paul has come, Paul has gone, Paul has written. But Jesus has not returned. Some members of the assembly have died. Paul had not prepared his converts for this with any teaching, so they develop some of their own. They believe they have already taken up their kingdom. They are then on a straight path to their thrones in heaven. Those who have died have moved on across the threshold. They are not dead; they are more alive than ever. Why, then, should the dead be roused from their foul graves?

Paul responds only at the climax of his present letter, for here is his foundational claim and the Corinthians' foundational error. The Corinthians are still separated from that future by the return of the Anointed and their own transformation. There is a gulf to be crossed; and unless they see it ahead of them, they may not cross it successfully at all. Why does Paul not point this out straightaway? Because the Corinthians are not ready to hear it. Before he corrects their error Paul must equip the Corinthians with the capacity to make the judgments that its correction will call for. And for that they must relearn, above all, that for the good news they need they are wholly dependent on himself and his instruction.

So how were Paul's converts to live, in these last months or years of the present order? What of their humdrum needs and pleasures and cares?

CELIBATE ANGELS

As for what you wrote, it is good for a man not to touch a woman (1 Cor. 7:1). This has long been a famous line. It appears to set celibacy unambiguously above married life. As we saw in Chapter 8, modern readers have found it easy enough to look behind such a verse for Paul's suppressed sexual urges, but the verse itself calls for more careful reading. The recommendation is now generally read as a quote from the Corinthians' own letter. *As for what you wrote: "It is good for a man not to touch a woman."* This, then, is not Paul's own motto at all.

We may need, however, to turn the screw tighter still. Here is the sequel to that quotation: *But because of* [the danger of] *sexual wrongdoing let each man have his own wife and each woman have her own husband. To his wife let the husband give what is due, and similarly the wife too to her husband. The wife is not in charge of her own body, but her husband is. And similarly the husband too is not in charge of his body, but his wife is* (7:2–4). If they are to deny each other, it is to be by agreement and for a period of prayer, so that Satan should not tempt them by the urgency of their desire. *I say this as a concession, not as an order. And I wish that all humanity were just as I myself am; but each has their own gift from God, some in this way, others in that* (7:6–7).

Paul does not rebut that opening motto of the Corinthians. Far from it. He refines it with a concession to his converts' weakness, that is all. Where did the Corinthians get the motto from that they should be citing it to Paul? Perhaps, of course, from other emissaries: from Peter, perhaps, or the Apollos of whom we shall hear more in a moment. But the slogan chimes in so closely with Paul's own recommendation, which follows it, that we can be pretty sure the Corinthians learned the slogan from Paul himself. From him, they will have learned as well of the "spiritual marriages" that he addresses in the same chapter: unconsummated unions undertaken with the restraint proper for these last days before the Lord's return.

Why, then, did the Corinthians need to write to remind him of his earlier instruction? Had the restraint proved too difficult to maintain? On the contrary. Paul had taught a rigorously ascetic ethic when in Corinth, but he had likely modified it in the first letter that followed his departure. For some of his converts, however, this would not do. They had followed his first instruction and had carried it through—and had been richly rewarded in the gifts of their new life. Paul had made it as much a promise as a demand, and his ascetic converts had found him in this as good as his word. These gifted ascetics—however few or many they were in the assembly—wanted no weakening in his stance.

Wrote Paul to Corinth: *The sanctuary of God is holy, which you are* (1 Cor. 3:17). No one, whether priest or layperson, could lawfully take any part in the rituals of the Temple without prior sexual abstinence. The assembly is now the Holy of Holies. No wonder some of Paul's converts felt called to celibacy. At least some Qumranites were celibate too; and there too—if the Jewish historian Josephus, writing about the Essene sect, is writing about Qumran—there was an emphasis on prophecy.

There are traces of such sexual renunciation in the gospels too. Matthew's Jesus discusses divorce. Matthew connects his instruction with another saying, one about celibates. It is carefully framed, for it had clearly been contested; Matthew recognizes how abhorrent it would be to those who are not called to celibacy themselves. *"Not everyone,"* says his Jesus, *"receives this word, just those to whom it is given: There are eunuchs who were born that way from their mother's womb; and there are eunuchs who have been made eunuchs by men; and there are eunuchs who have made themselves eunuchs on account of the kingdom of heaven. Those who can receive this, let them receive it"* (19:11–12).

So much for sexual life in this present order, in the gestation of the kingdom. What about such life at its fruition? There was scope here for deep disagreement. Mark—and thanks to him, Matthew and Luke—record Jesus' response to a carefully phrased question. Some Sadducees quizzed Jesus on the rising of the dead. The Sadducees thought any hope for such a resurrection was fantastical. To reduce it to absurdity they imagined a woman married in turn to each of seven brothers; as each died, she married the next. *"At the rising, whose wife shall she be? For all seven had her as wife."* Jesus' answer turns on angels' immortality; they have no need to procreate, and so no need for marriage. Jesus answered his sly Sadducean questioners: *"When they rise from the dead, they shall neither marry nor be given in marriage, but shall be as angels in the heavens"* (Mark 12:18–27).

Angels have no need to marry. Nor, of course, have the Corinthians, for the Anointed would return before any children could grow up or grow old. In the whole chapter on marriage Paul does not mention children. *They shall be as angels in the heavens*—some at least of Paul's converts believe they have this glory well before the rising of the dead.

THE GLORY OF THE ANDROGYNOUS ADAM

We have heard only the opening verses of 1 Corinthians 7. They are the opening salvo in a long chapter of advice on sexual activity and restraint. Paul calls throughout for reciprocity: neither partner should divorce the other. A believing husband married to an unbelieving wife has just the same duties and opportunities as a believing wife married to an unbelieving husband. But better still, an unmarried man can concentrate on pleasing the Lord, a married man must please his wife; an unmarried woman can concentrate on pleasing the Lord, a married woman must please her husband.

Here is Paul establishing equality. In one area of the assembly's life, however, such "equality" had already gone too far. We hear in 1 Corinthians 11 that something in the Corinthians' worship was upsetting Paul. The passage is obscure. Paul could be brisk where he and his addressees knew exactly what he was talking about; at our distance we are left floundering for clues. It is once more possible that Paul is now opposing a practice that he allowed, or even established, when he was in Corinth. We heard something of Paul's argument about this in our Chapters 8 and 9. But we were kneading Paul, then, into a modern mold. Let's follow the contours, this time around, of his own thought and priorities.

Paul speaks here again of men and of women in closely parallel terms. This time, however, it is to draw a distinction. When a man prays or prophesies, he must have his head uncovered; when a woman prays or prophesies, she must have her head covered. In the rituals of the Corinthian assembly, this distinction between the sexes was being erased. Women were dressing their hair as men. To reestablish the distinction, Paul appeals to the God-given order of things: *A man should not have his head covered, being as he is the image and glory of God; and the woman is the glory of man* (11:7).

At the beginning *God created them male and female* (The Beginning [Genesis] 1:27). Paul seeks to recover the true import of the distinction. But it was possible to look or hope for a more radical recovery. The Corinthians know Paul's proclamation of the new Adam and the restoration in the Anointed of all of Adam's long-lost glory. *All of you who have been baptized into Anointed, you have clothed yourselves with Anointed* (Gal. 3:27). Paul's addressees have been baptized. They have been stripped of the clothing of the old Adam, fallen and degenerate. They have been washed clean in baptism and have emerged to be clothed in the garments of the newborn, to mark their renewal in knowledge *according to the image of their creator* (Col. 3:10). They have recovered the glory that belonged to Adam before the Fall. What form does that glory take?

The Jewish philosopher Philo, writing in Alexandria within a few years of Paul, tells of Adam, Eve, and their first sight of each other. "Love follows, it brings together the two divided parts, as it were, of a single creature and fits them together, setting up in each a desire for fellowship with the other in order to generate others like themselves" (*On the Creation of the World* 152). The two divided parts of a single creature—Philo knows the story of androgynous Adam, of the Adam who was both male and female, who contained within one person all that is human. The image of a first androgynous human stems (without any link to the Jewish story of Adam) from the Greek philosopher Plato in the fourth century B.C.E. If we were to read the creation stories in The Beginning as a single narrative, we too would look for a distinction between the two "stages" in the creation of humanity: *God created them male and female* in chapter 1, but in chapter 2 God takes a rib from the sleeping Adam and from it creates Eve (The Beginning 2:21–22). Well after Paul's day the hints of the Old Order and of Plato were combined in some manuscripts (now lost) of the Greek translation of the Old Order: instead of the clause *God created them male and female* these read *God created him*—a single figure—*male and female* (The Beginning 1:27).

As in the beginning of creation, so at the end. Paul's converts believed themselves to be members of the new Adam, his glory restored at this end time to the glory of creation's first days. The distinction between the sexes, perhaps the most basic distinction in human life, was overcome. How were these Corinthians to live out this primordial state for themselves? So much was intractable. The order of the fallen world still dominated the bodies of the converts and the different roles that they had to play as men and women in society. The laws, heavily patriarchal, did not change; nor did patterns of employment and civic power.

But at home? Some Corinthians were clear—they were called to celibacy. And in the assembly? Its times of worship here on earth were the times at which the assembly itself could represent the truth of the new order, for the assembly was the Body of the Anointed in which all the crude distinctions of fallen humanity were brought to nothing. Rituals mattered. And the forms of the assembly's rituals could—and should—embody the truth that the rituals were there to celebrate, including the one that said in the new creation men and women were one. Women were therefore wearing their hair as men did. Women were praying and prophesying in the assemblies too, as men did.

The Corinthians believe themselves to worship in the company of angels. Paul does not deny it. But he and the Corinthians draw very different conclusions from the angels' presence. The Corinthians are looking to live, themselves, as the angels who are with them. Paul finds in the angels' presence every reason for good order and the observance of proprieties. *For this reason the woman ought to have a covering on her head on account of the angels* (11:10).

The Corinthians were not the only followers of Jesus to seek—and in their own minds to find—that primal unity between men and women. The Gnostic *Gospel of Thomas* imagines its restoration:

> Jesus said to his pupils:
> When you make the two one,
> and when you make the inner as the outer and the outer as the
> inner, . . .
> and when you make the male and the female into a single one,
> so that the male will not be male and the female not be female . . .
> then shall you enter the kingdom.
> GOSPEL OF THOMAS 22

A NEW TEACHING FROM A NEW TEACHER brings a new community to life and stirs new powers within that community. The teacher's claims fuel the members' new life. The life itself leads to new claims. These lead in their turn to a life richer still. The members look for words and rituals to do justice to their status, to their present halfway life, to the consummation of that life, and to the relation between them. Borders, as we saw in the Galatian assemblies, are difficult places to inhabit. It is hard even to define the relation between the land left behind and the land that lies ahead, for each country has a language suited to itself and its ways. A new community on the borders must—in a nonorganic, even artificial way—develop hybrid forms and rituals. They will seem to a visitor far stranger than those of any well-established neighbor.

Once the teacher has left, the converts must carry on the search for themselves. Nothing is finalized or set in stone. The converts will almost certainly draw once more upon the old traditions, hopes, and rituals in which they had been brought up and had lived before their conversion, for these bring with them a rich vocabulary of terms and experience. They bring too the warmth of a well-known and well-loved lifestyle. And they ensure some order, both within the community and in its relations to that old, unconverted world that hems it in.

We can, at our distance, look with bemusement at the dreams of a new creation fostered and ritualized in Corinth. We can look, as well, with admiration at the vigor and honesty with which some at least pursued these dreams. They misunderstood Paul, as they filled out the map of the strange borderland they lived in, but they did not misunderstand him by much.

These converts lived an unsettled life on the margins between one life and another. The churches have laid deep foundations on this borderland and have built on it vast monuments to the faith. The churches and their people have settled there. We just belong there now and hardly remember that it is a threshold at all.

And so we too have misunderstood Paul, far more deeply than his converts ever did, who joined, in their assembly, the worship of the angels in heaven.

The Conduits of Power

BAPTISM AND THE BAPTIZERS

"Jesus is cursed" (1 Cor. 12:3) may well have been a slogan current in the Corinthian assembly. It summed up dramatically one view of the Anointed himself and so of his followers too. The earthly Jesus was no concern of theirs. Such converts had a full and consistent view of themselves. The death of Jesus needed no emphasis—still less, how cruel and undignified that death had been. What mattered was the route that his death opened up for his followers, the route, here on earth, to the life and knowledge of heaven. Here was an offer to match or surpass all the offers of all the religious cultures that surrounded the Corinthians. Here was freedom from the turmoil of this brash, hectic, rootless city of

Corinth and access to a world from which that city and every part of its life could be seen afresh.

The power of tongues, prophecy, healing, miracles—how did an individual Corinthian acquire any of these gifts? They were gifts of the Breath. And the Breath was a gift that converts expected to be given at baptism. Paul says, alluding to a baptismal cry:

> You have been washed,
> you have been made holy,
> you have been found just
> in the name of the Lord Jesus Anointed
> and in the Breath of our God.
>
> 1 CORINTHIANS 6:11

Note the climactic recognition in the last line. Given the usual link between baptism and the Breath, it would not be long before a more specific connection was made. On the one hand were the gifts imparted at baptism; on the other, the powers held by the person who conducted that baptism. It was easy to surmise that *any* special gift was channeled through the person who had performed the baptism of the person so gifted. The greater the gifts of the baptizer, the greater the power that could be transmitted to the candidate. Comparisons were made between the different preachers, and judgments were passed.

Here was scope for competitive pride and for factions. The converts were not only assessing each other but their emissaries too, and these included Paul himself. No wonder Paul, as he berates the Corinthians' divisions at the beginning of the letter, distances himself from the act of baptism. He had his own adherents, but he had his detractors too. In one of his few baptisms he had baptized the household of Stephanas; but as we have seen, no great gifts followed. And apart from that one household? *I give thanks that I baptized none of you except Crispus and Gaius, so that* (as Paul now realizes with relief) *no one might say that you had been baptized into my name* (1 Cor. 1:14–15).

The gifts were valued that might publicly and clearly follow baptism; these were signs of the angelic life to which baptism had introduced the baptized person. But a far deeper hope was fostered—that baptism actually guaranteed this new and heavenly life. Toward the end of the letter

Paul is countering the conviction of some Corinthians that *there is no ris-ing of the dead*. They see no need for it; they are, after all, growing into the life of heaven here and now. But if there is no rising, asks Paul, *what will those people do who are being baptized on behalf of the dead? If the dead are simply not roused, why are these actually baptized on their behalf?* (15:29). People were baptized on behalf of the dead so that the dead who had died unbaptized would be given the sight of God that Jesus' living fol-lowers were longing for. Paul does not condemn the practice or the expectation that it would be effective. He just points out here that the practice makes no sense without belief in the rising of the dead. We may again wonder how the Corinthians had been led to the practice in the first place. Almost certainly by the baptismal teaching of Paul.

It is easy for us, at our distance, to patronize Paul's Corinthians. They were, it seems, so clearly deluded and arrogant. They were caught up in the flashy, ruthless style of first-century Corinth. They had failed to reach the heart of Paul's preaching, that all the standards, pride, and aspirations of this world are overthrown in and by Jesus. And only if the converts let these standards be overthrown in themselves, their outlook, and their lives can they play their part in God's plan. Only then can they acquire the wisdom God offers and be transformed as God calls them to be.

And by the end of 1 Corinthians the assembly should be in no doubt of this. But Paul had to write 1 Corinthians precisely as a corrective to resolve the misunderstandings to which his own preaching in Corinth had given rise. The Corinthians may have been wrong about their pas-sage, half completed, through to life in heaven, but they had taken seri-ously only what Paul had promised them. They may have misused and misunderstood the gifts that baptism had brought them, but they had believed only Paul's claims for the ritual and its power.

APOLLOS AND THE BREATH

Luke tells us that Paul stayed in Corinth for eighteen months, long enough, we might think, for him to choose leaders and establish guide-lines that together could maintain a peaceful, united assembly without him. Far from it. Paul and two friends from Corinth, Aquila and his wife, Prisca, probably sailed off to the east, for Ephesus, in the late summer of 51. The great city of Ephesus, on the coast of Asia Minor, was—and, as a site of extraordinary ruins, still is—as impressive and beautiful as any ancient city. It would become the center of Paul's web, the point from which he could keep in touch with east, south, west, and north. On this first occasion, however, he stayed only briefly. He then moved on around the coast to Caesarea or to Antioch and so to the fateful council in Jerusalem. Aquila and Prisca stayed in Ephesus. There, we hear from Luke, they met Apollos, a preacher from Alexandria who was Jewish, highly educated, and already teaching about Jesus *accurately in all details* (The Mission [Acts] 18:25).

Luke's account of Apollos is strange and may be confused, but the upshot, that Apollos wanted to cross over to Greece, is plausible. The believers in Ephesus—and among them, no doubt, Aquila and Prisca—endorsed the plan in Paul's absence. They gave him a letter of recommendation to ensure his acceptance there. He made for Corinth. There he had a dramatic effect. He offered a style and sophistication of teaching that Paul conspicuously lacked. He was an effective orator. He had mastered both Jewish belief and Greek philosophy in the remarkable—and immensely appealing—fusion of the two that flourished in Alexandria. He may only have been explaining, with a philosopher's care, the teaching of Paul that Aquila and Prisca had relayed to him, but he was an experienced teacher already. His preaching took on a momentum of its own, and he won adherents.

We know nothing of Apollos's teaching itself. But from Paul's contemporary Philo we know a great deal about the philosophical Judaism of Alexandria in the first century C.E. By the time Paul writes 1 Corinthians, the Corinthians value just those qualities that Philo praises in the heavenly, as opposed to the earthly, human being. If Apollos shared Philo's milieu, we may well have discovered the stream that fed such philosophical terms into the Corinthians' river. From Paul they have learn to see themselves as living the life of angels. From Apollos they learn how Greek philosophy describes such a state.

These converts are half freed already from the confines of this life. When at last their liberation comes and they see God face-to-face, why should they want or need the body that has weighed them down? "The body," writes Philo, "is wicked and a plotter against the soul and a

corpse and a thing dead forever." Who can see this? Only God and anyone dear to God. "For when the mind soars aloft and is being initiated
into the mysteries of the Lord, it judges the body to be wicked and
hostile. . . . So when, O soul, will you fully realize that you are a
corpse-bearer? Then, when you are perfected and are held worthy of
prizes and crowns. For then you shall be a lover of God, not a lover of
the body" (*Allegorical Interpretation* 3.69–71).

First Paul comes to Corinth, then Apollos and Peter (or his assistants) too. Three different teachers with quite different styles. But each
offers gifts from God that give the converts an authority of their own.
The converts grow in confidence. They compare their teachers. It is
not clear that Paul is the most prestigious. Apollos has all the skills and
education that are fashionable in the Greek world. Peter has the authority of Jesus' own closest follower. The assembly is coming to see itself as
largely independent of Paul. Some at least of its members do not hesi-
tate to stand in judgment over their emissary and founding father. This
is a dangerous presumption. Paul must quell it—as brutally as need be.

1 CORINTHIANS: SHAPE AND PURPOSE

We are about to follow this letter, blow by blow. First Paul undermines
the Corinthians' authority and reasserts his own. They have presumed
to sit in judgment on Apollos and himself. But to undertake such a
divisive assessment betrays, in itself, a lack of the sound judgment that
any assessment needs. If anyone should be assessing and judging, it is
Paul. Paul uses high rhetoric, sarcasm, and dire warnings. By the end of
chapter 4 he expects the Corinthians to be humiliated and scared. He is
ready to use the most powerful weapon in his armory. The Corinthians
have written to him about the ethics of marriage and sex, but they have
not told him about a sexual scandal in their midst. They presume to
judge Paul, yet have failed to act against a crime in their own assembly
that calls for instant judgment. Paul demands the culprit's expulsion
from the assembly. He had condemned the Corinthians near the beginning of the letter as infants, able to digest only the milk of the most
elementary teaching. He has by now reduced them to utter infancy,
wholly dependent on their father.

Paul has swept away the building of their pride and confidence. What he has demolished he will now rebuild. At the start of chapter 7, his tone changes. At issue in the letter's next section are not just the individual cases. What decision should they make here or there? Paul sets out to teach a far more ambitious program—*how* to make such decisions here, there, and for the future. He will not create for the Corinthians a single building, with all its pieces in place and prescribed for ever; he will show them the principles on which to build.

Paul tapers his arguments to his needs. In writing to the Galatians he used the language of opposition, of flesh over against the Breath, because he had to detach his converts from those whom he opposed. But in writing to Corinth he uses the language of unity, of the single body that he is writing to reunite. To the Galatians he insisted that he was their sole authority on earth and was himself answerable to no other. But to the Corinthians he talks of the traditions he has received and passed on to them and of the practices of other assemblies. He had to draw the Galatians out of the orbit of Jerusalem and Antioch. But he had to counter the conviction in Corinth, however few or many held it, that an individual, a small group, or even a single city's assembly is self-sufficient in its progress to God's kingdom.

We expect a letter of Paul's to teach us or persuade us. He has a far more ambitious aim. His addressees are baptized. As a community they are the sanctuary of God, and the Breath of God lives in them; and the body of each individual is a sanctuary of the holy Breath (1 Cor. 3:16; 6:19). But they have fallen short of their calling. Paul will bring them, in and through the reception of his letter, to be by its end what in principle they were at its start, a community of "spiritual" adults enlivened by the Breath. Their gifts were not given for the benefit of their holders, stand-alone heroes of prophecy, tongues, or healing; they were given for the benefit of the community. And they were given within the limits of earthly life, limits that the Corinthians have lost sight of. The Corinthians have misunderstood the function of the Breath and the promise offered in the life it brings. If they are to be filled with the Breath, as they can be, they must learn first what such fullness is *not*. They will learn it from 1 Corinthians, the most dramatic of all the letters that have reached us from Paul.

CHAPTER 18

A TIME TO KNOCK
DOWN . . .

SETTING THE TONE

I give thanks to my God at all times about you, for the grace of God that has been given you in Anointed Jesus: in all ways you have been made rich in him, in all eloquence and in all knowledge; for the testimony of Anointed has been made secure in you, so that you are lacking in no gift of grace as you await the unveiling of our Lord Jesus Anointed; who will secure you to the end, to be faultless on the day of our Lord Jesus. God is faithful, through whom you have been called into partnership with his son Jesus Anointed our Lord.

1 CORINTHIANS 1:4–9

ONCE MORE, IN THE OPENING LINES OF 1 CORINTHIANS, Paul introduces the themes he will pursue; once more he expresses confidence in just those qualities and beliefs of the Corinthians that are causing him most acute concern. He praises his addressees and lulls them. This is what they want to hear. Within a few pages he will turn the tables—all that they have they are using wrongly.

Rich in eloquence and knowledge, lacking in no gift of grace: these are the endowments of which the assembly is immensely proud. Interwoven are the themes of Paul's own preaching. His converts await the unveiling of

Jesus Anointed anytime now. It is Jesus Anointed himself who will keep them blameless until that day comes. God is faithful, through whom they have been called to partnership with—even to have a part in—Jesus Anointed. Paul expresses the confidence in them that they have in themselves.

Such favorite themes will give Paul too the ammunition with which to check his converts' independence. They are not so rich, he will soon tell them with heavy irony, as they think they are. They are still waiting for Jesus' unveiling and have not reached safety yet. Until they do they should take the greatest care, for they are far from faultless now. Yes, God is faithful; but if they maintain a partnership with demons, are they?

We are going to follow the flow of Paul's thought through the early chapters of the letter. We might expect Paul's argument to rise as a wall, each layer of bricks resting and relying on the rows beneath. But a building is static: we can look at one part, at another, at the whole; we can look at the parts in any order and revisit those we have already seen. We need to see that Paul's letters have not just a shape, but a momentum too. We will see him catch up the addressees in the current of his thought and sweep them onward to his destination. They are to think carefully, of course, and to learn. But far more than that, they are to be flattered, awed, impressed, embarrassed, and humbled. Paul will take them in quick succession through broad tranquil waters and through bruising rapids. He links every paragraph as it concludes with its successor; there is no moment at which the addressees can stand back and take stock. The river gathers power as more waters join the stream. The addressees can be soothed one moment, standing steadily and gazing around them, and be swirled off balance the next by a change in the current. They can be heartened by their steady progress as they go with the stream, and be all the more frightened when it sweeps them suddenly into a different course. And the cumulative effect of all this turmoil? Paul's addressees will be unsettled, anxious, and increasingly dependent upon him, upon his teaching, commands, and approval.

We have no sense, as modern readers, of Paul's own presence in his words, when they are read and heard, as words directed precisely at us to praise, mock, exhort, or condemn us. No sense, that is, of the presence of our father, a man who can berate us for being childish, send an older brother to inspire us, reduce us to infancy by his criticism, or exhilarate us by his praise.

For his addressees, by contrast, Paul himself was inescapable. The impression of Paul's *presence* in his letters was not an accident or a by-product of his writing. He speaks of his own coming in the terms he uses of the coming of the Lord, and of his letter's coming in terms of his own. Not that this presence in the letter was a straightforward substitution that we can expect his addressees simply to have recognized and relaxed with.

We will keep an eye on this relation between the person and the letters of Paul. By the time of 2 Corinthians 1–9, the Corinthians have grown dissatisfied with this ersatz arrival of their emissary. They want their father. He promises to come, and then sends a letter promising another, later visit instead. Is he avoiding them? Does he not care, after all? Or does he know how much more effective he is in writing than in person, and so make the most of his letters? By the time he writes 2 Corinthians 10–13 he has to acknowledge such a suspicion (10:7–11). He must defend his authority against detractors and rivals. But once more he does not visit; he sends a letter instead. He declares that he will be as effective in person as he is in his letters—in yet another letter. His currency could have bought him any result he wanted when he wrote 1 Corinthians. But no longer. As time goes by, Paul's person and his letters are both devalued; and they reach their weakest at the very moment he must write 2 Corinthians 10–13 and most urgently needs all the strength he can muster.

"NOT IN PERSUASIVE WORDS OF WISDOM . . ."

And I myself, when I came to you, came in no superiority of speech or of wisdom to announce the mystery of God. For I did not judge it right to know anything among you except Jesus Anointed—and him crucified. And I myself was in weakness and fear and much trembling in my behavior toward you, and my speech and my proclamation were not in persuasive words of wisdom but in the display of breath and of power, so that your faith might not rest on the wisdom of humans but on the power of God.

1 CORINTHIANS 2:1–5

Paul has praised the Corinthians in his greeting for their eloquence and knowledge; so he wins their goodwill and secures a hearing. He has set up his addressees, and he is about to knock them down. They are divided—precisely by their pride in and reliance on that skill and knowledge. The criteria applied by the assembly are shown up for what they are, the standards of this world's praise and dignity. So Paul reminds his converts how he himself has renounced all worldly wisdom and eloquence, for by any worldly standards his good news is insupportable; it is *a stumbling block to the Jews, folly to the Gentiles* (1:23). Paul vindicates that good news, however, in a striking passage, formally and beautifully composed in a series of dazzling contrasts. Let the Corinthians be in no doubt that Paul has at his fingertips all the skills of speaking they take pride in—and more. To the Corinthians such skills are a sign of authority; the spell they cast is a sign of power. But to Paul? They are bagatelle.

It is telling that Luke, when he introduces Apollos, describes him as *eloquent* (The Mission [Acts] 18:24). To master such skills in public speaking was an important part of Greco-Roman education. No wonder they were valued by the "wise" in Corinth. A good speaker has an unnerving power over his or her listeners. Convictions, ideals, and hopes, if forcefully expressed, are infectious. When Apollos made wisdom so appealing, he attracted others to it, just as he should have. When he described and imparted it with dignity and skill, he brought honor to himself and to his followers, just as he should have.

Paul must make it clear that such rhetorical skills are not the qualities needed to proclaim and win acceptance for the good news. And he does so by using them himself. Paul prepares to deny he relied on eloquence in Corinth, in a passage appealingly eloquent:

> *Look back on your call, brothers:*
> *not many were wise after the fashion of the flesh;*
>> *not many were powerful;*
>> *not many were high-born.*
> *But the foolish things of the world—*
> *God chose them to put to shame the wise;*
>> *and the weak things of the world—*
>> *God chose them to put to shame what is powerful;*

> *and the low-born of the world and the things counted as*
> > *nothing—*
> *God chose them, the things that don't exist,*
> > *so that he might deny the things that do,*
> > *so that no flesh should have any boast before God.*
> *And as a gift from him you are yourselves in Anointed Jesus, who*
> > *became wisdom*
> *for us from God: justness and holiness and redemption,*
> > > *so that (as it is written), "Whoever boasts, let them boast in*
> > > *the Lord."*

1 CORINTHIANS 1:26–31

". . . BUT IN THE DISPLAY OF BREATH AND OF POWER"

We have already encountered Paul's various uses of the use the first-person plural, "we." Sometimes he clearly refers with it to himself alone, as a figure of special dignity. Sometimes he refers to himself and all his addressees. And sometimes he uses it ambiguously, perhaps to refer just to himself, perhaps to them too. He describes now the inspiration under which *we speak* (2:6). His primary reference, then, is to himself as preacher. It is he who has access to the truths he describes. But how keen the Corinthians are to associate themselves too with these gifts. They too, after all, have been baptized; they too have the Breath of God. Paul is speaking of gifts that his converts believe themselves to have.

And how do they use these gifts they are so proud of? To pass judgment on each other and on their teachers. The themes of discernment and sound judgment, which Paul dwells on here, are his concern through the rest of the letter. Who has the capacity and the right to assess and pass judgment on whom? The assembly's members are assessing the relative standing of Paul, Peter, and Apollos. As we would expect, they speak in terms of wisdom. Whether thanks to Apollos himself, to Peter, to Corinthian culture, or to a fertile combination of them all, wisdom is in the assembly a term of pride and praise. And its members are claiming a wisdom sufficient to judge the wisdom of the missionaries who brought to Corinth God's wisdom in the first place.

No wonder Paul heads to the central question: Who in this scenario has the real wisdom that comes from God? And how do they have access to this wisdom? Paul has his hand on all the ammunition offered by the poetry of the past. "Who has known your plan," the poet of the Wisdom of Solomon asks God, "if you have not given them wisdom and sent your holy Breath from the heights?" (9:17).

Paul must fend off the claims of those teachers who rely upon their own exclusive access to the secrets of heaven. There are doors that other seers left locked, the keys in their own powerful hands. Paul has opened those doors to his converts. But how many of these converts have walked through? Paul talks strikingly of *the perfect* among whom he speaks wisdom (2:6). Does he, then, have a second and higher set of teachings offered only to a privileged few, teachings higher even than the teaching he has already relayed in Corinth about the Anointed? No. He must teach his addressees the humility to know how much they do not know—and the eagerness to learn it. Then they too will be among the perfect who hear him speak wisdom.

As it is written:

> *What no eye has seen and no ear has heard*
> *and what has never come into the human heart,*
> *what God has prepared for those who love him—*

> *but to us God has unveiled it through the Breath.*
>   1 CORINTHIANS 2:9-10

Here is a route to knowledge entirely within God's gift. Who are the *we* to whom this knowledge has been unveiled? Paul himself; Paul and his assistants; or Paul, his assistants, and the Corinthians? Paul lets the ambiguity stand for now.

All Paul had thought to know when he was in Corinth was *Jesus Anointed and him crucified* (2:2). This is itself the wisdom he speaks, *in a mystery, the wisdom which was hidden, which God ordained before all ages for our glory* (2:7). But this is the good news that is *a stumbling block to the Jews, folly to the Gentiles.* How can it ever be accepted by anyone? At issue is not just what we know, but how we can know it. And the means of knowledge is itself an indispensable object of knowledge—the Breath of God.

> *For the Breath fathoms everything, even the depths of God. For who among humans knows the depths of a person except the Breath of that person, that is within? In the same way for those things of God—no one knows them except the Breath of God. And we ourselves have not received the Breath of the world but the Breath that comes from God, so that we might know the things freely given us by God.*
>
> 1 CORINTHIANS 2:10-12

A long tradition claimed that like knows like. Paul raises the stakes. Self, he maintains, knows self. Paul is exploiting a theory of knowledge familiar throughout the ancient world. But he is using it not to define what makes possible any knowledge held by any human. He is defining what makes possible the knowledge of God for those chosen by God.

As only the individual knows the depths of that individual, so God alone knows God. If we have been given knowledge of God, it is because *the Breath that comes from God* has informed us. It is no accident that Paul speaks of *the depths of God*. The tradition of the seers spoke of those who "descended" to the throne-chariot. *The Breath that comes from God* offers Paul's converts, with no vision or journey, all that a seer could claim to know.

> *These things we speak of as well, not in words taught by human wisdom but in words taught by the breath, interpreting things of the breath in language of the breath* [or *to the people of the breath*]. *But people who live out the life of the human soul do not accept the things of the Breath of God. These are folly to them, for such things are discerned in the realm of the Breath. But those who live by the Breath assess everything, and are themselves assessed by no one.*
>
> 1 CORINTHIANS 2:13-15

Assessed by no one: here's the rub. The Corinthians have been presuming to judge Paul—Corinthians who have no conception of the knowledge that Paul has and they lack, for Paul himself, body and mind, is the re-presentation of the Anointed:

For [as Isaiah asks] *"Who has learned the mind of the Lord, to instruct him?" But we, yes we, have the mind of Anointed.*

1 CORINTHIANS 2:16, QUOTING ISAIAH 40:13, GREEK VERSION

WE HAVE THE MIND OF ANOINTED. Does this *we* include the Corinthians? They would certainly have thought so. They would have been alert, as they listened, with satisfaction. But Paul moves in to the attack. In a sudden shift to the first-person singular, "I," he rounds on their presumption. *And I myself, brothers, was not able to speak to you as to those who live by the Breath* (3:1). On the contrary, they were bound by and to the flesh. They had wanted Paul, when he was with them, to relay to them the very deepest mysteries. They had wanted solid food, but they had been like infants, able to digest only milk. And as then, so now.

To show his converts' incapacity, Paul returns to the factions he condemned near the start. The wisdom and the knowledge on which Paul's converts pride themselves are, they are sure of it, the wisdom and knowledge of heaven, for they are living the lives of angels. They are already slipping off the constraints of earthly life. No one can deny or remove their gifts. They are their own masters. They are surely entitled to assess, compare, and judge the different missionaries who have worked among them. Here, then, the Corinthians' claimed wisdom comes to expression, in this competitive assessment of Paul, Apollo, and Peter.

Paul's response is withering. The Corinthians have disagreed in their assessment. This is hardly surprising; each missionary had his own allies. The disagreements have led to divisions. And the divisions themselves show that the Corinthians have quite failed to understand the character and effect of the wisdom they boast of. Paul is not concerned with the rightness of one faction or the other, but with the divisions themselves. The Corinthians are fit to judge no one—let alone those who have planted and nurtured them in the faith.

TURNING THE TABLES

Where Paul uses humor, it has a bitter taste. Public speakers of his age knew how to flatter their listeners—and how to shame them. Paul turns on the Corinthians with caustic derision. The assembly is divided into factions. Each lays claim to special gifts from God. Where the factions see God-given privilege, Paul sees only arrogance. Any gifts from God are just that: gifts, freely given, for which the Corinthians can claim no credit. Paul reminded them at the start how few of them had been by earthly standards wise, powerful, or well-born. He comes back to the theme. Look how they have left their own emissary behind: he is still foolish, weak, and without dignity; they already have the "wealth" and empire he had promised them. He compares their presumption with his tireless work and the scorn it earns him.

What do you have, each of you, that you did not receive? And if you received it, why do you boast as if you did not? Oh, you Corinthians are already filled to satiety, you have already become rich, without us you have become kings! How I wish you had become kings, so that we ourselves, as well, might become kings beside you! (4:7–8). We might find such sarcasm hard to stomach. It seems so wearing—and, we might suspect, so counterproductive.

The Corinthians, says Paul, are *puffed up.* We need not imagine the whole assembly as his target. Far from it. The more he elaborates, the clearer it will have become to the listeners which group or groups of them he has in mind. Such public humiliation may well bring his targets to heel; it will do nothing to win their hearts and minds in the longer run.

Paul mocks and shames the Corinthians into the humility they should feel. And then, when they are reduced to an embarrassed guilt? *I am not writing to rebuke you but to warn you as my beloved children* (4:14). Paul has changed tone again. He embraces them as their father. They are still loved. He is even sending them, in Timothy, a brother from whom they will do well to learn: *Timothy, who is a beloved child to me and faithful in the Lord, who will remind you of my ways in Anointed, just as I teach everywhere in every assembly* (4:17). The disappointed father sends the steady older brother to the troublesome adolescent siblings who are striving for independence. An effective move, perhaps, but another insult likely, in the longer term, to stir up an angry rebellion.

The father still loves his children. The Corinthians must have needed that assurance. Paul has unsettled everything that his converts thought precious and blessed about themselves. He does not deny them their angelic life. Of course not—it was Paul's good news that had first enthralled them with this offer. But all that it had led them to—all the confidence and new perspective that made a difference to their daily lives—all this has been brought tumbling to the ground. At this stage in the letter their confidence has been dissolved into the frightened dependence of children. They can look only to their father—and to the favored brother Timothy—for guidance and right judgment. And if any of them still presume upon their own gifts, let them beware. *On the basis that I am not coming to you, some of you have got puffed up. But I am coming to you soon, if the Lord wants it so, and it will not be the words I will discover of those who are puffed up, but their power. For the kingdom of God is not a matter of words but of power. Which do you want? Shall I come to you with a rod to chastise you with or with love and a breath of mildness?* (4:18–21).

His listeners are looking ahead with trepidation, yes, but with time to correct the errors that their father has so ferociously exposed. They have breathing space. Or do they? In an extraordinary moment, Paul now catches them off guard. He orders them to expel a wrongdoer from the assembly. The culprit had taken his father's (widowed?) wife as his own. Paul is horrified.

Far more is at stake than this one delinquency. Members of the assembly have been sitting in judgment on Paul, but they have failed to pass any judgment on this flagrant wrongdoing. The leaders have written to Paul to ask or tell him about the rules to follow on sexual morality, but they have failed to mention this glaring moral failure in their midst. Paul knows more about the assembly than they think he knows. They have every reason to be embarrassed. They think so highly of their discernment and its application, but where these are most obviously needed, the Corinthians have failed. It is time for them to relearn their real standing and to follow the instructions of their father without question or qualm.

And you are puffed up? Have you not rather gone into mourning, so that the man who has done this deed might be taken out of the midst of you? I myself, absent in body but present in the Breath, I have already passed judgment on the man who has done this in this way—in the name of the Lord Jesus—when you and my breath have gathered together with the power of our Lord Jesus, hand the person in question over to Satan for the destruction of the flesh, so that his breath may be saved on the day of the Lord.

1 CORINTHIANS 5:2–5

Paul is not as absent as he seems. He has asked mockingly what power have those who are puffed up. When the assembly and his breath are together he leaves no doubt what power he himself can speak with: *the power of our Lord Jesus.* This is already a far cry from the human assize the assembly had mounted when they assessed their missionaries; it is a prelude to the great trial on the day of the Lord. How the Corinthians have been boasting. And how wrongly: *It is not good, this boasting of yours* (5:6).

And the culprit himself—was he present in the assembly when the letter was read aloud? Or had the leaders, when they had heard the letter privately, ensured that he was already at arm's length from the assembly? Either way, Paul is playing for high stakes. If the assembly refuses to obey a command of such solemnity, his position is far weaker than it would have been if he had never made it. But if the assembly does his will, he has in the most vivid and indisputable way regained his authority.

There is an irony in Paul's invoking his presence here and the obedience it calls for. His own absence has given space for this scandal to arise. And yet in that absence lies Paul's most powerful lever to the scandal's resolution. When he is present his power can be tested. It is visibly deployed, yes; but it is visibly open to challenge too and to the danger of failure. But when he invokes his power in a letter? Who is going to challenge the authority he claims and the power with which it invests him? Who will dare deny them? In the boldness of Paul's present demand lies its strength. He is laying claim to a present, ineluctable power. And it is precisely his absence that will protect the demand, if anything can, from challenge by a confused and diffident assembly.

Paul has interpreted the Corinthians' pride and self-assertion as presumption and grounds for shame. If they have been so blind up until now, what confidence can they have to reject or question his present instruction? Paul has laid his ground carefully. He is ready to demand the assembly's unquestioning obedience. This obedience—and at such a distance, with no means of an immediate visit, only such an obedience—will embody for Paul and for the assembly the recovery of a right relation, as Paul sees it, between them. The Corinthian children must obey their father.

It is a bold, risk-laden move by Paul. We will never know if it was successful.

THE CORINTHIANS HAVE FAILED to reach the judgment so obviously called for in one case. But they have called upon outsiders, we now hear, to reach it for them in another. Can Paul's converts, who will sit in judgment on humans and on angels, need to go to pagans for arbitration or redress? His position is stronger now than it was when he condemned their presumption; he can be blunt. *I am not writing,* he said earlier, *to rebuke you* (4:14). This time he says *I am telling you this to rebuke you* (6:5). They should if necessary suffer injustice themselves rather than be unjust to their fellow believers. Yet again Paul's concern is not just with the specific case, but with the failure of which it is an example—a failure of wisdom and knowledge. Over and over the Corinthians show by their actions that they lack what they so proudly claim.

And these are the Corinthians who have been passing judgment on their father in the faith. They will really show the discernment they claim when they use all their skills to maintain and strengthen the assembly as the one *body of Anointed.* The Corinthians are now ready to learn that discernment for themselves. They are about to hear how a person inspired with the Breath—such a person as each of them aspires to be—will address the questions of life and worship in these last days of the world's present order.

Paul has reduced the assembly to a total dependence upon himself, his insight, and his rulings. Where he has demolished, he is now ready to rebuild.

CHAPTER 19

. . . AND A TIME TO BUILD UP

JUDGMENTS AND HOW TO MAKE THEM

Love builds (1 Cor. 8:1). With a loose but clear symmetry, Paul runs a second time, beginning in chapter 7, through the arguments he has conducted in the opening chapters of 1 Corinthians. There he has condemned the Corinthians for their arrogant folly; now he offers them examples of the insight that they have so conspicuously lacked. He deals first with marriage, where he takes trouble at every stage to clarify the source or ground for his instruction. Then he deals with meat from sacrificial animals; this time he stresses the responsibility each convert bears for the fellow members of the assembly. Last, he looks at worship and at the order it calls for. He has brought to heel the factions centered round the baptizers and their power and their offer of great gifts; now he turns to the gifts themselves and the arrogance to which they have given rise. In all three cases Paul must reignite the sense of that unity that makes the community what it is.

His bitter sarcasm fades away. What Paul had claimed for himself in the earlier chapters he now puts to use. *We have the mind of Anointed,* he had said. And now, as he gives instruction on marriage, he lays out what his standing has taught him. In case anyone is still inclined to dispute it, he rounds off (with a last touch of irony): *I think I too have the breath of God* (2:16; 7:40). He had described himself as a steward who must be *faithful*. When he now gives his opinion, he reminds the Corinthians that he speaks as one who is, thanks to God's mercy, *faithful* (4:1–2; 7:25). Paul had urged his addressees at the letter's darkest moment, *I urge you, become imitators of me* (4:16). And now that they are making progress under his instruction he can say again: *Become imitators of me, as I have become of Anointed* (11:1).

Paul picks up the threads that had colored the letter's first half and weaves them into the second. But how differently they appear here. In the first part of the letter we hear how the Corinthians had dared stand in judgment over Paul and his fellow emissaries. He had mocked such pretensions. *It is not of the slightest importance to me, that I should be assessed by you. . . . We are fools on account of Anointed, you are sensible in Anointed* (4:3, 10). But he believes in his letter. It is surely having the effect he intends. In its second half he speaks calmly of his role as an emissary and of his own restraint, freely undertaken for the sake of others. By this point he can admit a question without irony and will answer it fully: *My answer to those assessing me is this* (9:3). Drawing a comparison between the people of Israel (punished in the desert) and his own assembly (liable to punishment), he asks for their attention: *I am speaking as to sensible people; judge for yourselves what I am saying* (10:15). The Corinthians are being equipped at last to exercise the judgment they have been so proudly—and disastrously—misusing.

In the first part of his letter, as he closed his dire warning against overconfidence, Paul picked up and corrected a slogan of the assembly: *Everything is permitted to me—but not everything is advantageous. Everything is permitted to me—but I will not let myself be overpowered by anything* (6:12). He is attacking the exultant misuse of that permission. He will return to the theme at another moment of warning, but his tone has changed. He is not demolishing now, but building. In this second half of the letter he writes, *Knowledge puffs up, but love builds up the household* (8:1). As he draws to the section's end, he will sound the theme again. *Everything is permitted—but not everything is advantageous. Everything is permitted—but not everything builds up the household* (10:23). Paul has started, even as he writes, to build the household of God—the sanctuary that the Corinthians are. And so, by following his instruction, must they.

Paul is equipping the Corinthians to become the moral agents they should be. What matters in the examples he gives them is partly, of course, what Paul decides, but partly how he decides it. He is giving his assembly the wherewithal to make such decisions for themselves. He has just lambasted his converts for sexual immorality, so he turns first to instruct them in that morality as it should be. He draws careful and quite clear distinctions between the kinds of authority he claims for his different rulings. *I say to those who are unmarried . . . And to the married I pronounce (not I but the Lord) . . . To the rest I am speaking myself, not the Lord. . . . About the virgins I have no command from the Lord, but I give an opinion as one to whom the Lord has granted the mercy to be faithful. . . .* And finally for widows, they should remain unmarried, *in my opinion; and I think I too have the breath of God* (7:8, 10, 12, 25, 40). Paul leaves no room for confusion when the command is his and when it is the Lord's. Here is a model example of good judgment exercised by an emissary who has—as so few of the Corinthians yet have!—*the mind of Anointed.*

And so on to the divisions that were crippling the assembly. He has attacked them. Now it is time to heal them. The rich still treated the poor as second-class members of the community they shared. Paul will have been disappointed, but surely not surprised that his converts still drew the old distinctions between their patrons, their peers, and their dependents. The patterns and expectations of patronage—on all sides— would take time to unravel. That may, ironically, have given Paul a badly needed breathing space. The bonds of patronage had their faults, but where Paul had worked any of them loose, he had introduced no other ties with which to keep the assembly united. The result was quickly seen. The highly gifted saw no link between themselves and those less startlingly endowed. All too readily they competed with each other and ignored everyone else. For this problem there were no precedents, and it was all the more dangerous for that.

Paul insists that all the gifts flowering in the assembly are due to one and the same Breath of God. There is no competition between different sources of different gifts:

To each is given the manifestation of the Breath with a view to the best: for to one is given a word of wisdom through the Breath; to another a word of knowledge according to the same Breath; to another faith in the same Breath; to another gifts of healing in the same Breath; to another

*the working of miracles, to another prophecy, to another the discernment
between different breaths, to another various kinds of tongues to speak in,
to another the interpreting of tongues.*

1 CORINTHIANS 12:7-10

Now for some serious building, and the Corinthians must help in
the work. Paul plays down the speaking in tongues of which the
Corinthians are so proud. He extols prophecy instead. *Those who speak
in tongues build up themselves; those who prophesy build up the assembly*
(14:4).

Only a person's own breath, Paul had said near the letter's start,
knows the deep truth of that person; only the Breath of God knows the
depths of God. Those who are informed by that Breath assess everything and are assessed by no one. How far the Corinthians had been,
even from such knowledge as this about knowledge itself. But Paul
envisages at the letter's end an assembly of prophets who will assess any
newcomers to the assembly, for they will be given knowledge of the
secrets of the hearts of humankind; and the newcomers will recognize,
thanks to their knowledge, that God is among them (14:24–25). This is
not yet the knowledge of God given by the Breath of God, but the
Corinthians can grow perceptibly toward the stature they had wrongly
thought was theirs to boast of all along. It is among the *perfect,* Paul had
said, that he speaks wisdom. He had been unable to speak to the
Corinthians as he would to those informed by the Breath. They had
been infants, able to digest only milk. But now, as the letter comes to its
end? *Do not be toddlers in your thoughts; but in wickedness be as infants, and
in your thoughts become perfect* (14:20).

These chapters (8–10 and 11–14) are built around two general
themes: first, the ethics of eating meat likely to have been used in a
pagan sacrifice; and then the unity that should be represented—and not
undermined—in the assembly's worship. The two sections share a striking structure. In each case Paul first lays down a position. His argument
then seems to ramble, and even at times to support positions starkly at
odds with his opening statement and his final conclusion. At the center
of each section Paul launches into an apparent digression, a block of
self-contained material that interrupts his flow. And finally he returns to
the opening theme and refines the instruction he gave there.

The first of these two sections shows Paul's aims and techniques to fine effect. At its end he seems just to confirm his opening instruction about food. But at the start he had been giving voice to the arrogance of a Corinthian who took no care for the other members of the assembly. However right in principle, such a decision reached without regard for fellow believers is a decision badly taken. The central "digression" is a section on the freedom that Paul himself enjoys as an emissary, and on the care and restraint with which he uses it. And so, by reference to himself, he assesses freedom and its proper use. Far from being a distraction, these central paragraphs show once more how the right decision can, at the section's end, be rightly taken.

The fame of the second section rests on its own central paragraphs. They are on the nature and work of love. Here, in love, is the basis for any right decision in the church's life. It outranks any other consideration, motive, or disposition. No worship is apt worship that subordinates love to any pride in special gifts. This central block of material, then, has its place at the heart of Paul's argument. And it cries out too for our attention on its own. Paul's grand, poetic praise of love has become the most famous chapter in all his writings.

"IF I SPEAK WITH THE TONGUES OF HUMANS AND OF ANGELS"

The lines on love found in chapter 13 can easily be detached from their context. Perhaps they did start life as a self-contained "hymn" and were just ready for Paul to slot into his letter. Perhaps, then, they were not composed by Paul at all; he could have incorporated—and perhaps adapted—a poem that suited his theme well. But as we shall see, the poem as it stands is linked, in almost every clause, with the rest of the letter and with conditions in Corinth. We are more likely watching Paul at work in another of the styles he has at his disposal. Here is a master at work, giving his converts an unforgettable poem to dwell on long after the details of his argument have been absorbed or forgotten.

Paul has undermined the Corinthians' pride and extolled the role of love. He has contrasted the effect of the two in the particular case of the eating of meat. Now he treats pride and love side by side.

Paul confronts first the most telling claim of all, the clearest signal that his converts have of their privileged standing before God:

> If I speak with the tongues of humans and of angels,
>   but have not love—I am. become a sounding bronze or ululating
>   cymbal.

Bronze jars the Corinthians would have seen in niches round the edge of their theater to amplify the sounds from the stage; bronze gongs they would have known from pagan temples. Gongs were linked especially with Dionysus and Cybele, cymbals with Cybele. Paul links the cries of the devotees and the cymbals' reverberations as a single ringing, incoherent ululation. Once devoid of love, the Corinthians' greatest pride is no better than the pagan chaos they have left behind.

> And if I have prophecy and know all those mysteries and all that
>   knowledge
> and if I have all that faith so that I move mountains,
>   but have not love—I am nothing.
> Even if I divide up all I own and hand over my body so that I might
>   boast [or be burned],
>   but have not love—I have no benefit at all.

From the language of angels to prophecy and so to knowledge—Paul is stripping down, one by one, the pride his converts had built upon the foundation of these gifts. And in each case these are gifts that Paul himself enjoyed. The gifts themselves are as important as ever; it is their misuse against which he warns.

Paul has moved beyond the Corinthians' slogans toward a slogan of his own. He had praised the Thessalonians for *the work of your faith, the labor of your love, and the endurance of your hope* (1:3). As he writes to the Corinthians about love he thinks of faith. No wonder his next clauses embrace hope too:

> Love waits patiently, love shows kindness. It is not jealous, does not brag,
> is not puffed up, is not ill-mannered, does not seek its own interests, is

not goaded, keeps no score of wrong, takes no pleasure in injustice but cel-
ebrates the truth. It supports without limit, has faith without limit, hopes
without limit, endures without limit. Love never falls apart.

Every contrast hits home. Paul's converts have variously been jealous
of each other's gifts, puffed up in pride, selfish with their wealth, and
litigious against fellow members. He has had to warn them: *let no one*
seek their own interests, but the interests of the other (10:24). They need
Paul's example: *not seeking my own advantage but the advantage of the many,*
so that they might be saved (10:33). And then from negative to positive.
Paul thinks again of his favored triplet, faith, hope, and love. He knows
which of them is foundational—it is love that generates faith and hope.
So much for the present. What of the future?

> *But as for prophecies, they will be brought to nothing;*
> *   as for tongues, they shall cease;*
> *   as for knowledge, it shall be brought to nothing.*

There is still a chasm between present gifts and future fulfillment.
Paul's converts are no longer the children they were at the letter's start,
but they are still far from the adulthood that will be theirs at the consummation of all things. There is no seamless gradation from the gifts of
angels here and now to the angels' company in heaven before the face
of God.

> *For we are coming to know in part and we prophesy in part;*
> *   but when completeness comes, what is in part shall be brought to*
> *   nothing.*
> *When I was a child, I spoke as a child, I reasoned as a child, I reckoned*
> *   as a child;*
> *   now that I have become a man, I have brought to nothing childish*
> *   things.*
> *For now we see through a mirror, in a riddle;*
> *   but then [we shall see] face-to-face.*
> *Now I come to know in part;*
> *   but then I shall come to know just as I am known.*

I spoke as a child. Paul has his mind on the Corinthians' pride in speaking in unintelligible tongues, to outsiders a childish babble. He is looking back too to his attack near the start of the letter in which he could speak to them only as *to children in Anointed; I fed you,* he said, *with milk, not solid food; for you could not yet take it—and you still cannot take it even now* (3:1–2). Their fondness for tongues betrays their continued childishness. But Paul has also in mind their progress. *Now that I have become a man, I have brought to nothing childish things.* If the Corinthians have learned what the letter offers them, they can follow his example. In the next chapter Paul will return to the theme of tongues. He can speak with confidence this time of their growth: *Brothers, do not be toddlers in your thoughts; but in wickedness be as infants, and in your thoughts become perfect* (14:20).

Not even the Corinthians imagined themselves already face-to-face with God. But this is their final calling; and Paul reminds them how wide a gulf there is between their privileges now and those that are yet to come. Corinth was famous for the manufacture of mirrors, and mirrors were a familiar image for indirect knowledge, sometimes clear, sometimes opaque. Who has come nearest to that final and total knowledge? Paul himself. God promised that he would speak to Moses *mouth to mouth, in a [visible] form and not through riddles; and he has seen the glory of the Lord* (The Census [Numbers] 12:8, Greek Version). Paul is the Moses of the New Order; as he is privileged above Moses, so will his converts be.

So what shall last and not be brought to nothing?

So now these three are abiding: faith, hope, love.

Will there still be need for faith, when all that we believe in shall be at last before our eyes for us to see? Or need for hope, when all that we currently hope for is fulfilled and attained? Scholars have long asked why Paul keeps all three elements of his triplet in view. About the final future he seems to be saying too much. He may of course be thinking still of the present times; but in these times, as the whole passage has confirmed, far more is still active, evident, and valuable than just three favored dispositions. About the present times he is saying too little.

Paul has surely turned in these last lines to the end of the present order. This end is approaching even as he writes. The glories of the new age are emerging, here and now, in the letter and its recipients together.

And the greatest of these is love.

"Where, Death, Is Your Sting?"

Maranatha, "Our Lord, come." In worship, the kingdom of heaven—the dominion of God—is more nearly realized on earth than at any other place or time. Nowhere is the expectation of Jesus' return more vivid or immediate. Paul, then, is ready for his final move. The Corinthians believe themselves to be growing into heavenly beings. They are already living half the life of heaven and will, when their transformation is complete, find themselves in the perfect sanctuary as they are themselves the earthly sanctuary here and now. Where will they attain their final transformation? On a renewed earth? Or in a heaven elsewhere? The geography of this fulfillment matters, for them, far less than its perfection.

And their way is clear to this great fruition. Nothing is an obstruction, not even death, for the death and rising of the Anointed has brought them, while still alive on earth, into the life that only the righteous dead had formerly enjoyed.

And so the Corinthians can deny the rising of the dead. To envisage the rising of putrefied corpses was grotesque. They can rather look forward to being freed from their earthly bodies. They will surely then find themselves, perfect and unencumbered at last, in the company of heaven. There they will gaze upon the glory of God, and they will use as their mother tongue that language of angels, which they catch in tantalizing fragments now.

A deep truth has led the Corinthians into a deeper falsehood. Paul may well have misunderstood their position; he may well, after all, have been getting confused reports of the differing views taken by different factions in the assembly. From all that he has heard, he knows that he must hold before them a drastic transformation still to come. It may be death that they will undergo; it may be, while they are still alive, the return of Jesus. Either way, each person will then have a spiritual body informed and enlivened by the Breath. And only then will the Corinthians be spiritual through and through. This side of the change, let them beware: they are not yet so near to their goal as they believe.

Paul turns twice to Adam, and in each case to the first Adam and then to the second. *For since death came in through man, so through man the rising of the dead. For just as in Adam all die, just so in Anointed shall all be made alive* (1 Cor. 15:21–22). The two accounts of creation in The Beginning [Genesis] had led Philo to think of two Adams: the first, incorporeal and at home in the mind of God; the second, the Adam of flesh and blood. Paul turns any such schema back to front. He declares the "the first Adam" to have been a living soul, made from the dust of the earth. The first *Adam had a son in his likeness, after his image, and he named him Seth* (The Beginning 5:3) It is the image of this earthly Adam that we, his descendants, bear. There is nothing here for the Corinthians to boast of. The earthly Adam is not the figure whose glory they should seek or claim. On the contrary, a far greater glory awaits them. It is the last Adam who was a life-giving breath, sprung from heaven. *As we have borne the image of the man of dust, so we shall bear the image of the man of heaven* (1 Cor. 15:49).

The image the Corinthians should long for is not yet theirs to have. The Corinthians are not angels yet. Their reclothing is not yet complete. Baptism has not transferred them to the realm of heaven. And how are they to attain that life? They are not due to rise, in smooth continuity from the present order, like seers into heaven:

I say this, brothers, that flesh and blood cannot inherit the kingdom of God, nor does corruption inherit incorruption. Look, I tell you a mystery:

We shall not all sleep, but we shall all be changed,
in an instant, in the twinkling of an eye, in the sounding of the last trumpet;
for it will sound and the dead shall rise incorruptible,
and we shall be changed.
For this corruptible must put on incorruption
and this mortal must put on immortality.

1 CORINTHIANS 15:50–53

There is still an awesome transfer to be undergone. And when it has been completed, only then will death have been defeated.

And when this corruptible has put on incorruption and this mortal has put on immortality, then shall the word be fulfilled which is written [by the prophets Isaiah and Hosea]—

> *Death has been swallowed up in victory.*
> *Where, death, is your victory?*
> *Where, death, is your sting?*
>
> 1 CORINTHIANS 15:54–55, QUOTING ISAIAH 25:8 AND HOSEA 13:14

"HAVEN'T I SEEN JESUS OUR LORD?"

We have encountered Jesus crucified and Jesus in glory. But what of Jesus risen? In particular, what did Paul believe had happened at Easter?

Paul reminds the Corinthians of the tradition he had relayed to them on his visit. I have put in quotation marks the clauses that are most likely Paul's quotation of this tradition.

> *I handed over to you, first and foremost, what I also received,*
>   "*that Anointed died on account of our wrongdoings*
>   *according to the scriptures,*
>   *and that he was buried*
>   *and that he was risen* [roused, but as an attained state] *on the third*
>   *day according to the scriptures*
>   *and that he appeared to Cephas* [Peter], *then to the twelve*";
> *Then he appeared to more than five hundred brothers at once,*
> *of whom the majority remain* [with us] *to this day, but some have fallen*
>   *asleep;*
>
> 1 CORINTHIANS 15:3–6

Perhaps we should see the next lines too as a formula, inherited from James's circle and tagged on by Peter's to the formula they already knew; Peter's priority is not challenged. It is only with the last lines of all that we will undoubtedly hear Paul's own voice:

> *then he appeared to James,*
> *then to all the emissaries;*
> *and last of all—just as if to the child discharged half formed from the*
> *womb—he appeared to me too.*
> 1 CORINTHIANS 15:7-8

Our first reaction nowadays is to compare this tradition with the stories of our four gospels. Did Paul believe, for instance, that Jesus' tomb had been empty on Easter Day? Almost certainly. A Jesus whose body was still in the tomb would not have been *risen* or *roused;* he would have been a ghost. Then we wonder about the apparently careful ordering of the list of witnesses. As the list now stands, more than chronology is at stake. Peter has precedence, then the Twelve, the closest followers of Jesus named in the gospels. We do not hear elsewhere of the appearances to the five hundred brothers or to James, the brother of Jesus. James is not recorded in the gospels as a follower of Jesus at all. The formula suggests James was one (and probably the leader) of the emissaries. This was clearly a wider group than the Twelve, whatever the overlap between them.

And then Paul's own sighting. Was it similar in character to the sight given—in different ways, perhaps—to any of those higher on the list? He uses the same verb for his sighting as for the others'. There were likely those who thought that only a person to whom Jesus had appeared could properly be described as an emissary. *Aren't I free?* Paul asked the Corinthians, linking himself with emissaries far better established than he was himself. *Aren't I an emissary? Haven't I seen Jesus our Lord? Aren't you my work in the Lord?* (1 Cor. 9:1). Paul describes himself with a most striking phrase: one who came prematurely to birth, whether alive or dead. It may have been an insult cast at him by his opponents: his much-vaunted call had been sudden, had lacked all preparation, and had brought him forth as a malformed child.

What is Paul trying to achieve by this formula and its expansion here? As throughout this letter, he is embedding the Corinthians among the Anointed's other assemblies. They are part of a greater whole. Whoever has led them into their strange beliefs about resurrection, Paul has no part in the error. And for the substance of their beliefs? A list of witnesses provides no proof of Jesus' resurrection, but it makes startlingly clear who the Corinthians are disbelieving—the very followers of Jesus without whose preaching the assemblies would not exist at all.

Paul has his eye on the Corinthians' own hopes too. The assembly has, so far, been little concerned with the death of members. Paul has interpreted some such deaths as a punishment. Those who eat and drink the Lord's Supper unworthily are liable to judgment. *Therefore many among you are weak and sick and a fair number are falling asleep* (11:30). But Paul has as well a longer view. More will likely die, and with no special intervention from God, before the last great transformation when the mortal shall put on immortality. The Corinthians should not be surprised. Some of those have already died who saw the risen Jesus. A generation of Jesus' followers is already passing; another may yet live and die before the final victory over death. The Corinthians, self-absorbed, must draw back from their dreams. They must see how large is the landscape in which they are set and how small their part in it.

These are answers, well tested by scholars, to well-known questions. But in this book we are turning our eyes to a different *sort* of query. Paul has before him the life of the Anointed: at Easter, and at the time of Paul's writing, and at and beyond the Day of the Lord itself. He has in mind as well the life of his converts: now, and after their death, and at and beyond the Day of the Lord. What, as Paul sees it, is the relation between these various forms and stages of life?

To understand any one of these categories, we must understand its links—in the mind and purposes of Paul himself—with the rest. None can be expounded on its own. Paul's converts were offered straightaway something of the risen and of the glorified life of the Anointed. And conversely, what they believed about that life was drawn in part from their own present experience, self-consciously related to it, as the Body of the Anointed and the sanctuary of God.

Again, these converts were encouraged in the life they were already living by the prospect of their life yet to come, their life, that is, in the prelude to judgment if they died before the Day of the Lord and then (a different condition) their life in its aftermath in the court of heaven. Once more, those prospects were fleshed out by the converts' experience as members of the Body—and so part of the present life—of the Anointed. They are already growing into the life of heaven.

Paul needed to encourage and restrain—and simply to define—the self-understanding of his addressees, their experience, and their hopes for the future. He had to call upon their self-reflection and imagination—and, first and foremost, upon his own.

Paul knew more than most about these various forms of life, but even he glimpsed only fragments of the links and likenesses between them. Or rather, he had precisely and only such imagined links and likenesses as the basis for most of his claims about them. Paul had to extend and amplify what he inherited. He needed to surmise on the basis of what he had experienced for himself. The hall of mirrors that resulted—a magical place in which every image is related to every other—is testimony to Paul's extraordinary mind. Does this weaken the impact or credibility of what he has to say? On the contrary. This *is* its impact. His converts have deployed their self-understanding and imagination, but wrongly. They have failed to maintain crucial distinctions. The mistake has had dire results. So the converts must look again. And learn to see aright what Paul the seer was well equipped to show: the links between present and future, earthly and heavenly, which make them one complex but coherent—and quite beautiful—whole.

PURPOSE AND PROGRESS

The Corinthians believed themselves at the letter's start to be inspired by the Breath of God, to be spiritual. From that belief sprang, as Paul saw things, arrogance, willfulness, and factions. The Corinthians were proud of their knowledge and judgment and used both so badly that they stood condemned, from their own actions, of ignorance and folly. Instead of informing the old creation with the standards of the new, they were interpreting the new by the standards of the old. Paul has checked their abuses, brought them to heel, exemplified right judgment, and shown the priority of love over knowledge. Finally he has shown them the gulf between themselves and the heavenly life they boast of. If they learn what the letter has to teach them, they will at last be the spiritual beings they had imagined themselves to be. They will be set to inherit the empire they had believed to be theirs already.

Paul's chief concern is not the Corinthians' errors themselves, but the route they took into error. To correct those errors he does not simply counter them; he demolishes the self-understanding that has caused them. To replace it he does not show the Corinthians just some sound judgments, but how to judge soundly for themselves. We all too easily read off Paul's instructions and ignore the lessons in discernment of which they are examples.

At the start of the letter Paul distinguishes two categories: the "spiritual," those informed by the Breath; and those who simply live out the life of a human soul. It is among the first, the perfect, that he speaks God's wisdom in a mystery. And the second? The Corinthians themselves, dreaming of the kingdom they believe they already have, are hardly even among these. The Corinthians are bound up in the flesh, in the realm—or better, perhaps, under the power that dominates the realm—of this life, its ambitions, and standards. By the end of the letter the Corinthians will be ready to see what was quite beyond their comprehension at the letter's start.

How easily we miss this progress that Paul intends the Corinthians to make, for we project the tenor of our own reading into the reception of his letters. Nowadays when we assess a book's claims we think of ourselves as free from moral pressure, from partiality, and from the demands of loyalty and self-assertion. We are generally free, when we read a book, from the weight of a present imposed and inescapable moment of decision. We are free from the fear of betrayal, of false servitude, of a dangerous future and a vengeful God. As we know no such pressures in our reading, they go unnoticed in our study of Paul's letters.

But this context of decision is critical if we are to understand the first part of 1 Corinthians. Paul is not setting out a balanced argument to be assessed stage by stage and then again at its close. He is dismantling the Corinthians' image of themselves, each other, and their missionaries; he is bringing them, here and now, to confess his own authority. Their false self-image must be unsettled and undermined, their new understanding publicly and unambiguously confirmed. Within this movement Paul demands, in that first solemn climax, that the assembly expel a particular wrongdoer. Far more is at stake than a single punishment. If the Corinthians obey, they have acceded to Paul's reading of their status and his own. If they disobey, they have denied that Paul has any hold on them. Upon that one act of obedience by the assembly, now listening to his letter, hangs the whole relation between this father and his children.

What are we, as modern readers, to make of Paul's letter? Was Paul an inspirational father to his converts? This, then, was a Paul who steered his children safely past the shoals into which they had been led by a dark mixture of misunderstanding and worldly standards. Or was he a bullying father? This Paul left his converts to nurture his strange teaching without him, was bitterly defensive when they showed some independence, and brought them to heel by any means he could.

Which was he? He was both.

CHAPTER 20

THE TRANSFORMATION OF AN ASS

PAUL'S LETTERS REACH US AS JEWELS, cut and polished, on display against a plain black background. They seem to shine all the brighter for that. But we will understand them only when we travel to the mine, see the rock in which they are set, and extract them for ourselves. Two thousand years ago, Corinth was the city that never slept. What did the city already have to offer, when Paul arrived, that would help his first listeners to place his good news? Was it philosophy, teaching, a mystery, or magic? We need an impression of the alternatives jostling for attention. They met more needs than we might now give them credit for.

No one who has enjoyed Christmas in New York City should belittle the buzz of a city in celebration: chatting crowds at the ice rink in Rockefeller Plaza, excited children in Toys R Us, families around the tree in the Metropolitan Museum of Art, young and old hushed at a candlelit service on Christmas Eve in one of the city's cathedrals. In different settings we find ourselves in different moods and open to different influences. We go to Times Square for a noisy celebration, to a darkened church for quiet solemnity. Paul's world knew as well of solemn rites in solemn settings and the awed devotion they inspired. Such rites were held throughout the empire in different forms and in honor of different gods. They were certainly not uniform.

331

Some details of some such services have come down to us. We would be eager to know more, in particular, about the rites of the "mysteries," accessible only to those who had undergone distinctive rites of admission. (Our words "mystery" and "mystic" are derived from Greek words whose root is the verb *my-ein*, "to initiate." A *mysterion*, or "mystery," was a cult open only to its *mystai*, or "initiates.") Such initiates were under orders to tell no outsiders of their secret knowledge or rituals. Paul himself uses the word "mystery" to describe insights granted to him, but not yet to his assemblies.

The initiates of these pagan mysteries kept their secrets well, but the existence of the cults was well known. We have heard briefly of the great procession, at the start of the sailing season, held in the Corinth harbor by the initiates of Isis. Scholars have long wondered whether Paul was influenced by any of these pagan mysteries. In particular, when Paul writes to the Romans of baptism, this initiation looks strangely similar to the movement through which, at initiation, the pagan mysteries took their members. Might Paul have attracted converts by an apparent similarity between the cult of his Anointed and the mystery cults? Or more dramatically, in his account of baptism has Paul drawn on motifs that he and his readers had picked up from popular knowledge of those mysteries? Has Paul actually reshaped the assemblies' earliest faith to echo the rituals, devotion, and beliefs well known and respected throughout the gentile world? No wonder, then, Paul won gentile converts to his cause.

As I stressed in Chapter 16, at issue is not a close dependence on arcane details of belief that Paul is unlikely to have known. Nor is any mimicry of the mysteries' rituals themselves. They were elaborate and expensive. Paul would, if anything, have been offering an invitation to a mystery freed from the cost and snobbery of a famous cult such as that of Isis. My concern in the next couple of pages is chiefly with Paul's addressees. How would the good news of Paul have looked to Corinthians who knew what we know about the mysteries?

A faith that we do not share can seem very distant, nothing more than a hodgepodge of wild stories, superstitions, and strange rituals. Could anyone have taken them seriously? The mysteries offered insights and inspired devotion. They were immensely attractive. They spoke of the most important things of all, life and death. They told stories and took initiates through the stories' drama. They offered a god's protection and care; and their temples, in cities all across the empire, offered a welcome and familiar ways of worship.

We are about to follow just one story of initiation, told in Latin around 170 C.E. It appears as the conclusion of a fantastical novel by Apuleius, *The Golden Ass*. The hero Lucius, the story's narrator, had been transformed near the novel's start into the shape of an ass; at its end he recovers his human form. How could anyone, we might ask, have taken seriously such an obvious and playful fiction? Yet two hundred years after it creation the novel was still well known. Augustine, the greatest of all Latin theologians, wondered whether Apuleius might indeed have been turned into an ass. Augustine warns his readers not to be fooled by those who claimed Apuleius was a magician whose powers surpassed the powers of Jesus Anointed himself. We shall soon see why.

Lucius had gone to Thrace, famous for its magicians, in search of sorcery and sex. Much of the novel is bawdy, but Apuleius is a master of many styles. He can tell a delicate romance as well as a bedroom farce. As the novel itself teases us, so its function eludes us. Is Apuleius leading his readers from the errors of Lucius to the life of an initiate? Or is he simply telling a story? Is he a wry but impassioned teacher? Or a literary juggler?

The story's denouement is in Cenchreae, a harbor town that served Corinth. Lucius, in the shape of an ass, has escaped from a show in which he was due to be a prize exhibit. He has run away to Cenchreae, site of a temple of Isis. He falls asleep on the seashore. He wakes up with a start and describes, in a beautiful passage, how he is affected by the sight of the rising moon. As ever, pagan worship acknowledges and responds to power. How apt that a man longing for a change of fortune should invoke the mistress of the tides, the ever-changing moon:

> "About the first watch of the night [in the late evening], awakened in a sudden fright, I see the full circle of the moon glistening with extraordinary brightness, just emerging from the waves of the sea. And coming as I did upon the silent secrets of dark night, certain as well that the preeminent goddess wields her power in her outstanding majesty and that human affairs are ruled by her providence, and that all creatures and lifeless things are

quickened by the divine assent of her light and might and that individual bodies on land, in the sky and in the sea now grow in consequence of her waxing, now lessen in obedience to her waning; since fate, it seemed, was sated with my sufferings and was offering, however late, the hope of deliverance, I decided to pray to the majestic sign of the goddess, present before me."

Lucius must purify himself before prayer. Washing our bodies clean is an image of inner cleansing as powerful now as it was then. Into the sea goes Lucius, submerging his head seven times. Why seven? It was a number, says Lucius, invested with special significance by the ancient philosopher Pythagoras. Our hero is drawing on all of the sacred traditions he has to hand. Wisdom was not the preserve of a single school or sect.

Nor was the ability to recognize a god. In the modern West we wonder how the ancient world could have revered its vast array of gods. Of course, power is seen in different forms in the different elements of nature and in the different centers of human activity—in individuals, in groups, and in societies, but a mature religion, we believe, will see in this diversity the power of a single all-creating, all-powerful God. To distinguish, as pagans did, the power of the sun from the power of the moon—and then to revere them separately and under different names in different regions—this seems to us a childishness we are glad to have left behind.

Where we see folly, the ancient world saw a fitting humility. Back then it was acknowledged that humans do not know how all the world's different powers are related. People couldn't be sure their own experience or tradition had recognized them all. They expected others to have been as perceptive in their worship as they were in their own. They knew other nations or groups used their own names for the powers over their lives, and they acknowledged whatever connections they could see between their gods and others'. Lucius, therefore, in a poetic plea, addresses the goddess of the moon by the various names that might be appropriate. Lucius comes finally to his plea for help, throwing himself on the grace of the goddess:

"By whatever name, with whatever rite, in whatever image it is proper to invoke you: *you,* now defend me in my uttermost tribulations; *you*, strengthen my fallen fortune; *you,* grant me rest and release from the cruel mischances I have endured."

Lucius is given a vision of the goddess rising from the sea. She addresses him. Apuleius writes again in the richest, most poetic style of his time:

"Look," says the goddess, "I am here, Lucius. Moved by your prayers, I, the mother of the universe, the mistress of all the elements, first offspring of the ages, mightiest of powers, queen of the dead, foremost of the inhabitants of heaven, the single, universal image of the gods and goddesses, I who rule with a nod of my head the starry heights of heaven, the freshening breezes of the sea, the deep-mourned silences of hell, I whose single power the whole world worships in such varied forms, with such varied rites, under such varied names."

She lists some. Lucius had been right in the four names he had used—and there were far more that would have been as apt. One of her titles was "Isis of a Thousand Names." She is invoked on a papyrus from the second century C.E. that lists a dozen names for the goddess as used in Egypt, and as many again from other countries: her names in Arabia, Syria, Greece, and Rome, her names among the Amazons, Indians, and Persians. Among many aliases—such as Aphrodite, Athene, Themis— are epithets: Trusty, Bountiful, Savior, Initiate, Divine. Some places used both; in one city Isis was known as "Intelligence, Ruler, (the goddess) Hera, Holy." Here names and epithets are equivalent. It was not only Jesus, the "Anointed One," whose epithet became his name.

The Greeks recognized the frailty of human affairs in their reverence for Fortune, personified as a goddess. Lucius revered Isis as the goddess with power over Fortune itself. And the goddess has not come just to confirm to Lucius who she is. She will use her power on his behalf. She says:

"I am here in pity at your misfortune, I am here in sympathy and good will. Now put by your tears and put aside your sorrowings. Banish your grief. Now by my providence the day of health and deliverance is dawning upon you."

Isis gives him instructions to join the great procession in her honor and, still in the form of an ass, is to eat the garland of roses held, as part of the ritual, by a priest. (Such a wreath, on a large scale, can be seen on the statue of a priestess of Isis found at Cyrene in North Africa; it rests on her right shoulder, and passes across her left arm.) Lucius will then be transformed back into his human shape. For this kindness, the goddess expects Lucius's loyalty in return.

> "You will clearly remember and will always keep hidden in the depths of your heart this instruction: that the rest of your life's course, right up to the limits of your last breath, is pledged to me. Nor is it unjust that you should owe all the life you have to her by whose help and goodwill you return to the world of men. And you will live in blessedness, you will live in glory under my protection. And when you have completed your life's span and travel down to the dead, there too, where I shine among the shadows and reign in the depths, you will be dwelling in the Fields of the Blessed and, for my favor to you, will constantly worship me."

In the deep gloom of the Underworld, where the dead flit like shadows and gibber like bats, is one quite different realm, the Fields of the Blessed, for the favored few. Apuleius is ascribing more power to Isis than is she is normally given. She is usually the chief power on earth; only a couple of hymns know her as "the fire of hell" or "the glad face in the land where all is forgotten." One of the great riddles of these ancient mysteries was what they offered their devotees after death. Perhaps it was less than we might expect. But as Isis can promise a better life in the next world, so she can offer a longer life in this. An inscription in Egypt praises "Isis who bestows life, . . . who lengthens the years of him who is devoted to her and causes his rule to last for ever."

Lucius's sexual appetite had landed him in his present trouble; from now on this appetite had to be curbed. This demand will for a while check his enthusiasm to be initiated into the goddess's mysteries. Isis says:

> "But if by assiduous allegiance and by worshipful service and by determined chastity you win the favor of our godhead, you will

know that it is permitted to me—and to me alone—to prolong your life beyond the limits laid down by your fate."

Lucius is told of this power of the goddess again, by a priest advising him on his initiation:

"For both the gates of death and the care of our health and deliverance are placed in the hands of Isis, and the actual transmission of the mystery is celebrated in the likeness of a voluntary death and a deliverance obtained by prayer. In fact those who had finished their life's span and were already set on the very threshold of light's end, those, though, to whom the great unspoken mysteries of the cult could be safely entrusted—the power of the goddess tends to choose these and by her providence they are in a way reborn and set once more on the course of a new health and deliverance."

Lucius's dream comes to an end. He wakes up, the sun rises, and the great procession starts. Lucius eats the wreath of roses and is cured; he is human again. The priest who had held the wreath speaks to him: "Lucius, you have come at last to the harbor of Peace and the altar of Mercy." Random Fortune had tormented him, but has now "brought you to this holy state of happiness. . . . Let unbelievers see! Let them see and recognize their error! Look: Lucius, freed from his former troubles and rejoicing in the providence of great Isis triumphs over his fate. . . . Lucius, dedicate yourself today to the observance of our cult and take on the voluntary yoke of our goddess's service. For as soon as you become the goddess's slave you will feel more fully the fruit of your freedom."

All who see the miracle are agog. "It is doubtless," they say, "because of his past innocence and faithfulness that he has earned such remarkable patronage, to be in a way reborn and immediately engaged to the service of the goddess's cult." Our author has not lost his sense of irony. Lucius's earlier life had been anything but innocent or faithful. The people are misguided, but Lucius himself is under no delusion.

What a striking claim this is. Lucius has been "reborn" by the goddess's own election into her cult, reborn into humanity. This rebirth must be complete before he can be taken any further into the goddess's mysteries. "Lucius, how fortunate," he is told, "how blessed you are, that the august power so greatly favors you with her benevolent will." Crowds gather to honor Lucius with gifts. The uninitiated are dismissed. Lucius is clothed in an unused linen robe and led by the priest into the innermost part of the sanctuary. By now Lucius feels immense loyalty and debt to this priest, who has guided him to this initiation. Such friendship could last a lifetime and beyond: we have an inscription from Rome commemorating the gift of a burial site to be shared by a priest, his initiates, and their descendants. The donor could expect the families to remain closely linked.

Lucius goes on:

"Perhaps you are anxious to learn, eager reader, what was said next, what was done. I would tell if to tell were permitted, you would learn if it were permitted to hear. But both ears and mouth would incur equal guilt: the mouth for being so impiously talkative, those ears for being so boldly inquisitive. But perhaps your suspense is a matter of religious longing, so I will not crucify you with ever-longer torment.

"Listen, therefore—but believe: these things are true. I came to the boundary of death. I trod the threshold of Proserpina [the wife of the god of death; she was snatched from the living]. Carried through all the elements, I returned. In the middle of the night I saw the sun flashing with a brilliant light. I came face-to-face with the gods below and the gods above and worshiped them from close at hand. Look, I have told you things that you may hear but cannot know. So I shall relate only what can be divulged to the uninitiated without calling for propitiation.

"Morning had come and the rituals been completed. I came out, wearing twelve robes as a sign of consecration. This is very holy clothing, but I am not forbidden to speak of it, since a great many people were there and saw it. For right in the middle of the sanctuary, I stood as ordered on a wooden platform set up in front of the statue of the goddess."

The ritual that follows is remarkable. Lucius is dressed and adorned to "be" the sun:

"I stood out because of my clothes: they were only linen, but elaborately embroidered.... From whichever direction you looked, I was marked out with animals, portrayed on every side in various colors. Those who have been consecrated, the initiates, call this the robe of heavenly Olympus. Now in my right hand I carried a flaming torch, and my head was beautifully bound with leaves of gleaming palm, the leaves standing out like rays of light. In this way I was decorated in the likeness of the sun and set up in the guise of a statue. Suddenly the curtains were drawn back, and the people wandered around to view me. Next I celebrated my birthday as an initiate, a most festive affair: a delicious banquet and a cheerful party. The third day too was celebrated with a similar ceremonial ritual: a holy breakfast and the official conclusion of the initiation."

How warily historians have scrutinized this story. Many of them have been historians of the New Order, asking what linked the cults of Isis and of the Anointed—and what divided them. Even the summary given above could be accused of pandering to this interest. Any links need careful treatment.

But we do better to acknowledge the appeal of Isis's cult on its own terms, both its appeal to the wealthy who could afford the initiation with its moments of private awe and of public fame, and its appeal to the crowds who watched the procession, knew their debt to its patrons, and came to see the initiate robed as the sun. We might well wonder how any Lucius viewed himself, as he returned to the daily round after his celebration, and how his neighbors viewed him. We look for categories in which to describe his death and rebirth, his journey through all the elements, and his final display as the sun. What did an initiate hope for, in this world and the next? Apuleius gives us the most meager of clues. The initiation had been an expensive business. He was encouraged to think it all worthwhile by the unexpected return of his lost horse. And the story closes with a quiet satisfaction. All his expenditure is beginning to bear dividends in Rome. He is becoming well known as

an attorney. He is better able now to withstand the slander of his opponents. Isis, he believes, has displaced the fickleness of fortune. We
should not mock. A book promising prosperity will always be a best-
seller; all the better, if it comes with a religious air.

So much palaver for so little. Or so it may seem to us, confident that
Christianity has raised us above such superstitious rigmarole. But let us
leave Lucius at prayer in the days after his initiation, gazing upon the
image of the goddess and pledged to serve her in gratitude for her favor
to him. Paul would look on such a figure and see an idolater, prostrate
and in tears before a lifeless image. He would not have come close
enough to hear the prayer—or its devotion, gratitude, and loyalty.

But we will do justice to Paul's achievement only if we recognize
what options for prayer his good news, over time, absorbed or over-
came. Lucius prays:

> "O holy and eternal protector of the human race, always bounti-
> ful in the nurture of mortals, you apply the sweet affection of a
> mother to the misfortunes of the wretched. Not a day or a night
> or the slightest moment passes empty of your blessings. You pro-
> tect men on sea and land. Driving away the storms of life you
> hold out your saving hand, with which you unwind even the
> threads of fate, inextricably wound together. . . .

> "The fullness of my voice is inadequate to say what I feel about
> your majesty, as a thousand mouths and as many tongues would
> be inadequate. I will then do the one thing a devout but poor
> man can do. I will guard your divine face and your most sacred
> godhead in the secret places of my heart, and there will I picture
> it to myself."

CHAPTER 21

HONESTY OR POLICY?

Boasting on the Day of the Lord

THE ABSENT EMISSARY

Before things in Corinth get better, they get far worse.

In the spring of 54 Paul writes 1 Corinthians from Ephesus. He is already planning a visit that summer to Macedonia; he expects to turn southward next, down Greece, to see the Corinthians in person. But Timothy returns to Ephesus with dire news: Paul's opponents in Corinth are gaining strength. Paul likely skips Macedonia and comes straightaway to Corinth. It is a disastrous visit. His rivals belittle him, and the assembly does not back him. He retreats in disarray.

By the end of the summer he is back in Ephesus. To his recalcitrant Corinthians he writes a letter, now lost, that costs him, he will later say, *many tears* (2 Cor. 2:4). Did he expect to winter in Ephesus? He does not stay there. He has already had trouble there in the spring, *fighting*— he says in a vivid image—*with wild beasts* (1 Cor. 15:32). And there will be worse to come. Luke gives a stirring account of a riot in Ephesus shortly before Paul leaves the city. The cult of Diana—and the employment of all those who made a living from the cult—is threatened by Paul's success. The silversmiths lead a demonstration that endangers Paul's companions and could have cost him his life. Luke will not state—even if he knows—that Paul was driven out of the city by pagan opposition, but scholars have long suspected he was. He heads north, to Troas, a port city as well placed as Ephesus for links to east and west.

The autumn of 54 in Troas was likely the lowest point in Paul's whole life as an emissary. He had established two bases: Ephesus in the east, Corinth in the west. He has lost Ephesus and perhaps, to judge from Timothy's news, Corinth too. And if the center of operations is lost, its satellites are threatened. In Ephesus and through Asia Minor the representatives of Jerusalem have been winning the respect and adherence of Paul's converts. Paul's good news is exhilarating, but the Law offers a clarity, structure, and honored antiquity that Paul cannot match. You can be sure with the Law; with Paul you can only hope. With Paul out of Ephesus, these rivals have the clear field in the city and eastward through Galatia that they have been hoping for. He will tell the Corinthians of the *tribulations we had in Asia: we were under extraordinary pressure, beyond endurance, so that we despaired of life itself; we thought we had received a sentence of death* (2 Cor. 1:8–9).

Is it missionaries from the same stable with the same appeal that have won over the Corinthians? Perhaps. There is a group declaring its loyalty to Peter, as prestigious as any figure in Jerusalem. And the hero of Paul's opponents is Moses, the great prophet and lawgiver of Judaism. But the Law's observance—as far as we can tell from Paul—is not itself the principle over which the factions divide. The issue is more personal. Paul's good news has encouraged a grand enthusiasm. Apollos has given it a philosophical basis. Peter himself—as we have seen—is a loyal pupil of the seer Jesus. However different their messages in detail, they combine to make a heady cocktail. Which of the preachers would be given the credit for its extraordinary results? It had never been clear that Paul would prevail. And when he writes his sad, angry letter from Ephesus, he seems likely to have lost once and for all.

Paul writes through many tears. He promises to visit. He does not arrive. Instead, his converts hear of the danger and rejection to which he is exposing himself across the Aegean in Asia Minor. He has been preaching openly, indiscriminately, but not, it seems, with success. On the contrary, this emissary of the Lord has been rejected, derided, attacked. This is humiliating for the good news, for Paul, and for the Corinthians themselves. There are quite enough in Corinth who are waiting to treat him with the respect their own father, emissary of the

Anointed, deserves. But even these are beginning to wonder if Paul is quite the figure they have believed him to be.

And now Paul writes again. Titus brings the letter, which is our 2 Corinthians 1–9. It is a poor substitute for a visit from their "father" in the faith. Paul is clearly unreliable in his plans. Is it just the pressure of circumstances that has kept him away or is he not, after all, quite honest? Does this ever absent father really love them as much as he had claimed? Why then does he avoid them? The assembly—his own foundation—suspects that he is easily swayed. Confidence in Paul, we have found, is confidence in the good news he brings. And in turn distrust of Paul soon leads to distrust of his good news.

Once more Paul uses an opening paragraph to introduce the letter as a whole; in it are the main themes laid out in order, as a guide for his addressees through the argument to follow. Whatever has gone amiss between Paul and the Corinthians so far, the bond between them is reciprocal and deep.

> For our boast is this, the evidence of our conscience [or of our knowledge of ourselves]: We have behaved in the world in sincere care and godly integrity, not in worldly wisdom but in the grace of God—and especially in our relationship with you. For we write you nothing other than what you read and even realize. And I hope that you will realize fully—just as you did realize about us in part—that we are the ground for your boasting just as you too are ours on the day of the Lord Jesus.
>
> 2 CORINTHIANS 1:12–14

We are the ground for your boasting: this will occupy Paul for the letter's first six chapters. He will have to work hard. In 2 Corinthians 1–6 we have Paul's fullest account of his own calling and role. What the Corinthians need for their own transformation from glory to glory is before them in Paul himself: here in his own person, illumined by the glory seen on the way to Damascus, is the re-presentation of the glory of the Lord. This could so easily lead to idolatry—as Paul well knows: It is not ourselves that we preach but Jesus Anointed as Lord, and ourselves as your servants on account of Jesus (4:5).

And so to the letter's second part, 2 Corinthians 7–9: You are the ground for our boasting too (7:4). Paul and the Corinthians are to rely on each other. What have the Corinthians to offer Paul? Their contribution to Paul's great collection, his tribute from the nations to Jerusalem—*this* is what they should bring to the relationship. Paul reminds them of the Macedonians' generosity; surely they remember the money brought by Silas and Timothy that made possible his full-time preaching. He reminds them too of their own undertaking, of the embarrassment to all concerned if they renege upon it, and of the pride that he—and they—will rightly take in the collection's success and their part in it.

Paul and the Corinthians have argued. He must heal the relationship between them, and he has found the way to do it. But as we read Paul's self-defense and his encouragement, we will be struck by the voice and authority with which he speaks. He insists on his utter transparency. He sets up a stark contrast: either he will be totally open to everyone or he will betray the good news with which he has been entrusted. There is no third way. This is not a matter of policy; it is determined by what he and his good news are. When the Corinthians once understand his role in God's plan, their distrust will turn to pride. It is then—and only then—that Paul turns to the collection and uses every means he can to cajole and shame the Corinthians into generosity.

Paul is a driven man. He is under a pressure we cannot share for the success of his collection. We see him only from a distance. And from where we stand, he seems to have been open only for a purpose—a purpose about which he is not open at all when he speaks so proudly of his openness at the beginning of the letter.

SIGNPOSTS

We are the ground for your boasting just as you too are the ground for ours on the day of the Lord Jesus. In this opening fanfare Paul declares the letter's overarching theme; at its midway point and at its conclusion he sounds the same motif again. And so he provides a set of signposts for his addressees; he has no wish to lose them in the passionate intricacies of his argument. Here are the equivalent, offered by Paul himself, of the section breaks and headings that we value in modern Bibles. Paul knows, quite as well as any editor today, how important such guidance can be.

As we follow Paul's argument we will make full use of these sign-posts. There are several sets. Paul is working to reestablish in the Corinthians a sense of mutual reliance, so he unfolds to them his understanding of himself and of his role: *the evidence of our knowledge of ourselves* (1:12). Over and again he will bring up this knowledge of himself to mark the Corinthians' increasing knowledge of him—and of themselves, for they will understand him when they understand themselves, and themselves when they understand him.

Is Paul then commending himself to them? The question recurs, once more steering us through the letter. A missionary could expect to bring with him, to a city he had not visited before, a letter from a well-established assembly to introduce and recommend him. *Are we starting to commend ourselves again? Or—surely we do not need letters of commendation, as some people do, to you or from you?* (3:1). The relation between Paul and the Corinthians is far too close for that. They cannot stand apart and offer or invite a cool assessment. *Our letter—that is what you are, written on our hearts, known and read by all humankind* (3:2). This letter is open for all to read. The Corinthians are disappointed that Paul has exposed himself to derision. But Paul's preaching can no more be kept from the view of others than they can themselves. They are wholly implicated in the good news and in its proclamation to the world at large.

The Corinthians want Paul to avoid rejection and humiliation, but he allows just two alternatives: either to preach openly to all, as he is called by God to do, or to betray the good news. As he is open to the Corinthians, so must he be open to others. *Therefore . . . we renounced the secret ways of shame, not operating in craftiness nor falsifying the word of God, but in the disclosure of the truth commending ourselves to every human awareness in the sight of God* (4:1–2).

The themes of boasting, commendation, and mutual knowledge shape the letter. All are determined by one need, the need to reunite Paul and his assembly. So he reminds them, at three climactic moments, of the work in him and them of the Breath of God: by their baptism in the past; through their present transformation; and in their future glory, *when all of us must appear openly before the judgment seat of the Anointed* (5:10).

First, then, we hear of the past and the endowment that God has given to all the baptized: God *has also put his seal on us and given us the down payment of his Breath in our hearts* (1:22). Next, of the present transformation to which the Breath gives rise. *And we—all of us—with unveiled face gazing as in a mirror on the glory of the Lord, are being transformed into the same image, from glory into glory, just as from "the Lord,"* which a famous passage in the Old Order speaks of, that is, *from the breath* (3:18).

And finally the Corinthians hear of the glory to which this transformation is leading them. Paul's converts are following the route of Paul the seer himself. In baptism they passed through the veil that separates this life from the next, this world from the courts of heaven, humanity from God. They are now in the sanctuary itself; they *are* the sanctuary. In this new life they are transformed from glory to glory as the seer is transformed who draws near to the throne of God. And at the last they will reach their destination. They will put on the garments of glory that await the righteous dead—and that Isaiah the seer saw waiting for him in the seventh heaven.

> *We who are in this* [mortal, earthly] *tent are groaning with the weight. Not that we want to put this off, but to put more on top, so that the mortal might be swallowed up in life. And he who has wrought us for this very thing is God, he who has given us the down payment of the Breath.*
>
> 2 CORINTHIANS 5:4–5

Past, present, and future—this whole section of the letter is steering the Corinthians toward the final future. *All of us must appear openly before the judgment seat of the Anointed, each one to receive* recompense for *the things done through our bodily existence, in proportion to what we have done, whether good or evil* (5:10).

Paul is taking them onward through the transformation he speaks of. Onward toward the moment of which he can say with ever greater confidence, *we will be the ground for your boasting just as you too are the ground for ours—on the day of the Lord Jesus.*

LETTER OR LETTERS?

For all their forward movement, Paul's letters have an architectural grandeur. His recurring themes are the girders, placed at critical points and carefully charted intervals, that shape and support Paul's building. They make clear the plan of the house and our architect's "vision." We are nearly ready to look more closely at the walls and windows around and in between these structural elements, but one preliminary needs some care first. We have spoken of 2 Corinthians 1–9 as a single letter. What about its last four chapters, 10–13? It has long been thought that these are likely a different letter or part of one. These are fraught, angry pages. Some scholars have suggested that in these chapters we have the letter Paul wrote on his sad return to Ephesus in the autumn of 54. (This is a view I do not share.) He reminds the Corinthians of it. *It was out of much distress and anguish of heart that I wrote you, through many tears, not so that you might be sorrowed but so that the love—you might know the love that I have especially for you (2:4).*

But this possibility prompts an additional, rather anxious question. How many other fragments, smaller houses in an uneven terrace, might have been patched together to make our one grand house, 2 Corinthians 1–9? Are these chapters really a single letter—a single building—at all?

First, then, let's consider the letter as a whole. Second Corinthians is spell-binding, but it is not uniform. Paul jumps from theme to theme; he covers some ground and then covers it again; he writes one part in a mood of careful confidence, another in a tone of angry warning. It has been over two hundred years since a great scholar asked: Might a number of letters have been bundled together to make this one letter, the 2 Corinthians of our Bible? Perhaps we have here a patchwork of letters or fragments of letters brought together by an assembly that was determined to preserve, as best it could, all that was of lasting value in the letters from Paul. Paul's words were precious; it was more important to preserve and use them than to honor their original arrangement.

Where, then, might editors have been at work sewing together the most helpful excerpts of different letters and making out of them a single, artificial "letter" from Paul? We can find possible seams in almost every letter of Paul's. Some scholars see, in each of 1 Thessalonians, 1 Corinthians, 2 Corinthians, and Philippians, a jigsaw of ill-fitting fragments whose original contexts and order are now heavily disguised.

If we can identify the various components, perhaps we can identify as well the original order and contexts. We might have expected, in 1 and 2 Corinthians, to study a full picture of the assembly's life at just two moments. Perhaps, instead, we have a series of snapshots that reveal all the ups and downs of a turbulent two years. This is a fascinating possibility. All our evidence is here before us in 1 and 2 Corinthians themselves. There are four or even five points at which we could reasonably take our 2 Corinthians apart. Most striking of all is the end of 2 Corinthians 9, and I gladly follow the consensus that 2 Corinthians 10–13 is part of a different letter.

And so to a closer focus on 2 Corinthians 1–9, acknowledging the break points that might disrupt these chapters. Let's look at just two such points; our decision on these affects all that follows. In order to reassure the Corinthians, Paul must explain—or explain away—his recent movements:

> *Going to the Troas* [by the Hellespont, at the northeast corner of the Aegean Sea] *for the good news of the Anointed—and a door was open for me in the Lord—I had there no respite for my spirit, because I did not find my brother Titus, but I made my farewells to them and went away to Macedonia* [westward to the north of Greece, at the northwest corner of the Aegean].
>
> 2 CORINTHIANS 2:12–13

After the travel information, Paul's topic and tone change abruptly. He launches into a long defense of his work and status. He has spoken openly to all. His audiences have not always been persuaded; he has often enough been derided or worse. Is he for that reason unworthy of the commission he claims to have? Far from it. We will return later to his remarkable self-defense. When it ends after several pages Paul changes tack again, and just as suddenly as before:

> *And on our going to Macedonia our flesh had no respite, but in everything we were tormented: battles from outside, fears from within.*
>
> 2 CORINTHIANS 7:5

Any reader might wonder whether the story of this journey should really be interrupted by four chapters devoted to a quite different theme. Perhaps the whole intervening section once belonged to a different letter altogether.

Scholarship moves in tides. For decades the search for break points and fragmentary letters swept all before it. The waters are receding now, and in this I am a child of my time. Other scholars are mounting their arguments for the letter's unity; I advance mine. The arguments are quite different from each other, but any observer will see that we are all of us, however independent we believe ourselves to be, part of a new current that is sweeping the waters back into the channels they occupied fifty years ago.

Readers will discover, then, within the next couple of pages, why we will be treating all these opening chapters together as part of one long letter. Paul, as ever, puts down markers for his listeners, to help them anticipate and then follow the course of his argument. These markers unite all of chapters 1–9 (except eight verses) in a single dense, poetic movement.

IN CHAPTER AFTER CHAPTER OF THIS LETTER Paul explains and defends his mission and himself. There are moments of dazzling teaching too. It is easy to pick these out from the letter as a whole and to savor them in isolation. To do so, however, is to misunderstand both Paul's teaching and the defense of himself in which he has set it. It will not do, however, to rejoin that old tradition that dealt first (and briskly!) with Paul the person and then turned to the real business of his letters—his teaching. Paul writes to the Corinthians precisely to *overcome* this distinction. If they are to grasp the good news he brings, they must look at Paul himself, who brings it. He does not bring the message in his words alone, but in his person. Paul himself is the re-presentation of the Anointed.

We will eventually, of course, want to stand back from Paul's self-presentation and assess it coolly. He has good reason to lock himself and his good news together, because only in this way can he remain indispensable to an assembly that is attracted by other emissaries, their message, and their claims. But in sending 2 Corinthians 1–9 Paul likely makes a drastic mistake. The Corinthians are edgy; they are in part humbled before Paul, in part unsettled by his own humiliation. They really want to see Paul himself, not his assistant. Paul insists he is wholly open to the Corinthians as to God himself—but how much he keeps hidden until he is sure the Corinthians believe him. Only then does he tell them what this openness requires from them as he urges and shames them into being generous. It is a dangerous move. What if they see through it?

"We Are the Ground for Your Boasting . . ."

SHARED ENCOURAGEMENT

Paul's opening verses, as so often, set the tone for what follows. *Blessed be the God and father of our Lord Jesus Anointed, the father of mercies and God of all encouragement* (2 Cor. 1:3). Paul mentions *encouragement* ten times in as many lines. God has encouraged him so that he can encourage others. If he is afflicted, it is for the sake of their encouragement. If he is encouraged, it is again for their encouragement as they go through the sufferings he has endured. *And our hope in you is firm: we know that just as you have a share in the sufferings, so you have a share too in the encouragement* (1:7). He has been in danger of death and has had to rely on the God alone who rouses the dead. And the Corinthians have helped too by their prayer, *so that from many people thanks may be given through many for the grace shown to us, for our sake* (1:11).

The prayer, help, and thanksgiving come full circle. It was God who encouraged Paul in the first place, and to God that the Corinthians will give thanks for Paul's rescue from the danger of death. Paul involves the Corinthians, from these very first words of the letter, in the great cycle of God's work and of his own. Paul supports them, and they support him. Paul's, it is clear, is the chief work. The relationship is reciprocal, but not symmetrical. This is enough for Paul's purpose. Not for a moment, in this letter, will he let the Corinthians stand outside the rhythm of God's work undertaken by himself, to view it as dispassionate observers (1:3–11).

Paul does nothing to disguise the danger he has been through. The Corinthians want honesty and dignity in their emissary. Paul insists that honesty will reveal in his work and suffering none of the worldly dignity that they value—but a dignity far greater than the world can imagine.

BAPTISM AND THE BREATH

We have seen how often Paul had changed his plans. He knows how badly the Corinthians have responded. In forming the last plan to be changed,

> *Did I act in a fickle way? Certainly not! Or do I decide what I decide in a worldly way, so that with me there is the "Yes, yes" and the "No, no"? As God is faithful, our word to you is not "Yes" and "No." For the son of God, Jesus Anointed, who was preached among you through us— through myself and Silas and Timothy—he was not "Yes" and "No," but "Yes" has come about in him. For as many as are the promises of God, in him is their "Yes." Therefore through him too is the Amen to God to [God's] glory through us.*
>
> 2 CORINTHIANS 1:17-20

It is a remarkable defense. Paul has been accused of changing his mind. He recalls the promises of God, which all find their "Yes" in the Anointed. How have the Corinthians come to know of these promises and the "Yes"? Through Paul and his collaborators. The assemblies respond with their own "Yes," their Amen. How does this Amen reach God? Back through the Anointed, in whom is the first "Yes," and through his missionaries. This is the route—the indispensable route— for the promises from God to the assemblies, and for the Amen from the assemblies to God. In each direction is a double conduit, the Anointed and the missionaries.

Paul does not advance an argument here. He lays down a challenge. To believe that Paul plans in a worldly or fickle way is to believe that the conduits from and to God are corrupted. God's promises might then have been misrepresented. Their "Yes" in Jesus, their supposed fulfillment, might have been wrongly relayed. The Corinthians' own "Yes" in response, their Amen, might have gone astray. If the Corinthians distrust Paul, they distrust the whole structure of their newfound relation with God. They cannot afford to believe ill of their emissary.

Paul is rebuilding relations with the assembly. He knows better than to leave so stark a challenge in the air. He moves from confrontation to an embrace. Paul has thus far paired himself with the Anointed: they are the conduit together, for the Corinthians' advantage. He has a commission from God that sets him alongside the Anointed and quite apart from his converts. *Through Anointed too is the "Amen" to God, to [God's] glory through us.* It is time now for him to turn his viewpoint around. He aligns himself no longer with the Anointed, but with his converts. Paul has been using "we" and "us" to speak of himself and perhaps of his collaborators and "you" to refer to the Corinthians. But from speaking of the commission that sets him apart he turns to the great commission that he and the Corinthians share. He and they together are marked with the seal of the Anointed: they are baptized. *And the one who confirms our relation, with your own, to the Anointed and who has anointed us— is God* (1:21). Paul silently reembraces his converts and draws them into the privilege of God's service. *God has also put his seal on us and given us the down payment of his Breath in our hearts* (1:22).

Paul draws on metaphor after metaphor. In the first hint of baptism, he talks of anointing; Luke links anointing and baptism too. Paul uses as well the terms of commerce: once a *down payment* had been handed over by a purchaser, the vendor could be made to *confirm* the sale; to *put one's seal* on an object was to assert one's ownership. The metaphor will surface again in the mid-second century as an image for baptism. We can surmise the source of the connection: the Jewish ritual of Sabbath still includes a clause perhaps known in Paul's own day, of God who in circumcision has "sealed his offspring with the sign of the holy Order."

Once more the Corinthians' concerns are defied, not answered, by an appeal to their own life within the faith The stakes are high. If the Corinthians believe in their own endowment with the Breath, then they believe that God had indeed anointed Paul for his task of bringing it. The only evidence, then, that the Corinthians have of their emissary's commission and of his loyalty to it is—themselves. And on the other hand, if they reject Paul, they deny their whole existence as an assembly. To doubt Paul is to bring their Christian life tumbling down about them.

Against the Corinthians' concern Paul has brought to bear all the authority he can muster: the authority of God's faithfulness, of the Breath, and of Paul's own oath. Could Paul not find a defense that relied less strongly on just that reliability—Paul's own reliability—that was being questioned? There is a telling hint here of the conditions under which the good news can be accepted. How is Paul to convey to others the assurance he won through an experience they have not shared? How are they to see in their lives and standing what is clear to him only in the light and terms of his vision of the Anointed? They are already members of the assembly, yes, but they have far more to experience and acknowledge than they yet know. So he describes them to themselves. In three climactic passages he tells them, "This is how you have been, how you are, and how you will be." And it is Paul—Paul alone—who knows it. This letter itself will reveal them to themselves and so enable them to become the new creation that Paul knows them to be.

BUT WILL IT WORK? Has Paul even managed, in these opening paragraphs, to vindicate his travels and his absence? Clearly not. He turns suddenly to a more personal defense born of the Corinthians' particular history. *I call on God to be my witness, upon my life: It is to spare you that I have not come to Corinth* (1:23). This is as strong an oath as any we ever hear from Paul. He clearly doubts whether the assembly will believe him. The grand image of his role next to the Anointed will not, he suspects, reconcile his converts to his absence. But his oath presumes too much. Who is he to spare or not spare the Corinthians? He backtracks quickly: *Not that we are the lords of your faith, but we are fellow workers promoting your joy; for in the faith you stand secure* (1:24). But does this leave Paul with the authority he needs? Within a moment his instinct for command comes to the surface once more. He had written his fraught letter, he says, *so that I might know your character, proving if you are obedient in all respects* (2:9).

Over and over we will encounter in Paul a striking combination of the humility of one who believes himself to be wholly dependent on God for his power and effectiveness and the assurance that he is authorized by God to use this power unflinchingly. His use of this power is repeatedly baffled. His teaching is misunderstood, challenged, or misapplied. He relies on a deeply personal relationship with his assemblies, but the relationship is stormy, and the assemblies forever want more of Paul than he can give them.

MOSES AND PAUL: THE LETTER AND THE SPIRIT

The Corinthians are worried that their emissary has been preaching to all and sundry. Should he not be more aware who will accept his good news and who will not; and so avoid the humiliation of rebuff? But Paul insists he is called to preach without distinction.

> *We are a fragrance of Anointed rising to God among those being saved and among those being lost: for the one group, a scent arising from death and leading to death; for the other, a scent arising from life and leading to life. And for this, who is adequate?*
> 2 CORINTHIANS 2:15-16

For the task he has been given, asks Paul, *who is adequate?* We have seen Paul draw upon the prophets for his self-understanding, on Isaiah and Jeremiah themselves and on the Servant of God of whom Isaiah spoke. In the coming pages he has one more comparison to draw—with the great prophet and leader Moses. Almost certainly he could not avoid it; there were opponents in Corinth who were drawing the comparison already, to Paul's discredit. But once under way, Paul makes the most of it. He must confront the challenge. How could he claim for his good news a stature to compare with the good news brought from Sinai by Moses? Who was Paul to compete with the greatest prophet of them all? Paul is picking up the gauntlet. He knows he is not adequate, but what had Moses himself said when God gave him his commission? *"Lord, I am not adequate"* (The Escape [Exodus] 4:10). Here in Paul is the Moses of God's new order.

The passage on Moses is remarkable even by Paul's standards. In all parts of 2 Corinthians Paul's language is bursting at the seams, but nowhere does it do so with greater density and power than in these paragraphs in which he dwells on Moses' great commission—and on a far greater commission: his own.

PAUL: FROM GLORY TO GLORY

For the task ahead, *who is adequate? For we are not as the majority, hawking the word of God, but we speak as from sincerity, as from God face-to-face with God we speak in Anointed* (2 Cor. 2:17).

Moses was the greatest of the prophets, the leader of his people, the hero of the Old Order. Moses had been ordered by God to lead his people out of Egypt. Had he leapt at the chance? Far from it. Moses finds excuse after excuse, reasons why God should not choose him. *"I beg you, Lord, I am not adequate. I was not yesterday nor the day before nor from the time when you started to speak to your servant; I stutter and am slow of speech"* (The Escape 4:10, Greek Version). God brooks no contradiction: *"Who has given mouth to man, who has made him deaf or dumb, seeing or blind?"* (4:11). Moses was no speaker. Nor was Paul; *the presence of his person*, said the Corinthians, *is weak and his speech is contemptible* (2 Cor. 10:10). Later tradition remembered how Moses' hand suffered from a skin disease (traditionally translated as "leprosy"); Paul in turn speaks of the scourge in his flesh, which God refused to remove (12:7–9).

Such is the Moses who will lead God's people out of Egypt and to freedom. For two prolonged visits he ascends Mt. Sinai to receive the commands of God. On his descent from the first such visit he finds that the Israelites, in his absence, have built themselves an idol of gold. Moses pleads with God to forgive his people. He speaks *face-to-face* with God. *"Now, if you forgive them their wrongdoing, forgive; but if not, blot me out of your book that you have written* (The Escape 32:32). In his letter to the Romans Paul will have to confront the apparent obstinacy of his own people—why have they not accepted the good news? As Moses interceded for Israel, so does Paul: *For I have prayed to be accursed, I myself, cast out from the Anointed on behalf of my brothers in the flesh* (Rom. 9:3).

Moses rose to the top of Sinai. Or did he rise far higher? From the first century C.E. onward there is a steady tradition that Moses went up from Sinai to heaven, to receive there the Law and to bring it down to earth as a gift for his people. In heaven he was shown the secrets that are normally associated with the seers. He went to the place where the light of the sun and the moon is. He was shown the ways of Paradise. And at Moses' death God reminded him of the heaven into which he had entered. Paul had good reason to think of Moses' commission and his own long before the Corinthians compared the two and found Paul's wanting.

Moses had relayed *commands* from the Lord. Paul rounds off an argument in 1 Corinthians with: *All those who think they are prophets, let them recognize what I am writing to you: it is the Lord's command* (1 Cor. 14:37). God promised Moses that he, God, would do many *signs and wonders* and gave Moses *wonders* to perform himself, not least of which was defeating the Egyptian magicians (The Escape 7:3; 4:21; 7:8–9:12). Moses himself gives an account of God's commands to Israel and of Israel's years in the wilderness (The Second Law [Deuteronomy]), and he tells of the *signs and wonders* God wrought there. The phrase becomes almost a slogan for God's dramatic acts of power. And Paul? He in turn reminds the Corinthians of his *signs and wonders and acts of power* (2 Cor. 12:12) and hints to the Romans of all that the Anointed had done through him *by word and by deed, in the power of signs and wonders, in the power of the Breath of God* (Rom. 15:18–19).

Moses' own brother and sister had criticized him. *"Has the Lord"* they asked, *"really spoken only to Moses? Hasn't he spoken to us too?"* (The Census [Numbers] 12:2). God summoned them to the Tent of Meeting in anger. Paul knows the passage well, both in its Greek form (from which Paul generally draws his own citations from the Old Order) and in the Hebrew original. In the Greek version, God says:

> Listen to my words: If there is a prophet among you,
> I will make myself known to them in a vision and will speak to them in
>   a dream.
> But not so, my servant Moses. In my whole house he is faithful.
>
> THE CENSUS 12:6–7, GREEK VERSION

Paul has already written of himself to the Corinthians as the steward of God's household, whose task is to be *faithful* (1 Cor. 4:1–2).

About Moses, God continues:

> With him I will speak mouth to mouth, in a [visible] *form and not
>   through riddles;*
> and he has seen the glory of the Lord.
>
> THE CENSUS 12:8, GREEK VERSION

Moses *has seen the glory of the Lord*—just as Paul himself has seen it in his turn. Paul knows The Census too in Hebrew. Here are the last lines of our passage, in the version Paul appears to have known:

> *He is entrusted with my whole house.*
> *With him I speak mouth to mouth, in a mirror and not in riddles;*
> *and he sees the form of the Lord.*
> THE CENSUS 12:7–8, VARIANT

This is the passage Paul had in mind when he wrote to the Corinthians about love: *now we see through a mirror, in a riddle* (1 Cor. 13:12). There he envisaged a mirror as opaque and the knowledge it offers as partial and clouded. The Census had thought of mirrors quite differently; in it mirrors offer clear, dazzling knowledge. For centuries the surface of mirrors had been polished bronze. Glass mirrors were introduced in the age of Paul himself. A mirror's clouded, dented, or dirtied surface gave just a hint of the figure before it, but a mirror's well-polished surface was the vehicle for a glittering—and uncanny—image. Such is the image that Moses had seen and, centuries later, Paul saw. And now, thanks to Paul, his converts are coming to see it too.

So much links Moses and Paul. All the more striking, then, is the contrast that Paul draws between himself and Moses in this letter to Corinth. Paul's detractors have compared Paul and Moses and found Paul wanting. Paul turns the tables.

Moses came down from Sinai with the commands of the Old Order inscribed on two tablets of stone. But the New is written not on stone; it is written on the hearts of believers. The letter kills; the Breath gives life. Paul can draw for this theme on the great prophecy of the prophet Jeremiah. Through Jeremiah, God says:

> *Look, the days are coming,*
> *when I will make a New Order with Israel,*
> *not like the Order which I made with their forebears,*
> *when I took them out of Egypt, the Order which they broke.*
> *This is the Order which I will make with Israel after those days, says God:*
> *I will put my Law within them,*

and I will write it on their hearts;
and I will be their God, and they shall be my people.

Let's, then, follow Paul's contrasts through the following paragraphs. We are about to disentangle a tight knot of images and associations. We will identify one leading sense in each, and so are in danger of leaving other hints and associations as discarded loose ends. We will need, eventually, to reweave the bundle. Paul's style matches the point he is making. These dense, overladen verses are hardly offering information. They offer in themselves the cryptic, half-grasped images of an unveiling—about the greatest unveiling of all. To borrow a phrase we know well, in these images is the likeness as the appearance of the truth Paul is speaking of.

It is as well to say at the outset that Paul's attack on Moses and the Order he brought has no basis in the text of the Old Order itself. Paul is waging war here on his own account and with weapons of his own. Any rival preachers, extolling Moses, have a counterargument ready to hand: Paul is unspeakably arrogant. Paul's most powerful argument, as we have already seen, remains the lives and gifts of his converts themselves. No wonder he turns the Corinthians' attention back, at every opportunity, to themselves and his relation to them. Whatever Paul's detractors claim for the life ordained by Moses, Paul expects it to seem paltry beside the gifts that he himself has brought the Corinthians.

HERE, THEN, IS THE OLD ORDER'S ACCOUNT of Moses and the glory of his face. So dear to God was Moses that on his second long visit to Mt. Sinai God gave him a glimpse—just a glimpse—of God's own glory. While God was speaking with him, Moses' face was suffused with glory. And when Moses came down from that second visit his face was shining. From then on he wore a veil over his face. Moses continued to receive commands from God down on the plain. He had a Tent of Meeting, a tent pitched outside the camp, *where the Lord spoke to Moses face-to-face, as a person speaks to their friend* (The Escape 33:11, Greek Version). He removed the veil only when he went into the tent to speak with God.

And Aaron and all the elders of Israel saw Moses and the appearance of
the color of his face was glorified, and they were afraid to approach him.
And Moses called them and they turned to him, Aaron and all the lead-
ers of the prayer house, and Moses spoke to them. And after this all the
sons of Israel approached him, and he commanded them everything that
the Lord had told him on Mt. Sinai. And when he stopped speaking to
them, he put a veil onto his face. But whenever Moses went in before the
Lord to speak with him, he would take off the veil until he came out
again. And coming out he would tell all the sons of Israel whatever com-
mands the Lord had given him. And the sons of Israel saw the face of
Moses, that it shone with glory.

THE ESCAPE 34:30–35, GREEK VERSION

Paul takes up the theme of the veil that had covered the face of
Moses. The glory of Moses' Order, Paul claims, was fading; so in turn
was the glory on Moses' face. Moses, then, veiled his face to hide not
the glory itself, but the fact of its fading away. But the Order served by
Paul is eternal; its glory is unfading—and any glory that it gives to its
prophet or people will be unfading too. Paul uses the motif of the veil
in many ways. He speaks of the veil on Moses' face and a veil on the
Jews' hearts, of the veil removed when Moses turned to the Lord and a
veil removed from the face of Paul's own people.

We are ready to hear Paul's great comparison of the Old Order and
the New. Here is a translation of the crucial passage. I have glossed (in
brackets and in roman, not italic, type) some of Paul's most concentrated expressions. The density of his metaphors makes room for other
readings too—too many to explore here. We can only admire a passage
so alive with hints and possibilities.

On the one hand, Paul has explained, is Moses' ministry; this leads
to our condemnation. On the other is Paul's own; thanks to this we will
be found just. However great the glory, then, attached to Moses' ministry, it will be far outshone by the glory attached to Paul's.

Having, then, such hope we speak quite openly, and not as Moses used to
put a veil onto his face so that the children of Israel might not gaze at the
conclusion of what was passing away.

But their minds were hardened. For right up to the present day the same veil rests on the reading of the old order, without the lifting of the veil, that in Anointed it is passing away. And up unto today whenever Moses is being read, a veil lies on their hearts.

"But [as we read in The Escape] whenever he turns to the Lord, the veil is removed." Now "the Lord" here is the Breath of God; and where there is the Breath of the Lord, there is freedom.

And we—all of us—with unveiled face gazing as in a mirror on the glory of the Lord [that is, on the Anointed], are being transformed into the same image [the image of God that we gaze on, the glory of the Lord that is the Anointed himself], from glory into glory, just as from "the Lord" [the one Moses turned to, that is], the breath.

2 CORINTHIANS 3:12–18

What is Paul's own role in this unveiling and the transformation it offers? The beginning of the comparison is striking but readily envisaged: Moses had seen the glory of God. His face glowed thereafter with reflected glory. This glory was recharged whenever Moses went into the Tent of Meeting *before the Lord*. This was the reflected and fading glory on which the children of Israel gazed. And Paul? He is the Moses of the New Order. He has seen the glory of God in his vision of the Anointed, the image of God. And he now bears that glory in his turn. It is this reflected but increasing glory, in the ministry and person of Paul, that the Corinthians can gaze on now.

This is already striking enough. Paul, however, does not rest here. He envisages the veil on the face of Moses and then a veil on the hearts of Moses' people, the Jews. What was true of Moses as history was as metaphor true of his people. Paul has in mind both Moses himself and Moses as the representative of his people.

Whenever he turns to the Lord, the veil is removed. Paul has here joined together two moments in this story from The Escape. As we have heard, Moses called the elders of the people, *and they turned to him* and saw his face aglow with glory; and a few lines later Moses *went in before the Lord to speak with him*, and at these moments *would take off the veil*. But in Paul's paraphrase it is Moses himself who turns; he turns to the

Lord. In Paul's imagination Moses again represents his people. Paul is evoking far more here than just this one passage in The Escape. To "turn to the Lord," throughout the Old Order, was to acknowledge him as God and seek to do his will. As Paul envisages the setting, all the Jews have the same opportunity now to turn to the Lord that Moses himself had then to enter the Tent, remove the veil, and see the glory.

But who in Paul's day takes up that opportunity? It is Paul's people, his converts, who turn to the Lord. And what do they see when they do?

Paul imagines looking into a mirror. What do we most commonly see there? Ourselves. Most of us look most often in a mirror to see our own image. Paul imagines his converts seeing such a sight, but not in this case the dull tarnished image of Adam that normally confronts us. He imagines their turning physically to the Lord, as the elders turned to Moses, and seeing the face of the Anointed as Paul himself has seen it— the face of Adam restored to his first glory. They are looking on the *likeness as the appearance of adam*—on a "human" figure. Here, facing them as they look in a mirror, is a dazzling, metalled image of themselves. A mirror reflects onto its viewer the light that falls on it. The Corinthians are gazing on the image of God in which they were themselves created, and from that gaze their own faces will be illumined with reflected light. They will recover the glory that Adam lost.

But let's ask a blunt, overly literal question. Where shall Paul's converts see this image? Who or what do they "turn" to, as the elders had turned to Moses outside the Tent of Meeting and as Moses inside had turned to the Lord? Paul's metaphors are in danger of losing all real reference in the lush jungle of their own allusions.

Paul lets himself come full circle, back to that first simple contrast he drew between himself and Moses. In The Escape the leaders of the Jews had *turned to Moses* and seen his face aglow. And Paul's converts shall turn to the new Moses, to Paul himself, and see one who re-presents the Anointed, the new Adam, the image of God. This, then, is the mirrored image, dazzling like metalled glass, in which the Corinthians shall see the glory. And the sight will transform them into that glory. What Paul saw on the road to Damascus, the Corinthians shall see in Paul. Here, right before them, is what they need for their own transformation—Paul himself.

Moses ascended to the heavens. So has Paul. Moses' glory faded. Paul's is growing brighter. The seer is transformed as he ascends through the heavens, through ever greater glory toward the throne of God. The Corinthians are being transformed here on earth, by their gaze here on the glory of God in the face of the Anointed—represented by Paul himself.

And so Paul brings his passage to a climax. He returns to the Breath. He has already introduced it as a gift received at baptism, that first movement from the fallen world toward the glory beyond. Now he signals its importance again in the ongoing transformation of the Corinthians. *And we—all of us—with unveiled face gazing as in a mirror on the glory of the Lord* [that is, on the Anointed], *are being transformed into the same image* [the image of God that we gaze on, the glory of the Lord that is the Anointed himself], *from glory into glory, just as from "the Lord"* [the one Moses turned to, that is], *the breath* (2 Cor. 3:18). The Corinthians may have expected to hear in this letter about transformation, but Paul aims far higher. In the understanding they are winning here, they can see for the first time who and what is the Paul they have so belittled.

The more clearly they see in Paul's letter what is there to be seen— the more fully they grasp from the sight of Paul himself the Anointed, his standing, his death and its effect—the more brightly they reflect the glory they are gazing on. The Corinthians' transformation is under way.

"NOT OURSELVES BUT JESUS ANOINTED"

In 2 Corinthians 3:12–18 we find a fanfare of confidence, but Paul's imagery gives rise to a terrible danger. He must fend it off at once.

Paul insists he is in every way open, as his good news requires. *If our gospel is veiled at all, it is veiled among those on their way to destruction, among whom the god of this aeon has blinded the thoughts of the faithless, to prevent them seeing the light of the gospel of the glory of the Anointed, who is the image of God* (2 Cor. 4:3–4). With this, Paul has said enough for his argument. But he quickly sounds the same theme again.

Of course it is the Anointed who is the image of God, but the Corinthians have not had sight of the Anointed; they have had no chance to gaze on him. They have had Paul, himself anointed by God (2 Cor. 1:21). They have been able to gaze on *him*. And what more might that lead to? To idolatry. Surely Paul is moving himself too close to the Anointed and so to the image and glory of God? Unless care is taken, the Corinthians could come to worship Paul himself.

Paul averts the danger with an emphatic reprise of that last and most dangerous sentence. *For we do not proclaim ourselves but Jesus Anointed as Lord, and ourselves as your slaves on Jesus' account. For the God who said "Light shall shine out of darkness" is the one who shone in our hearts, to bring about enlightenment, the knowledge of the glory of God in the face of Jesus the Anointed* (4:5–6). Idolatry must be prevented, but the conditions cannot be avoided that could—by error—give it rise, for as we have heard, *God was pleased to unveil his son in me, so that I might preach him among the Gentiles* (Gal. 1:16).

Like knows like. Only *the likeness as the appearance of Adam* on the throne makes accessible to human minds what humans can know about the God in whose image they were made. Words will never be enough. And in turn, only a person can re-present that likeness to those on earth who have never seen it. Words, once more, will never be enough.

WE ARE READY TO LEAVE this extraordinary passage behind. We do well to close with a footnote to the whole discussion. Paul and the Corinthians are all subject to the transformation from glory into glory. So much the more striking, then, is an ancient tradition that saw and emphasized just how high a status Paul is claiming here. I have so far translated the text adopted by all modern editions of the Bible: *We, all of us, . . . gazing . . . on the glory of the Lord, are being transformed.* But the oldest of all our surviving manuscripts, a papyrus written around 200 C.E., omits the words *all of us* in that sentence.

When Paul at the start of this section said *as from God face-to-face with God we speak in Anointed* (2:17), it is clear he had in mind his own exclusive role as an emissary. The privilege enjoyed by Moses in the Old Order is enjoyed by Paul in the New. For the scribe of our papyrus Paul was still using "we" at the end of this section (3:18) without any reference to anyone except himself. All the complexity that we have seen in Paul's images is dissolved. The subject of this paragraph is Paul and Paul alone. Two other differences, small in themselves, confirm the different tenor of the passage. This Paul is alone in gazing on the glory and alone in his transformation. *And we with unveiled face gaze as in a mirror on the glory of the Lord,* [that is, only] *we who are being transformed into the same image that we gaze on* (2 Cor. 3:18 in Papyrus 46).

Paul the emissary reveals the transformation, for Paul the seer is undergoing it. And in this tradition, Paul alone.

IN VESSELS OF EARTHENWARE: RE-PRESENTING THE ANOINTED

The Corinthians can dwell on Paul himself; they can "gaze" on him with faces and hearts unveiled. He has led them step by step through and past their own misunderstanding. He now takes them deeper into the disclosure and his role in it. They have clear vision at last. But what will they see?

Paul generates a striking contrast. He moves sharply from his poetic account of God's glory to the degradation he himself suffers in his ministry. *We have this treasure in vessels of earthenware, so that the extraordinary character of this power might be God's and not from ourselves* (4:7). Paul recalls the sufferings that have never confounded him. He is forever on the cusp, on the verge of disaster—but never defeated: *in everything pressed hard but not trapped, nearly desperate but not wholly desperate, struck down but not destroyed* (4:8–9).

These sufferings are not simply his alone. The Corinthians can now see at last Paul's role for what it is. *We always bear the dying of Jesus in our bodily person, so that the life too of Jesus might be made visible in this bodily person of ours* (4:10). To see Paul is to see into the great drama of salvation itself. The Corinthians have, in Paul, the death and life of Jesus himself re-presented before their eyes.

We always bear the dying of Jesus in our bodily person. Paul speaks not of the Anointed, but specifically of Jesus. He is reminding the Corinthians of the man of flesh and blood. Paul repeats his point with a contrast still more extreme: *for we ourselves who are alive are always being handed over to death on Jesus' account, so that the life too of Jesus might be made visible in our mortal flesh* (4:11). By the same token, when the Corinthians had been ashamed of Paul's sufferings, they had been ashamed of Jesus' sufferings too. We remember the low value put, by some in the Corinthian assembly, on the body of flesh and blood; it was irrelevant to life in the Breath here on earth and would—as they claimed—be abandoned to decay when the true self could at last enjoy that life in the Breath, unencumbered, in the age to come. Paul stood against such a view in 1 Corinthians, and once more stands against it here. In the despised suffering of his flesh and blood lies the true disclosure of Jesus. The Corinthians who so value knowledge are blind to the most important knowledge of all—the knowledge offered to them in the person of Paul himself.

So that death is at work in us, but life in you (4:12). The Corinthians too have their part in this great drama. Paul knew already when writing 1 Corinthians how readily his converts could misunderstand the life they enjoyed in the Breath of God. But it is Paul himself who introduced them to that life. He must correct their confidence, not undermine it.

We, naturally enough, compare Paul with his converts. In 1 Corinthians Paul calls upon his converts to imitate himself. *Be imitators of me, as I am of Anointed* (1 Cor. 11:1). But here in 2 Corinthians 1–6 Paul is the object of awed contemplation, not of imitation. He does not, therefore, suggest that his converts bear the dying of the Anointed; that burden is his alone. And conversely, we contrast Paul, just as naturally, with the Anointed. He can imitate Jesus, nothing more. But here in 2 Corinthians 1–6 Paul re-presents Jesus in his own person. Paul is not looking at Jesus and copying him; Paul finds himself living out, in every part of him and every action, a role that has become himself.

From baptism in the past to transformation ongoing in the present, Paul is shaping this first part of his letter around the great movement into which God draws God's people. And where will this transformation end? Paul has moved on from his commission to the suffering intrinsic to it. As we have seen him do before, he speaks of himself (and perhaps his assistants) as "we"—and then quietly lets that "we" embrace his addressees as well. As he thinks of his present suffering and of God's plan for him, so he thinks too of God's plan for his converts. Neither he nor they will forever be weighed down with the fleshly "tent" that is our home and our burden on this earth. *We groan with the weight, we who are in this tent, because we do not want to take it off, but rather to put on another on top of it, so that the mortal may be swallowed up by life. And the one who wrought us for this very thing is God, who gave us the down payment of the Breath* (2 Cor. 5:4–5). The garments of glory are waiting for Paul and for his converts as they will be waiting for the seer Isaiah. The destination lies ahead.

At the beginning of the letter, Paul declared his aim: he would show the Corinthians that he was the ground of their boasting as they were the ground of his. As he was aware of himself and his honesty, so he wanted the assembly to be aware of them too. The first part of his task is nearly done; they know now why they can—and should—be proud of him. His awareness of himself and theirs now coincide. In this they have not just won a knowledge of external things. So deep is the effect that Paul has had upon them that they can—and must—look inside themselves if they are to understand him. And at him, if they are to understand themselves.

Paul's whole demonstration is set within the great movement of God's plan for Paul and for the Corinthians themselves. Only one boast is of value—the boast with which Paul and the Corinthians can stand before the judgment seat *on the day of the Lord Jesus.* As this first part of Paul's letter draws toward its climax, all the themes we have already heard return in a grand symphonic recapitulation:

> *All of us must appear openly before the judgment seat of the Anointed, each one to receive recompense for the things done through our bodily existence, in proportion to what we have done, whether good or evil. Knowing, therefore, the fear of the Lord we persuade humankind but we stand open before God; and I hope we stand open too in the awareness of each of you. We are not commending ourselves to you again, but giving you an opportunity for boasting on our behalf, so that you may have some reply to those whose boast is in outward appearance and not in the heart.*
>
> 2 CORINTHIANS 5:10–12

THE NEW CREATION

Paul has still to round off this first part of the letter, and it is a ringing conclusion to all that we have heard so far. He presents his own credo to the Corinthians who are now ready to hear it. He has taken them in imagination from their past through the present to their future at the bar of judgment. And in more than just imagination. As they have become aware of their progress into glory, so they have made greater progress. Paul has designed the letter to effect what it describes.

How much they know and understand now, that they could not at the letter's start. Paul can now lay bare before them the principle that underlies all he has said so far. For the last time in this chapter we are going to navigate a single passage, 5:14–21, finding as we go some of the streams that feed into its swirling current.

> *The love of the Anointed controls us, because we have made this judg-*
> *ment: one died on behalf of all, so all died; and he died on behalf of all,*
> *so that those who live should no longer live for themselves but for him*
> *who on their behalf died and was raised.*
>
> 2 CORINTHIANS 5:14-15

The paragraph is strangely introduced: *the love of the Anointed controls us, because we have made this judgment*—the judgment that we shall see next. Making a judgment? What a cool appraisal this suggests. As Paul has "made sense" of his calling, so he is inviting his addressees to "see the point" of all that he has said in this letter so far. *The love of the Anointed* may be the love he now sees that the Anointed has for him, or the love he feels for the Anointed as a result; or both. For Paul's love follows his recognition, what the Anointed's love has done.

The image of God on which the Corinthians gaze is Adam restored to glory. All *adam*, all humanity must be embraced in what he has done. *One died on behalf of all, so all died.* As Adam died, so did all *adam*. Those involved, then, are not just the converts to the Anointed at their baptism *into the death of Anointed* (Rom. 6:3); all humanity has died, past, present, and future. Paul had told the Galatians as the individual Paul: *I have been crucified with Anointed* (Gal. 2:19). Here to the Corinthians he speaks as the emissary: *All died.* But not everyone has moved through this death to the new life beyond. Just those who are in the Anointed are therefore ready to enjoy, here and now, a version of the life enjoyed in heaven by the righteous dead.

> *So that we ourselves, from the present onward, know nobody after the*
> *fashion of the flesh. Although we have known Anointed after the fashion*
> *of the flesh, yet now we know him in this way no longer.*
> 2 CORINTHIANS 5:16

Paul now knows no one *after the fashion of the flesh*. That was how the Corinthians had known Paul before they heard this letter, and how they had known the Anointed too. They had thought in this world's terms, in terms of pride and public dignity. Paul too, before his conversion, had misunderstood the Anointed in just the same way.

Might Paul be telling us that he met Jesus before the crucifixion? We are bound to speculate on the possibility, but this is not Paul's point here. (He is more likely, if anything, picking up and belittling a claim made on Peter's behalf by his representatives in Corinth.) It is not acquaintance that is at stake, but "knowledge"—the knowledge that Paul's conversion has brought to him and that Paul himself brings to others.

> *So that if anyone is in Anointed, there is a new creation. The old things*
> *have passed away, look, they have become quite new* [or, *the new has*
> *come to be*].
> 2 CORINTHIANS 5:17

Adam restored belongs in Eden restored and brings *adam* with him. Jesus was on earth, just as Paul is, so that he might take his followers where he himself belongs—and where Paul has already been. Those baptized into the Anointed and so now *in him* are on the trajectory that has shaped the whole letter so far. They are being transformed as they move toward the judgment seat, the throne of God, just as Paul was transformed as he passed through successive heavens to the glory of the court of God. The journey—of their transformation and of this letter—began with their baptism. It will come as no surprise when Paul describes baptism to the Romans as baptism into the death of the Anointed. The baptized are buried with the Anointed and so are ready for the life of heaven.

But Paul's converts need neither "journey" now nor the privilege of a seer. It is in the daily life of the assembly that Paul's converts (the

Body of the Anointed) can dwell on Paul (who re-presents the Anointed) to grow into the glory of the Anointed, who is himself the image of God.

And how did the Anointed do what he has done? We are reaching the conclusion to the letter's first half. Every instrument in the orchestra is playing:

> *And all of this is from the God who reconciled us to himself through Anointed and gave us the service of reconciliation, as follows: God was in Anointed reconciling the world to himself, not counting their infringements against them, and had put in us the word of reconciliation. We are therefore ambassadors of Anointed, with God himself, we may say, offering encouragement through us: "On behalf of Anointed, we make our plea: Be reconciled to God. The one who did not know wrongdoing—God made him into wrongdoing on our behalf, so that in him we might become the justness of God."*
>
> 2 CORINTHIANS 5:18-21

We have heard in our Chapter 4 of the Day of Atonement. Paul thinks once more of such rituals. Here he speaks generally; he does not dwell on that day itself. And specifically; he studies the details and nature of an atoning sacrifice. God offers forgiveness when an unblemished sacrifice is offered. In the Greek version of the Old Order the word "wrongdoing" is used both for the wrong and for the sacrifice that secures God's forgiveness for it:

> *If the ruler does wrong . . . and his wrongdoing becomes known to him, . . . [he will sacrifice an animal, and] it is [an animal of] wrongdoing. And the priest with his finger will place some of the blood of [the animal of] wrongdoing on the horns of the altar of the offering. . . . And the priest will make atonement in respect of him from his wrongdoing, and it shall be forgiven him.*
>
> THE LAWS OF RITUAL [LEVITICUS] 4:22-26, GREEK VERSION

Once more Paul takes over an ancient image and remolds it. The Old Order speaks of atonement. Paul speaks of reconciliation. This is a secular word, unfamiliar in any talk of sacrifice and its effects. Now if such reconciliation is to take place at all, we will expect God to make the move. It is for God to let go his anger and be reconciled. But God, claims Paul, has made a more roundabout move. It is for humans to be reconciled to God. It is for them to let go their wrongdoing, and God will accept their offer, for in the Anointed, the new Adam, God has enabled the old *adam* to make a move they would never have undertaken for themselves. For *God was in Anointed reconciling the world to himself.*

Over and over we have heard Paul stretch his language to say what he needs to say. In one of his boldest sentences Paul now takes up the description of a sacrificial animal as itself *the wrongdoing* for which its death atones. Paul had earlier told the Corinthians that the Anointed had become for them wisdom from God—justness and holiness and redemption (1 Cor. 1:30). Now he tells them to what they themselves are called. Jesus' movement to a life on earth has made possible their movement toward the life of heaven. *The one who did not know wrongdoing—God made him into wrongdoing on our behalf, so that in him we might become the justness of God.*

". . . Just As You Too Are Ours"

THE COLLECTION FOR JERUSALEM

The letter's second part, chapters 7–9, is a shorter section than the first and will take us fewer pages here, but without it we understand nothing of Paul's self-presentation or aims.

Great is my openness toward you, great are my grounds for boasting in you (2 Cor. 7:4). Paul has given the Corinthians good reason for pride in him. Now for his grounds to take pride in them. Paul turns the letter upon its great axis and launches its second part. Titus has brought him good news.

And besides our own comfort we took even more and special joy in the joy of Titus, because his breath has been set at rest by you all. For if I have expressed some pride in you, I was not put to shame. But as we

*have said everything to you in truth, so too our pride expressed to Titus
has proved true.*

2 CORINTHIANS 7:13-14

But there is more to be done. Paul has launched his collection for
Jerusalem. Here is the tribute that his Gentiles shall bring to the Holy
City in these last times before the Lord's return. In Macedonia, he says,
the response has been immensely encouraging. And in Corinth? A year
before, the Corinthians had set to with a will. Has their enthusiasm fal-
tered? Paul has taken trouble over the administration of the fund and
starts by making the arrangements clear. There had been suspicions in
Corinth that Paul or his associates were not handling the money honestly. Paul himself must make it clear that he is innocent of misdoing.
With these doubts laid to rest, Paul can get back to his own concern,
the raising of additional funds.

Paul has had in mind, throughout, the pride that he and the Corinthians can take in each other, but they are not alone in such links.
Paul now shows the Corinthians how many threads are interwoven
in this life and enterprise. The Corinthians have received from the
Anointed, from Titus, and from Paul himself. They have been held up
to the Macedonians as an example and have in turn the Macedonians'
response before them as an inspiration. How are they to react?

When listing the paradoxes of his own role, Paul had ended: *as griev-
ing but always rejoicing, as poor but making many rich, as having nothing and
possessing everything* (2 Cor. 6:10). Paul was not alone. How had the
Macedonians responded to his appeal for the collection? Once more in
Paul's imagination the literal and the metaphorical merge. *The abundance
of their joy and their deep poverty have overflowed into the wealth of their sincere concern* (8:2). The same fundamental example for Paul, the Macedonians, and now the Corinthians is forever in sight: *You know the grace of
our Lord Jesus Anointed: on your account he became poor who was rich, so that
you, yes you by his poverty might become rich* (8:9). It is time for the
Corinthians to join this rhythm of generosity and care.

Titus too is offered as an example. Titus had *made a start* on this collection, so Paul has urged him *to bring it through to completion.* The
Corinthians had *made a start* in their desire to help a year before; now,

urges Paul, they should *bring* the act itself *through to completion*. Titus had been well received in Corinth; he has seen the Corinthians' *eagerness* to resolve their disagreement with Paul (7:13–8:17). Paul vouches for their *eagerness* too, as he reminds them of the *eagerness* of the Macedonians, for the Macedonians had given generously *of their own choice*. And so back to Titus:

> *Thanks be to God, who has put the same eagerness toward you in the heart of Titus. He has had that comfort, and now, all the more eager, has of his own choice left to come to you.*
>
> 2 CORINTHIANS 8:16–17

Paul rounds off. The Corinthians are to give proof of their love and of the good grounds Paul had for taking pride in them. Here chapter 8 ends. It has often been asked whether chapter 9 was once part of a different letter. It reintroduces, with a flourish, just the same theme that Paul has been discussing. Shouldn't the letter contain either chapter 8 or chapter 9—but not both?

If it has been added by a later editor, we can see why. Paul has already established the grounds for reciprocal pride, and here he pleads once more for the Corinthians to vindicate their founding father. In Macedonia Paul has spoken of the Corinthians with pride (9:2); Greece as a whole had already been ready to help for a year, and it was the commitment of the Corinthians that had fired them. Now, vice versa, he praises the Macedonians to Corinth; they have given far more than he had hoped. The Corinthians have been an example to others. Now those others are an example for them. Instrument after instrument picks up the theme.

The Corinthians are playing in a great symphony of generosity and commitment. Once they can hear those around them and can sense their role in this great sweep of sound, they will surely not fail the other players—or their conductor, Paul.

> *I have sent the brothers, so that the pride we have in you may not prove vain in this side of things, so that you may be prepared, just as I have been saying you would be. Otherwise, if some Macedonians come with*

me and they find you unprepared, we ourselves might be put to shame—
not to mention yourselves!—in this essential thing.

2 CORINTHIANS 9:3-4

From all this will grow not just material help for the *saints* in Jerusalem, but another round in the spiral of thanks upon thanks offered to God by Paul's churches. We have heard of the thanks that Paul gives for the Corinthians and the Corinthians give for Paul, but there are more instruments in this orchestra than just these. Titus, the Macedonians, the church in Jerusalem—the theme of thanksgiving is picked up and passed on, wider and wider through the church:

For the support of this civic service does not only supply the wants of
the saints, but is also abundant through many thanksgivings to God.
Through the proof provided by this service you [or they] give glory to
God for your obedience in confessing the good news of the Anointed and
for the sincere care of the fellowship shown to them and to everyone.
And in their prayer for you they will be longing for you on account of
the surpassing grace of God in you. Thanks be to God for his indescrib-
able gift!

2 CORINTHIANS 9:12-15

HIDDEN MOTIVES FOR OPENNESS?

Paul has worked tirelessly to reassure the Corinthians that they can trust him. He has been wholly honest with them throughout, and he can no more hide his good news from others than the Corinthians themselves—who are his "letter"—can hide themselves. As he and they are bound inescapably together in the good news, so are they bound as well in mutual encouragement and care.

Paul's modern readers, however, may find that his presentation raises more questions than it resolves. Paul declares that he has been and is being wholly open to the Corinthians. But this openness has one aim that he does not admit to when he speaks of it: to bind the Corinthians so closely to him that they cannot refuse his request for money. So much for the balance of mutual care, so carefully wrought, between the emissary and his assembly.

And what of his tactics? If he succeeds, he has knit the assembly and himself together again, more tightly than ever. But if the Corinthians once unravel Paul's construction and ask what is he trying, through its elegant balance, to get out of them, then their suspicion and anger will be greater than ever before. Paul, they will believe, is using them. He has tried to awe them, and he has. But all for an aim he did not admit—to rescue himself from the shame of a failed collection.

WE ARE ABOUT TO MOVE to quite different circumstances and a quite different sort of letter. This is a good moment to stand back and survey the portrait that is emerging of our emissary.

Small and fragile communities have needs in common. Paul ends each letter with a plea for unity. To back his instruction Paul holds out to the Corinthians an image of the Anointed and his Body on earth. This is a standard metaphor for the body politic. Paul has elevated it into a principle and aim impervious to any critic. Paul has appropriated for his version of the good news all that is harmonious and has decried all that oppose or misrepresent him as the cause of division. Paul has described to the Galatians the fruits of the Breath, all the virtues that lead to and foster social harmony, and by contrast the works of the flesh, all the behavior of faction and bitterness. To the Corinthians he extols everything that would build up the Body: considerateness, carefulness, self-restraint, good order.

But Paul himself broke ranks in Antioch. Paul insisted that he was answerable to God alone and to none of the authorities in Jerusalem. Paul excoriated the teachers in Galatia and humiliated the wise in Corinth. Paul insists on peace and unity among his addressees, but only on his own terms. It is always those who disagree with him who are breaking up the Body of the Anointed. The Galatians must break off relations with the teachers from Antioch or Jerusalem. The Corinthians must accept his authority as supreme. Paul forever resists schism, but Paul is the schismatic.

Did Paul not see the danger that he was creating the divisions he so bitterly condemned? No, for he is fired by his own vision. It authenticates itself and brooks no contradiction. Paul is utterly single-minded.

He is taking his addressees along the path that he himself knows well. And his eye is forever, come what may, upon the goal.

And he expects his converts to follow him, for he is their father. He tells the Corinthians: *I am writing to you as to my much-loved children. For if you had thousands of attendants, guiding you in Anointed—you do not have many fathers. For in Anointed Jesus through the good news it was I that was your father* (1 Cor. 4:14–15). Paul presents himself as parent to the Thessalonians, Galatians, and Corinthians. Such a claim would have surprised no one. Of course a teacher could be a father to his pupils. How much weight would anyone attach to such a familiar claim? A convention can, with time and overuse, become trite, but on any one occasion it may be used with all the expressive intensity that made it so popular in the first place. Paul's claim to be father to his assemblies does not trip lightly off his tongue. He is fostering and protecting a relation that was central to his mission. And it was not ready-made. It involved a strange mixture of intensity and artifice. Both parent and children, after all, had only recently entered this relation, and all of them as adults.

The most revealing moments are those in which the relation is under threat, where the father is absent and where his love—past and present—is no longer trusted. Such moments of danger introduce a crosscurrent to the parental theme. Paul must struggle to maintain the relation through prolonged separation and by letters whose attempt to bridge the distance only reminds both sides of it. Ironically, Paul gains an advantage by his absence and the opportunity it gives him to write. When he is present his power can be tested and challenged. When he is absent it is more than just his rhetoric that grows more compelling. Who would dare deny his demand to expel the culprit of 1 Corinthians 5?

Yet over time this advantage becomes transparent and is thereby undermined. How will Paul, in the last letter to the Corinthians of which we have a fragment (2 Cor. 10–13) reassert the strength of his personal presence that the Corinthians so despise? (I adopt the view, frequently taken, that these chapters were written some weeks or months after 2 Corinthians 1–9 and as part of a separate letter.) He has only one means—a letter. He must use just the advantages of this now distrusted medium to rebut the charge of its misuse. The medium of Paul's authority has itself become a weapon in the challenge raised against it.

Paul is now angry, sarcastic, anxious. What happened after the arrival of 2 Corinthians 1–9 that called for such a fierce response? More preachers had likely arrived, under commission from Jerusalem, to undermine Paul's standing and good news. They were sowing on fertile ground. Is Paul, they can ask, avoiding the Corinthians? Is he finding, yet again, excuses to stay away? Can this puny figure, so often subject to humiliation, really be an emissary of the Anointed? Paul knows what they are saying about him: *His letters are weighty and powerful; but the presence of his person is weak and his speech is contemptible* (2 Cor. 10:10). What can he do? He must write again.

He will be back among them, he insists. He says it once, twice, three times, at ever greater length and with ever more virulent warnings. *If I come again, I will not spare* any wrongdoers (2 Cor. 13:2). But he protests too hard. The Corinthians know full well how readily Paul talks of visits he will never make and when he does, how feeble a figure he cuts. The powers of these new arrivals may be no greater than Paul's, but they flaunt such gifts as Paul had not. They see no value in weakness, nor do a good many of the Corinthians. The new arrivals are likely not denying—they are trumping—Paul's authority and the gifts that confirm it. Everything he does, they do better. They are, he can say mockingly, superlative emissaries, commissioned by Jerusalem and endowed with gifts galore.

What can Paul invoke—something practical, demonstrable, immune to denial—to set himself apart from these rivals? How striking that he chooses his refusal to accept any income for himself from the Corinthians. It is a desperate move. His strange independence had been open to suspicion; he had needed to defend it. But in 2 Corinthians 10–13 he must turn the tables. With this principle—and perhaps with this alone—he can set clear blue water between himself and the new arrivals, for he knows they will not follow his example. *Superlative emissaries?* No. They are *false emissaries,* agents of Satan whose disguise need slip only once for the Corinthians to see them for what they really are.

Twice Paul runs the argument that shapes this (fragment of a) letter: once to attack his rivals (10:12–11:15) and once to vindicate himself (11:16–12:18). He is aggressive and defensive in turn. There is no mention here of love or mutual dependence, of the bonds he has so carefully woven between the Corinthians and himself. His talk here is of power and his willingness to use it. The letter may well have had the effect he needed; within eighteen months he will be back in Corinth, writing from there to Rome. But it is telling—and perhaps sad—that the last words we hear from this relationship between Paul and the Corinthians are the words of 2 Corinthians 10–13, the words of a father raging against the mutiny of the children whom he has, over years, loved and nurtured, maneuvered and bullied, instructed and inspired.

THE CORINTHIANS HAD SEEN different sides of Paul. 1 Corinthians 1–6 revealed an aggressive figure. He knew his power and was single-minded in its reassertion. He swamped the Corinthians in the immediacy of his own claims and the absurdity of theirs. It was the response of a father fed up with the clever ignorance with which his adolescent children hurt themselves and him. And yet there was something almost brutal in that letter. Such a weight of experience and skill, so neatly disowned, was brought to bear against errors so reasonably sprung from Paul's own teaching.

In 2 Corinthians 1–9 Paul presents his converts with himself and his mission as the key to their own self-understanding. He sees danger in the assembly's search for independence. He likely does not see that his own absence is quickening this search. More likely still, he cannot see that the danger seems so threatening because of his own hurt and confusion, for his own children are struggling to be free from their father. Paul pleads for the reciprocal pride that he shall take in his converts and they shall take in him. The relation is reciprocal, but not symmetrical. Paul must remain forever the parent, and his converts the children who need him.

The presence of Paul matters. He is the figure that unites and energizes his assembly. He has generated—and in his letters is still generating—an intimacy between himself and his assemblies that binds them together in a mutual dependence. When this relation is endangered, he pulls out all the stops. His converts are longing for the Lord's return, and they are longing for Paul's. And Paul can fill the gap left by the Lord. But only by his own presence, not by his protestations in writing that he longs to be with them himself. The arrival of the Lord and the arrival of Paul; the same word in Greek covers both. The Lord never comes; their emissary never comes. Just a letter arrives. The absent Paul proclaims the absent Lord.

Paul himself is the central focus for his addressees, their unifying and sustaining figure. And he is now as elusive as the Lord whose coming he proclaims.

PART VIII

PAUL AND ROME

CHAPTER 22

"THE POWER OF GOD FOR DELIVERANCE"

PAUL'S MASTERPIECE

Paul's letter to the Romans is his masterpiece. In the vast sweep of its subject matter, Paul surveys the will of God for all humanity; Jew and Gentile are embraced, from Adam to the final disclosure of God's kingdom. In its magisterial structure, it is a mountain range marked by peaks of tremendous grandeur. In its style, we have in quick succession snappy "dialogues," measured arguments, and their resolutions rich in poetry. And finally, it seems, in its detachment from the ups and downs of a particular assembly, at last Paul can paint for his addressees the whole landscape of his thought from a viewpoint he himself has chosen, undistorted by the errors or agitation of others. At last we can surely lean forward and simply listen to what Paul himself wishes to say.

Paul wrote to the Romans from Corinth in the winter of 55–56. Jesus' followers had already been in Rome for ten years or more. One of our earliest reports of the assembly there is from the Roman historian Suetonius: the emperor Claudius expelled the Jews from Rome, probably in 49, after repeated riots "instigated by Chreestus." Suetonius is almost certainly referring to Jesus the "Christ," the "Anointed." The trouble may have arisen within the prayer houses between members who revered Jesus and those who did not. Or the rioters may have sought targets well outside their own communities. If this Anointed hero was God's agent to bring about the empire's end, then that empire's heathen, idolatrous capital was ripe for attack at his followers' hands.

The Roman authorities were always suspicious of foreign religions. The Jews themselves had been expelled before: in 139 B.C.E. and again in 19 C.E. We cannot be sure how effectively any of these rulings were imposed or for how long. If our sources are to be trusted, that edict in 49 marked the second brush between Claudius and the Roman Jews in a decade: he had barred them from assembling—and so from attending prayer houses—soon after the start of his reign in 41.

We have heard already of one couple who left Italy for Corinth *because of Claudius's edict that all the Jews should leave Rome*, the Christian Jews Aquila and his wife, Prisca (The Mission [Acts] 18:2). By the time Paul writes to Rome, they are back in the capital. They head the list of allies to whom Paul sends his greetings; they had risked their lives for him. Prisca and Aquila have come full circle, and thanks to that exile in 49 they are now among Paul's closest friends.

In between such occasional repressions the Jews were well treated under the law: both Julius Caesar and Augustus had granted them special privileges in Rome, which later emperors confirmed. By the 60s C.E. there were probably thirty to forty thousand Jews in Rome. We hear of different Roman prayer houses serving different Jews: those in the emperor's household, for instance; those connected with the government of Judea and Syria; those speaking Greek; those speaking Aramaic; those from southern Italy or from Africa. Some or all of the congregations would likely have met in the houses of wealthy members; there is still no clear evidence in first-century Rome of a purposely built prayer house or a building converted to such use.

As elsewhere, in these Jewish congregations lies the origin of the Roman Christian assembly. We cannot now know how many of these prayer houses, before 49, had Jewish members or gentile affiliates who revered Jesus or exactly what role—or how central a role—he played in the faith of these different admirers. These followers of Jesus gravitated no doubt to the prayer houses whose own leaders shared their conviction and welcomed Christian teachers. And then came the edict of 49, and the Jews were ordered out of Rome. Gentile affiliates, whether

Christians or not, had good reason to lie low. Gatherings at the prayer houses were suddenly few and far between. The gentile followers of Jesus still wanted to meet together. A new form of assembly may long have been thought of; now it was needed. An assembly of gentile Christians was coming to birth.

AT THE END OF HIS LETTER TO THE ROMANS Paul sends an extended greeting to twenty-five of his friends and associates and to the members of two households. Some manuscripts of the letter lack this chapter. Scholars have asked whether it has been tacked on. Might the letter have been intended for some other city? It is more likely, after all, that Paul knew this many people in Ephesus, the base of his mission in Asia Minor, than in Rome, which he had never visited. And first on the list come Aquila and Prisca, of whom we last heard with Paul in Ephesus. Here we will adopt the view more generally held: Paul is indeed sending greetings to Rome itself. Aquila and Prisca are safely back in the city after Claudius's death (in 54 C.E.) and the lapse of his edict.

Rome was a magnet. More than half Paul's list commends people likely to be immigrants; their various names were popular in quite different corners of the empire. Nine of those mentioned are women. Rufus and his mother, *who has been a mother to me too,* remind us of the story of Jesus' death itself. The readers of Mark's gospel were clearly expected to know the Rufus whose father, Simon of Cyrene, had carried Jesus' cross to his crucifixion (Mark 15:21). Mark's gospel is traditionally linked with Rome; we might well suspect that one and the same Rufus was known to the gospel's first audience and to Paul. The family's link with Cyrene is telling. In The Mission we read that preachers from Cyprus and Cyrene made the first gentile conversions at Antioch; the good news, they insisted, was for all nations. Their activity led to Barnabas's visit to Antioch, and so to Paul's. Had Rufus's family been among those who preached "Pauline" good news before Paul himself? No wonder they had taken this new ally to their hearts.

Almost a third of Rome's inhabitants were present or former slaves; it is no surprise, then, that at least ten of Paul's addressees have slaves' names. Paul greets the Christian members of the households of Aristoboulos and Narcissus; the second master may be the Narcissus, himself a former slave, who had been a close aide to the emperor

Claudius and amassed a fortune of his own. His slaves would have joined the emperor's when their master fell from favor; several names in Paul's list are matched among the known members of the vast imperial household.

Paul picks out just three of his addressees as Jewish. By the early 50s the assembly may have been made up almost entirely of Gentiles, those who in 49 had avoided any suspicion that they were Jewish and those who had joined since. Claudius died in 54. We would expect his decree against the Jews to have lapsed, at the latest, on his death. On return to the city the Christian Jews will have sought out the gentile affiliates of their old congregations, but these would by now have formed assemblies of a new character. These assemblies will have had gentile leaders and fostered a life that had grown independent of Jewish ways. Even the most liberal Jews will have been unsettled. Paul's whole letter confronts the tensions to which these developments gave rise. In such an assembly will have been some well-established Gentiles and some newly returned Jews. No wonder they were divided over the Jewish Law. There may before long even have been separate assemblies, each owing allegiance to Jesus but badly in need of reconciliation.

The troubles of 49 have made Paul wary. To judge from the letter, trouble is brewing again. Members of the assembly are nursing grievances against Roman authority. In the 50s there were, we know, widespread protests in Rome against the unjust exaction of taxes. A regime ready for God's punishment was allowing gross extortion by its agents. The assembly's mood was volatile; Paul must head off any explosion. He writes sharply. Nothing, he insists, must disrupt the assembly's standing in official eyes. He knows only too well from Prisca and Aquila and their exile in 49 how brutally the police could respond. *Every single person,* orders Paul, *must obey the governing authorities. There is no authority that is not from God, and the powers that be were appointed by God. Anyone, then, who resists that power is in rebellion against God's decision and such rebels are bound to be punished. . . . You want to be free from fear of the authorities?—Do what is good, and you will have their praise. They are there in the service of God for the general good* (Rom. 13:1–4).

Few lines in the Bible have had more troubling consequences than have these. Written for a beleaguered community, they urged the steadiness necessary for survival. Within three hundred years they would be read and preached by an imperial church as a command for submission to this world's powers that be. Such a reading, in various forms, shaped Europe for over a thousand years and can still be invoked today by a government seeking complaisance or by a church endorsing it. These lines by Paul—long since detached from the febrile assembly in Rome—run like a thread through these knotted arguments.

Rufus and his mother, Epainetus, Andronicus and Junia, Ampliatus, Urban, and Stachys—the friends that Paul greets were among the tens of thousands of ordinary people who crowded the tenements of Rome and made a living as artisans, small merchants, and manual or clerical staff. Here were citizens and slaves, locals of Rome, an emissary from Jerusalem, an early convert from Asia. This list of Paul's greetings is a rare and welcome snapshot of an assembly finding its feet less than thirty years after Jesus' death.

Writing to Rome

FORM AND FUNCTION: THREE SKETCHES

Paul's message, as we have seen, is not taken on board just by the grasp of an argument or the acceptance of proofs. His addressees must learn to contemplate a wonder too great for normal speech. Paul had been exposed to this wonder in the most dazzling and immediate form in his sight of the risen Jesus on the road to Damascus and on his journey to Paradise. Paul in turn must make it present in and as a person. His presence is open to dire misunderstanding—but is intrinsic to his converts' Christian life.

Paul has nearly thirty friends in Rome, and that is how he writes— as their friend. Whether or not any had been his converts, he claims no authority over them. And over the other leaders and members of the assembly he could claim no authority even if he wanted to, let alone the distinctive authority that he alone, as far as we know, ever claimed. The Romans will not recognize in him the re-presentation of the Anointed. Paul's coming will not prefigure, for them, the coming of the Lord. The letter simply cannot have the function of those other letters written to Paul's own converts. What, then, does he set out to *achieve* in writing to the Romans? The question has vexed scholars for over a hundred years. In the following pages I will outline three answers. In each case, we will start by aiming our arc lamp at particular parts of the letter.

Paul has written here a letter of extraordinary complexity. Once more he is stretching his language to say what he seeks to say. Every word counts. Images of life and death, slavery and freedom are reflected from mirror to mirror and back again. Almost every paragraph has given rise to a scholarly book, and each of the climactic passages to dozens. We need a path through the jungle, just as the letter's first recipients needed one before us. And Paul knew it. He has marked quite clearly the overall structure of the letter; he has highlighted his main themes, built up to climaxes, and closed each section with a flourish. His style varies dramatically during the letter; he knows how important, for listeners, a variety of tone and speed can be. A grand, formal, heavily laden sentence; a dramatic cry of moral agony; an outburst of poetic praise—with these Paul draws attention, unmistakably, to the high points of his argument.

Let us sketch this structure. We will take up the pencil three times, to produce the portrait in three stages. We will not be able to give equal attention to all parts of the letter. Some will remain in outline even when we have finished. But the letter's shape, at least, will by then be quite clear.

The first draft introduces the classic reading of the letter, familiar to generations of churchgoing readers. This finds in the text as much a treatise as a letter. Paul has written a summary of his faith. He is setting out his theology as completely and systematically as he can. He is—in this alone of all his letters to have reached us—writing without any pressure from disputes or opponents or anxious converts.

At the letter's center, in this first reading, is the tension between the Jewish Law and the good news, between the obligations of observance and the blessings brought by faith. In this tension, we may well think, lies Paul's deepest contribution to our understanding of God and humankind. On the one hand is the human urge to be in control. We long to establish a claim over God. We will put all our effort into the observance of rules, chalk up credits, and earn our own salvation. On the other hand is the acceptance of a free gift, the salvation offered to those who know their utter dependence on God's good will and who throw themselves on his mercy. Here is the heart of Paul's preaching, the engine that has driven all the instruction we have heard from him so far. And the letter to the Romans is the place to find it stated clearly and without distortion. What, then, is Paul trying to achieve by the letter? He is expounding his position, and perhaps, we shall see, as much for his own benefit as for the benefit of his addressees. With this conclusion our first sketch will be complete.

It will then be time to add some details to our sketch and so to create our second version. This time we notice hints of a far more personal agenda than we have seen so far. We are only adding to the first outline; nothing is being erased. But we will find how different the portrait looks with the addition of shading and details. Paul, it seems, is actually responding to a credible but disastrous misreading of his good news. He is not, then, writing a self-contained overview. The letter is not shaped as he, left to his own devices, would always have shaped his proclamation. He is, to use a phrase from the English game of cricket, "on the back foot," defending himself and his wicket from an unexpectedly fast ball. This does not affect just the incidentals of the letter, a sentence here and there, a few caveats and short asides. It shapes the whole letter. It determines what he needs to say and how he needs to say it. It was over the Jewish Law and the role of the Jews that the argument has arisen; it is, then, to the Law and the Jews that he turns his attention. Such a letter *may* summarize Paul's thought in a balanced, systematic way. But no reader should bank on that in advance. What, on this reading, is Paul trying to achieve? He is fending off a particular reading of his good news that would make that news, as Paul wholeheartedly agrees, a scandal.

And so, last, we will fill in the details that complete our sketch in its third and final version. We will watch the markers that Paul puts down of the progress he expects his addressees to make during and thanks to the course of the letter's reception. They will encourage us to look at the subject of our sketch in a quite different way. In our search for a systematic presentation of the good news, we have been reading the letter as a treatise and have quite forgotten the drama of its delivery: read out loud, chapter after chapter, it is an ever growing wave that swept its addressees from the first warning of God's wrath to the final offer of hope. Paul sets out not just to describe his gospel, to ground or defend it, but to make it effective, within the letter itself, as God's power at work on his listeners as they hear. The good news *is the power of God for deliverance for everyone who believes* (Rom. 1:16), and this letter is that power in action. To take Paul's message on board is to be transformed by and during the reception of the letter itself.

How far this finished portrait seems from the outline of our first version. We had been looking for exposition; we are being summoned to transformation. And now that we have seen Paul's aim? We will still be following Paul's route on the map, free to glance to and fro across its features, assessing and comparing. But we should never forget that Paul was taking his addressees, step by step, through the terrain itself. In this case—above all others—we will understand Paul only if we look beyond what he is trying to say. We must grasp what he is trying to *do*.

Let's start our first sketch of the letter's shape, and then catch from our later versions a sense, ever fuller, of its movement.

Starting the Sketch: "Justness from Faith"

"THOSE WHO ARE JUST FROM FAITH . . ."

We begin with that classic reading of the letter as a treatise. Paul's introduction ended, he sets to with a ringing declaration:

> *I am not ashamed of the good news. For it is the power of God for deliverance for everyone who believes, first for the Jew and then for the Greek. For the justness of God is being unveiled in it, from faith to faith, as it is written: "Those who are just from faith will live."*
>
> ROMANS 1:16–17, QUOTING HABAKKUK 2:4

Those who are just from faith is the theme for Paul's opening chapters. He surveys Gentiles and Jews alike. Gentiles are sunk in idolatry and in the evils to which it leads. Among the Jews too—so proud of the Law and its observance—there is no shortage of evil. Faced with the impending Day of Wrath, this cannot be a nation confident of its acquittal by God. Do the Jews rely on their observance of the Law? But the Law itself makes clear: no one is held just by God through *works of the law.* On the contrary, through the law comes just the knowledge that we do wrong. Are we then left beleaguered and in despair? Far from it. Paul lays out the first climax of the letter in a passage we heard in our Chapter 4.

> *Now without the law the justness of God has been made clear, born witness to by the Law and the prophets, the justness of God through Jesus Anointed's faith for all those who have faith.*
>
> ROMANS 3:21-22

Abraham is the prime example of such faith. When Abraham and his wife were childless and both already old, God promised Abraham that he would be the *father of many nations.* Abraham believed the promise, and *it was accounted to him for justness* (The Beginning [Genesis] 15:6). This was before Abraham was circumcised and generations before the Law was given to Moses on Mt. Sinai. What counted was Abraham's faith. And he did become, as promised, the father of many nations: the father of the uncircumcised who have faith; and the father too of the circumcised who do not rely simply—or at all—on the observance of the Law but who walk in the paths of the faith taken, before he was circumcised, by our father Abraham.

". . . WILL LIVE"

Those who are just from faith—will live. Paul is ready at 5:1 for the transition to his next section on the life to which God is bringing us through this faith and the justness it brings. We have been held just thanks to faith and we have peace with God. So much has been effected by the death of the Anointed. *If, when we were enemies of God, we were reconciled to him through the death of his son, all the more, now that we have been reconciled, we shall be delivered in his life* (Rom. 5:10). Paul contrasts Adam and the Anointed; the former brought wrongdoing and death and the latter, justness and life. Paul explores that "death" in full and plangent detail. The power of wrongdoing has made use of an opportunity offered by the Law. The Law itself is holy and just and good. But we are caught up in the desires of the flesh; and the prohibitions of the Law itself, in a bitter irony, have been used by wrongdoing to spur us into evil. *What a wretch I am! Who shall rescue me from the body of this death?* (7:24).

Once more Paul has laid out the grounds for despair. The spring is tightly wound. Paul releases it with a chapter of triumph. *There is now no condemnation for those who are in Anointed Jesus. For the Law of the Breath of life in Anointed Jesus has freed you from the Law of wrongdoing and of death* (8:1–2). In place of the Law Paul now speaks of the Breath and its effect: we are no longer slaves, but children—and so are fellow heirs with the Anointed. The whole of creation is longing for the unveiling of the children of God, for creation itself will be freed at last from the slavery of destruction and brought into the freedom of the glory of the children of God.

We might well feel, as chapters 5–8 draw to a close, that the letter has really run its course. And yet we are only just over halfway through the text. The mountain peak of chapter 8 has been the center of the range, towering above the hills on either side. Paul starts his next section at 9:1 in a quite different tone—he is agonized in his care for his own people, the Jews. Why are so few of them accepting the good news? Three chapters follow (chapters 9–11), leading up to the next climax.

"FROM FAITH" OR "FROM DEEDS"?

Once more, in chapters 9–11, the Law is at issue. The letter's first section had a moment of striking grandeur at its center, when Paul spoke of God's work in the Anointed *without the law;* and now at the center of this new section he speaks once more of the Anointed, the Law, and the Jews' reliance on the Law. *What shall we say, then? That the nations who are not pursuing justness have obtained justness—justness, that is, that comes from faith; but Israel, in pursuit of the law of justness, has not attained to the law. Why? Because they pursue it not from faith but as from deeds* (9:30–32). The distinction is being sharply drawn. A human search undertaken by human strength to satisfy a human urge has missed the point. *I bear witness to them that they have a zeal for God, but not based on knowledge* (10:2). Is this the most dangerous zeal of all? It is the highest human aim. It attracts the deepest thought, greatest care and bravest determination of which humans are capable. But on this reading of Paul, such zeal is an error: a terrible error of human pride and our longing for self-rule, self-sufficiency, and the right to make demands of God. *For they are ignorant of the justness of God and seek to set up a justness of their own—and so have not been subject to the justness of God* (10:3).

The role of the Law was brought to prominence during the Reformation in the sixteenth century. The heirs of that Reformation have dwelt on it ever since. The Reformers diagnosed the church of Rome as preaching a gospel of good works in which credits (for acts of worship and of charity) must be earned and set against debits (for wrongdoings). The Reformers found here an analogy with the Jews' observance of the Law as they found it presented and assessed by Paul. A link was readily made between a Judaism that denied the free gift of justness at the time of Paul and the Roman church that denied it still in the sixteenth century. Paul himself had berated the one and could be called into service, at a time of fierce polemic, to attack the other. At last, we can hope in the twenty-first century that we have exhausted this bitter legacy. Thanks to the scholarship of the last thirty years it is clear that to present the Law's observance in this way is to present a parody. At the heart of Judaism, then as now, is the blessing that God has chosen to bestow by his own gracious gift upon Israel; and within that blessing are the clear routes of obedience, reparation, and forgiveness that God has opened to enable his people, frail and fallible as we all are, to remain within his favor.

For over three hundred years two distortions fueled each other: a parody of ancient Judaism and a parody of the contemporary Roman Catholic church. They may, by a strange irony, have sparked or fostered an insight of incomparable importance—an insight into the quite spurious claims that religion seems to offer us on God. But this does nothing to justify the parodies themselves. So how did Judaism come to be so deeply misunderstood? We are bound to ask of Paul again, as we asked when reading his letter to the Galatians: Did Paul misunderstand the Judaism in which he was himself brought up and to which he had been resolutely loyal as a young man? Surely not. Did he, then, come to see this Judaism in such a light only after his conversion? And in this development did the polemics of his mission—not least in Galatia—distort his presentation of the Law and its demands? If so, it was a fateful distortion, for in the hands of a powerful church it became a weapon against Jews. Paul, it may seem, has given the Western world a distorted view of his own ancestral faith that has for centuries fueled antagonism against his own ancestral people.

God has given promises to Israel that cannot be broken. How, then, is he keeping them in this age of the Anointed? As we saw in Chapter 12, it was believed that God would rescue his own people from oppression and so bring all the nations of the world to recognize God as the one God and the Jews as his own people. The nations would flock to Jerusalem to pay obeisance. Paul closes his argument with a mystery, a truth disclosed to him by God. God has inverted the order of these great events. It is the Gentiles who shall be converted first. *A hardening* [of the heart] *has come in part upon Israel until the fullness of the nations has come in—and in this way all Israel will be saved* (Rom. 11:25–26).

> *Oh, the depth of the wealth*
> *and the wisdom and the knowledge of God!*
> *How his judgments are quite unsearchable*
> *and his ways are quite inscrutable!*
> *For* [as Isaiah asked] *"who has known the mind of the Lord?*
> *Or who has been his adviser?"*
> *From him and through him and to him are all things;*
> *to him be the glory for all ages. Amen.*
>
> ROMANS 11:33–34, 36, QUOTING ISAIAH 40:13

Here is the clearest climax and closure of all. The letter now winds down. Paul launches upon more particular instructions about the payment of taxes, the eating of various foods, the dangers of division. The tone has changed again from the praise of God to brisk advice. Paul is ready to round off the letter. He confirms that the good news is for all nations. He outlines his own role in the spread of the good news and his own plans to visit Rome. And with a list of greetings to his friends in the city, he is gone.

Why might Paul have written such a letter as this? Oddities in some of its oldest manuscripts suggest the letter once lacked that last chapter of greetings and all mention of Rome itself. These give the impression that the letter was once a "circular," a letter sent to various assemblies whose individual copies were personalized by the mention of a destination and the people there known to Paul. This gives us all the more reason to read the bulk of the letter without reference to a particular community or its relation to Paul. The theory that the letter was written as such a circular has not been widely accepted, but what the letter had not been in origin, it might well have become. Such a general and systematic letter, after all, would have been of value to assemblies wherever Paul himself was welcome. We can imagine its distribution by Paul and his close allies. The references to Rome, we may conclude, were not added to the Romans' copy of the letter to make it more personal. They were deleted from the other copies to make it more general. Letters were certainly circulated. Paul's pupil concludes the letter to the Colossians: *When this letter has been read among you, see that you have it read in the assembly of the Laodiceans too, and that you read the letter from Laodicea* (Col. 4:16).

But we are still left wondering why Paul wrote this letter to Rome. When Paul wrote, he was planning a visit to Jerusalem and then an expedition to Spain (Rom. 15:24–25). In Jerusalem he would face entrenched distrust; in Spain he would be moving way beyond his previous area of operations. He had good reason, before either journey, to codify his thoughts. There were few Jews in Spain and few Greek-speakers; if he preached in Spain as he writes to Rome, he would have left his audience utterly confused. But Jerusalem he knew well, and he knew where he would come under suspicion. So much the better if he could have, ready and in order, his answers to any looming attack. And here these answers are, in his letter to Rome. What was the role of the Law in God's plan and what was the role of the Jews? Where was the justness of a God who appeared to have jettisoned his promises and the people to whom he had given them? In Jerusalem these would be burning questions, and the answers he was rumored to give laid him open to bitter opposition. No wonder he prepared himself well for his visit.

THROUGHOUT THIS CHAPTER AND THE NEXT I will refer to Paul's addressees without qualification as the Romans, as the members of an assembly or assemblies in a single city. But there is none of the intimacy between Paul and these addressees that has inspired his letters to

Thessalonica, Galatia, or Corinth. He knows more than twenty-five of his addressees; we will never know how many more members of the assembly or assemblies there were. It seems there were enough, though, to ensure that Paul can make no call upon the loyalty or dependence of his addressees in general. He does not expect the Romans to see what duty or right he has to instruct or visit them. He offers explanations, at the letter's start and finish, of his writing and his plans. At the start he realizes that he might seem arrogant and stumbles as he corrects the impression; at the end he works to undo any offense caused by his forthright intervention (1:11–12; 15:15).

This does not empty the letter of all personal reference or passion. Paul opens his heart to the Romans in his account of the Jews. And he may be offering himself, in some way, as the exemplary subject of the turmoil described at the letter's heart (9:1; 10:1; 7:7–25). But in all this he is not pleading for—still less, appealing to—any intimacy or confidence between himself and his addressees. Here is an emissary who knows his distance and expects to keep it.

Here, in turn, we seem to have a letter freed from the heights and depths of human relations. The turmoil of such relations throughout the other letters may seem in this context to have been the static that obscured a broadcast we were straining to hear. In the letter to the Romans we are free at last to hear the good news, clear and without distortion. We have strong incentives to discover such clarity. We cannot, after all, stand in relation to Paul as his own foundations did. We are (and any Christian readers need to be) confident that we do grasp his good news. For such a grasp, therefore, any dependence upon the personal relations between Paul and his addressees must be incidental. Paul spoke across the Aegean to strangers in Rome and can speak no less directly across the centuries to us. And all the better, if we can present such a transmission of the good news not simply as possible but as ideal, as the setting that allows the good news to be heard, as a broadcast freed from static at last.

What a powerful statement the letter becomes. It is just what is needed by any modern church. This in itself should make us wary. We all too readily find what we want to find. We long for a full, clear statement of Paul's thought. And more especially for a sight of the star at the center of its solar system. That star will shape the orbit of all the dependent planets and their moons; its light and heat will engender all the system's life. For a sight of such a sun, the grand, stately letter to the Romans is clearly the place to look; and there at its heart we find a careful and passionate account of the Jews' Law, the Anointed's faith, and their contrasting roles in God's plan.

But what have we failed to find? Two central features of this extraordinary letter. We will bring one to light as we take up our pencil for the second version of our sketch: the vehemence with which Paul is rebutting a distortion of his own good news. The other will come into view when we finish off the sketch at the end of the next chapter. There we will capture the dynamic of the letter. Paul wrote the letter as he did to transform his addressees, even as they heard it.

CHAPTER 23

"I AM NOT ASHAMED OF THE GOOD NEWS"

PAUL WAS NOT AS IMMUNE to circumstances when he wrote to Rome as we might think at first. His good news had been misunderstood. People were claiming it as a charter for libertines, some with enthusiasm, some in horrified opposition. So let us for the moment imagine ourselves as worried but nonpartisan listeners of the first century, listeners who know enough of the Old Order to recognize Paul's allusions to Adam, who rely enough on the Old Order to find in Adam the forefather and template of all humanity, who know the dark rumors about Paul's good news, how it appeals to but threatens the justness of God. Above all, let us imagine ourselves as listeners to whom this confusion *matters.*

Such disagreements would in any case be bitter. Circumstances in Rome may have conspired to make them sharper still. There is persecution in the air. God is due to rescue his faithful people, but it is the faithful who are threatened. Has the assembly misunderstood God's will, flouted it, and angered him? Is the assembly itself the target of God's wrath? If there is any such danger, its cause will soon be diagnosed in the airing given to that scandalous message of Paul. Paul must clarify his message, and he must bolster the hopes of the assembly. Thanks to the peace we have with God, says Paul at the start of his central section, *we boast in the hope of the glory of God. And not just that; we boast too in the tribulations, knowing that tribulation effects endurance, and endurance a properly reckoned character, and such a character hope* (Rom. 5:2–4). Suffering and hope both feature again in the climactic central chapter: *We share in Anointed's suffering so that we might share in his glory. In hope we have been delivered* (8:17, 24). And once more at that chapter's end, in a famous conclusion, Paul offers a stirring reassurance:

> *What will separate us from the love of God? Tribulation or distress or persecution or hunger or nakedness or danger or the sword? As it is written,*
>
> *On your account we are killed all the day long,*
> *we are accounted as sheep for the slaughter.*
>
> *But in all these things we are more than victors through him who loves us. For I am persuaded that neither death nor life nor angels nor powers nor things present nor things to come nor height nor depth nor any other created thing will be able to separate us from the love of God in Anointed Jesus our Lord.*
>
> ROMANS 8:35–39, QUOTING PSALM 43:23, GREEK VERSION [44:22]

No wonder Paul rounds off the letter's final section, of instruction for the assemblies' daily life, with a prayer on the same theme: *May the God of hope fill you with all joy and peace in your keeping the faith, so that you might overflow in hope in the power of the holy breath* (15:13).

I AM NOT ASHAMED, SAYS PAUL at the beginning of the letter, *of the good news* (1:16). Could his good news, then, be shameful? He is said to belittle the Law and to encourage wrongdoing; such a good news as that—as Paul is the first to maintain—would be shameful. So Paul, we have seen, must make it clear at the outset that he is not soft on wrongdoing. And to prove his distance from any such error, he links God's justice with its counterpart, God's anger, right at the letter's start. God's justness and God's anger are being unveiled in a spiral of crime and punishment, vividly described in the very next verses. Paul moves into an elaborate condemnation of wrongdoing, of idolatry and its consequences. Here is a formal, balanced presentation of punishment that fits the crime. There is no complaisance with evil here.

From the outset, Paul's letter is shaped by his need to correct the rumors of his libertine proclamation. As the crime above all crimes, he targets idolatry. He has chiefly in mind the pagan world, but he keeps Jews on their toes too, hinting at their ancestors' idolatry when they worshiped the Golden Calf. .

The motif is familiar in Jewish texts. In general the worship of false gods and their idols set Gentiles apart from God's own people and convicted them, in itself, of blindness and folly. Its consequences deserved to be dire, and were. Paul himself works up an elaborate paragraph to make such consequences clear. He swings from crime to a punishment that fits the crime. Or, rather, perhaps from crime to the consequences that fit it less by God's action than by his letting things take their course.

> They have exchanged the glory of the imperishable God for the likeness of an image of a perishable person and of birds and animals and reptiles. Therefore God has handed them over in the desires of their hearts to impurity, for them to dishonor their bodies among themselves; those who have exchanged the truth of God for a lie, and revered and worshiped the creature instead of the creator, who is blessed for ever, Amen! Therefore God has handed them over to dishonorable passions, and their women have exchanged natural relations for those against nature; and similarly the men have abandoned their natural relations with women and burned in their lust for one another, men committing shameful deeds with men and being paid in their own bodies the wages suited to their error.
> ROMANS 1:23-27

Homosexuality was as repellent to the Jews, as it was not to the Greeks. The term, it must be stressed, is our word, not Paul's. It is our general term for a range of dispositions and practices familiar in the Greek world, but not covered by a single Greek term. And for a good reason. These different dispositions and actions were differently viewed and were informed by views we do not share on the physiologies of men and women and on their nearness to—or distance from—the ideal of (male) humanity. Our single word "homosexuality" would be far too clumsy for use by a Greek thinker.

In general terms Paul's argument would have been well known to any Jewish addressees and to any former pagans who have been weaned from idolatry. We meet with it, for instance, in the Wisdom of Solomon, a prolonged praise of wisdom that was written within the couple of centuries—and perhaps within the decades—before Paul's missions. Paul knows the book's themes well, and perhaps the book itself. The author is developing an image well known from the Old Order. Sexual immorality is evoked there as a metaphor for infidelity to God. It was not difficult to rework the connection to diagnose such immorality, in practice, as a result—or a symptom—of that infidelity. We hear:

> The invention of idols is the beginning of prostitution,
> Their discovery is the ruin of life.
> It was not enough to be in error about the knowledge of God,
> but living in a great war of ignorance
> they call such great evils peace.
> Everything is confusion: blood and murder, theft and deceit,
> destruction and faithlessness, . . .
> defilement of soul, interchange of sexual roles,
> disorder in marriage, adultery and debauchery.
>
> WISDOM OF SOLOMON 14:12, 22, 25-26

Paul, then, is drawing on a tradition he knew well, but he gives it a quite striking emphasis. The Wisdom of Solomon lists fourteen crimes (I have abbreviated the passage); one of them is that "interchange of sexual roles." Paul too is attacking humanity's neglect of God, and he will round off his onslaught with a similar list of evils. But he precedes it with his full-scale attack on this crime and this alone—male and female homosexuality. *Their women have exchanged natural relations for those against nature; and similarly the men have abandoned their natural relations with women and burned in their lust for one another.* Emphasis matters. Paul has one target in view above all. Why?

Paul has identified *the likeness as the appearance of a man* upon the throne of God—it is Jesus. As he writes to the Romans he sees and confronts the most radical charge that could be laid against him and his good news—that his reverence for a man has distorted the reverence that he owes to God alone. In his understanding of Jesus has Paul himself *exchanged the glory of God for the likeness of an image of a mortal person?* If he has, then it's no wonder there are those in Rome who have become so gleefully immoral. Here in human life, they can claim, is the disclosure of God. And in the good news of Paul humanity—with all its most powerful urges—has been unleashed at last into the free glory for which it was created. Paul's good news had become a charter for libertines.

Paul must put himself above all such suspicion of idolatry and all blame for its results. He charges others with the crime. And for its punishment? Paul, like the Wisdom of Solomon, has a dozen or more evils he could choose from. Among sexual offenses he could easily have chosen adultery, the image so often linked in the Old Order with idolatry. But all those other evils—and not least adultery—were condemned in Greek as well as in Jewish culture. It was just same-sex partnerships that occupied in the social, moral, and philosophical maps of Greek culture a general place they would never be granted in Judaism. They could plausibly be said to characterize one culture over against the other. So Paul pinpoints those partnerships as God's punishment upon that Greek world.

All or most of Paul's own addressees will, at least in theory, have renounced idolatry. In the letter Paul lambasts "them" for the crime, readily understood as people outside the assembly. Paul's audience would have relaxed as they heard his onslaught because they are out of the frame. But not for long. Where his opening attack had emphasized unconverted pagans, the next section homes in on converted Jews. So who escapes, by the end, the direct attack of this inquisitor? Only those converted pagans who have renounced idolatry and pagan immorality without taking up observance of the Law, for this is just the group that shows the faith and lifestyle Paul wants to nurture.

The old Adam had been the first idolater, blind to *what can be known of God* (1:19). The new Adam is himself precisely what can be known of God. Paul's good news of the Anointed, then, is the one teaching that can draw pagans from their idolatry. Because they have in the Anointed the image of the one true God, they need no other images, no statues. And the same good news can draw Jews from the golden calves that tempt them still, for the Anointed is himself the wisdom of God and discloses *what can be known of him*.

PAUL IS RESPONDING TO CLAIMS about his good news that he fiercely denies. The claims may have been made by his detractors; more probably they were made by people who had found in Paul, as they thought, an ally. They had misunderstood him, and even at this distance we can see how such a misunderstanding was possible. Now Paul himself may have chosen to make this most subversive (and perhaps most widespread) error the starting point for a systematic letter treatise. But no longer can we claim with any confidence that Paul is writing the treatise he could write only when he was not responding to errors and opposition. On the contrary, Paul, as far as we can tell, is taking his addressees in Rome across terrain that he has not chosen himself.

And Paul charts his course and theirs with the greatest care. At the letter's start he is keeping an equal distance to Jews and Gentiles; the good news, after all, was *for everyone who believes, first the Jew and then the Greek* (1:16). The Greeks, or Gentiles, he makes clear, have it in them to *show the work of the Law to be written on their hearts* (2:15); while the Jews who boast in the Law are found willfully and obviously to break it. Any supposed superiority in the Jews has been undermined. Now Paul steps back. His tone changes as he moves into a swift series of rhetorical questions. *What then is the advantage of the Jew or the benefit of circumcision?* Great, in every way. The Jews have been entrusted with the *sayings of God* (3:1–2). Some of those Jews may be unfaithful, but not God himself, for God, by contrast, actually demonstrates his fidelity in the judgment he passes on those who have proved false.

But this makes room for a sly counterargument. Our wrongdoing gives God a chance to show his justness. What, then, is wrong with the wrongdoing? Paul sets up a dialogue with an imagined objector who pursues this line of thought. *Now if our injustice establishes the justness of God, what shall we say? Surely not "God is unjust, who brings down his anger"?* (3:5). Paul balks even at suggesting such a thing, then dismisses the point. *Certainly not! Since, in that case, how will God judge the world?* (3:6). The objector, however, is not quelled yet. *"But if in my falsehood the truthfulness of God has overflowed to his glory, how can I still be judged as a wrongdoer?"* (3:7). This is a remarkable line of thought. Paul pursues it without flinching. At last we see why he must: these questions are all fired by a rumor about himself. *And surely it cannot be—as we are slandered and as some claim we say—that we are to do evil so that good may come of it? The judgment on them is just!* (3:8).

Brisk questions, impatiently answered. But Paul will eventually have to mount a fuller riposte than this. The power of wrongdoing, he says several pages later, was vastly strengthened by the arrival of the Law. All the more, therefore, is achieved by the countering grace of God. *What shall we say, then? Are we to remain in wrongdoing, so that grace may abound? Certainly not!* (6:1). He settles that question, but must confront its corollary. *What, then? Shall we do wrong, since we are not under law but under grace? Certainly not!* (6:15). Paul's rebuttal of these two questions leads us into the very center of the letter. They prompt the next challenge and shape Paul's response. *What shall we say, then? "The Law is wrongdoing"? Certainly not!* (7:7). We have heard of Paul's answer already, in the voice of his agonized "I" in thrall to wrongdoing. These are some of the most intense lines in all his letters. With these three questions and their answers Paul takes us painfully up to the mountain peak at the center of the letter; and so can show us, in a chapter of triumph, the landscape of hope beyond.

But even these questions and their answers—the whole central section of the letter—do not settle the issues raised in that early exchange about God's justness. Paul turns to it yet again, when he is asking what has become of God's promises to Israel. To whom has God given the sonship and the glory, the possession of the Law, the service appointed by God and his promises? To the Israelites. *What shall we say, then? Surely there is no injustice in God? Certainly not!* (9:14). God has mercy where he wishes. But this makes space for a new version of that old sly argument. *You will say to me, then: "What blame is there left, then? After all, who has ever flouted God's will?"* (9:19). These questions lead us in turn into the three fraught chapters, 9–11, of which we have heard on the Jews and God's will for them.

We have heard the same formulas, over and over, of rhetorical question and indignant answer. And every time Paul is rebutting the same rumor—that his good news implies injustice in the judgment of God. Modern Christians look to this letter to find how they might be found just before God. But Paul must demonstrate as well a prior justness, the justness of God himself. God has presented Anointed Jesus, declared Paul in that first ringing climax, *toward the manifestation of his justness at the present vital moment, for him to be just and to hold just those dependent on Jesus' faith* (3:26).

We can now at last see the importance of those chapters on the place of Israel in God's plan. God's justness is at stake, and God cannot be just if he breaks his promises to the Jews. This is far more, for Paul, than an abstract question of consistency. *I speak the truth in Anointed, I do not lie, my conscience bears me witness in the holy breath, that my sorrow is great and my pain is unremitting in my heart* (9:1–2). Here speaks again the new Moses whom we encountered in 2 Corinthians. He is offering his life in the Anointed as a sacrifice, to carry any punishment laid upon his people, if it will only help them. *For I have prayed to be accursed, I myself, cast out from the Anointed on behalf of my brothers in the flesh* (9:3). Our view of the letter can broaden out. The central section and its triumph mark one summit. But it is quite clear that far more is still to come in those chapters on the Jews than an appendix.

PAUL'S NAME AND GOOD NEWS have been brought into an argument. The position ascribed to Paul would have scandalized anyone in the Christian assemblies who valued the Jewish Law, primarily Jews, and with them the God-fearers. And could anyone seriously adopt this mis-understanding of Paul as their own understanding of God's will and promises? We remember the Corinthians' slogan: *Everything is permitted.* It was a slogan almost certainly derived from Paul's own teaching, which Paul himself, when writing to Corinth, had to refine. He is now writing to Rome from Corinth itself. No place had given more vivid proof of how his teaching could be skewed into a libertine position. It was not hard to hear in Paul's teaching the permission to throw over the traces and await the Lord's return in freedom from all restraint. The death of the Anointed has simply and surely reconciled his followers, whatever they may do, to God. They may as well—or are even called to—take advantage of the freedom this offers them.

Once more, factions. Factions had divided the assembly in Corinth; Paul's own version of the good news had been used to stir up trouble there. Paul fears factions will now divide the assembly in Rome, and once more his own good news is at the heart of the trouble. We might expect such arguments to be resolved by Paul's backing one side rather than the other. He left no doubt, after all, over his position in Gala-tia—and took no pains there to be conciliatory. In Corinth, however, we saw Paul adopt a quite different approach. He did not declare one group or the other to be right and its opponents to be wrong. The error lay in the fact of the dispute. The Body of the Anointed was breaking up. *This* was the crisis, and all the groups in Corinth were culpable. What mattered, above all, was to regenerate the Body as a unity.

We are sketching a portrait of Paul's letter to Rome. In our third and final version, we will see Paul do for Rome what he had done for Corinth. The members of two factions hold to different teachings and observe different lifestyles, but between them is a connection deeper than any of their differences. To be prized away from their current views will take far more than mere persuasion. Paul is about to *redefine* the members of each faction, to unpick and reweave the threads of their self-understanding. He will redefine each individual and the community itself. In seeing themselves afresh, the Romans will begin the process of their own healing—as individuals and as a community. Paul's letter to the Romans is therapy.

It is time to fill in the final details to our sketch of the letter's shape. It will take just a few touches with the brush, but the letter that we have so far seen will be transformed.

Finishing the Sketch:
The Healing of the Mind

Exactly how much we can know about God from the natural world, and how accurately, and how we know whatever we can know—these are central questions in all theology. They are fiercely disputed. But Paul insists that we can know enough. We must look again at that opening tirade against idolatry:

> For what is known of God is clear among them. For God himself has made it clear. For what cannot be seen of him is seen from the foundation of the world as an object of thought from created things: that is, his invisible power and his divinity. So that they are without excuse.
>
> ROMANS. 1:19-20

Humankind has *exchanged the glory of the imperishable God for the likeness of an image of a perishable person and of birds and animals and reptiles* (1:23). He is thinking throughout this passage of Adam, made in the image and likeness of God and endowed with his glory—a glory lost at the Fall. Adam had been the master of all the creatures, but in his obedience to the serpent he had allowed one of them to master him. And so Adam's successors—all humans of all times and places—are liable to turn from worshiping God to serving, with heart and mind and utter devotion, some power or ambition of this world. Idolatry was, for Jews and for converts to Christianity, the universal and fundamental wrong of the pagan world. Pagans, then, are Paul's chief target. He does not, however, let Jews off the hook. He takes care to evoke Israel's own idolatry: while Moses was on Sinai, the people worshiped a Golden Calf.

We have followed the threads in the elaborate web of crime and matching punishment in which Paul sees such humans bound. After a page of expansive eloquence, he changes gear:

> *As they have not reckoned to keep God in their awareness, God himself has consigned them to an unreckoning mind, to do all kinds of wrong, filled with every injustice, wickedness, malice and evil, full of malice and murder, strife, craftiness and spite, tale-bearers, slanderers, God-haters, insolent, haughty, boastful, contrivers of evil, rebels against parents, without sense, without sensibility, without care, without mercy. They know the just verdict of God: that people who do such things deserve death. But not only do they do these things themselves, but they share in approval of those who do them.*
>
> ROMANS 1:28–32

They, they, them. Paul's culprits are outside the assemblies and beyond the reach of his letter. Paul is describing a vast delinquency of mind, will, and flesh. But his own audience—in particular, Jews who would never succumb to idolatry—can look on, only grazed by his attack. Or can they? Paul turns to the attack. He catches them quite off balance: *So you are without excuse, yes, you, everyone who judges others. For when you judge others, you judge yourself. For there you are, judging—but you do the same yourself* (2:1). He is broadening his view to cover all humankind. And so he can declare in the great formula of faith that marks the first summit among the letter's mountains: *All have done wrong and fall short of the glory of God* (3:23).

An *unreckoning mind* at the letter's start (1:28), a mind restored by its central climax. At the letter's midway point, that central, soaring peak in the mountain range, Paul looks back on the progress made possible by the letter so far. It is an unforgettable moment when the mind is sufficiently healed to recognize the limits of its own power. The mind is no longer in rebellion against God, but is still unable to counter the power of wrongdoing. That will take more than any mind can do. The inner person is ready now to endorse God's law, but sees a rival law at work in the body and battling against *the law of my mind. So then I myself serve the law of God with my mind—but with my flesh the law of wrongdoing* (7:22, 25).

But restoration is under way. Those who are children of God are heirs of God, fellow heirs with the Anointed. Those, then, whom God has chosen *he has determined beforehand to be conformed to the image of his son* (8:17, 29). Their transformation is being wrought even as they hear the letter. Here is the good news in action, the power of God for deliverance. The Romans are to grow into a self-conscious determination to obedience and to faith. And in that growth they will discover the limits of their own power—and the rescue offered at the crucial moment by God's.

Paul's last chapters (12:1–15:13) are dedicated to the practicalities of the Romans' daily life. How easily we stop reading once the serious business of the letter is over and done with and Paul turns to the nitty-gritty of an assembly whose problems have nothing to do with us. And how completely, by such neglect, we miss the result of Paul's work. As Paul reaches the last section of the letter the effects of the change, in the individual and in the assembly, are already apparent. Now the Romans have a sound mind and can begin to reckon aright. Their transformation has started in their reading of the letter itself.

> *I urge you, brothers, through the mercies of God to present your bodies as a living, holy sacrifice, well-pleasing to God, the service guided by your reason. Stop fashioning yourselves as at one with the present age. Keep*

up your transformation in the renewal of your mind, so that you might reckon aright what is the will of God: what is good and well-pleasing and perfect.

ROMANS 12:1–2

Keep up your transformation in the renewal of your mind. Paul has not been just persuading, teaching, informing. He has set out to heal the Romans. Paul aims to trigger the power that will move his readers from the downward spiral of God's anger to an upward spiral of obedience. The good news, activated here and now in the letter's reception, is God's present *power for deliverance.*

CHAPTER 24

THE AGONY AND THE ECSTASY

Dying to Death

The good news is the power of God for deliverance (Rom. 1:16). And in the reading of the letter to the Romans this power is active here and now. It is at work. The Romans' response to this very letter, then, will be a benchmark of the gospel's power among them. They have in themselves the chance to break the cycle of evil and to recognize for themselves the sign of their healing in their own response to Paul's words. Such self-consciousness matters; to see the progress under way brings the confidence and energy that drives the progress onward. There is, then, an offer in Paul's letter. There is a warning too. If the Romans fail to heed Paul's letter, they will confirm that they are caught in the cycle of evil that leads to death.

We have outlined what Paul sets out to do in this letter. It is time now to see how he does it. We will watch him unravel the Romans' errors, offer them knowledge, and remold both their understanding and their will. Paul works deep down in their self-understanding. He calls on the description of a human that would have been familiar to any thoughtful Jew or well-taught God-fearer. He locates his individual within a familiar matrix defined by figures famous from scripture. Paul's individual cannot deny his or her links with these figures. But he or she can decide how to respond to them, how to view the figures themselves and how to live out their example, legacy, offers, and demands. There are Adam and Eve, bringing to life all the constraints and freedoms that humans feel around them and within them and yet find hard to specify. There is the exemplar Abraham, who brings circumcision, long before Moses, and so sets the Jews apart as God's people. And there is Moses, who brings the Law that regulates and sustains Jewish life and confirms its separation from the gentile world.

Most readers of this book will be, as I am, gentile. We, no less than ancient Jews, need to define our place among others and to specify ourselves over against those others. Many of us still do so, in part, by reference to our cultural links with great figures from the distant past. And some of us look specifically to the heroes of our religion: to Jesus himself; to saints with a modern following, such at Vincent de Paul or Thérèse of Lisieux; to great figures in a tradition we value, such as Martin Luther or John Wesley.

But most reference points are for most of us, I suspect, the people and institutions that surround us today. The members of a multicultural society do not easily find unity in the experiences, countries, or cultures that their diverse forebears did not share. What we share is the present. And it is a kaleidoscope, dazzling in the variety and brilliance of what it offers us. We live in a world of wide knowledge and limitless communication. We can draw on ever more categories and examples to say about ourselves all that we want to say. We can skim ideals, hopes, and self-definitions from cultures of which we know only the surface that we glimpsed in school. Paul had a narrower range of stories and definitions than we have, but he plumbed them deeper and deeper, arriving at connections that a casual thinker, even then, would never sense or see. Paul had a concentration, a close focus, that may do more justice to individuals and their culture than a modern pick-and-mix.

The family unit by which we nowadays define ourselves is a family of seven generations at most, from our great-grandparents to our great-grandchildren. We can hardly imagine a sense of belonging and loyalty to forebears who lived a thousand years ago and more—and to all their other descendants. We are the poorer for it. We are so fascinated by the present that we are confused by our own deepest loyalties and dreams, for these are still secured and fed, in a dense tangle of roots, by the long histories from which we, our families, and our communities have grown. What Paul knew well, as the ground from which he grew, is for us a foreign land. This is his starting point. When he sets out on his journey, then, we can hardly see how dramatic is the route he takes.

Paul will redefine his addressees, as individuals, as a community, as part of creation as a whole. In their new understanding of themselves stand the trigger and the start of their transformation. In this redefinition Paul makes possible—and begins—the healing of his addressees—the healing of each mind, and so of each addressee as a whole, and so finally of the Romans' community.

Paul is engaging not just the Romans' intellect, to grasp the sequence of his thought, and not just their will, to apply the insights this thought leads them to. He needs their imagination. Paul evokes two sets of views. The adherents of each set are presented as types, not individuals. These types are characterized by beliefs and hopes that are strange to us now. We do not recognize the figures so lightly drawn by Paul, and so do not realize that he is sketching such figures at all. But to Paul's addressees—unless he had quite misunderstood the situation in Rome—the types would be well known.

We can envisage a modern equivalent. An author could introduce the contrasting views "typical" of a Republican and a Democrat, for instance, or of a conservative and a liberal Christian. Most of us—and far more than just political activists or committed churchgoers—would quickly recognize the views and their likely adherents. The author, with minimal "props," can stage a debate between these protagonists and be confident that readers will follow its course. But put the debate before a foreign visitor, perhaps, or a young person with no knowledge of these well-worn disagreements—and he or she will find the text wholly bemusing.

Paul evokes two such types. They represent two groups, well known within the assemblies of Asia Minor and Greece and familiar, Paul believes, in Rome too. The groups' members are clearly and consciously opposed to each other. Paul redefines the types—and so the groups—to show that they are not opponents at all. In relation to God they are structurally identical; each is in error and, in their mutual opposition, wholly destructive.

At the letter's central point these two types are merged. The

Romans have already undergone the death to death that baptism was, but they have not grasped that death as Paul believes they should have. In their imagination they must undergo it again. This is to be the central moment of their transformation. Even in speaking of such an aim we find ourselves hard-pressed for terms. Paul's letter can and will no more duplicate baptism than Paul himself duplicates Jesus. We need subtler words to say what needs saying. Paul knows as much himself. He is again straining the limits of normal learning and growing so as to unveil truths that are, he believes, far beyond such apprehension.

Paul is seeking a change in the Romans so total—in self-understanding and way of life—that its subject could speak freely of its result as his or her transformation. We have caught a glimpse of this aspiration in 1 Corinthians and 2 Corinthians 1–9. Here in the letter to Rome it is seen most clearly. But what exactly will constitute such a change? What will count as success? As in the letter's reception, so in its analysis: only at the end of our journey will we have before us the full sense of such terms as "transformation," which we have had to use on loan from the outset. We must evoke for the moment an effect whose character we are not yet able to define; it will otherwise remain, even at the end of our reading, unseen.

Let's listen, then, to the letter's earlier chapters with our ears open not just for the thoughts presented, but for the effect of their presentation. Of course we expect Paul to judge what the Romans need to hear for the successive stages of their healing. More telling is his judgment about when they are ready to hear it.

To Heal the Mind

"AN UNRECKONING MIND"

For the last time we are drawn to that opening tirade at the letter's start. Paul has diagnosed a willful blindness in the world around him. They know enough, these culprits. But they cut off their intellect and their will from acknowledging what they know. And the consequences are dire for that intellect and will alike. The culprits are *filled with every injustice, wickedness, malice and evil, full of malice and murder, strife, craftiness and spite. . . . They know the just verdict of God: that people who do such things deserve death* (1:29–32). Paul's addressees can wholeheartedly agree. Or can they? Paul turns the tables on them. They too should beware. *So you are without excuse, yes, you, everyone who judges others. For when you judge others, you judge yourself. For there you are, judging—but you do the same yourself* (2:1).

The Romans are showing the signs of the punishments Paul has just listed: they are bitterly divided. So are they guilty of the crime? They too know enough to recognize and worship God aright, but they are ignoring what they know. And the result within the assembly is the result they should expect—a breakdown into bitter division.

Knowledge—this is the theme of the letter's opening chapters. If the Romans have lost sight of the knowledge they really have, then they must first be reminded of what they can and do know. They have the knowledge to be what we would call responsible moral agents, but their mind is diseased. So Paul sets out to heal it. This is the aim of the whole letter. The mind here, Greek *nous,* is just that ordered constellation of thoughts and knowledge that we draw on and generate in the course of our daily lives, what we have in mind and use. But how can Paul's addressees use a diseased mind to heal its own disease? A mind so corrupt has no bootstraps or grip by which to pull itself up from its own corruption. Paul, then, must first reassure the Romans that they do have the capacities they need; they do have the knowledge and the wherewithal to use it.

Those who observe the Law will think they have the advantage. Not so, insists Paul. There are Gentiles without the Law who nonetheless *do what the Law requires* (2:14). They have an active and discriminating conscience or knowledge of themselves. There are Jews, meanwhile, who boast in the Law and yet betray it. We saw in the classic reading of the letter how such *boasting* is the characteristic wrong of "the Jews," the "religious" people. They take pride in their obedience to the Law and believe themselves to earn their place in God's kingdom. But that classic view ignores Paul's emphasis. The pride that Paul is attacking here is specifically pride in the knowledge that the Law brings. The chief object of boasting is not an achievement, but a knowledge that, he says, is not being applied. *You rely on the law and you boast in God and you know the will of God and you reckon up what is important, taught by the Law,*

and you are confident that you are a guide of the blind, a light for those in dark-
ness, a tutor for the foolish (2:17–20).

Scholars have long wondered about this early section formed by
chapter 2. It is so prominent. Surely such an opening passage should set
out the character of Paul's good news, in particular, in the classic reading, the need for us to rely wholly on God's mercy and the faith of the
Anointed. But Paul does not mention the Anointed once in this section. He insists that *on the Day of Anger and of the unveiling of God's*
judgment (2:5) we will all be judged simply by our deeds. Those who
maintain a good life will get the glory and honor and immortality that
they seek. It is as simple as that. Paul is writing, of course, to Christians.
Surely they know that all he promises is dependent on their prior confession of the Anointed. Is he assuming, then, that they will be alert to
this, the heart of the good news, throughout? No, this is not Paul's
point. He wants his addressees, Jews and Gentiles alike, to acknowledge
by the end of this passage that they have no excuse for the evil that
infects them. They are—and now they will know they are—responsible
agents and not so sunk in error that they cannot take the first steps out
of it. What they *cannot* do will soon enough become clear.

THE FAITH OF FATHER ABRAHAM

Abraham was promised he would be the father of many nations. He
believed the promise, *and it was accounted to him for justness* (Rom. 4:3,
quoting The Beginning [Genesis] 15:6). Why does Paul devote a chapter to the story of Abraham? Abraham believed the promise, as we have
heard, before he was circumcised. Converts to Judaism, then, had good
reason to regard him as a model and forefather. And so had the Jews
themselves. We have already seen Paul, when writing to the Galatians,
rework the promise God made to the seed of Abraham. He insisted it
was no longer a promise to the Jews alone—or even to non-Christian
Jews at all. Here in the letter to the Romans is the same maneuver
again: Paul takes up a view starkly at odds with his own and reworks it
to his own advantage.

For Paul, Abraham is a model of trust. God promised him an heir.
He believed in the impossible and hoped against hope. *Without any*

weakness in his faith he disregarded his own body, already the body of a dead *man—he was a hundred years old—and the death in which our mother Sarah* *lived* (4:19). His faith was proved when he believed the promise; fulfillment followed.

Here is the order of the Romans' own movement into faith. They have heard a promise and believed it. The fulfillment of the promise, however, is yet to come. The Romans must hope against hope. And to help them do so, Paul offers the encouragement of an example: of the patriarch who himself hoped against hope and who had faith in *the* *God who brings the dead to life and who calls things that don't have being—* *things that do* (4:17). The Romans have taken on a belief as drastic and as strange as Abraham's—that God raised Jesus from the dead. When they credit the great claims and promises of the faith, the Romans are doing no less and no more than Abraham himself—and not by circumcision at all.

Process and Progress

We are about to dive into the letter's central chapters, 6 and 7. Paul combines a small group of images with dazzling intricacy. When we nowadays read or hear these chapters, we can readily imagine them as a challenge laid down by Paul that is still before Christians today: to be a Christian, this is what you must believe. After so many years of Paul's recitation in church, it is hard for Christians to ask the question most natural to any non-Christian reader: What do these chapters actually mean?

Paul sketches an adherent of each of two factions. There likely were such groups in Rome, but we cannot assume they were as important in the assembly as they were to Paul. His concern is neither to give an accurate summary of the Roman assembly, nor to address just those members of the assembly who recognize themselves in one of his descriptions. Far from it. He needs to target just those errors—in their purest, most vivid form—that are, he believes, dividing the assembly. Any member will recognize the views he evokes.

THE LIBERTINES

It is not just Paul's verbal dexterity that is confusing. He speaks boldly of what has happened in baptism. It is over and done. Its effect is in place and independent of the future conduct of the baptized. And yet some of those who have been baptized believe they can, without any qualms or ill effect, carry on as evilly after baptism as before—more evilly still, if they once think that baptism has guaranteed God's favor, come what may. God's mercy and grace are all the more active, the more there is to be forgiven. We are permitted, then—even encouraged—to do wrong. Why does Paul take so seriously such an extraordinary view? Because he is said to preach it himself.

Do you not know, Paul asks the Romans, *that all of us who have been baptized into Anointed Jesus have been baptized into his death?* (6:3). He expects them to answer yes. How much of what follows would have been familiar to them, we cannot now know. *So we were buried together with him through that baptism, into his death* (6:4). Paul needs the Romans to believe that something has happened to them, once and for all. If they will once see themselves as dead to the Law and to wrongdoing, as corpses beyond the influence of either, they will look elsewhere for the source of their life and liveliness. Paul is stretching language into the most emotive images he can find. He must startle or shock the Romans into seeing themselves—and so into living—as they never have before. He is writing not to clarify a position, but to change it.

We can ourselves see how strange Paul's position is. He has to urge the Romans, *So you too, account yourselves dead to wrongdoing but alive to God in Anointed Jesus* (6:11). They have not grasped what has already happened to them and must be told to make a deliberate effort: to make themselves think of themselves as *dead to wrongdoing.* By this conscious self-assessment they will come to see what is true of themselves already. Paul pursues the theme. The Romans must work at the image that they have of themselves. *Present yourselves to God as if alive from the dead* (6:13). All the grandeur of the baptismal rites and formulas has not secured the converts in the way of life to which they have been called. They must now view themselves from a distance, so that they can see their failure and the grounds for it.

We might have some sympathy for any Romans drawn to that libertine view. They have died, Paul tells them, and been buried. This is already strange enough, and a test for their imagination. Paul carries on. He talks of life and death: physical life and death; life under the power of wrongdoing and the death to which this leads; death to the power of wrongdoing and the life to which that leads; and the state of the Romans themselves meanwhile, sharing in the burial of Jesus and looking to share his life

But the libertines, as the Romans now hear, are so far from recognizing such experience as their own that they have to envisage it, by an act of imaginative will, in order to become what Paul tells them they already are. Ever further into the letter they go, hearing from Paul just a dazzle of strange images and a psychological fiction they are expected to impose upon themselves. Why should they agree to do so?

THE LEGALISTS

Enough, for now, of those libertines, who were following through—they believed—the logic of Paul's own good news. Others in Rome saw in the Law's loyal observance—and in the clarity it provides, day by day—the precious offer and demand of God to be undertaken by anyone who seeks God's blessing and rescue from the wrath to come. This view too may well have smoldered, even without the intervention of rival preachers, in most of Paul's own assemblies. It will have burst into flames in response to libertines such as those Paul has just evoked. Two such flints, struck together, will have ignited bitter divisions.

These loyal legalists as well have good reason to find Paul confusing. Paul tells them, in a notoriously odd image, that their death with the Anointed has freed them from the Law as certainly as a husband's death frees the wife from her marriage. They are free then to go with another man, the Anointed. These Law-observant Romans, as Paul himself insists, have had no grasp of this husband's death and their new freedom. Paul wants them to abandon their dearest principle for this intricate series of metaphors.

• • •

WHY SHOULD PAUL'S LETTER be more successful than baptism had been itself? How can Paul expect such exhortation to *work?*

Paul writes as if to an assembly aflame with the dispute between these two factions. But the chief delinquency of the assembly, he maintains, is not the error of one faction or of the other. Freedom to do wrong and obedience to the Law are slogans. Their adherents, fiercely opposed to each other, fail to see that the two positions are in fact equivalent. In the face of the good news, the power of wrongdoing and the power of the Law are parallel in their role and in the end to which they lead—to the division that is breaking the Roman assembly apart.

It takes Paul to show how closely parallel to each other the members of these factions really are. Paul first evokes those who think themselves free to do wrong. *What shall we say, then? Shall we remain in wrongdoing, so that grace may increase? . . . Shall we do wrong, because we are not under the law but under grace? Certainly not!* (6:1, 15). All those claiming such privilege have failed to grasp what they have undergone in baptism. In wrongdoing there is no freedom; the guilty are putting themselves under the power of wrongdoing and becoming its slaves. *We have died to wrongdoing,* so that we might live *in newness of life.* The person we were, *our old man,* was crucified *so that the body of wrongdoing might be brought to nothing.* Thanks to baptism, wrongdoing *will have no lordship over us.* A far cry, this is, from the old slavery to wrongdoing and its *fruit* of death. Now the Romans are *enslaved to God* and have instead the *fruit* that leads to holiness (6:4–22).

So much for the libertines. Paul next turns to those who rely on the Law's observance. Any such members of the assembly likely defined themselves, ever more strenuously, by opposition to those libertines. But are they fooling themselves? Paul creates a moment of real drama: he defines their status in terms and a structure precisely parallel to those that define their antagonists'. The Law *has lordship* only over those who are alive. *You have died to the Law.* And so this faction too can *bear fruit* to God and no longer *bear fruit* to death (7:4–6).

We seem to have two groups with two outlooks and clear distance between them. The groups' members see only the differences. Paul insists that they are inseparable. Those who adhere to the Law are not free; they extol just that which gives power to the wrongdoing they are the most vehement to resist. Those who flout all law are not free; they are slaves to the wrongdoing that draws its power from the Law. The two factions are caught up in the whorls of each other's error. Their members are fueling what they claim to resist.

Why has Paul worked so hard to generate this symmetry? He works to rebut both positions in Rome by showing they are interdependent. Each can be so destructive precisely and only because of the other. And so he will heal the adherents of each. The factions are united in the error that divides them and in its effect upon their own and each other's lives. The conflict itself between two such positions, each clamorously and divisively maintained, is betraying the good news and dismembering the Body of the Anointed.

The Agony . . .

How clear Paul makes it seem. But to see the neat patterns in a knot does not yet free the person tied with it. Paul has laid bare the power and shared character of wrongdoing and the Law; but he has not enabled his two types to overcome them. And so we come to the most remarkable paragraphs of all. They will occupy our next couple of pages. Paul invites his addressees ever more deeply into the world of the two imagined types. He will demonstrate, in his monologue of the tortured self, what the death is to which wrongdoing and the Law together are subjecting them all. In this demonstration their mind at last comes to itself. Will and intellect are healed. The mind is no longer pitching the self into the crimes portrayed at the letter's start.

> *What shall we say, then? That the Law is wrongdoing? Certainly not! But I would not have known wrongdoing if it were not for the law. For I would not have known desire if the Law did not say, "You shall not desire."*
>
> ROMANS 7:7

Every generation of readers asks: Who is the "I" of these paragraphs? The question was already an issue for Origen, writing in the third century, and has been ever since. Is Paul really speaking of himself? As he now is or as he was before his conversion? Or as he can see himself since the conversion—and only since then—to have been before it? Does such an "I" expand to include all other Christians, all other Jews, or all other Christians in their retrospect upon their pre-Christian life?

Of course we think initially of just Paul himself, but the identification is not so easy. This self of the letter is tortured by an inability to keep the Law; Paul, by contrast, will tell the Philippians that he himself had been blameless before the Law. Again, his self says, *Without the law I was once alive* (Rom. 7:9). What an odd claim (about his childhood, perhaps?) for the Jewish Paul to make about himself. To some readers this self has seemed to be in agony too sharp for any Christian, let alone for Paul; to others, in an agony just right for a Christian. The debate goes on.

Here we have been looking for the solution in a quite different way. Paul is not doing obscurely what we modern readers would expect him to do; he is doing clearly what we would never have foreseen. Paul creates in his letter a world of its own. His addressees had antennae alert to the situation within their own assembly. Beyond that, when they listened to the letter's recitation, they had only the clues they could pick up from the letter itself. Paul spins a web around the Romans, within which the types in his dialogues and monologues emerge and play their part and disappear again. When he speaks as the self in the following paragraphs, he evokes Adam and Eve, the Law given at Sinai, and all the language he has just used of the two factions in turn.

And in this way he evokes a person, an "I," who exists only in the letter—the figure in whom the members of each imagined faction, brought gradually and now finally to a right mind, will converge for the last movement toward their death to death, their baptismal rebirth. For ease of reference, I will call this "I" the "self" without any further qualification or quotation marks. We need only to remember that it is a self defined in and by the letter alone.

And why does he write as "I" at all? Paul associates himself with the self of the factions he has evoked and opposed, for the Paul who will heal the divisions in the Body is a member of that Body himself. There is a unity—deeper than any division—between those groups that their members cannot see, and a unity between them all and Paul himself. We learn much of what Paul believes from what Paul says about the Body of the Anointed, and far more from how he acts within it.

THE INDIVIDUAL, THE ASSEMBLY, HUMANITY, AND THE WORLD

At stake is more than a sum of individuals. Paul's addressees are *in Anointed*—in the realm of his power, and within his Body. To be in this Body is to be in an assembly. No wonder, then, that Paul's focus on the "I" is framed and informed by his still more central concern for the assembly as a whole. Paul speaks of communal breakdown at the start. The assembly will be at unity by the end. And in between, we hear Paul's most famous teaching on the self's standing before God. The movement is as important as its parts: the community is nothing without the individuals that make it up; and only within the assembly, in turn, can those individuals fulfill God's will as limbs of the Anointed's single, united Body.

So far, so good. But we have still not mastered the shape of Paul's thought. At the center of Paul's letter his vision embraces all humankind: he is speaking of Adam and Eve. And at this very moment he sets his lens to the closest, tightest focus of all to speak of the individual self. Paul speaks of the single self precisely by speaking in terms of Adam, of the first human and so all his heirs, and of all *adam* by speaking of the individual self. The most intimate and the most universal—the two belong inseparably together.

Paul does not rest here. At the moment of transfer to hope and glory, Paul will pull back: from "I" to "you" in the singular, to "us," and then once more to the plural indefinite "you," and so outward to all the children of God—and beyond. For more is at issue in this new Adam than humanity. Creation itself is groaning in childbirth as it waits for its final liberation. The whole creation that was molded by God's Wisdom at the beginning will be redeemed by God's Wisdom at the end.

The light that Paul saw shine on the road to Damascus was the light, until Adam fell, that illumined all creation. It has shone again. Humanity can see in its brilliance what humanity was created to be—and in that very knowledge begins to become it once more.

THE HEART OF THE LETTER

What a tightly packed passage chapter 7 is. We shall see the skill with which Paul embraces in this one monologue himself, his addressees, and the self-definition to which he has brought those addressees.

Surely some of Paul's Roman addressees will have looked on as he redefined the factions and their opposition, confident that they themselves were uninvolved. Here was an argument that affected only the members of those factions, however few or many they may have been. It did not affect the restrained members of the assembly who followed Paul's good news as he intended it should be followed. Has Paul, in this part of the letter, got these in his sights at all? Yes, indeed he has.

Paul has seen in those factions a failure to grasp what the Anointed has achieved and what his followers have, in the gift of the Breath, received. (It is striking to see him present the questions of his libertine opponents as if they made the good news an object of clever calculation.) Those in error have not been specious; they have defined themselves in the most fundamental of all terms, but they have misunderstood those terms. To dire effect.

There were those who defined themselves by the template of Moses' Law. *"Look,"* said Moses to the people of Israel, *"I have put before you today life and death, good and evil. If you listen to the commandments of the Lord your God, which I am ordering you today, to love the Lord your God, to follow in all his ways, to keep his just requirements and his judgments—then you will live* (The Second Law [Deuteronomy] 30:15–16). These followers of Moses looked to the Law for life. But they forgot that the Law brought Adam—and so all *adam*—to death.

And there were those who defined themselves by the template of Adam before the Fall, and so of Adam now restored. They thought of themselves as free to flout all law. But Adam himself was subject to a commandment that was in force long before Moses lived. Adam broke it, and so died.

These templates have been misused. They must be properly combined and understood. And then they will define all humankind. At last Paul's addressees—all of them—will have the terms to hand in which to understand themselves and their place in the sight of God.

To bring them to this understanding Paul will not argue or expound. He will stir the depths of their imagination.

> *I would not have known wrongdoing if it were not for the law. For I would not have known desire if the Law did not say, "You shall not desire." But wrongdoing, taking its opportunity through the commandment, effected in me every desire. For apart from the law, wrongdoing is dead. And without the law I was once alive, but when the commandment came wrongdoing sprang to life, and I died, and the commandment—the commandment issued for life,—this was found to be for me a commandment for death. For wrongdoing, taking its opportunity through the commandment, deceived me utterly and through it killed me.*
>
> ROMANS 7:7–11

God gave Adam a commandment in Eden not to eat the fruit from one tree, the tree of the knowledge of good and evil, for on the day that he ate of it, he would surely die (The Beginning 2:17). But the serpent *deceived* Eve. She ate the forbidden fruit, and Adam ate too. What was the crime represented by the Fall? Improper desire or covetousness was widely seen as the root of their wrongdoing.

It is no surprise, then, that Paul's self has invoked the tenth of the Ten Commandments, relayed to Israel by Moses: *You shall not desire the wife of your neighbor. You shall not desire the house of your neighbor . . .* (The Escape [Exodus] 20:17). Paul knows the tradition that the Law relayed to Moses existed before the world was even made, and he makes good use of it. He allows Adam—all *adam*—to be implicated in the Law that was relayed only to Israel and only centuries later.

It is worth our standing back for a moment. Can any of us believe that such desire is stirred in us only by the arrival of a law against it? It's true, forbidden fruits are sweeter. Adam "did not want the apple for the apple's sake," wrote Mark Twain. "He wanted it only because it was forbidden." But if this is Paul's account of the origin of human evil, it sounds to modern ears bathetically trite. It also convicts God of strange folly, that he has instituted a Law that will do exactly the opposite of what he planned it to do. So why does Paul seem to take such a route?

Because his chief concern is not to evoke a single individual, but to merge into one the templates of Adam and of Moses, and so to reveal the template that defines all humankind.

Thanks to the first half of the monologue (7:7–13), the addressees can recognize the combined voices in the second (7:14–25). In Paul's "I" there speaks Adam, the voice of all humanity and the voice of the man who first encountered the power of law. There the Jew speaks too, from a self-understanding formed by God's promise relayed by Moses. There the would-be libertine speaks, who has relished freedom from all law. There Paul speaks, linking himself with the Romans in this final stage of their restoration.

Every imagination needs fuel to feed its flames. Paul offers none of the material familiar to our modern minds, informed by the psychology of the last two hundred years. He picks up, from the ideals of the Roman factions themselves, the defining heroes of the past and reworks their roles into one.

Any members of the assembly who were resolute in the Law's observance were quite sure what they were doing; they were following the Law that brought life; they were resisting the wrongdoing that led to death. Their antagonists who renounced all law were quite sure what they were doing, living out their freedom from condemnation in reliance on God's promise to Jesus' followers.

And they were all wrong. Paul has unpicked these two supposedly independent groups and has rewoven them into a single whole. The first group, relying on the ramparts of the Law, is giving every opportunity to the power its members claim to resist. The second, which has left all such protection behind, is stirred to action by the very Law from which its members claim to be independent. They are both deluded. And their delusion has mired them, both alike, in death.

Let the Romans once recognize that, and what follows?

So that the Law, on the one hand, is holy and the commandment is holy and just and good. Did the good, then, turn out to be death for me? Certainly not! But wrongdoing did, so that it might clearly be wrongdoing, in

effecting my death through the good, so that wrongdoing might be wrong
beyond measure through the commandment.
ROMANS 7:12-13

The members of both groups now have a mind ready to watch itself
in action. They are reaching a clear self-consciousness, free from the
delusions that had led them into the delinquency of Paul's opening
condemnation.

Here, then, the addressees can hear themselves speaking, characters
themselves in the world of this drama, a chrysalis from which the fully
formed butterfly is struggling to emerge:

For we know that the law is filled with the Breath, but I am made of
flesh, sold [like a slave] under wrongdoing. For what I am effecting, I do
not know. For what I want—that's not what I do; but what I hate—
that's what I do. And if what I don't want, that's what I do—then I say
"Yes" to the Law, and agree that it is fine. And now it is no longer me
effecting this, but the wrongdoing that lives in me.
ROMANS 7:14-17

Paul runs this line of thought once, and then he runs it again. We
might think he is just repeating an important point for emphasis. Far
from it. That distinction between himself and his wrongdoing makes
possible an insight that changes everything. His self can now specify
where the good and the evil lie. His intellect and will are no longer
sunk in the old conspiracy against their own knowledge of God. The
self can now spot the conflict between mind and deed and so comes to
understand its own will. For the first time, the self recognizes in itself
the workings of the conscience—of the will and the self-conscious
intellect—that Paul introduced at the start of the letter. The self sees its
own mind in action, healed; here it is analyzing, assessing, and deciding.

This gives to the self the distance from itself to scrutinize its two
centers of action. The mind has a new lesson to learn, the lesson of its
own limitations. It will discover the power within the self over which
the mind itself is powerless—the *flesh.* The self-consciousness to which
the self has come is not enough. It remains ineffective. There remains

an opposing center of action that leaves powerless this healed and knowing will. The agony must get greater still:

> *For I know that the good does not live in me, I mean in my flesh. For to want it, that is close to hand, but to effect what is fine—that is not. For I don't do what I want, the good; but what I don't want, the bad—that is what I do. And if what I don't want, that's what I do—then it is no longer me that is effecting it, but the wrongdoing that lives in me. So I find the Law, for me who wants to do what is fine—I find that for me what is bad is close to hand. For I share the delight in the Law of God, in my inner person; but I see another law in my limbs, waging war against the Law of my mind and taking me prisoner in the Law of wrongdoing which is in my limbs. What a wretch I am! Who will rescue me from the body of this death?—But thanks be to God through Jesus Anointed our Lord!—So then: I myself in my mind am a slave to the law of God, but in my flesh to the law of wrongdoing.*
>
> ROMANS 7:7-25

The self can see for itself the death of which Paul has been speaking, but it can see no escape. The mind is now doing all it can, and it is not enough. The self is watching its own death from the power of wrongdoing.

Only death can undo such a death. Paul has asked, *Do you not know that all of us who have been baptized into Anointed Jesus have been baptized into his death? . . . Our old person has been crucified together with him, so that the body of wrongdoing might be brought to nothing, to the end that we be no longer enslaved to wrongdoing* (6:3, 6). Dead to wrongdoing; and dead to the Law that gave wrongdoing its power. And from this death comes life. Paul continues: *So we were buried together with him through that baptism, into that death, so that just as Anointed was roused from the dead through the glory of the father—so we too might walk in newness of life* (6:4).

The Romans are ready to undergo once more this death to death and to come through to the life beyond. What the mind cannot do, the Breath does. The Romans, in Paul's diagnosis, could not grasp what was happening at the time of baptism. Now they can. So Paul triggers the move from the body of this death to newness of life. Here is the effect of baptism, at which the Breath was given, made present in the reception of Paul's letter. As Paul in his person re-presents the Anointed, so his letter re-presents the gift of the Breath.

> *There is now no condemnation for those who are in Anointed Jesus. For the Law of the Breath of life in Anointed Jesus has freed you from the Law of wrongdoing and of death.*
>
> ROMANS 8:1-2

Paul has wound the spring tight. He releases it in a chapter of triumph.

. . . and the Ecstasy

A downward spiral at the letter's start is matched by an upward spiral at its end. In the letter's first half Paul had constructed for the Romans a mirror image of the state to which he hopes to bring them; everything in Rome that he will address at the letter's end is already in his mind at its beginning. We heard, for example, how the Romans have had to follow Abraham, who *had faith in the God who brings the dead to life and calls things that do not exist as things that do. . . . Without any weakness in his faith he disregarded his own body, already the body of a dead man—he was a hundred years old—and the death in which our mother Sarah lived* (4:17, 19). In their turn the Romans *have faith in the one who roused Jesus our Lord from the dead* (4:24). That hope against hope will save even their body too.

> *If the Breath of him who roused Jesus from the dead dwells in you, then he who roused Anointed from the dead will bring to life your bodies too through his Breath that dwells in you.*
>
> ROMANS 8:11

They need such hope. Paul hints again at the danger facing the assembly. Individual followers of Jesus, Paul reminds the Romans, have the assurance to address God as Jesus addressed him: *Abba*, Father. Now, *Abba* is a cry of anxiety. Jesus, we are told by Mark, addressed God as *Abba* in the Garden of Gethsemane, in his turmoil on the night before his death (Mark 14:36). It is no surprise, then, that Paul reminds his addressees what they in their turn must expect to undergo. *We are heirs of God, sharing the heritage of Anointed, if indeed we share in his suffering so that we might share in his glory too* (8:18). Paul had said earlier, *We boast in the hope of the glory of God* (5:2), whatever *tribulations* may arise. And now he can take up the theme. *In hope we have been delivered* (8:24), whatever the sufferings we know now.

Far more than individuals are involved. The followers of Jesus are not mere viewers of an unveiling; they are themselves to be unveiled as what they really are, for the whole of creation *is going to be freed from the slavery of mortality into the freedom of the glory of the children of God* (8:21). These children are leading creation into its new state. And as creation groans in childbirth until now, *so we too, having the firstfruits that are the Breath, we ourselves too are groaning in ourselves as we wait for our full adoption, the redemption of our bodies* (8:23). The Corinthians have the down payment; the Romans have the firstfruits. Israel in the past had presented to God the firstfruits of the harvest; so now, with an inversion so typical of Paul, we hear that in the Breath God has given his people the firstfruits of the glory that is to be theirs.

AND AS THE CORINTHIANS WERE ON THEIR WAY TO GLORY, so are the Romans. They need no journey to get there. The transformation of a seer is theirs to have, here and now. The Romans, like the Corinthians, are growing from glory into glory, transformed into the likeness of the image they gaze on. The glory is growing even as they hear and accept Paul's letter. And by the end of the letter the Romans will have learned, in practical terms, what Paul's talk of transformation means.

> *We know that for those who love God everything works together for good;*
> *for those, that is, who are called according to his foreplanning.*
> *Those whom he foreknew, he has foreordained to be conformed to the*
>   *image of his son,*
> *for him to be the firstborn among many brothers.*
> *And those whom he foreordained, he has also called;*
> *and those whom he called, he has also held just;*
> *and those whom he held just, he has also [and already] glorified.*
>
> ROMANS 8:28–30

"Heirs of God, Sharing the Heritage of Anointed"

Paul's addressees are now ready to hear what they could not grasp at the letter's start. Paul returns to the questions of that sharp questioner. What advantage have the Jews? At issue is God's own justness, his faithfulness to his own promises. *"God has set forth as the* [or *a*] *mercy-seat"—through faith—"in his blood for the manifestation of his justness on account of the remission of former wrongdoings in the forbearance of God," toward the manifestation of his justness at the present vital moment.* It is not enough for God to exercise his power to save as and where he will. Its exercise must be just. *For him to be just,* Paul continues, *and to hold just those dependent on Jesus' faith* (3:25–26).

Paul well knew what was at stake when he added that closing section to the formula he quoted. He will enable the healed minds of the Romans to recognize God's justness for themselves. When they have done so they will be free from the last remnants of the factionalism that Paul has had in mind throughout. At the letter's start the advantage seemed to lie with the Jews. They had the Law. Once that has been linked with wrongdoing, the advantage lies with the Gentiles. Had Paul, in leveling the playing field, overcorrected? Now he redresses the balance with the three dense chapters, of which we have already heard, on God's plan for the Jews and their final vindication.

And so to the letter's closing section, 12:1–15:13. All presumed superiority, in one faction or the other, has been dissolved. Paul now recalls the whole list of evils from the letter's opening condemnation and expounds their contraries. Love works for good, not for evil; it lives in friendship; it honors others; it serves the Lord; it succors saint and stranger alike. For all in all, the love that is the fulfilling of the law stands over against the discord whose punishment is death. How far behind we have left those agents of evil whom we heard of at the letter's start, agents who are filled with injustice and evil, with envy, trickery, and spite, who are libelers, hate God, and are devoid of love or pity. The evils that Paul listed were social; they would tear an assembly apart. Their contraries are social too; they will be the strength of this body, the assembly or assemblies in Rome.

Only and precisely at the letter's end can the assembly take on Paul's command: *Stop your conformity to the present age. Keep up your transformation in the renewal of your mind, so that you might reckon aright what is the will of God: what is good and well-pleasing and perfect* (12:2). Once more the mind, as at the letter's start; but this time, a mind healed. Once more a reckoning of right and wrong; but this time, uncorrupted. The community that was collapsing into bitterness can now recover the life to which it was called—as a single body of many limbs. It is Paul's letter itself, through the course of its reception, that has healed the assembly's judgment and so the assembly itself.

How will the addressees look upon themselves and others, once their mind is restored to health and the gift of the Breath inspires them? Paul turns in his last chapters to instruction. There is no anxiety now over the Law and its observance. Not because Paul is inconsistent, but because the Romans have been healed of the corruption that gave rise to the anxiety. The Romans have made progress and are now ready to hear what would only have deepened their confusion at the letter's beginning. *Owe nobody anything except to love one another. For those who love have fulfilled the rest of the Law. For the commandment, "You shall not commit adultery, you shall not kill, you shall not steal, you shall not desire"— and any other commandment—it is summed up in this: "You shall love your neighbor as yourself." Love works no harm to a neighbor; so love is the fulfillment of the law* (13:8–10).

In the instructions of these last chapters Paul returns over and over to a few related words. It is hardly possible to embrace all their senses in as few English terms. In the parentheses below, then, are the significant words of Paul himself. The limbs of this body are not united by patronage and dependence, by mutual honor, pride, or obligation. They are united by love. In the sensible moderation of the assembly's humdrum life, the Romans' newfound awareness is tested and realized.

The Romans are not to think too highly of themselves *(hyperphronein)*, but to think reasonably *(sophronein)*. Back to the theme Paul comes a few verses later. They are not to think *(phronein)* haughtily or be clever *(phronimos)* in their own eyes. And again after a couple of paragraphs, whoever thinks *(phronein)* of a particular day as holy thinks *(phronein)* in this way for the Lord. *And so may the God of endurance and encouragement grant to you to think (phronein) the same as each other, according to [the will of] Anointed Jesus, so that with one heart and with a single voice you may praise the God and father of our Lord Jesus Anointed* (12:3; 12:16; 14:6; 15:5–6).

We have heard often enough of love, faith, and hope. This familiar trio emerges yet again in these last chapters, as the threads that bind Paul's exhortation together. No wonder Paul ends: *May the God of hope fill you with all joy and peace in your having faith, so that you may excel in hope in the power of the Breath of God* (15:13).

CHAPTER 25

PHYSICIAN OF THE MIND

IT IS TIME ONCE MORE TO PAUSE and draw breath. Readers may well
have some pressing questions.

Paul has set out to induce a change in the Romans. He expects it to
show itself in their self-consciousness and that will change their behavior toward each other and the outside world. And is that all he
intended? He draws on baptismal imagery, yes. But we have seen more
than once how skillfully Paul can deploy an image over the course of
pages. Here, perhaps, he is simply drawing on baptism to make his
instruction more effective.

If we stop here we are doing no justice to Paul's aim. Looking for
words in which to describe Paul's procedure, I have spoken of his healing the minds of his addressees and re-presenting their baptism. It is that
last stage that is likely to unsettle us most. Paul is invoking the imagination of his addressees, inviting them to retrace in self-conscious reflection a process they have already undergone. He wants this process in
their imagination to be more effective than the event itself had been.
This is a remarkable aim. What does Paul expect his addressees to
undergo, to experience? What would he recognize as success?

Paul engages so much at once in the Romans' understanding: their
knowledge of the Old Order; their dispassionate self-description; their
personal commitment to a way of life and a community; their memory
of baptism; and their openness in all of these to dread, fear, hope, and
awe. He also engages so much in their imagination, fueled by the dense

whirl of images he evokes, and by the strange fusion of Adam, Moses, and the Romans themselves.

In this density Paul is evoking the atmosphere of ritual, the solemn, transformative air of a rite of passage. We know, in our own way, the standing of such rites and the effect they can have on us. And we know, in particular, how far removed such rites are from their description read or heard. The marriage service might serve as one modern example. It is awesome enough to read the words of the service, but there is a world of difference between studying the words of the marriage service in a book and standing with one's partner and making the vows for oneself. This comparison gives us just a glimpse too of the power Paul expects his own procedure to have. A couple whose marriage has been in difficulty might themselves head back to the words of their marriage and evoke—not just recall, but evoke with all their power of their memory and imagination—their marriage day and all that they undertook and felt and hoped for then. And they might find that they understand more in retrospect of what they said and did than they had understood at the time. *Here* is the style in which to read Paul. We are inclined nowadays to study his words, and so we miss their point. Paul did not intend his audience to study his letters, but to undergo them.

Not that Paul was naïve. *There is now no condemnation,* he exclaims in a burst of triumph, *for those who are in Anointed Jesus* (Rom. 8:1). The addressees come out of the darkness into the sunlight of the Breath. But within a few lines Paul is warning: *You are not in the flesh but in the breath, if indeed the breath of God dwells in you. But if anyone does not have the breath of Anointed, they are not his* (8:9). If, if, if—five times in as many sentences Paul tees up the question: Have the Romans really moved across to the life of the Breath? Paul takes nothing for granted.

SOME CHRISTIAN READERS will be unsettled by Paul's therapeutic endeavor. Too much, they will think, is being said about humanity and not enough about God. And too much is being left to human agency; it is as if we are limbering up to effect our own deliverance. Or it is as if Paul is limbering up to effect our deliverance, within the limits of his capacities and ours. Even when he takes his readers through from death to life, he is—it may seem—playing them like an instrument. He is ascribing to the Breath what might look to a cynical observer like the effects of his own manipulation. We have, it seems, ignored the work of God in this, and so the will of God as well, the freedom of God's decision that any one individual shall—or shall not—accept the good news.

We should certainly admit that Paul is in danger of stirring up the effects, within his readers, of a theatrical self-involvement. They could become excitedly self-conscious without being self-aware. It is for this reason that he enters all those warnings in his chapter of triumph. He is well aware that his readers may still be subject to the wrongdoing and the Law from which he has tried to free them.

But for the larger question. In this chapter, as throughout this book, we have been following Paul as he leads his addressees from a letter's start through to its end. In the first half of the letter to Rome, Paul is acting as the Romans' guide. He does all he can to enable the Romans to follow where God, as he sees it, summons them to go. So, what about his addressees' free will, autonomy, or dependence on God? What about the theory behind such change? Paul will come back to that theme in the letter's second half. First he exposes the Romans as best he can to God's offer. Only then does he ask in detail: Who does God make that offer to and on what conditions?

The Romans are to be healed as they hear the letter. What a striking aim for any author. It would be reassuring to know that this one letter is not alone, in all the documents from the ancient world, to adopt some such strategy as this. Is there any other document from Paul's day that employs anything like it? Yes, indeed. One of the most famous documents from the early church, the gospel of John.

John: Midwife of the Breath

For a page or two, I look back to my earlier book, *The Four Witnesses*. It will be possible here, as we concentrate on Paul, to give only a short-ened account of John's technique and aims.

The very first people to approach Jesus in John's gospel want to know where is he *staying*. It is the word that will be used in the gospel about Jesus' presence among his followers after his death. It is, then, already the right term—at the start of the story—for the gospel's readers to use, for this is the presence that such readers need to recognize and value—the presence of Jesus after his death. *"Where are you staying?"* they ask. Says Jesus, *"Come and see"* (John 1:38–39).

Within a couple of chapters Nicodemus, a leader of the people, comes to Jesus by night:

> *Jesus said to Nicodemus: "In God's truth I tell you, unless people are born again from above, they cannot see the kingdom of God."*
>
> *"How can people be born when old?" said Nicodemus. "Can they go back into their mother's womb and be born?"*
>
> JOHN 3:3–4

John calls for a revolution in the readers' understanding. They must undergo a change whose very description Nicodemus could not begin to understand. We have seen Paul at work on the Romans' mind, having to use the very organ that needs renewing to effect the renewal; a corrupt mind must see and correct its own corruption. John has just as deep and paradoxical a task—to effect a rebirth for which an embryo such as Nicodemus cannot see the possibility, let alone the need. In John's story, riddles and contradictions face the characters and the readers alike. These are the devices with which John sets out to confound his readers into new birth and its consequence—the life of the new aeon. John is the midwife of this new life.

John, then, does not want us to abandon the search for understanding. He is not just showing us what to think and know, but how to think and know it. A sort of knowledge is at stake that—as John's strategies make clear—stretches our daily language and logic to the breaking point and beyond. How are John's readers to attain it? And how will it function when they have?

As he speaks with Nicodemus, Jesus is unyielding: *"In God's truth I tell you, unless people are born from water and breath, they cannot enter into the kingdom of God"* (3:5). Nicodemus blunders through the dialogue. It gets no easier as Jesus carries on:

"God so loved the world that he gave his only son,
so that all who believe in him should not die,
but should have the life of the new aeon."

JOHN 3:16

Nicodemus is not the only figure in the story to be bemused. John's readers can recognize within themselves the questions, errors, and confusions of John's different figures. They are also to recognize within themselves the needs of those that Jesus heals or helps. A nobleman and the desert crowd, the cripple and blind man, Martha, Mary and Lazarus—the figure of Jesus in John's story heals, feeds, gives new sight, and brings to new life. And what Jesus does in the story, the story is designed to do in John's community. Healing, feeding, the gifts of new sight and of new life—these are just the images with which John does justice to the intended effects of his own text. The readers, baffled by Jesus' riddles and puns and strange ways, are being brought slowly to the new birth at the center of John's story. They are being made ready to undergo their baptism into new life.

The text of John's gospel itself offers readers new birth. This sounds grand. But a reader might well have asked then, as we can ask now: What does the language of new sight and new birth really signify? The bigger such claims are, the more carefully we will check them. As we have seen from Paul's letter to the Romans, high claims and ritual could leave the "reborn" Christian all too clearly untransformed. John gives no final answer to such a challenge, for he makes happen—but does not describe—the effect he wants his text to have.

John invokes the readers' imagination. He lays before his readers the process a candidate for baptism was invited, trained, and expected to undergo. And more still, the readers are invited to undergo that process for themselves in the reading of his text. A baptismal acclamation says:

Wake up, sleeper,
and rise up from the dead,
and the Anointed shall shine upon you.

EPHESIANS 5:14

Whoever is in Anointed is a new creation (2 Cor. 5:17). Philosophers of Paul's day spoke of ignorance and folly as death and of progress through philosophy as a movement into life. Paul and John claim still more. They are drawing on Jewish tradition. The rabbis would come to speak of conversion to Judaism as a new birth. "When someone brings a creature [the person who can hardly be called human before conversion] under the wings of the Divine Glory [see Ruth 2:12], then God counts it to them as though they had created and fashioned and formed that person," just as God created and formed Adam in The Beginning [Genesis] (1:27; 2:7). And again: "A proselyte just converted is [in innocence from past guilt] like a child just born" (a familiar motif, for example, at Babylonian Talmud *Yevamoth* 22a, 48b). The convert is at last a human such as God intends humans to be. There is room for ambiguity here: a conversion might be seen as a new creation or the true completion of the old. No wonder it is hard to spot the exact emphasis in a famous Jewish text that extols conversion. It may have been written within Paul's own lifetime. The hero, Joseph, praying for the heroine, says:

> "Lord, bless this virgin
> and renew her by your breath,
> and form her anew by your hidden hand,
> and make her alive again by your life."
>
> *JOSEPH AND ASENATH* 8:10–11

God himself is at work in conversion as he was at the start of creation. Within the assemblies of Paul and then of John the fulfillment of God's purpose in creation is in view. No, better still, it is within reach.

FIRST IN JOHN'S GOSPEL we encounter Nicodemus; then the cripple healed in John's chapter 5. In the ensuing argument Jesus must answer the charge that he makes himself equal to God:

> *"In God's truth I tell you,*
> *all those who hear my word and believe in him who sent me*
> *have the new aeon's life and do not come to judgment,*
> *but have passed from death to life.*

In God's truth I tell you,
the hour is coming and now is
when the dead shall hear the voice of the son of God,
and those who hear shall live."

JOHN 5:24–25

Then the man born blind is given new sight. And so finally we come to Lazarus. His sister Martha confirms her faith that Lazarus will rise again on the Last Day. But she must see in Jesus himself that Last Day. Jesus does not contradict Martha; he shows her the truth underlying what she believes. He answers Martha:

"I am the rising and the life:
all who believe in me, even if they die, shall live;
and all who live and believe in me shall not die, not for all aeons.
Do you believe this?"

JOHN 11:25–26

Martha gives a full answer: *"Yes, sir. I have come to believe that you are the Anointed, the son of God, the one due to come into the world"* (11:27). Martha speaks for herself. She speaks for her dead brother too. Lazarus is coming within the reach of the great promise that we heard from Jesus at the gospel's start.

"God so loved the world that he gave his only son,
so that all who believe in him should not die,
but should have the life of the new aeon."

JOHN 3:16

Jesus had spoken to Nicodemus about rebirth. Nicodemus had been bemused: *"People can hardly go into their mother's womb a second time and be born!"* (3:4). But this is not the womb from which Lazarus needs to emerge.

A rock has been used to close the mouth of Lazarus's tomb. *"Take away the stone,"* says Jesus. *"The hour is coming and now is when the dead shall hear the voice of the son of God, and those who hear shall live"* (5:24).

Over the darkness of the tomb the Word of God is spoken again. The Breath that was active at creation is moving once more over chaos. The readers have heard the cripple ordered to walk and the blind man ordered to wash. The commands were given as directly to the readers themselves. They have been restored to health and brought to sight. They have yet more to undergo. *"The dead"* said Jesus, *"shall hear the voice of the son of God."*

John's readers, buried in darkness, are ready to see the light of day and hear the voice of the son of God. *Wake up, sleeper,* rang the cry at baptism, *and rise up from the dead.*

Jesus calls out to the sleeper in the tomb:

> *"Lazarus, come on out."*
>
> JOHN 11:43

PAUL AND JOHN

John evokes the movement toward and through baptism. (Many of John's readers will have been baptized already. We must again recognize how deeply the evocation of a rite already undergone can stir a reader.) John takes his readers from death through rebirth before telling of the death and rising of Jesus that make it possible. It takes the first half of his gospel to prepare his readers for this rebirth. And this imagined death and new life will equip his readers to understand that enabling death of Jesus when its story is finally told. The readers must first be brought to new life; only then, according to John, can they hope to grasp its origin in the new life of Jesus.

Paul looks back on his readers' baptism and sets out to realize within them its latent, transformative power. He must use the corrupt mind to heal its own corruption. He knows that he must prepare the conditions that will make possible a new and purified understanding. His addressees must be made ready for the letter's climactic center. The mind is made open to healing, baptism is re-presented, and the obstinacy of the flesh is finally overcome by the Breath

John has told a story; Paul has offered teaching. They use terms as different as the forms in which they present their good news. But each has an extraordinary sense of human capacity and its limits, of the insights within our reach and the frailties that keep us from seeing them. And most important of all, they share an overarching strategy. Each text is to take its addressees once more "through" baptism. Each author uses his text to transform the readers or hearers during and through its reception.

The chief vehicle for Paul's good news is himself. Paul re-presents Jesus in the presence of his own person. Paul's letters re-present Paul himself and come with all his power; but he resorts to a written text only when need be. John's prime vehicle is a text, used precisely to present a person and his power to bring healing, new sight, and new life. John re-presents Jesus precisely in the presence and use of his text.

The Rituals of Rome

We have been immersed in Paul's thought and have adopted something of his tone, but we do well to listen at times from a distance. For one last time, let's leave the emissary's side, stand in the position of his Roman addressees, and listen, as nearly as we can, with local Roman ears. Here, then, is a practical, day-to-day question that would face every pagan convert and God-fearer as they heard the recitation of Paul's letter. What would they learn or decide to do?

Some pagan devotions were so low-key and domestic that we can at our distance forget they were observed at all. At the time, however, they were unmissable; and Gentiles would have wondered, as they listened to the Christian emissary, what would Paul's faith require them to do about these modest daily rituals. These rites had a public counterpart, strikingly ambitious and grand. We will attend first to a family's hearth and home and then to the hearth of the empire itself.

The family father of a Roman household was responsible for the rites of family religion. Rites of passage fell within the family's own responsibility, when a baby was accepted into the family or a child passed into adulthood or a death must be marked and mourned. The gods of daily life—the family gods, the gods of the store cupboard, the gods of the family fire—were all around the family, in the house itself.

Frequently found in Roman houses were small statuettes of the family gods, the *lares,* who protected the family and secured its prosperity. Some ancient writers identified the *lares* as the deified spirits of the dead. Such statuettes were standard in form, usually of an active figure (sometimes on tip-toe, sometimes with one foot raised) standing around seven inches high, with a drinking horn in one hand and in the other a wine bucket or shallow bowl. Larger houses had a shrine for the *lares,* which housed paintings or statuettes of the *lares,* memorials of the family's ancestors, and perhaps the figure of Vesta herself, goddess of the hearth. The shrine was prominently placed in the central courtyard of the house or its kitchen. This was the focus for the family's rites and sacrifices. Rituals inherited from the past had to be handed on from the present generation to the next. Where the Romans went, there went their rites. It is no surprise to find such a statuette in Italy or France, a shrine in Pompeii or the Greek island of Delos.

In the larder was the food for the family's children. Around the hearth, the center of the home, was the warmth of the family and household. In the ancestors lay the family's identity, and in their care lay the family's well-being. As we envisage these shrines and rites of devotion, it is worth asking: Did the Roman Christians abandon them on conversion? Did they put away the figurines, give up the offerings, and ignore their ancestors? We do not know how long it took for Christian families to stride or drift away from reliance on these age-old rituals of the family. But if we are to feel the texture of their faith, we must let the question stand. And I admit to my own suspicion that a good proportion of such family fathers continued to respect these rites for years or decades after their conversion.

So much for rites so domestic that we ignore them. Let's look for a moment at their public equivalent in Rome, the rituals and roles that affected the architecture of the city itself. Their influence is no easier to judge. Their symbols were everywhere, although for much of the time these called for no conscious recognition. What exactly, then, did they represent in the minds of individuals in good times and in bad, at festivals and on ordinary days? (We in our turn are surrounded by the public symbols of our nation. On every dollar bill is the Masonic pyramid and eye of wisdom, two Latin mottoes—one declaring a New Order of the Ages—and the affirmation "In God we trust." In ordinary times such images are rarely noticed, but how alert we would become, if anyone belittled them, denounced them, or threatened the values in America that we believe they stand for.)

We are turning from the father of the family to the father of the fatherland, to the emperor himself. The Christian assemblies were growing in the shadow of imperial propaganda. Once more we can only let the questions stand before us. How deeply influenced by imperial Rome were those who lived there? How completely and how quickly did its symbols lose their grip on Christian converts? In the rituals of imperial Rome we see the power of ancient stories reworked with immense sophistication. The emperor was the conduit for the gods' blessing and protection of Rome. He was intrinsic to its life. All this was represented to the people of Rome in rituals that echoed their own domestic rites. In such a setting as this Aquila, Prisca, Rufus, and their peers had to hold fast to their new faith and survive.

The emperor was called "Lord," "Savior," and "Deliverer," words that we link with the New Order and with Jesus; but they were terms used to praise the emperor before they were used of the Anointed. "Lord" had been applied to Augustus from 12 B.C.E. A region in Greece declared Nero to be "Lord of the whole world" in 67 C.E. As Nero rode back into Rome in triumph after one visit to Greece, the crowd cried out, "Hail to Nero, our Apollo! The only one from the beginning of time!" When the gospels record Jesus' triumphal entry into Jerusalem, they are setting up an unsettling competitor to the emperors and generals of the Roman world.

The emperor, as the father of the fatherland, protected the city's hearth. Augustus tells us himself how he was given the title "father of the fatherland" in 2 B.C.E. by the Senate, the knights (next in rank to the senators), and the whole Roman people. His successor, Tiberius (14–37 C.E.), refused the title; by the time Paul wrote, the emperors Caligula (37–41), Claudius (41–54), and Nero (from 54) had all accepted the accolade. Each family had its "father"; so had the empire. As the family father wielded total power over the family, so did the father of the fatherland over the Roman people and their empire.

Each household had a hearth. So had Rome itself. At the east end of the Forum was the round Temple of Vesta, goddess of the hearth. In it was no image of any god or goddess, just a fire that was always lit. Curtained off from the rest of the building was a storeroom entered only ever by the Vestal Virgins, the women chosen by the Great Priest to care for the hearth of the city and its perpetual fire. In this room were kept the most sacred relics of the city's ancient history. There stood the Palladium, statue of the goddess Athena. Legend had it that the founder of Rome himself, Aeneas, had rescued the statue from the burning city of Troy; only when the statue had been moved to the Temple of Vesta was Rome's status—and protection by the goddess—assured. Aeneas had brought as well the sacred flame from Troy to Italy; Romulus, said to be the city's founder and the forebear of Augustus, had brought it to Rome itself. The Jews were not alone in having at the heart of their temple a veiled and inaccessible sanctuary.

The Vestal Virgins tended the sacred fire and guarded and cleaned the storehouse with elaborate ritual; they gathered the first ears of corn from the harvest and made from them the sacred flour used at sacrifices. The Virgins did in public for the city what was done in private in every home. They were wholly separate from ordinary life—priestesses living together as celibates for the thirty years of their service, in the city's most public space—and yet they represented that ordinary life as lived in every household. They were virgins who secured the fertility of the land and of the nation itself. A phallus was kept in the Temple; from this—or even from a spark of the sacred fire itself—various heroes were held to have been conceived. Vesta herself was the sacred flame, the virgin, the mother. The safety of Rome depended on the safety of the flame, the Virgins, and the relics for which they cared.

Rome had long been divided into four areas, each subdivided into districts. At every crossroads in every district were shrines to the *lares*. In charge of these shrines and their sacrifices had been Colleges, in which political dissent had festered. Julius Caesar tried to suppress the Colleges. Augustus, by contrast, promoted these crossroad cults, knowing they were centers for the social life of slaves and the poor. He arranged theatrical performances in every district in 29 B.C.E. Twenty years later Augustus redivided the city to form 265 districts. The districts' cults were altered too, so that they were now dedicated to the *lares* of Augustus himself and to the emperor's own *genius,* or spirit. These cults' celebrations had traditionally been held on May 1. A new festival was then added on August 1, the start of the month newly named in the emperor's honor, when the object of reverence was to be the *genius* of Augustus. The spirit of the family father was honored in every household; the sprit of the city's "family father," the father of the fatherland, was to be honored throughout the city. The private rites of the emperor's own household were now the public rites of every district.

And the central household of the whole city, the Temple of Vesta? As Augustus spread his family's rites outward through the city at large, so he drew public pieties inward to his household and himself. From the start, Augustus enhanced his links with the Vestal Virgins. After Augustus's victory at Actium in 31 B.C.E. the Virgins headed the procession that greeted him. They were present at the dedication of the Altar of Peace in 9 B.C.E. and were among those responsible for the annual sacrifices there. In 12 B.C.E. Augustus had been elected Great Priest, responsible for the choice and supervision of the Virgins. The Great Priest had always lived in an official house in the Forum, next to the precinct of the Virgins. Augustus remained in his house on the Palatine Hill. But within two months of his election as Great Priest, an image and shrine of Vesta were dedicated in his house. This was not a takeover. The relics and sacred flame remained in the Temple of Vesta, but the focus was no longer solely on the Temple. Augustus, the Great Priest, could now be known as the Priest of Vesta; a story spread that he was descended from the goddess herself. A ramp linking the Temple and Augustus's house already ran from the Forum southeast to the Palatine. The hearth of Augustus was now the hearth of the city as well.

Augustus had already built, next to his own house, a new and outstandingly lavish temple to the god Apollo; by 18 B.C.E. it housed the venerable Books of Prophecies, in which Rome's destiny was inscribed. First with the temple to Apollo and now with the new shrine to Vesta, Augustus was gathering around himself—in the very layout of the city—the precious relics of Rome's past and guarantors of her future. We hear allusions to these changes in the literature of the time. The poet Ovid writes carefully, making it clear that Augustus had the Senate's approval for this latest move. But so dominant is the emperor and so clear the reference that Ovid need not even mention him by title or by name:

Vesta has been received in the house
Of her kinsman. So have the Senators rightly decreed.
Apollo has one part; to Vesta belongs the second part.
What still remains, the third has: he himself.
Stand firm, triumphant laurels of the Palatine;
Garlanded with oaks, may the house stand firm.
One house holds three eternal gods!

FASTI 4.949–54

What resistance could the Christians in Rome mount against such sophisticated and all-pervasive propaganda? They offered allegiance to a lord greater than any emperor; but a lord who revealed nothing of his power outside the gathering of his followers. We might ask of these followers, as we would of the Jewish communities too: Did any, many, or all those followers attend the performances at their local crossroads in honor of Augustus's spirit? Did they point out to their children the Temple of Vesta or rely at times of crisis on her protection of the city? And how did their neighbors respond if they did not?

We are about to turn our attention to Paul's letter to his Philippian converts. He will write in grand terms of the Anointed, terms that evoke great heroes and images of the Old Order. These terms will evoke the emperor too. Paul was more subversive and more dangerous to imperial order—and so put himself in more serious danger—than we can now readily see. He tells the Romans to obey all the city's powers that be. We think of him as keeping his own head—and their heads—beneath the parapet. But who could fail, in Paul's day, to contrast Paul's praise of the Anointed with the praise that any loyal subject or citizen would sing to the emperor's glory alone? Paul says:

Therefore, God has highly exalted him [the Anointed]
and has given him the name above every name,
so that at the name of Jesus every knee should bow,
and every tongue confess that Jesus Anointed is Lord.

PHILIPPIANS 2:9–11

PART IX

PAUL AND PHILIPPI

CHAPTER 26

A COMMONWEALTH IN HEAVEN

A PRISONER FOR THE ANOINTED

Paul did make his long-planned journey to Rome. As a prisoner of the Roman government.

In the spring of 56 he had left Corinth. He was making for Jerusalem. With him he had his great collection for the assembly there. Delegates accompanied him from various provinces of the empire: from Macedonia, southern Galatia, and Asia (The Mission [Acts] 20:4–5). No doubt they had brought their own assemblies' contributions. Luke mentions no delegate from Corinth itself or from the other assemblies in Greece. After all Paul's work there—and all the persuasion of 2 Corinthians 2:1–9—the Corinthians had still taken, it seems, no part in the collection.

Instead of heading straight across the Aegean eastward, Paul headed north to Macedonia, then hopped from harbor to harbor down the coast of Asia Minor. How strange that he did not call in at the great city of Ephesus. Luke tells us that it was to save time (The Mission 20:16). But Paul had good reason too to avoid the opponents there who had driven him out in the autumn of 54.

And so at last Paul brings his collection to Jerusalem. Luke makes no mention of its reception there. It may have been rejected. Paul, after all, was bringing the tribute of the Gentiles to Jerusalem; but he did not come as a suppliant or subordinate. He and his gentile assemblies owed their love and aid to the leadership in Jerusalem—but not their obedience. As Luke tells the story, Paul's visit stirred up the hostility of the non-Christian Jews in Jerusalem. And what of the Christian Jews there? Luke may not have known in full why James and the assembly did not come to Paul's help. Paul came on terms they would not accept, offered help they would not take, and landed in danger from which they would not help him.

Paul had to defend himself in Judea against both the Jewish and the Roman authorities. Luke insists that Paul could have been released without further investigation; for Luke, after all, it is important that Paul be innocent of any and all charges of which Theophilus might have heard. Paul is arraigned before the Roman governor in his capital, Caesarea. The governor would like to hand over the case to the Jewish council, apparently under his own presidency, in Jerusalem. Paul refuses. He is a Roman citizen; he will be tried by a Roman tribunal. And if the governor will not exercise his jurisdiction, then Paul will insist on a trial before the emperor himself. So to the emperor he must go—to Rome (The Mission 25:9–12). In the plan of history discerned by Luke, the days of Jerusalem are past. The Jews have rejected the good news, and Paul is on his way to the center of the gentile world. We hear he spent two years in Rome under guard, living in his own lodgings, receiving visitors, and preaching openly and without hindrance. Certain prisoners were, we know, permitted to live at home under guard.

Paul launches his letter to the assembly in Philippi: *My chains in Anointed are well known to the whole Praetorium and to everyone else* (1:13). The Praetorian Guard was a troop of imperial soldiers quartered in the Praetorium just outside the walls of Rome; as a prisoner brought from abroad, Paul would have been handed over to the prefect or to the chief administrator of the guard. But we need to bear in mind that other cities too, such as Ephesus and Caesarea, had a Praetorium, the official residence of their governor. Where, then, was Paul when he wrote to the Philippians? Ephesus, as we have heard, was a hub of his later missionary work, and it was readily accessible from Philippi. Paul certainly faced trouble in Ephesus, and it is possible he was imprisoned there. If our letter was written from Ephesus, it was written around 54, at the time of the Corinthian correspondence. I am here tentatively taking the alternative view that Paul wrote several years later, around 63, when he was under arrest in Rome.

Philippi was the first of all European cities to hear Paul's good news when he sailed westward across the northern Aegean in 48. Philippi was a Roman colony, refounded by Octavian (Augustus) after his victory at the battle of Actium in 31 B.C.E. Roman veterans had been settled in the city; its full citizens were citizens of Rome. We cannot know how many of Paul's converts were citizens themselves or shared in the civic pride of the veterans' children and grandchildren. The rest of the population—the indigenous noncitizens—looked in at the Romans establishment from the outside. But everyone in the city knew that the veterans' descendants were proud citizens of a commonwealth that embraced not just their own city, but the whole known world.

Paul offers to these citizens a far higher commonwealth than Rome could ever give them. To the indigenous noncitizens Paul offers a commonwealth far greater than that of the colonists, their families, and their privileged allies. He writes to an outpost of the empire from its center, the seat of the emperor, lord, and savior of his subjects throughout the world. But he writes about an emperor far greater than Rome's.

"The Name Above Every Name"

Paul writes of the Anointed:

> *Being in the form of God,*
> *he thought equality with God*
> *   not something to be seized;*
> *but he made himself empty,*
> *   taking the form of a slave,*
> *being born in the likeness of humans;*
> *and in fashion being found as a human*
> *   he humbled himself*
> *and was obedient to the point of death—*
> *   and death on a cross.*
>
> PHILIPPIANS 2:6–8

The Anointed goes from high standing before God to the lowest degradation, and so, as we shall see, through to installation in the highest dignity of all. Paul's letter to the Philippians contains the most beautiful "hymn" to have reached us from the churches' first hundred years. It is compact, rhythmical, balanced—and as striking a summary of early Christian belief as we could hope for. Perhaps it was actually used as a hymn, recited or sung in the public worship of the early assemblies. Paul may well have inherited it from those who acknowledged Jesus' exaltation in the very first years after Jesus' death. He may then have expanded it and given it just the emphasis most important to himself, but he left its rhythm and structure largely intact. These gave clear signals that it was a poetic unit and came with all the authority of the services in which such formal verse belonged. Did Paul expect the Philippians to know its words already? He gives no hint that they would. But the lines would have stood out strikingly then as now. Here is an elevated, numinous passage.

> *Therefore God has highly exalted him*
> *and has given him the name above every name,*
> *so that at the name of Jesus every knee should bow,*
> *of things in heaven and things on earth and things under the earth,*
> *and every tongue confess that Jesus Anointed is Lord,*
> *to the glory of God the father.*
> PHILIPPIANS 2:9-11

How readily we turn to this hymn and leave the rest of the letter to one side, and so we miss seeing the far larger "poem" of which the hymn is just one—crucial—part. From the start to the end of the letter Paul is unfolding the same movement of humility and reward in himself, in the Anointed, and in the Philippians. In these protagonists Paul does not present three independent units, casually or coincidentally linked. They are inseparable. As in 2 Corinthians 1–9, so here: Paul's addressees can understand themselves only if they understand the Anointed and Paul and the relation these stand in to each other and to the Philippians themselves.

What does Paul want his addressees to learn from his use of these suggestive lines? They are to discover a new *way* of seeing themselves.

Paul must enable the Philippians to give an account of themselves that will do justice to themselves. And for this they must draw on the models that Paul puts before them—the Anointed and Paul himself. And then in turn Paul can do justice to the Anointed only by drawing on the poetry of the past, on models from the Old Order that provide a setting for the Anointed and illumine his role by comparison, contrast, and analogy.

We will be listening to the poetry of the past and the poetry of Paul himself—not of course in rhyme or meter, but in the images that recur and evolve and introduce readers to a world of their own. In the following pages we will again be watching Paul's images and tracing the patterns they form. Once more these will reveal the shape of the letter itself and of Paul's thought within it.

As we have seen, oddities in 2 Corinthians 1–9 have led scholars to read the letter as a compilation, perhaps made in Paul's own lifetime, of sections preserved from various letters and sewn together. The same argument has been advanced for this letter to Philippi. But here too there are recurring themes offering well-placed signposts to steer Paul's addressees through this letter from section to section. Of course, Paul could have used the same images and motifs in successive letters to the same assembly, and the assembly could have arranged fragments of those letters, by chance or design, to create the patterns that are now visible in the letters as we have them today. But what a strange coincidence this would be. When we have before us a clear and elegant order, we need not look for muddle.

What was the letter to the Philippians *for?* Yet again, at our long distance, we learn much about the letter's origins from its end. In the final paragraphs Paul is ready to speak directly to the problems that he has been writing to resolve. Rivalry and contention had embittered the assembly. Now at last he can confront them directly. In the course of the letter he has dug through the foundations of the wall by which the assembly has been divided, group from group. He need now only nudge the wall and it will fall. *Euodia, I urge, and Syntyche, I urge: be of the same mind in the Lord. And yes, I ask you too, Syzygus* [Yoke-Fellow] *by name and nature: help them to do so. For in the good news they have competed alongside me together with Clement and my other fellow workers* (4:2–3). Paul does not join the argument between the women Euodia

and Syntyche. Far from it. He continues: *Rejoice in the Lord always.*
The theme has marked this letter's every section. And even here Paul
repeats it. *Again I say, rejoice* (4:4). Paul has a point to make: the Philippians are called to a life of rejoicing. Paul's instruction throughout has
been countering a quite different atmosphere, one that is sniping, competitive, and joyless.

Paul knows at his letter's start what he is to achieve by its end. Far
more is to be changed than relations between two local leaders, Euodia
and Syntyche. He will arm the Philippians with a vocabulary for their
self-description broader and deeper than they had dared use before. As
they looked for ways in which to think and speak of themselves, they
had been like fish snapping for flies at the surface of a pond; but they
can find their true character only down in the pond's depths. Paul offers
the Philippians knowledge of himself, knowledge of the Anointed, and
so—with the language and perspective that these give them—the
opportunity for knowledge of themselves. Paul has undertaken just as
grand and bold a maneuver in his letter to the Romans. At issue in
each case is not just what the addressees might come to think, but the
repertoire of thoughts and images in which they can come to think it.
To think what they should they must learn how to think it.

How abstract this can sound. But Paul is not offering the Philippians a theory. He is offering a model for living. There is a pattern, a
movement that their lives share with Jesus' life and with Paul's. For
those living out their obedience to Paul, to the Anointed, and to God,
this movement embraces everything—from the healing of wounds in
the Philippian assembly through to the humility and death of Jesus
himself. It has long been wondered how the hymn that speaks of
Jesus before his human birth and after his enthronement can possibly
provide a model for any "normal" human life. The worry betrays too
narrow a view of Paul's purpose. He sets out precisely to enlarge the
Philippians' perspective, to show them their place within a vaster landscape than they have ever thought to gaze on. And so he can launch
the hymn with a brisk command: *Have this in mind in yourselves, as in
Anointed Jesus too* (2:5).

From Degradation to Reward

SOUNDING THE REFRAIN

Yet again Paul binds his converts and himself together at the letter's start: *Both in my chains and in the defense and strengthening of the good news you all share in the fellowship of God's generosity to me* (1:7). Not that the Philippians are in captivity too; but from these very first lines Paul is weaving the link between his condition and theirs, his role and theirs—and between himself and them. Paul uses an extraordinary term for a feeling so deep it grips the stomach: *I long for you all in the visceral longing of Anointed Jesus* (1:8). And it should not be his alone. He will remind them later of *the visceral feelings of care and mercy* (2:1) that should flourish among them too as part of the Anointed. Time and again Paul speaks in this letter, in words he hardly uses elsewhere, of the experience that is or should be shared between himself and the Philippians: sharing in fellowship, sharing in imitation, sharing in effort, sharing in joy. And all of it requires the Philippians themselves to share one outlook with each other.

Paul's introduction is over. He picks up the grand movement that shapes the letter as a whole, from present humility to the glory yet to come. First, he thinks of his own humiliation. It is *for the advantage of the good news,* Paul insists, that he is in chains (1:12). The assembly in Rome is spreading the word with greater boldness than ever. Some, he says are doing so out of *jealousy* and *rivalry,* others *from goodwill; some from love,* others *from selfish rivalry* (1:15–17). Paul will later make quite clear which pattern the Philippians should follow. He will urge them to share a mutual *love* and to do nothing *in selfish rivalry* (2:2–3). It is God who is helping them to act *above and beyond goodwill* (2:13).

Paul seems strangely unconcerned by the motivation of these rivals in Rome. He admits to no tension here, however dark the motives of his detractors might be. And by his calmness he starts defusing the tension in Philippi. There is rivalry there too. Motives are being impugned. Euodia may distrust Syntyche and Syntyche Euodia. But here in the letter is Paul himself, acknowledging the work even of people who relish his own imprisonment. Whatever the disagreements in Philippi, the assembly's leaders should do no less.

Will Paul survive his time in chains? Paul turns from his present state to his future, from suffering to its reward:

For to me, living is Anointed and dying is gain. Living in the flesh? If that is what it is to be, it will bear fruit in my work. And which I shall choose I cannot tell. I am torn between the two, longing as I do to depart and to be with Anointed, for that is far preferable. But to remain in the flesh, that is more necessary, for your sake.
PHILIPPIANS 1:21-24

Here is a tone we have not heard in any other letter. Paul looks forward, as ever, to Jesus' return, but he knows he may not live to see it. Not because of his old age or Jesus' strange delay, but because of his own present danger. It is better, though, for the Philippians that he lives than that he dies. In his passage, then, through suffering to his reward, the last stage is for the moment postponed. And so is its description in the letter. In his life he will continue for now to share the expectancy of his converts; and within the letter he will keep their expectation open and undefined. The first bars of the letter's melody are sounded, but its harmonies are unresolved.

Listeners are quite sure there is more of this melody still to be heard.

THE COMMONWEALTH ON EARTH

From humility to glory—Paul plays through his theme a second time. Now he has the Philippians in mind. He wants to be sure that the Philippians are *standing secure in a single spirit, with a single soul sharing in the competition for the faith of the good news* (1:27). We shall hear of such contests in the letter again, of the strain and persistence they call for and of the garland awarded to the victor. Here at the start Paul thinks of the Philippians' strenuous efforts; in the letter's next section, of his own; and at its end, of the relation between them.

The Philippians have been unsettled by opposition. They have not seen what a blessing this is to such athletes in the faith as they are called to be. *The grace has been granted you to live your lives on behalf of Anointed: not only to believe in him but also to suffer on his behalf. For you are undergo-*

ing the same contest yourselves that you have known to be mine and now hear to be mine (1:29–30). Paul aligns their suffering with his own. They are caught up in the movement that defines his own life. It is taking them on part of a route first traveled by one far greater than them all—from glory through humiliation and so to glory once more.

Dangers from without, divisions within. Paul knows which is the poison more dangerous to the Philippians—the disputes and rivalry brewing in the assembly itself. Paul invokes his hymn, the grandest and most solemn of antidotes. To introduce it he urges the assembly:

> *If there is any comfort in Anointed, any encouragement in love, any fel-lowship of the breath, any visceral feelings of care and mercy—then fill up my joy: be of the same mind, having the same love, sharing one outlook, being of one and the same mind, thinking nothing in selfish rivalry or in empty opinions but in humbleness of mind thinking of each other more highly than of yourselves, each of you regarding not your own interests but, each group of you, the interests of others.*
>
> PHILIPPIANS 2:1–4

We hear in the hymn of the Anointed as emptying himself. To empty himself was surely to abandon the form of God. We tend, there-fore, covertly or openly to translate the hymn's first lines: *Although he was in the form of God, he humbled himself.* In the Greek there is no such *although.* The participle *being* is far more open. We can understand the hymn only when we make space too for the other sense that such *being* can bear: not "although" but "because" *he was in the form of God.* This is why the Anointed humbles himself—in such self-offering is the truest, clearest image of God. When Paul's converts undergo such humility in their turn they are not bidding farewell to the dignity of heaven that is surely theirs; they are entering upon it.

> *Being in the form of God,*
> *he thought equality with God*
>   *not something to be seized;*
> *but he made himself empty,*
>   *taking the form of a slave,*
> *being born in the likeness of humans;*

and in fashion being found as a human
  he humbled himself
and was obedient unto death—
  and death on a cross.

Therefore God has highly exalted him
  and has given him the name above every name,
so that at the name of Jesus every knee should bow,
  of things in heaven and things on earth and things under the earth,
and every tongue confess that Jesus Anointed is Lord,
  to the glory of God the father.

PHILIPPIANS 2:6–11

What Paul urges upon his converts is true already of their Lord. The Anointed *thought* equality with God was not to be seized, he *humbled* himself, and God exalted him *highly.* Then Paul continues, with his mind still on the hymn and on the Anointed *obedient* unto death:

And so, my beloved, just as you have always obeyed, so now—not just in my coming but much more now in my absence—with fear and trembling work at your own salvation. For the one who empowers in you both the will and the power to act above and beyond goodwill—this is God. Do everything without grumbling and disputes.

PHILIPPIANS 2:12–14

Paul is aiming every shot with care. He knows what dangers he must quell. No wonder he will urge his converts, at the letter's end, to make clear to everyone how *reasonable* they are, to make known their requests to God and *not to strive* on their own account. He promises them, if they will only obey, the one thing they most urgently need: *Then the peace of God, that is too high for any mind, will keep your hearts and the thoughts of your minds in Anointed Jesus* (4:5–7).

PAUL IS NOT ASKING HIS CONVERTS to resign themselves to the cheerless shadows of life in a deep valley. They are following in the footsteps of the Anointed. Do some of the Philippians think they are entitled to a grandeur that the world—and even fellow members of the assembly—

will not grant them? They should turn their gaze on the Anointed. He forsook far more than they could even imagine in order to lead where they now follow. And in this self-denial the Anointed did not lay aside the character that was his; he fulfilled it. And so will the Philippians fulfill theirs. Ahead of them is a sunlit mountain. They will reach it. But the route to it is along the valley in which they are so reluctant to stay.

The Anointed undertook a great movement in a single arc: down from glory, through death, and so to the throne of God. Paul, in his own life, has undertaken the first half of that trajectory in the hope of finishing the second. He has abandoned the grounds he had for dignity in human eyes. But what of his converts? Do they simply pick up the baton halfway through the race and run for the finish?

We learn little, from Paul, of the Philippians' troubles. Suspicion and arguments, it seems, were the worst they had to suffer. All the more touching, that Paul should dignify these self-inflicted wounds, setting them beside the wounds from others—the fatal wounds—that the Anointed freely underwent.

The Philippians see confusion in and around them; Paul gives them a map on which they can see their present point and chart their progress. If they once interpret Paul's route and their own as following this one great route taken by the Anointed himself, then the Philippians will understand their present position and the future to which it is leading them.

CIVIC SERVICE IN THE COMMONWEALTH

Live as a commonwealth, Paul tells the assembly, *worthy of the Anointed* (1:27). The image stays in his mind. We can watch a single image unfold and grow in his hands—the term for the civic service (or "liturgy") that was undertaken, at their own expense, by the leading citizens of any state. (Paul, as we know, is not afraid to use language familiar from the pagan nexus of sacred and secular duties.) This service would include the cost of public sacrifices. *It will be my pride at the Day of Anointed, that I have not run in vain nor have I worked in vain. But if my blood is actually poured out as an offering in the sacrifice and civic service of your faith, I rejoice and share in the rejoicing of you all. In the same way, you too—rejoice and share in my rejoicing* (2:16–17). Paul's service is the offering he can make of the Philippians' faith and of himself in its promotion; and in his death he may become part of the sacrifice itself. So be it. Such danger will not prevent him and his converts from being in balance, reliant on and helping each other.

The Philippians had sent a gift to Paul; one Epaphroditus had taken it. He had clearly become a valuable ally to Paul: he is *your own emissary,* Paul continues, *and civic servant of my need.* Now Paul sends Epaphroditus, *the brother who has shared in my work and shared in my soldiering,* back to the Philippians (2:25). Paul urges them to receive him with all joy; as the Philippians give Paul joy, so he will give them joy too.

Paul draws Epaphroditus into the network of shared service. Epaphroditus, emissary from Philippi to Paul, has been seriously ill. It did not stop him working. As the Anointed had been obedient *to the point of death,* so Epaphroditus *drew near to the point of death.* And Paul, emissary to Philippi, may well be near death too. In such mutual service the heart of the good news is heard beating. Paul is an offering in the civic service of the Philippians. Epaphroditus, in turn, has risked his life to do what he should: *to make up for what is lacking in the civic service that you owe me* (2:30).

A COMMONWEALTH IN HEAVEN

The Philippians are almost ready to hear the whole melody of Paul's letter in a single sweep of sound.

The assembly is being unsettled by claims that followers of Jesus must be circumcised. Paul once more interprets this demand as reliance on the flesh. He insists that he, more than most, could lay claim to any blessings dependent on observance of the Jewish Law. Here again is a high standing to be valued. But the Anointed thought equality even with God was not to be seized. The Philippians were to think of each other more highly than of themselves. And now Paul, part of this same movement, is clear: *Everything that was a gain to me, I thought it, on account of Anointed, to be a loss. No, more than that: I actually think everything to be a loss on account of the higher standing of the knowledge of Anointed Jesus my Lord* (3:7–8).

Paul has emptied himself of all the standing he had, so that he might have what he seeks for the Philippians and offers them in this very letter—the knowledge and insight they need to be blameless on the Day of the Anointed. *On his account I have suffered the loss of all things and count them as excrement, in order that I might gain Anointed and be found in him* (3:8–9).

Paul has told the Philippians, *Live as a commonwealth worthy of the good news of Anointed* (1:27). They know now how to do so. They have before them the paradigm of the Anointed himself:

> *Taking the form of a slave,*
> *and in fashion being found as a human*
> > *he humbled himself*
> *and was obedient unto death.*

And they have as well the example of the Paul who has counted all things as loss so that, as he now says, *I might be conformed to his death in case I might attain to the rising up from the dead* (3:10). The great melody of the Anointed himself is being played out in the life of Paul. Anointed Jesus, far more in origin than any mere human, took the form of a slave and died; Paul, never more than human, is in his daily life taking on the form of that death. And in his fellowship with that suffering of the Anointed, Paul already, here and now, knows something of the power at work in and unleashed by his rising.

The tune is to be played out in the lives of Paul's converts too. Here in Paul's letter is the score on which the Philippians can follow the music of their own lives, its shape and its destination. As they too undergo their degradation, so they too will have their reward. Their commonwealth on earth is a mere image of the commonwealth that is really theirs. At the letter's climax the title *Lord Jesus Anointed* emerges once more, the first time since the great hymn at the letter's start. This Jesus had been in the form of God; he was found in the fashion of humanity and humbled himself in obedience. And so he will refashion the Philippians from their humility into the form of his own glory. The last bars of the melody are heard at last. Its harmonies come to their resolution. The place of the Anointed, of Paul, and his converts converge.

For us, our commonwealth is in heaven, from where we are waiting for a deliverer, the Lord Jesus Anointed, who will refashion our humble body to be conformed to the body of his glory, in accordance with the operation of his power to subject everything to him.

PHILIPPIANS 3:20–21

In this is the victory for which Paul and the Philippians have been striving together.

Paul returns for a last time to the image of athletics. He imagines the Philippians in connection with himself and his own final victory in the games:

So, my brothers and dear friends that I long for, my joy and my garland, in this way stand secure in the Lord, dear friends.

PHILIPPIANS 4:1

CHAPTER 27

"In the Form of God"

The Servant of the Lord?

We have followed the threads of the letter to the Philippians to their final elegant knot. But modern readers—and likely ancient ones too—must still, at the letter's end, have in mind the grandeur of its hymn.

Was the hymn written by Paul or was it already the common property of his own and other assemblies? Did he perhaps adapt an already current hymn to give it just the accents that were most important to him? There have been many attempts to find its most natural line and verse breaks. Some of the most convincing find it hard, however, to accommodate the three Greek words that lie behind the phrase *and death on a cross;* these words "stick out" as an untidy addition to their verse. Paul puts enormous weight on the crucifixion itself. Perhaps these words are his own contribution to the hymn.

Let's assume Paul composed the whole hymn himself. Had he already provided it to other assemblies for their use in worship? Or did he write it for this one letter? He certainly puts the hymn to good use where it stands now. We might compare the poem on love in 1 Corinthians 13. There too we have a formal, highly wrought meditation. It could certainly have stood alone, but its themes and thrust, we have seen, link it tightly with the rest of its letter.

Questions, questions, and no clear answers. And it is time to ask yet one question more. It is perhaps the most important and yet the most elusive of all. Are we being invited, in this hymn, to see Jesus in comparison or in contrast with some great figure from the Old Order? With Adam, perhaps? Or with God's Servant, so important in Isaiah? Our hymn does not make any such links as obvious as it might. This is no accident. If Paul could expect the hymn's first users to recognize its allusions, he did not need to spell out the comparisons they prompted. He could play instead, and far more fruitfully, with contrasts.

The first Adam was made in the image of God. The hymn likely presents the Anointed as a second Adam. By contrast with the first, this second Adam existed, before being born as a human, in God's form. Paul's hymn, then, is hinting at a status for this second Adam greater than anything ascribed to the first. And again, in The Beginning [Genesis] Eve, and so Adam, were tempted to become like God; but the second Adam of the hymn had a chance, without any impropriety, to be equal to God. Whatever, then, could be said of the first Adam, far more could be said of the second.

But how much more? The first Adam was made in the image of God, but could never be confused with God. God alone can be offered the worship due to him.

> *I am God, and there is none other.*
> *I swear by myself:*
> *Justness comes forth from my mouth,*
> *my words shall not be turned aside;*
> *for every knee shall bow to me*
> *and every tongue shall confess God.*
> ISAIAH 45:22–23, GREEK VERSION

But at the name of Jesus, Paul's hymn tells us, every knee shall bow and every tongue shall confess that Jesus Anointed is Lord. How can the Anointed be given such reverence? The hymn sets up the question and implies its own answer: the status of God himself is being ascribed to the Anointed. Not with the formality of later doctrine, but in the practice—so the hymn implies—of worship. It is no accident that this claim is presented in the style and atmosphere of a hymn, for the worship of the assemblies did not simply express the doctrine of their leaders, but drove that doctrine onward. Doctrine and worship were the two horses, seemingly of very different kinds, that between them in these first decades pulled the cart of the assemblies. No one was better placed to yoke them together and to steer their strengths into a single onward movement than Paul the seer, for Paul thought visually, and the sight, above all, that informed his thought was the layout of the worship of heaven.

The first and second Adam—this is a motif we might expect Paul to use, but we have heard his love of other themes too. It is no surprise that the hymn recalls as well the Servant in Isaiah. *In humility he was judged and taken away,* just as the Anointed in our hymn *humbled himself.* The Servant *shall be exalted and glorified,* just as God has *highly exalted* the Anointed (Isa. 53:8; 52:13, Greek Version). In general, however, the words of the hymn seem almost to shy away from the words that Isaiah used of the Servant. The Servant is normally described or addressed as just that, a Servant; the hymn's figure, by contrast, took on the humility of a *slave.* Is this as well deliberate? The hymn, as it describes the new Servant, may well be deepening the degradation known to the old—and surpassing the height of his subsequent glory. As with Adam, then, so with the Servant—whatever could be said of the old Servant, far more could be said of the new.

Our hymn would certainly not be the only such text to draw upon Isaiah's Servant's suffering and future. The Servant *was led as a sheep to the sacrifice; and as a lamb makes no sound before its shearer, so he did not open his mouth* (Isa. 53:7). In Aramaic, the language of Jesus himself, the connection between lamb and servant was easily made: *thy',* "young one," could be used to mean either. In the book of Unveiling [Revelation], recording in Greek the visions of Jesus and his pupil John, the seer sees a Lamb at the center of the court of heaven. It bears the marks of a lamb killed in sacrifice. This Lamb is found worthy to open the book in God's hand. The creatures and elders around the throne break into a new song of praise: *"You are worthy . . . because you have been slain in sacrifice"* (5:9). Tens of thousands of angels take up the theme:

> *Worthy is the lamb that has been slain in sacrifice*
> *to receive the power and wealth and wisdom*
> *and strength and honor and glory and praise.*
> UNVEILING 5:12

And so all creation joins the song. Here is the Servant-Lamb of Isaiah, reimagined in glory. As Paul's Anointed is acknowledged and praised by all creation, so is the Servant-Lamb of Unveiling:

And every creature in heaven and on earth and under the earth and in the sea—I heard all of them saying:

> *To the one seated on the throne and to the lamb*
> *be the praise and the honor and the glory and the power*
> *for ages upon ages.*
> UNVEILING 5:13

In a vision of the court of heaven the seer sees the Servant-Lamb invested with his glory. Just such a scene is evoked by the hymn that Paul sends to the Philippians. The hymn takes the viewpoint of a seer who has watched Jesus invested by God, has seen the knees bow in heaven, and has had his ears opened to hear Jesus acknowledged by all creation. Only from heaven can so much be seen and heard. And only in heaven is the passage of time so strangely compressed: what the seer sees in heaven now "is" already the case, even if it remains as yet unfulfilled on earth.

As in Mark's gospel, so here: there was a long tradition of truths disclosed in heaven before they were apparent on earth. Mark disrupts the schema by disclosing a heavenly figure, the Son of Man, in the history of earth. The hymns of Paul's letter and of Unveiling disrupt the schema with the opposite movement—they disclose an earthly figure as the object of the worship of heaven. As ever, we do no justice to such dreams if we diagnose them as the refuge of a frightened fantasy. A language was needed in which to evoke a present and a future—a promise and its fulfillment—that stood in a relation to each other rarely conceived before. Even as we watch, thought and language are fueling each other's possibilities.

Images of the court of heaven were familiar enough from the Old Order, from the stories of seers and from the worship of the Temple in Jerusalem. It did not take a seer to envisage the scene of the book of Unveiling or to write its hymns; it did not take a seer to write the hymn sent to the Philippians. A poet or thinker could weave such a picture readily enough from the literature available. But a seer such as Paul, whether he wrote the hymn or not, had every reason to use it, for it spoke of a place he knew. He had been there. He had heard the praise. And he had seen the figure on the throne.

THE FORM OF GOD

The hymn reads well. So well that we might fail to see how strange are two terms in its first lines. The Anointed *thought equality with God not something to be seized.* Was it a standing that could be seized but should not be? Or a standing that he once had but was willing to forsake? *But he made himself empty,* or emptied himself—of what? Here again, perhaps, the author is trying to find words to say what has not been said before, that a figure once *in God's form* abandoned his standing. It is a strange claim in itself. And we might still ask: Why was this convoluted formula the best way to make it?

Just as striking are the expressions used for the figure's humanity: *being born in the likeness of humans* and *in fashion being found as a human.* It is if Paul grants the figure humanity, but only just. There is something uncanny in this man. And so there should be. If there was not, after all, it is unclear how he could be the "same" figure that has been described in the hymn's first lines as having been in the form of God.

The key to unlock these first lines is in their opening words: the Anointed was *in the form of God.* The phrase suggests, in Greek as in English, the visible shape of God, even more vividly than the Greek word for "image" that we have encountered already. Thus, in our hymn itself, the figure takes on *the form of a slave;* his status is there to be seen. In the mystery religions (which we have encountered in the worship of Isis, just one of many such cults) the essence of the god could be known, to the extent that it could be known at all, through the god's form and name. The Jews knew too of the importance of God's name. But God's form? Nothing of God, the Jews were sure, was revealed in any image that could be seen, touched, or measured. No such image could ever bear the form of God, the "features" that would identify God as God.

But what about Ezekiel, when he saw that mysterious figure upon the chariot-throne of God? Was he not gazing at the form of God?

(Even if Ezekiel had no clear equivalent, in Hebrew, of the Greek word for "form" that Paul would know.) It is a good question, but would not have been Ezekiel's own. Ezekiel is not being shown what the features are that identify God as God, but what we can know of God and how. And so indeed he clarifies what the form or appearance of this figure is, *the likeness as the appearance of adam*. But he does so not to speak of the form of God; it is, rather, to insist that these apparently human features do not identify the figure on the throne as a human being.

What, then, did Paul mean by *the form of God?* The clues lie elsewhere within the Old Order and its interpretation by seers. We will be looking, this time, at traditions that flourished long after Paul. It is from the hints in Paul that we can see how early these traditions were taking shape.

> *Thus says the Lord:*
> *"Heaven is my throne and earth is my footstool."*
> ISAIAH 66:1

God is sitting on heaven, his feet resting on the earth—if it were possible to imagine God at all, it would be with dimensions unimaginably huge. Human categories would be confounded, and precisely in that defeat the human mind would come to its deepest understanding. "I have seen the Lord's right hand motioning to me," we read in one book of unveiling, "and filling the heaven. You see how large my own body is, that it is just like yours. But I have seen how great the Lord is, that he is immeasurable, incomparable and has no end" (*2 Enoch* 13:3–10).

The Lord is beyond measuring. This is the conclusion we would expect. But it is reached through a vision of God's hand—a form that would in any creature be measurable. In measurement we compare, define, distinguish, and specify. To understand as humans is in some degree to measure and to measure is in some degree to understand. And if the subject of our thought confounds all measurement, we begin to understand—just as we should—the limits of our understanding. God, said the rabbis, had "a body of glory" or "self of glory," a Hebraism for "glorious body." Here is the form of God. It is futile to imagine the dimensions of such a form, but there is nothing futile at all in the humble, stark admission of that futility.

In one striking tradition from the seers of later Judaism, we are told the huge dimensions of God from the soles of his feet up past his legs, thighs, shoulders, and neck to the different parts of his head and then down over his shoulders to the arms, palms, fingers, and toes. The earliest such account admits, at its end, its own impotence. The editor has to fall back on the more ancient and venerable tradition that finds significance in God's names: "We have in our hands no measure, but the names are revealed to us."

No imagined form of God will give us the measurement of God. Is any other "measure" of God available to make him accessible to humankind? Here follows a beautiful passage from a commentary on *The Sayings of the Fathers,* the Mishnah's tract from which we learned in Chapter 14 about the generations that followed the Great Prayer House. At issue in this commentary are not just the measures revealed of God, but the conditions laid down for grasping them, for humans can share in these measures for themselves. To do so is to know God. This is not the knowledge of an external object. To acquire these measures, these heavenly beings, is to acquire something, in oneself, of the qualities of heaven.

Seven measures serve before the throne of the Glory. They are wisdom, justness, judgment, mercy, kindness, truth, and peace. As it is said [by the prophet Hosea, 2:21–22],

And I, God, shall betroth you to me forever;
and I shall betroth you to me with justness and with judgment
   and with kindness and mercy;
and I shall betroth you to me with truth and you shall know God.

Question from Rabbi Meir: Why does scripture use the words *and you shall know God?*

Answer: To teach that all those who have these measures in themselves know the knowledge of God.

THE FATHERS ACCORDING TO RABBI NATHAN, A 37

• • •

SEERS, WHO CLAIMED THE PRIVILEGED KNOWLEDGE to which the visions of heaven gave access, would always be open to suspicion. There was too much scope for an authority beyond control and so, frankly, for mere fraud. John writes at the start of his gospel, warning against such claims:

> No one has seen God, ever.
> It is God the only son,
> who is at the father's side,
> that has made him known.
>
> JOHN 1:18

John recognized, as clearly as Paul, that Jesus was the disclosure of God on earth that seers had aspired to see in heaven. John can discount any claims to have seen God. And Paul can play down his own. He invokes as rarely as possible his own visionary experiences, for what he has been granted, others do not need.

It could be hard to hold this line, and not just in Corinth. The letter to the Colossians is steeped in the language of the seers. Steeped too in opposition to such language, for such imagery is proving dangerous in Colossae. A close pupil of Paul's is writing to oppose a distinctive faction. Its members clearly value the Sabbath; they are likely Jewish in background. Its leaders acknowledge the Anointed, the head of the body, but *they do not hold to the head;* they are distracted by their errors. And where is their fault? The author homes in. He denigrates their teacher or teachers. *Let no one disqualify you by taking pleasure in humility* [in fasting and self-denial] *and in the worship of angels, the things he has seen in entering, puffed up without reason by his mind of flesh* (Col. 2:18).

The worship of angels is, almost certainly, worship shared with the angels in heaven. *The things he has seen in entering* are the sights granted upon access to heaven. The pupil of Paul the seer must denigrate the rival seers and prize the Colossians away from their claims. As dangerous as any threat to Paul's followers was the distortion of claims and offers that Paul himself had made. The measure of God, as it were, can be seen in the assembly and lives of his converts. They need no journeys to heaven or visions there. They have all they need, in and among themselves. They need only open their eyes and see.

THE GREAT ANGEL

As Paul was a seer, Jesus had been a seer too. As Paul traveled to heaven and saw the throne of God, so had Jesus seen the court of heaven too. We tend to think of Jesus' status, in the eyes of his followers, rising over time. It had been difficult to specify the similarity between him and God; it became increasingly hard to see the difference. Paul too knew of such a trajectory. He had before his conversion heard of Jesus as a seer, whose followers made wild claims for him on the basis of his visions and his knowledge of heaven. At Paul's conversion this view was turned upside down. His Jesus was not a seer visiting the throne; he was the figure seen upon it. Where Paul was a visitor, privileged and rare, Jesus belonged. Jesus was not a peer or a rival of Paul's; he was the object of all Paul's training and longing and meditation.

At the start of this book we heard of Enoch and of his journeys to heaven. He was envisaged as the greatest of the seers. He was an appropriate figure for such privilege. The Old Order does not tell of his death. *Enoch walked with God, then was no more; for God took him* (The Beginning 5:24). Ever greater glory was ascribed to him. And in this elevation some rabbis saw a threat to the sole godhead of God. Within the visionary tradition of the rabbis we hear claims being made for Enoch that are not so far from the claims that the assemblies were making for Jesus. The assemblies absorbed the Anointed into their worship of God as the Jewish prayer houses never absorbed Enoch. What the assemblies celebrated in Jesus, the prayer houses fiercely denied to Enoch.

The topography of heaven, vividly imagined, was not an end in itself. It was described to express relations of power and realms of authority. The philosophers of the pagan world had long wondered how to bridge the gap between a supreme god and his creation, for the most perfect power must surely be untainted by any contact with or responsibility for anything mutable, mortal, or evil. A solution was sought in an intermediary god who was active in the creation and rule of the world. That second god readily attracted attention, reverence, even fear. He was, for mere mortals, far more important than the god who kept his infinite distance from our squalid material world. Judaism responded, for the most part, without compromise: the one, true God did not share the creation or government of the world with any rival.

Decades—even centuries—after Paul wrote, a book of unveiling was completed that describes a journey to heaven by Rabbi Ishmael, who died around 130 C.E. Once more, as we hear of a vision, we are not hearing a story in which we might, with our greater sophistication, find the seeds of a philosophical idea. The story speaks, with a coherence and nuance quite equal to ours, of dangers we would be hard-pressed to express so vividly.

Ishmael, as narrator, tells of his encounter with the angel Metatron, Prince of the Divine Presence. Metatron, the great angel, had been Enoch, the human patriarch. God had taken him away from his sinful generation and had appointed him in the height as a prince and a ruler among the ministering angels. The angels prostrated themselves before him. God set him to serve the throne of glory.

Metatron tells his story:

In addition to all these, the Holy One, blessed be he, laid his hand upon me and blessed me with 1,365,000 blessings. I was enlarged and increased in size until I matched the world in length and breadth.

The Holy One, blessed be he, made me to grow on me 72 wings. He fixed in me 365,000 eyes and each eye was like the great light. There was no sort of splendor, brilliance, brightness, or beauty in the luminaries of the world that he failed to fix in me.

And the herald went out into every heaven and announced concerning me:

"I have appointed Metatron my servant as a prince and a ruler over all the inhabitants of the heights, apart from the great, honored and terrible princes who are called YHWH, by the name of their King. Any angel and any prince who has anything to say in my presence should go before him and speak to him. Whatever he says to you in my name you must observe and do."

The Holy One, blessed be he, revealed to me from that time onward all the mysteries of wisdom, all the depths of the perfect

Law, and all the thoughts of human hearts. All the mysteries of the world and all the orders of nature stand revealed before me as they stand revealed before the creator. Before anyone thinks in secret, I see their thought; before they act, I see their act.

Metatron was given a majestic robe and a crown, and as God set the crown upon his head he named him with the name of God so holy that it was almost never spoken at all. Wherever YHWH is written in the Old Order a Jewish reader will read out Adonai, or "Lord." Metatron was named "The lesser YHWH": "as it is written [The Escape (Exodus) 23:21], *My name is in him.*" The angels trembled at the sight of Metatron, crowned by God. Metatron was transformed into fire: his flesh and hair turned to flame, his eyes to lightning flashes.

But trouble was in store. Another rabbi had been to heaven before our narrator Ishmael. This was Elisha son of Abuyah, who lived as well at the end of the first century C.E.; we have heard of him already as the archheretic who in contempt was often referred to (as here) simply as "Another." (One version of the story of the four rabbis in Paradise includes a brief account of Another and Metatron.) At the entrance to the seventh heaven Another saw Metatron at work, judging the princes of kingdoms, seated on a throne, and surrounded by angels ready to serve him.

This is a moment of terrible drama. How could there be a second throne and on it a second figure to perform the roles that were God's alone? Metatron continues his story: "The soul of Another was alarmed to the point of leaving him because of his fear, dread, and terror of me."

The climax of the story has reached us in various versions, because it was too dangerous for later scribes. One version omits all mention of the godlike appearance of Metatron and of Another's fear. Still other accounts warn directly against the worship of Metatron. With good reason. In Metatron Another should have recognized an image of God's power, a disclosure of the master within and through his agent. But instead he saw a power to rival God's:

And Another opened his mouth and said: "There are indeed two powers in heaven!"

Another has raised Metatron to the standing of God himself. The consequences were dire for Metatron himself. And a voice from heaven warns the followers of Another to abandon this false teaching and its teacher.

Just as any loyal Jew might have warned the followers of Paul.

JEWISH THINKERS—LONG AFTER PAUL—wondered at Metatron's strange name. One tradition derived it from the Latin word *metator*, "measurer." What a telling proposal. The great angel and agent of God could be envisaged as his measure, the accessible form of the God who is beyond our apprehension.

"Measure" appears in another and more striking etymology, known from the second century C.E. in the *Gospel of Philip,* a text found at Nag Hammadi in the 1940s. "The emissaries before us called him 'Jesus, the Nazorean, Messiah.'. . . Messiah has two meanings: 'Anointed' and 'the measured.'. . . Anointed is the one who was measured. The Nazarene and Jesus are those who measured him" (62:11–17 [Saying 47]). The derivation of "the measured" is false, but plausible. Two identical stems, *m-s-h,* are the basis for two verbs meaning "to anoint" and "to measure." And so we have the setting for a strange motto recorded by Christian thinker Irenaeus, writing around 180 C.E. He praises those who say that "The immeasurable father is measured in the son," for the son, says Irenaeus, is the measure of the father.

A tradition quite alien to us is bubbling to the surface in the *Gospel of Philip* and in Irenaeus. It flows underground but far more strongly through Paul himself and emerges in his hymn of the Anointed, who was *in the form of God.*

In the Anointed Paul's converts can take something of the unimaginable measure of the God who fills all creation.

"Sit at My Right Hand"

The Lord said to my Lord, "Sit at my right hand,
Until I put your enemies beneath your feet."
PSALM 110:1

From the earliest days of his assemblies these lines were taken to refer to Jesus. As his followers searched the Old Order for references to Jesus and for clues to his identity and function, ancient passages were seen in a new light. The praise that had until then been offered to God and God alone was being revisited and reapplied.

As we have seen, there was a long history of unveilings or visions of different thrones and angels, different levels of power and the different responses they should and could evoke from human viewers. Such visions echoed the rituals of kings' courts and of the Temple in Jerusalem. These rituals had been current in different places and at different times. Many of them had fallen from use by the time the visions themselves were undergone. The very empires, courts, and buildings in which they had belonged were long since swept away. Left behind in the Old Order itself was a rich store of imagery; rich enough to make possible some fine—and forever fluid—distinctions. Generation after generation reimagined and redescribed these motifs.

We have heard of Daniel's vision of one like a son of man, invested by God with power over every nation. *As I was watching, thrones were set in place* (7:9). Thrones? How many were there? And who was on them? Jesus can tell his pupils, *"You who have followed me, in the Regeneration, when the Son of Man sits on the throne of his glory, you too shall sit on twelve thrones judging the twelve tribes of Israel"* (Matt. 19:28). The Son of Man will have the throne to match his new authority. And his followers will have their reward too. In Unveiling [Revelation] we hear of a different arrangement in which there was, around the throne of God, a circle of twenty-four thrones on which sit twenty-four elders with white robes and golden crowns (Unveiling 4:4).

Out of Daniel's vision Rabbi Akiba developed a dangerous teaching. (Rabbi Akiba was one of the four rabbis who ascended to the heavenly garden; we heard of their journey earlier in this book.) This teaching is mentioned in the context of heresies. Here is a shortened paraphrase of the debate. *Thrones were set in place*—what is there to say? "One throne for God and one for the Anointed," said Rabbi Akiba. But Rabbi Yose said to him, "Akiba, how long will you profane the Glory? Rather, one throne is for justice and one for mercy." Akiba conceded the point. A third rabbi joined in, "Such interpretation as this is not Akiba's forte. He should stick to the study of the Law" (Babylonian Talmud, *Sanhedrin* 38b). No wonder the dispute was remembered. Akiba had claimed that Simon son of Kosiba, the leader of the great rebellion against Rome in 130 C.E., was the Anointed. Was the second throne in heaven, then, prepared for Simon?

To occupy a throne was to have huge power. A throne, perhaps, at the entrance to the seventh heaven, where Another saw Metatron. Or a throne beside the throne of God. Or more telling and more dangerous still, a place *sitting at God's right hand* on the throne of God himself. This could leave, in a style well known in the ancient Middle East, two figures on the one throne. How telling that a second derivation is possible for the name Metatron from two Greek words, *meta-thron,* "with-throne." This Metatron would be the figure "With-God-on-the-throne."

But it was not here that Christian thought would come to rest. Within this new sect emerges the far bolder claim that there is just a single figure on the throne, at once God and his perfect, total self-disclosure in human form to humankind. This thought indeed forestalled the illusion of a second and lesser god. But at what a price. Such a confusion of categories—for anyone not captivated by the claim—was beyond blasphemy. It could not be called "thought" at all.

PAUL WELL KNOWS THE DANGER of those imagined thrones around the throne of God. When he wrote our 1 Corinthians he had to steer his converts away from presumption. We remember the sarcasm with which he brought them down to size. *Oh, you Corinthians are already filled to satiety, you have already become rich, without us you have become kings! How I wish you had become kings, so that we ourselves, as well, might become kings beside you!* (1 Cor. 4:8).

What had encouraged the Corinthians in this folly? Almost certainly Paul's own good news, promising a glorious future: *Do you not know that* the saints will judge the world? And if in you the world is judged, are you unfit to form the most everyday courts? Do you not know that we shall judge angels—let alone everyday matters? (1 Cor. 6:2–3). And what could have been the basis for such a promise? The status, already attained, of the Anointed himself. Where he has led, his adherents will follow.

Paul handles this imagery differently in different settings. In Corinth he must check a confidence that is claiming too much too soon. The reign of the Anointed is misleading those who will share in it to claim too much—here and now—for their own.

At the end of our 1 Corinthians, Paul is ready to correct the Corinthians' errors on their own present attainment and on death. However they had imagined the role of the Anointed and their own part in it, Paul now makes clear that the reign of the Anointed himself will end. So those who have their kingship in the Anointed will lose their kingdoms too. And when? At the final defeat of death. The Corinthians think they have moved through death to their kingdom. Paul insists that they are far from it. They will have their time of power. But the final victory, the victory over death, will not secure them their kingdom; it will mark the end of all kingdoms except God's alone.

To make clear Paul's reliance here upon the Old Order, I have put his citations from the Psalms in roman, not italic type:

> As in Adam all die, so also in Anointed all shall be made alive. And each in their own order: as firstfruit, Anointed; then those in Anointed at his coming; then the conclusion, when he gives over the kingdom to God the father, when he has brought to nothing every realm and every authority and power. For he must reign until he has put all his enemies under his feet. The last enemy being brought to nothing is—death. For he has subjected all things to him, under his feet. And when it says that all things are subject to him, it is clear that this is apart from the one who has subjected all things to him. And when all things have been subjected to him, then the son himself will be subjected to the one who subjected all things to him, so that God might be all things in all.

1 CORINTHIANS 15:22–28, QUOTING PSALMS 110:1 AND 8:7, GREEK VERSION

Paul faced one vivid danger in Corinth; he faced a quite different need in Philippi—and a quite different opportunity. In Philippi, a

Roman colony proud of its Roman identity, there was every reason to remind the assembly that there was a lord greater than any emperor to be revered. But did such an emphasis lead Paul and his assemblies to just the danger into which the rabbis will see Another fall? As Paul extolled his emperor over Rome's was he heading his converts toward the worship of the Anointed as a god beside God, a second and independent power?

The hymn *Being in the form of God* (Phil. 2:6–11) frames the description of Jesus' glory with great care; the glory comes from God and it redounds to God. If Paul inherited the hymn, he himself may well have added the last line; he will have wanted to keep God inescapably in view. And within that framework Jesus is given all there is to give: the name, the power, the praise.

It is within the images and formulas of worship that the assemblies confronted the question: What role and standing had the Anointed? Worship did not embody and solemnize the conclusions of cool thought; it drove thought onward with its own visual and imaginative logic. The worship of heaven and of earth were at one. And in Paul's hymn his assembly came as near as it could on earth to seeing the court of heaven itself. What, then, was to be seen there? The place of Jesus on the chariot-throne of God and his worship by all the powers in creation.

It had taken centuries for the figure of Wisdom to assume a life and character of its own. Here in Paul's hymn a similar movement of ideas is realized in a meditation on Jesus' human life. Paul's achievement, in this crossing of categories, is dazzling.

Here in Jesus, then, is no second power or rival to God on a second throne, for this enthronement is the return of the Anointed to the heaven in which he belonged. The Anointed has assumed in Jesus a life and character of his own and can now be acknowledged at last.

> *Therefore God has highly exalted him*
> *   and has given him the name above every name,*
> *so that at the name of Jesus every knee should bow,*
> *   of things in heaven and things on earth and things under the earth,*
> *and every tongue confess that Jesus Anointed is Lord,*
> *   to the glory of God the father.*
>   PHILIPPIANS 2:9–11

PART X

"A LIGHT TO THE NATIONS"

CHAPTER 28

THE FUTURE OF THE PAST

TRANSFORMATION IS PAUL'S TERM, and in it we have found a key to Paul's thought. To engender, deepen, and steer the transformation of individuals and their community is Paul's grand ambition. But how much—and how little—might such transformation have amounted to in his different converts, assemblies, and addressees?

It is worth asking first: What can be transformed in an individual? Outlook, morals, standards, understanding. All these, in any talk of such change, are likely to be linked. And in a community, however large or small? Relationships of affection, respect, and power. And in the relations between the members of a community and those outside? Respect, care, and the perceived boundaries of the community itself.

What distinguishes the grand effect that is "transformation" from the day-to-day changes that we all undergo and see in others? It is largely a pragmatic issue of the scale of the change and the words that seem to describe the subject before the change and afterward. There comes a moment (hard to define in particular cases, impossible in abstract) when we want to recognize the subject of the change as a new person or community. The old descriptions—which once amounted as a cluster nearly to a definition—simply will not do anymore.

There is no preset limit to change. For the emissary or preacher, there is great value in this open-ended road. Grand terms fuel grand hopes and aspirations. To talk of transformation is to aim high, and a high aim can help a high attainment. Attainment leads to confidence and so to an attainment higher still. A virtuous circle is under way. The self-consciousness of the person undergoing the change gives additional momentum to the change. This is the engine that will have driven any success that Paul had in the reception of our 1 Corinthians, 2 Corinthians 1–9, and the letter to the Romans.

We have caught glimpses of the changes—emotional, intellectual, spiritual, social, and economic—that conversion was likely to bring. Some at least of these converts were stepping well outside the normal routines and expectations of household and family life. Some undertook to be celibate. Some, to share their property. Such sharing was important. It protected the members who suffered economically as a result of their conversion: those who lost customers, employment, or a patron. Members of the assembly depended on each other's support, and those who gave the support relied, in turn, on the others' honesty and industry. Members made a great commitment themselves and had to trust other members to have made the same. All being well, there was a tightening knot of commitment; the greater the shared worry, danger, and support, the stronger the members' bonds to each other. No wonder Paul worked so hard to maintain the unity of each assembly, for there was danger in disagreements, suspicions, and—worst of all—distrust of Paul himself. Such divisions loosened the ties of love and loyalty. Hearts, minds, and wallets would all close.

Pagan patronage and friendships, we must suspect, were slowly or suddenly, partly or completely withdrawn. How quickly and how totally would have varied widely. It is worth comparing Paul's converts with the Romans attracted to Judaism, seventy years later. These Romans are lambasted by the poet Juvenal. He writes on the bad example set by fathers who take up Jewish ways; their children take things even further and convert to Judaism itself. Paul's converts would have seemed to their neighbors as disreputable as those God-fearers and their children seemed to Juvenal.

Juvenal thinks of a change that takes a generation to complete. We can readily imagine, at one end of the scale, a pagan with a penchant for the Sabbath (and a sympathetic employer) or, at the other, a convert to Judaism who has accepted its legal implications and earned its privileges. But we need to imagine as well the slow move from one to the other, the gradual adoption, spread over years or decades, of Jewish ways among Jewish friends. And enough Gentiles defied such enemies as Juvenal to make his venomous attack worthwhile.

If Juvenal had his way, the social stigma of such behavior would prevent any father from setting such a bad example. But to strengthen his attack he has, it seems, no further sanction up his sleeve, no threats from Roman authority, no pogroms, no danger of unemployment or penury.

> Some, who have a father that reveres the sabbath,
> Worship nothing but the clouds and the divinity of heaven,
> And find no difference between human flesh and pork
> From which the father abstained, and soon they remove their
>   foreskins too.
> Used to despising Roman laws
> They learn, follow and revere the Jewish justice,
> Whatever Moses has handed down in his secret book:
> Not to show the way to any but a person who observes the
>   same rites,
> And to guide only the circumcised to drinking water when it is
>   asked for.
> But it is the father who is at fault; for him every seventh day
> Has been idle and has lacked contact with any part of life.
> SATIRE 14.96–106

Juvenal was bitter enough about these Judaizers; Paul's antagonists would have said far worse about his converts to the strange sect of Jesus. And Paul's converts will have been more badly damaged by such jibes, for Paul's converts likely lacked the moral and practical support of the prayer houses on which, for instance, James's Law-observant converts could rely. Moses' Law, after all, had the dignity of an ancient wisdom; Paul's good news, at first sight, did not. Converts to Judaism joined a community that made up over 10 percent of the empire's population; converts to Paul's assembly did not. Converts to Judaism had all the time they wanted to make their move; if Paul was right, his pagan addressees did not.

Let's keep, nonetheless, a broader picture in mind. Of those attracted to Paul's good news, many for much of the time likely kept their heads down, took mockery in their stride, and won no more hostility from the powers that be than they had before conversion. Most managed to make their living in the hurly-burly of the empire's cities largely undisturbed, in part, perhaps, because they drew lines less sharp than we would expect between their former and their present loyalties. We have already heard of Erastus. He was a high official in Corinth. His position gave him a leading role in the city's endless round of pagan sacrifices, but he was a member of the assembly nonetheless. The ritual and devotional life of paganism was no private matter for an individual's choice, such as membership in a church is generally today. On every journey at the roadside shrines, at every festival and civic celebration the assembly's new members could stand out by their inaction or their absence, but not all of them did. Erastus was not alone in observing, as occasion required, either Christian or pagan rituals.

How many of Paul's converts had been God-fearers before joining an assembly? We cannot know. But the prayer houses had good reason, after conversion, to be wary of them. It is telling that for decades some Christians (if only the Jews and proselytes to Judaism) remained within reach of the Jews' jurisdiction and punishment. It was an uneasy relationship. Some forms of allegiance to Jesus would lead by the 90s—and perhaps, in places, even by the time of Paul—to expulsion from a prayer house. John anticipated this enmity within the narrative of his gospel. He wrote about Jesus' lifetime in terms that were more likely suited to his own day. The local authorities in Judea, he says, *had already decreed that anyone who acknowledged him as Anointed should be expelled from the prayer house* (John 9:22). Only those needed to be expelled who had not left of their own accord; to revere Jesus was not, in itself, to turn one's back upon the prayer house, its people, or its ways.

And if neighbors became suspicious of this new sect, and opponents became violent, and the authorities took note of its wild claims for its Savior and Lord? Then there was real danger. Mark's Jesus tells the gospel's readers in the 60s or 70s of both Jewish and gentile opposition: *"They will hand you over to councils and you will be beaten in prayer houses and you will be put before leaders and kings because of me"* (Mark 13:9). Fears could be more personal still. In a poignant warning, Mark's Jesus goes on: *"Brother will hand over brother to death, and fathers their sons, and children will rise up against their parents and will put them to death. And you will be hated by all on account of my name"* (Mark 13:12–13).

No one would underestimate the fears and the facts of opposition. But far greater, for anyone impressed by Paul, was the danger posed by God's anger, about to pour out his punishment upon an evil and idolatrous world. Striking too—and convincing, exhilarating support of the good news Paul brought—were the gifts of the Breath. Strange powers were at work in the assembly. Paul himself performed miracles. Converts spoke in tongues and prophesied. To be at the worship of the assembly was to be in the court of heaven, to join its hymns and to learn its hidden truths. So close, so palpable was the dominion of God—and so total were its offer and demand—that some converts abandoned work to prepare for it. Some set up in their own lives, as they saw it, the lifestyle of the androgynous Adam. If Paul re-presented the Anointed as he had been on earth, so would they, as a living symbol, make present his glorious Body in their lives. The Adam who had been glorious before the Fall was now dispelling the world's darkness once more. Everything must be seen—could only be seen—in the light of that glory. And its present signs, awe-inspiring as they were, would soon pale before the final disclosure of God's power as a candle pales before the rising sun.

Transformation and the Life of Gods

Paul is not alone in speaking of transformation. The Roman philosopher Seneca wrote letters of moral instruction in the mid-first century C.E. He describes his own progress. Here is a cool Latin version of the progress that Paul seeks for his Romans, right through to the subject's self-consciousness, the awareness of failure, and of the need for improvement.

> I feel that I am being not only reformed but transfigured. I do not yet, however, assure myself or indulge the hope that there are no elements left in me which need to be changed. Of course there are many that should be curtailed, reduced, or removed. And indeed this very fact is proof of a spirit that has been altered into something better: the fact that it sees its own faults, of which until now it has been ignorant. Some sick men are to be congratulated since they themselves perceive that they are sick.
>
> *LETTERS* 6.1

Seneca promises to send his fictional correspondent, Lucilius, some improving books (with the best passages marked!). But most effective of all instruction is the living voice and shared life of those whose example Lucilius should follow. Such improvement is central to Seneca's aims. "Those who have learned and understood what they should do and avoid are not wise until their mind is transfigured into those things that they have learned." He exclaims to Lucilius, "You are my work of art!" (*Letters* 94.48; 34.2).

From blindness to sight—philosophers could describe the results they sought in terms of vision. Let's hear Seneca again. In this praise of philosophy he keeps inseparably together the good life and the knowledge that makes it possible:

> Philosophy shows which things are evil, and which only seem evil. It frees the mind of idle nonsense. It gives solid greatness, while checking swollen greatness which takes airs without justification. . . . It sets forth what the gods are and what their nature is, what are the souls given a permanent existence in the second shape of deities, what are their powers and desires. These are the initiatory rites of philosophy. They do not open some local shrine but the vast temple of all the gods, the universe itself, whose true images and true likenesses philosophy has brought within the mind's eye.
>
> LETTERS 90.28

There was no doubt among philosophers that ambition, care, and the turmoil of the passions were based on a false understanding of humanity and led to deeper falsehood still. The philosophers offered therapy, a healing regime that might take months or years to have its full effect and was even then liable to be undermined by the worries or opportunities that could seduce the patient back into old, addictive ways. It is no accident that Paul's letter to the Romans is designed as therapy.

This philosophical therapy took different forms in different schools. To take an example that contrasts with Seneca's, the Epicureans combined teaching, a reverence for their founder, Epicurus, and the cohesion of an identifiable community. In friendship they found the heart of the life they extolled and actively pursued. They were roundly derided—perhaps even feared—for insisting that the gods took no active interest, let alone any active part, in human affairs.

But how were the Epicureans to describe the state to which their knowledge and community brought them? All power, in more conventional thought, was evidence of divinity; the greater the power, the nearer was its holder to the gods themselves. The chief characteristic of the gods, for Epicurus, was their detachment from the passions that distort humankind. The more detached from such passions any humans became, the nearer they came to the divinity of those gods. "The things, then, that I gain," wrote Epicurus to his mother, "are not small or of little force. They are of a sort that make my life equal to a god's, and show me as a man who does not—even by his mortality—fall short of their imperishable and blessed nature. For while I am alive, I know joy to the same degree as the gods" (in Fragment 65, ed. Arrighetti).

What Epicurus attained, his followers could attain too—a form of divinity. How was such a standing, whether his or their own, to be acknowledged? By celebrations that mimicked the formulas of traditional worship. Epicurus had died in 270 B.C.E. His followers knew him, in Paul's day, as their Deliverer or Savior. His figure was to be found on the rings and cups of his followers. Plutarch, in the second century C.E., mocks this reverence. The Epicureans, who denigrated the rites offered to the gods, appeared to treat their founder as such a god himself. Just listen to "the roars of ecstasy and cries of thanksgiving and tumultuous bursts of applause and reverential demonstrations and all that apparatus of adoration you resort to in supplicating and hymning Epicurus."

Epicurus's pupils knew that they could be defined only by contrast with the religions around them. His favored disciple, Metrodorus, using the familiar language of the mysteries, spoke of "all but sinking away by communion of experience and exchanging this earthbound life for the secret rites of Epicurus, as those that truly reveal god"—by contrast with the secret rites of those mystery cults that fostered illusion.

Epicurus himself likely had a wry awareness that his own community parodied the rituals it despised, but both Epicurus and his followers were bound by the possibilities of their time. He had necessarily adapted—not rejected—the traditional scale on which all humans stood between the human and divine. And so his followers could only adapt—not reject—the language in which to acknowledge his and their ascent on it. Such rites and celebrations provided the only language in which his followers could say about him and themselves what they needed to say. The pupil Colotes had once knelt before Epicurus and embraced his knees. This was a form of reverence due only to a god or to a monarch well on the way to godhead. What else could Colotes do? But then comes the next question. What was Epicurus to do, in the face of this extravagant gesture? "You have caused me," said Epicurus, "to consecrate you in my turn, and to demonstrate my reverence. Go about as one imperishable in my eyes, and think of me as imperishable too" (Plutarch *Against Colotes* 1117A–C).

It was not just the assemblies of Jesus that had to use the language of their age to wean their people from the beliefs and rituals served and fostered by that language for centuries. Nor was it these Christians alone who took over such language to make for their leader and themselves the boldest claims of which the language was capable.

PAUL IS NOT AIMING for the formation of a young man such as Seneca's Lucilius, making his ambitious way in Roman life. Paul offers nothing to such aspirations. We have caught glimpses of the changes to which Paul steers each and every member of his assemblies—a quite new perspective on dignity, achievement, and grounds for pride. In a Pauline assembly run as Paul would have it run, every social relation—within each family and within the assembly as a whole—would have been informed by mutual love and service. Married life carries on as before; slavery remains as before. But the outlook of every individual upon every other individual is the outlook of one new creature upon another, a fellow member of the Body of the Anointed.

We have tried to capture something of the excitement that fired the early assemblies, something of the single-minded hope that ensured their survival. It is as well, before we leave these assemblies for the last time, to admit what might have been ambiguous in their Christian lives. What remained stubbornly bound by the standards and expectations of the converts' old life? How many converts occupied a gray area between their new community and their old, and for how long?

In every chapter of this book we have heard how difficult it was to leave old ways of thought and behavior behind. Members of any culture are shaped by the ways of that culture. Paul himself and his converts, working to imagine and create something new, could only draw on the old and adapt it. And how easy it was for the old material, however recut, to resume the folds and fall of its old use.

We have glimpsed the grand Erastus on duty at a public sacrifice and have watched a normal Roman family before the shrine of its household gods. We do not know how long it took such families, after their conversion, to ignore the figurines, to put them out of sight, or to destroy them. Paul himself acknowledges to the Corinthians the existence of demons. What harm could there be, a Corinthian family might ask, in doing justice to these minor powers that had for so long been integral to the household? What greater harm might not befall the family, if the protection and goodwill of these powers were once foregone?

We have watched the wealthier members of the assembly in Corinth pushing their cases through the courts and reasserting in their hospitality all the old gradations of wealth and patronage. We have watched the Corinthians' leaders ignore a case of blatant immorality. As we envisage such an assembly, we should not assume it was run by the standards of a new creation; it was forever at danger from the standards of the old.

And what of Paul himself? We have watched him undermine in his assemblies the principles of pride and esteem that oiled the wheels of pagan society. No more, he hopes, will the dependence of the poor add luster to their patrons; no more will the grandeur of their patrons lend dignity to the poor. But Paul himself, we have seen, is the sponsor who can win for his suppliants the benevolence of a patron far greater than the emperor. Paul's converts are his pride as he is theirs. Paul can imagine, preach, and try to create a world in which those patrons are displaced whose hierarchy shaped the lives of almost every family in the empire. He can cut out rung after rung on that ladder of access and prestige, but he can imagine only what can be imagined by a person of his time and place. He still has to conceive a conduit from God's people to their God. Paul is the patron of his converts.

Paul's assemblies revered the Anointed, but they depended on Paul himself. He too was a founder, welcomed as an angel and sometimes as an agent greater still. In his talk of transformation Paul is using a motif familiar to his age, and with it he clearly enhances his own authority, for this much-vaunted transformation depends on Paul. To be its channel gives him power; and he uses it. However we view Paul, we do well to admit that the fierce trials of the new creation serve, in unexpected ways, aspirations well known to the old.

TRANSFORMATION THEN–AND NOW?

I write as a historian, but I have no wish to be disingenuous. Most readers of this book will have an interest in Paul that is more than historical. You may well be wondering by now if Paul has slipped through our modern fingers like a wraith and returned to his own age, strange in his inspiration, language, and hopes. With him, back to his alien world, goes his good news. It is hardly any longer the doctrine that we have always known and that some of us have for a long time loved, revered, resented, or disbelieved.

We have despaired too soon. We will never know as our own the tradition of visions and journeys and the court of heaven; we will never speak in such terms of the knowledge of God, its conditions, and limits. But we can, as we come to envisage such journeys, "see their point." If we are to recapture the doctrine of Paul, we should look to its origin, to the insight that blinded Paul, as Luke tells the story, on the road to Damascus. Paul realized, in defiance of any logic that his ancestral faith could allow, that the figure on the throne of God—Ezekiel's *likeness as the appearance of adam*—was the figure of Jesus. This figure remained the subject, in Paul's imagination, of his lifelong gaze. And he would eventually be rewarded with a "journey" to Paradise, the place of God's court and his throne. Can this glorious figure be the subject of our gaze too?

There are dangers here. Paul speaks of a reflection. All too easily, as we have already discovered, the figure we see of Jesus can be recognized—if only in regretful hindsight—as the reflection of our own ideals and hopes, for the image in Ezekiel of *the likeness as the appearance of adam* is only too apt. The likeness shines with a generalized brilliance. Who except ourselves is to fill in the details, to provide the model we need for our particular aspirations? Of course we can hope that the fig-

ure of Jesus, known from the gospels, gives us some clear features, independent of our own, to revere and emulate, but his memory and example have proved endlessly malleable in the service of human hopes and
designs.

The metaphor of this mirrored image is inescapably dangerous. And
by the same token it is poignantly honest. The dangers in the mirrored
image well match the limits of our knowledge, the conditions under
which we might reach that knowledge, and the likelihood of error.
Centuries of church life have made us believe that Paul forever pre-
scribes what we should and should not do, but he does not. First and
foremost he describes how we are, our capacities and limits. To accept
his good news is to acknowledge the description he gives of ourselves
and of the dangers that lurk within ourselves. Then we can recognize
that we are called by his good news not to deny our humanity or tran-
scend it. We are called to realize it, to overcome the dangers and
become the humans that we were created to be.

WE ARE TRAVERSING A SLIPPERY SLOPE, with a long steep fall to one
side. How readily we might forget the Anointed in this gaze upon
Ezekiel's figure and simply praise the potential of humankind. "Man,"
said the Greek philosopher Protagoras, centuries before Paul lived, "is
the measure of all things." It is a dangerous ploy so clearly to encourage
the self-aggrandizement of humanity. It is dangerous in practice. The
history of the last hundred years has shown that humankind is capable—in the name of its own purity and advance—of unlimited evil. It is
dangerous philosophically. Human thought has been bedeviled by the
assumption that human capacities and interests are of higher value than
those of anything else in the universe. And it is dangerous for Christian
faith. Far too much in Western culture already encourages our self-
reliance. The churches, above all other institutions, should surely be
turning hearts and minds toward our frailty, mortality, and utter dependence upon our creator and redeemer. The danger, in Christian eyes, is
clear. We might well pick up from the stories of the first and second
Adam—and from our movement from one to the other—only our
capacity for change, and not the conditions, in God's will and our obedience, that must nurture the change and shape its result.

It is deep, the chasm of self-reliance into which that steep slope falls away. Martin Luther described it in the sixteenth century. He saw the dire danger of a "theology of glory." Such a theology rings out with the praises of the Anointed in glory and of the humankind that is growing into his image, exultant in its own powers and potential. But such theology forgets the crucifixion and its horror, the humility and suffering of Jesus. Luther, then, called for a "theology of the cross," for it is on the cross that the Anointed, the son of God, most fully revealed his father. That is where we will see the image of God, not through an other-worldly contemplation of the splendor on the throne. At the cross too we will discover our total reliance on the Anointed and so on God. It is only the death of Jesus the Anointed that will repair the relation we have broken between God and ourselves. Here all the illusions of our independence or rights are stripped away.

One of the greatest students of Paul in the twentieth century, the Lutheran Ernst Käsemann, argued after World War II that there are few generations who can understand Paul. Only at our culture's darkest hours can we see what Paul saw: the depravity of humankind and its utter, unqualified dependence on the grace and mercy of God. Even those who challenge Käsemann's reading of Paul at point after point have acknowledged that Käsemann might have seen and laid bare, through his distinctive and Lutheran reading, a truth as deep as any seen by any theologian of his time.

HAVE WE YET CAUGHT A GLIMPSE of the transformation that Paul's good news might hold before us today? We have examples to hand more vivid and valuable than we might have dared hope for, for we have before us one individual acutely conscious of his own transformation, Paul himself, and one cluster of assemblies undergoing transformation, Paul's assemblies.

First, Paul himself. He declared himself to be transparent to his converts. He could be no less, for he re-presented the Anointed in his own person. To disguise that person was to keep the Anointed from his followers. All that the Anointed was they could see in Paul without distortion. Or could they? Here we have the advantage on Paul. Despite our distance—and because of it—we can see about Paul what he himself could not. Paul's life was changed on the road to Damascus. His character was not. This is a man who kept undimmed his fervor, energy, and courage, his unshakable reliance on God and commitment to God's cause. But at moments of crisis we see more. Paul longed deeply for his children's love and loyalty. He would use any means to secure it. He could bully, threaten, and maneuver. He could be covert at the very moment that he declared his openness. And all of this was integral to his mission. We can see, more clearly than could Paul himself, what the authority of a leader—both secure and threatened—can bring that leader, in the name of the good news, to do.

And Paul's assemblies? We see only the dangers that Paul addresses and only the account he gives of them. This does the assemblies no justice, but his converts were likely as divided as he claims. They were still shaped by the standards of the life they had left behind. At least some had misunderstood the good news that Paul had brought them. He had, they thought, encouraged them to look straight past death and beyond. They gazed from the hill brow of their present experience across to the mountain peak of the life to come. The air was so clear they could almost touch the snow. They did not see the road from one summit to the other winding through the deepest valley in between. But what they did see gave them a new outlook on themselves and on the world, and the courage and energy to define their lives by it. The new communities survived, matured, and grew. These are the assemblies, in all their light and shade, who were being transformed by their gaze on the image of God re-presented by Paul.

We are the heirs of this Paul and these assemblies. Their examples give no ground for complacency or for despair. They offer us no full or rigid template for transformation in ourselves. They fulfill no ideals and lay down no limits. Their help is far more modest, and for that very reason far more helpful. We are called to follow in our way the road Paul and his converts traveled in theirs. And thanks to their example we can watch our supposed transformation more acutely than they could their own. We can better see where we are still intractably unchanged, where the world around exerts its influence. We can recognize, most poignant of all, how deeply and bitterly the followers of the Anointed can be divided in their heartfelt, honest obedience to his call.

Paul Then, Paul Now:
The Future of the Past

PAUL: THE RE-PRESENTATION OF THE ANOINTED

For most of this book we have kept our eyes on Paul and his life and times. It is far beyond our scope to trace his influence through succeeding centuries to the present day. One of our results, however, calls out for more attention. We have compared Paul's strategies to those of Matthew and John. Their connection, two millennia ago, throws a bridge across one of the deepest divisions between the different churches of America today. A page or two on the construction of this bridge will be pages well spent.

In Paul we find the re-presentation of the Anointed. Paul's good news is inseparable from Paul himself. He is intrinsic to his message and to his assemblies. As a pastoral, practical point we can see why. He was the assemblies' focal point. In his legitimacy lay the legitimacy of his community. In him resided all authority. From him stemmed all authorized teaching. To him flowed the respect and love that united all the members who revered him. In him—the members' father, mother, nurse, brother, and friend—all the needs of the family were met.

Paul himself, however, claims more than such analysis can grant him. He raises himself above the needs of a fragile, divided, diffident new community and declares himself the nodal point between the Anointed in heaven and his Body on earth. Paul, himself anointed, is with the Anointed the conduit of God's blessings upon his converts and of those converts' thanksgivings to God. He is the object of his assemblies' gaze, the face that reflects the glory of the Anointed and imparts glory to his converts in their turn.

MATTHEW: GOD-WITH-US IN THE GOSPEL

We have seen in earlier chapters how John's Jesus functions in John's story as John's gospel is intended to function within his community. John's gospel re-presents Jesus. In this overarching strategy, John is not alone. A comparison with Matthew will stand us in good stead.

In his story of Jesus' conception Matthew invokes a prophecy of Isaiah:

"Look, the virgin shall conceive and shall bear a son,
and they shall call his name Emmanuel"—

which is, interpreted, With us God.
MATTHEW 1:23, QUOTING ISAIAH 7:14, GREEK VERSION

With-us-God. With this phrase we know, from the time of Jesus' conception in Matthew's story, that Jesus is to act as God's agent working on behalf of his people. As Isaiah's Emmanuel did, so Jesus is to do—from one end of Matthew's story to the other. After Easter, right at the end of the narrative, Jesus' pupils, obedient to the angel's command, have gone to Galilee. There on the mountain Jesus meets them and says:

"All authority has been given to me in heaven and on earth. Go out,
therefore, and make pupils of all the Gentiles, baptizing them in the
name of the father and of the son and of the Breath of God, teaching
them to keep all the commandments that I have commanded you. And
look, I am with you always, every day, until the aeon's completed end."
MATTHEW 28:18-20

On a mountaintop, near the beginning of the story, Jesus had refused the devil's offer of a kingdom; on a mountain, at the start of his teaching, he had taught his pupils and the crowds; and here on a mountain, at the story's end, he declares his investiture with unprecedented power. And now he can declare himself "Jesus with us." God was "with us" in the life of Jesus, and this is the same Jesus who is with us still. But where and how is "Jesus-with-us" to be found?

Jesus speaks at the gospel's end with all authority in heaven and on earth; he speaks with the authority of God himself. From With-us-God, therefore, at the gospel's beginning to *I am with you* right at its end—every word between these poles describes, with all the force the name can bear, With-us-God; and every word makes present the Jesus who is with us still. To draw too blunt a distinction: it was the life described in the gospel that was With-us-God; and the description in the gospel that is with the readers now. Jesus-with-Us is the text of the gospel itself.

Matthew's whole strategy falls into place at last. Matthew's Jesus so often seems to speak to Matthew's assembly even more than to the audience around Jesus himself. And with good reason, for underlying Matthew's Jesus, in the story of his time on earth, is the Jesus that after Easter he will be declared to be. Only at the gospel's end can readers see the force of that opening "Emmanuel." All Jesus' words and deeds bear the imprint of his "new" authority, from the gospel's opening chapter to its close.

This strategy prompts questions that Matthew himself did not need to face. What change in Jesus' standing is marked by the gospel's closing lines? What is the authority given to Jesus at the gospel's end that was not already his to claim at its start? Has Matthew been consistent in his view of Jesus then and now? Matthew ignores these questions. He faces instead, with the greatest care, the central challenge to Christian thought: how the extended course of a human life could be the disclosure of the unchanging Wisdom of God. The transition itself, then, from the earthly to the Easter Jesus is not Matthew's chief concern. He is looking back on Jesus then and now, on the single figure presented in his single story who was With-us-God and is now Jesus-with-Us.

The presence of With-us-God, then, is in the stories that Matthew puts before us in the text of his gospel itself, and most trenchantly of all in the words we hear there of Jesus-with-Us. Here was and is, speaking to us, the Wisdom of God.

THE PRESENCE OF JESUS IN THE CHURCH

The issue of authority has been with the church from the first century to the twenty-first. One of the bitterest disputes during the Reformation was over authority and its application in practical power. A sharp and misleading distinction defined the issue then and still colors its discussion now. The Roman church appealed to the authority of the apostolic priesthood, of men ordained by bishops in unbroken succession from the great emissary St. Peter. The reforming churches appealed to the authority of scripture. Let's look at each tradition in turn, with a full admission in advance that such a brisk survey can do justice to neither.

First, then, the apostolic priesthood. Matthew draws on Mark for the moment at which Peter acknowledges Jesus: *"You are the Anointed, the son of the living God."* Mark's Jesus responded with a command to tell no one about him. Matthew's Jesus gives a more ringing reply: *"I, I tell you that you are Peter, and on this rock I will build my assembly and the gates of death shall not have power against it. I will give you the keys of the kingdom of heaven; and whoever you bind on earth shall be bound in heaven, and whoever you release on earth shall be released in heaven"* (Matt. 16:18–19).

In our own day, Pope John Paul II has vigorously reaffirmed the role of Peter's successor in the church's life. The pope is not just a useful focus for unity in an ancient, scattered, and divided community. The pope is intrinsic to the church; the church is not the church without the pope. This is never clearer than at the Mass. A short extract from a document by the Congregation for the Doctrine of the Faith will make Rome's position clear. The italics are in the document; the quotation marks indicate quotations from other official pronouncements from Rome.

In this Roman tradition the Anointed, the head of his Body, the church, is represented by the head of the body of bishops, that is, by the bishop of the Church of Rome, the church that is the head of the churches.

The unicity and indivisibility of the eucharistic Body of the Lord implies the unicity of his mystical Body, which is the one and indivisible Church. . . . The existence of the Petrine ministry, which is a foundation of the unity of the Episcopate [the bishops] and of the universal Church, bears a profound correspondence to the Eucharistic character of the Church.

In fact, the unity of the Church is also rooted in the unity of the episcopate. As the very idea of the Body of the Church calls for the existence of a Church that is *Head* of the Churches, which is precisely the Church of Rome, *"foremost in the universal communion of charity,"* so too the unity of the episcopate involves the existence of a bishop who is Head of the *Body or College of Bishops,* namely the Roman Pontiff. Of the unity of the Episcopate, as also of the unity of the entire Church, *"the Roman Pontiff, as the successor of Peter, is a perpetual and visible source and foundation."* This unity of the Episcopate is perpetuated through the centuries by means of the *apostolic succession,* and is also the foundation of the identity of the Church of every age with the Church built by Christ upon Peter and the other apostles. . . .

For each particular Church to be fully Church . . . there must be present in it, as a proper element, the supreme authority of the Church: the Episcopal college *"together with their head, the Supreme Pontiff, and never apart from him."* The Primacy of the Bishop of Rome and the episcopal College are proper elements of the universal Church that are . . . *interior* to each particular Church. Consequently *"we must see the ministry of the Successor of Peter, not only as a 'global' service, reaching each particular Church from 'outside,' as it were, but* as belonging already to the essence of each particular Church 'from within.'"

> *ON SOME ASPECTS OF THE CATHOLIC CHURCH UNDERSTOOD AS COMMUNION,* 11–13

Now nothing in the claims outlined above denies the authority of scripture. It was, after all, the churches, and not least their priestly hierarchy, that confirmed in the second and third centuries what was to count as scripture. The canon we have in our Bibles now did not emerge without thought, dispute, and public authorization. And the Roman church, for centuries to come, then mediated that canon to its people, for scripture, claimed the church, must be interpreted. And those who are to interpret must be trained and authorized to do so.

It is clearly naïve to believe the meaning of scripture to be self-evident. Only the most self-righteous of readers would claim that his or her reading of scripture is transparently correct and that all other readings are fueled by ignorance, self-interest, or folly. For a glimpse of scripture's ambiguities, we need look no further than that commission to Peter, itself recorded in scripture. The disputes are still with us to which it has given rise, for that commission offers power. And its meaning affects the legitimacy and extent of the power of all those—on all sides—discussing it.

Enough, for our purposes, of the Roman tradition. Let's turn to the Reformers' counterclaims for the supreme authority of scripture alone. We might start again where we have just left off, with questions of power and interpretation. If a self-appointed and unaccountable hierarchy controls the reading of scripture, who will head off the self-aggrandizement to which any monopoly is prone? Who will check the interpretation of those who alone are authorized to interpret? To the Reformers, any filter between scripture and the people invited the abuse of power.

Worse still, any such filter stood between God's people and the Word of their God, and nothing could justify that filter. The Word of God must reach the people complete, in the people's own language, and without restriction. *The word of God,* we read in the letter to the Hebrews, *is alive and in action and sharper than any two-edged sword.* In Greek "word" is a masculine noun, like "man" in English. (A majority of nouns in Greek are masculine or feminine.) The pronoun used to refer to a "word" will be masculine in form: "he" and "him," not "it." How easily the author of the letter to the Hebrews can think of the Word both as an object wielded by God and as the person to whom we shall be accountable. *The Word pierces so deep that he separates soul and breath, joints and marrow. He passes judgment on the reflections and thoughts of the heart. No creature is hidden from him; everything is uncovered and stretched fully open before his eyes, to whom we must give our word of account* (Heb. 4:12–13). The Word of God, claimed the Reformers, must be allowed to speak to his people as directly at the Reformation as fifteen hundred years before.

To translate or not to translate—the story of the Bible's translations into English and their distribution, in the sixteenth century, is as poignant as the stories in the Bible itself. Among Reformers who wanted, like Luther, to put the Bible in the hands of ploughboys there was the passion that makes for martyrs. Most famous of those who died for their work was William Tyndale, betrayed, imprisoned, and executed in the 1530s. His translation of the New Order was the foundation upon which the King James Bible was built, but his work was contentious for decades. Among conservatives such as Henry VIII there was a continuing horror that the "most precious jewel, the word of God, is disputed, rhymed, sung, and jangled in every alehouse and tavern."

An English law of 1543 permitted the reading of scripture by nobles and the gentry, but not by the common people. Three years later one Robert Williams, a shepherd in Gloucestershire, in the west of England, bought a book of instruction as a substitute for the New Testament. He had paid 14d (10 cents) for it. He wrote a note in it. Here was a literate shepherd (a protégé, it seems, of a forward-looking minister who had recently died) who wanted to use his skills to read the Word of God for himself. A world is written in this simple note. Such men as Williams were the forebears of the modern church. "I bout thys boke when the Testament was obberagatyd [abrogated, forbidden], that shepherdys might not red hit. I prey God amende that blyndness. Wryt by Robert Wyllyams keppynge shepe upon Saynbury hill, 1546."

The law of Henry VIII has long since been abrogated in its turn. The churches have evolved, and so have the differences between them. The Jerusalem and New Jerusalem Bibles, endorsed by the Roman Catholic church, are among the most distinguished of modern translations. That is not to deny that there are deep differences still. In the 1960s the Second Vatican Council maintained, as the Council of Trent had maintained in the sixteenth century, that at the Mass the Anointed offers one and the same sacrifice that he offered when he died, "the same [Anointed] now making the offering in the ministry of priests who then offered himself on the cross, with only the form of the offering changed." No member of a Reformed church would agree. But Vatican II continues: the Anointed is also "present in his word since it is he himself who speaks when the holy scriptures are read in the Church" (Vatican II, The Constitution on the Sacred Liturgy, chap. 1, par. 7). Here is common ground. The different churches now gladly share the territory they can, while they still circle round the areas of their disagreements.

But it is time for these disagreements themselves to be redefined. On the one hand is the Roman claim that an apostolic presence is internal to every part of the universal church. And on the other is the Reformed claim that the voice of Jesus is still present in scripture today. As we can see, looking back over this book, both traditions are loyal to the instinct of the earliest assemblies. Seen as the modern expressions of this ancient instinct, the claims are not incompatible or in competition; each in its own way answers to the church's need, known from the very start, for the re-presentation of the Anointed in the church.

There is an irony in this heritage, its different forms, and the battles to which they have given rise. On the one hand are the heirs of Paul, the hero of the Reformers. But it is Paul who offered his assemblies in his own person the "presence" of Jesus. From this insight of the apostle Paul, there stems the understanding of apostolic ministry which is now most vividly expressed in Rome's focus on the pope.

On the other hand are the heirs of Matthew. This is the gospel that offers Rome the scriptural basis for Petrine supremacy. But it is Matthew who offered his assembly, in his text itself, the presence of Jesus-with-Us. From this insight of Matthew, there stems the under-standing of scripture the Reformation churches have made their own— that the Bible's text can function as the presence of the Lord.

One need, two ways to meet it; and the difference between them has kept the churches apart for centuries. Underlying the two answers, however, lies one and the same claim. It is the claim of Paul himself. *It pleased God to unveil his son in me*—in Paul's own person and presence. And in the absence of that unveiling is the letter from heaven. *The good news is the power of God for deliverance*—in the presence of Paul's letter, here and now.

CHAPTER 29

"TO THE END OF THE EARTH"

THE WORK OF OUR PAUL, emissary, prophet, and seer, is nearing its end.
He has come a long way from those meditations on Isaiah and Ezekiel.
that led to his conversion and his years of mission. So have we.

> *I saw the Lord sitting upon a throne, high and lifted up. . . . Above him*
> *stood the seraphim; each had six wings: with two he covered his face, and*
> *with two he covered his feet; and with two he flew. And one seraph called*
> *to another and said,*
>
> > *"Holy, holy, holy is the Lord God of hosts;*
> >
> > *The whole earth is full of his glory."*
>
> *And the foundations of the threshold shook at the voice of him who*
> *called, and the house was filled with smoke.*
>
> ISAIAH 6:1–4

The Mission [Acts] ends quietly. Paul is in Rome under house arrest.
Did he ever get to see the emperor? Not that we hear. Why does
Luke not give us an obviously dramatic close to his work? Perhaps he
expected his Theophilus to know what had befallen Paul in his final
years and so to need no further information. Now any such Theophilus
has had good reason to ask throughout his reading of Luke's work:

Why, if the assemblies were the heir of God's promises to Israel, had Israel itself not accepted the good news and kept its title to these promises? The question confronted every assembly. And in the assemblies' search for an answer that same vision of Isaiah was soon brought to bear. Isaiah had been ordered,

> "Go and say to this people:
> 'Hear with all your might but do not understand,
>   look with all your might but do not see.'
> Make the heart of this people fat,
>   and their ears heavy, and shut their eyes;
> lest they see with their eyes and hear with their ears,
>   and understand with their hearts,
> and turn and be healed."
>
> ISAIAH 6:9-10

This fierce command became well known among Jesus' followers. Mark and Matthew record its use by Jesus himself; John deploys it in his own voice as author; and Luke has it used by Paul in the very last lines of The Mission. The placing is important. Mark's Jesus invokes the command most darkly at the start of his work. We have encountered just a handful of miracles, the first disputes, and one parable. Enough has been said to show what resistance the good news will meet with. Mark tells us:

> When Jesus was alone, those around him with the Twelve [his closest followers, given powers and authority of their own] asked him about the riddles he used. "To you," he said, "the secret of the Kingdom of God has been given. But to those outside, everything happens in riddles, so that
>
> > 'Looking with all their might they may not see,
> > and listening with all their might they may not understand;
> > lest they change their ways and God forgive them.'"
> >
> > MARK 4:10-12

Those "outside" are positively excluded, it seems, right from the start and by God's own plan. This Jesus does not seek to persuade his audience. On the contrary, he makes his teaching obscure to ensure that they remain in darkness, *"lest they change their ways and God forgive them."*

Can Jesus really have applied this prophecy so starkly, in the sense of our present Greek text of Mark? In the Aramaic version of Isaiah the prophecy of Isaiah itself is softened. This is the version that was used in the prayer houses of Jesus' day and that Jesus would have known; this, then, is it argued, will be the sense in which he himself spoke. In this translation, those to whom Isaiah is to preach will indeed be blind and deaf, *"unless they see with their eyes . . . and turn and be healed."* Not *lest,* then, but *unless.* This is far more encouraging to general readers.

This is not, however, the sense in which Mark recorded Jesus' words. We might well ask, then: How could Mark believe that Jesus sought the condemnation of his audience? The answer lies in Mark's setting. The parables that Mark records were well suited to an assembly that was beleaguered and opposed, whose mission had met with scant success. The words of Isaiah would have been a comfort and encouragement to those inside, not the least by being so stark a condemnation of their enemies. The great prophet had faced the same resistance centuries before. And God himself had warned of it—in just the words that we find so hard to hear from the mouth of Mark's Jesus. Mark himself, as we have seen, issues a warning as well in these words. His whole gospel is a parable, and his readers must take care not to stay, blind and deaf, among those outside.

And Luke? He addresses Isaiah's prophecy, by contrast, right at the end of his book, in the closing lines of The Mission. This is no longer a prophecy taken over by Jesus at the story's start. It is expounded by Luke's Paul as a prophecy now fulfilled. This Paul looks back over the whole course of his mission. He sees how he has been the Isaiah of this later age, preaching to Israel as Isaiah had so many centuries before. Speaking to the Jews in Rome, this Paul cites his predecessor:

> *"You will listen with all your might and you shall not understand,*
> *you will look with all your might and you shall not see."*
> THE MISSION 28:26

There is a sad finality here. This is the third time in The Mission that Luke's Paul has declared that he will from now on preach to the Gentiles. And this time the die is cast—not because the Jews reject the good news outright, but because they cannot agree on their response. Here, we may suspect, is Luke's final glance at the setting that Theophilus knew well. The Jews were not all rejecting the good news any more than all Gentiles were accepting it. Least of all, perhaps, in Rome; we might well suspect, from Paul's letter to the Romans, that the assembly there included at least some Jews. It is enough, for Luke's final move, that the Jews of Rome are divided.

Luke, then, presents Isaiah's dark words in retrospect. All those in or around the assembly would have wondered why so few accepted the good news about Jesus. Here at the close is Luke's answer to this enigma. His solution has cast a long, dark shadow over the centuries since. All of Paul's passionate care for his own people is lost in this conclusion, and all of his quicksilver thought. Luke had his own viewpoint, insights, and needs. He was master of them all. But they were not Paul's. And in telling the story of Paul, Luke does scant justice to his hero, to this new Moses, new Isaiah, new and radical seer.

The Mission ends:

Setting up a day with Paul at his lodgings, a good many came to him, to whom he expounded and testified to the kingdom of God, seeking to persuade them about Jesus from both the Law of Moses and the prophets, from dawn to dusk. And some of them were persuaded by what was said, and others did not believe. They were in disharmony with each other, and disbanded. Paul said just one thing: "The Breath of God spoke well, when it spoke though the prophet Isaiah to your ancestors, saying,

> *'Go to this people and say:*
> *You will listen with all your might and you shall not understand,*
> *   you will look with all your might and you shall not see.*
> *For the heart of this people is hardened*
> *   and they have heard dully with their ears*
> *   and have closed their eyes,*
> *in case they should see with their eyes*
> *   and hear with their ears*
> *   and understand with their hearts*
> *and turn—and I should heal them.'*

So know this: to the Gentiles has this deliverance been sent. They will hear it, yes, they will."
THE MISSION 28:23–28

Paul: Emissary, Prophet, Seer

Who, then, was this Paul, whom Luke for all his skills quite failed to understand? We all have various pigeonholes in mind, when we first open his letters. Paul will surely, after all, fall into one of the categories familiar to us, even if it was not current in his own day.

But now, at the end of this book, we find ourselves far better helped by the categories, however strange to us now, inherited and developed so self-consciously by Paul himself. So be it. We *may* not have the pigeonholes ready to hand, in the twenty-first century, into which Paul fits. Here, perhaps, is no dove to coo tamely from a niche of our making. Or perhaps it is just too soon to know. We will do best to let this newly rediscovered Paul take flight and to watch his movements through page after page of his extraordinary letters. We may come to wonder if we have ever seen the patterns of such flight before. Paul had to rethink the categories he knew, to describe his Anointed, himself, and his work; perhaps we will need unfamiliar categories to describe him too.

PAUL WAS A SEER. The figure he saw on the throne of God was Jesus, crucified and elevated to bear the name above every name—the name of God. In his own person Paul re-presented this figure, his death, and his glory. Paul's own visions were set within a tradition that knew not just of journeys to heaven, but of the transformation they wrought upon the traveler. And so his converts in their turn would be transformed not by a heavenly journey of their own, but by membership of the Anointed and by his re-presentation in the person of Paul. And when Paul was not present in person? Then by his letters. They arrive with all the authority of letters from heaven and bring Paul in his breath to the assembly itself. They come with the power in themselves to work transformation, *the power of God for deliverance.*

Paul was not just an added extra to the life of the assembly. He was intrinsic to its life—its father, mother, brother, and friend. His assemblies needed him. And the more deeply we look into the letters, the more acutely we see that Paul needed his assemblies. He will bind them to him in every way he can, for he is a maverick, isolated from the other emissaries and adamant that he and his assemblies are answerable to the Anointed and to God alone. Just once we hear him write to a community whose members do not know him; over them he has no hold. Here we see most clearly what Paul aims to achieve in his letters. He is working to heal the mind of his addressees during the course of the letter's reception. As John is the midwife of the Breath of God, so Paul for the Romans is the doctor of the mind.

"The Full Number of the Gentiles"

At last Paul reached Rome. And then? He had told the Romans, before the turmoil he stirred up in Jerusalem, that he was planning to visit them on his way to Spain. Did he ever get there? We do not know. By the end of the first century Clement writes that Paul went "to the extreme west." Paul had a more pressing reason to go than we readily see now. Paul wrote to the Romans of *the full number of the Gentiles* that must *come in* (Rom. 11:25). He must preach, but not where the Anointed had already been named, for he will fulfill a prophecy of Isaiah about the suffering Servant of God:

> *Those will see to whom no message has been sent about him,*
> *and those shall understand who have not heard.*
> ROMANS 15:21, QUOTING ISAIAH 52:15, GREEK VERSION

The book of Isaiah's prophecies ends with a great vision in which the nations shall finally acknowledge God:

> *I am coming to gather all nations and tongues*
> *and they shall come and see my glory.*
> *And I shall send survivors to the nations,*

> *to Tarshish, to Put and Lud, to Tubal and Javan,*
> *to the coastlands far off that have not heard my name nor seen my glory;*
> *and they shall declare my glory among the nations.*
>
> ISAIAH 66:18–19

Put and Lud are linked with Africa, Tubal with Asia Minor, Javan with Greece. In all of them the good news was already known. And Tarshish? Paul's generation likely thought of it as Tartessus in southern Spain, on the westernmost fringes of the known world. Here was Paul's final duty. He had headed ever farther west, from Asia Minor to Greece and so to Rome. And to complete the arc of his mission, across the whole northern side of the Mediterranean, he must head westward still and bring the farthest Gentiles of Isaiah, from the end of the earth, to acknowledge God and his Anointed.

Paul has seen a great inversion in the order of deliverance. Before his conversion he would have expected God's Holy Land and holy people to be purified by a return to their God. Then the nations would gather in obeisance. Now, by contrast, he sees the Gentiles gathering to the Anointed. This, then, is the first stage in God's final intervention.

> *I do not want you to be ignorant, brothers, of this mystery: A hardness, in part, has come upon Israel until the full number of the Gentiles comes in. And in this way all Israel will be saved, as it is written:*
>
> *From Sion will come the rescuer,*
> *he will turn away impieties from Israel,*
> *and this will be the Order with them, from me,*
> *when I take their wrongdoings away.*
>
> ROMANS 11:25–27, QUOTING ISAIAH 59:20–21

At last God's full justness will be unveiled, and his own beloved people—Paul's own people—will be redeemed. And then at last the end can come.

Once More to Rome

"There was a group," wrote the Roman historian Tacitus around 110 C.E., "loathed for its vices, that the people called Christians. Responsible for the name was Christ; he had been put to death by Pontius Pilate when Tiberius was emperor. This checked the horrid superstition, but not for long; it burst out again, not only in Judea where it had started, but in Rome too, a sink into which everything vile and shameful flows and finds its vogue" (*Annals* 15.44).

In July 64 a fire broke out in Rome that would destroy a fifth of the city and damage twice as much again. The Christians were blamed. Tacitus tells the story of the Christians' arrest and execution. The historian loathed the emperor Nero as deeply as he despised the Christians; only Nero could have been so cruel that the Christians' punishment won them sympathy.

> Derision accompanied their end: they were covered with wild beasts' skins and torn to death by dogs; or they were fastened on crosses, and when daylight failed were burned to serve as lamps by night.
>
> Nero had offered his gardens for the spectacle, and gave an exhibition in his stadium. In the dress of a charioteer he mixed with the crowd and paraded on his chariot. And so for these culprits who had earned the most severe and exemplary punishment there arose a feeling of pity: they were being sacrificed, it seemed, not for the welfare of the state but to the ferocity of a single man.
>
> ANNALS 15.44

"Thus a beginning was made [in 64] of violent persecution of the Christians," writes the Christian historian Sulpicius Severus, around 400. "Afterwards also laws were enacted and the religion was forbidden. Edicts were publicly published: 'No one is to profess Christianity.' Then Paul and Peter were condemned to death. The former was beheaded, Peter was crucified." Sulpicius apparently believes Peter and Paul to have been killed after the main persecution. The church historian Eusebius, almost a hundred years earlier, put their deaths in 67. If the report is accurate, Paul must have stayed in or returned to Rome in full knowledge of the danger. And he paid the price.

And so Paul and Peter both fade from our sight. Perhaps in Paul's case it is not surprising. He was, after all, a loose cannon. His message was subtle, careful, deep; it was soon represented wrongly or wrongly understood. It is no wonder that he was held in such suspicion. *Some things in Paul's letters,* warns the second letter of Peter, *are hard to understand; the ignorant and unstable twist them to their own destruction* (2 Pet. 3:16).

Paul had his own agenda, own vision, own assistants. He had cut himself off from the main missions of Antioch and Jerusalem. And so their preachers sought influence in his assemblies and subverted his good news. Where a rival mission did not threaten his converts, their old familiar paganism threatened instead. As Isaiah's Servant of God had lamented, so could Paul lament in his turn:

> *"Vainly have I worked and to no avail,*
> *and for nothing have I used up my strength."*
> ISAIAH 49:4, GREEK VERSION

It would be years before Paul's influence began to grow beyond his own assemblies. It would be decades before the power of his thought was rediscovered. At his death he left behind just a handful of letters and a few fragile assemblies.

They were enough.

> *Says God* [in reply to Isaiah's Servant]—
> *God who formed me from the womb to be his slave,*
> *to bring Israel back to him: . . .*
> *"Look, I have made you to be an Order for the people,*
> *to be a light to the nations,*
> *so that you might work for deliverance to the end of the earth."*
> ISAIAH 49:5–6, GREEK VERSION

SOURCE
ACKNOWLEDGMENTS

(For Scriptural and Subject Indices, see the Web site
www.thegospelaccordingtopaul.com)

All translations from the New Testament and from the Greek Old Testament are my own. Translations from Eusebius, Josephus, Philo, Seneca, and Tacitus are my own, with a debt to the translators in the Loeb Classical Library editions. For the apocalypses I have used J. H. Charlesworth, *The Old Testament Pseudepigrapha* (Darton, Longman and Todd, 1983–85), with reference as well to R. H. Charles, *The Apocrypha and Pseudepigrapha of the Old Testament* (Oxford University Press, 1913), and M. Black, *The Book of Enoch* (Brill, 1985); for texts from Qumran, F. G. Martínez and E. J. C. Tigchelaar, *The Dead Sea Scrolls* (Brill, 1997–98), and G. Vermes, *The Complete Dead Sea Scrolls in English* (Penguin, 1997); for the Mishnah, H. Danby, *The Mishnah* (Oxford University Press, 1933).

All modern study of the seers and their visions of the chariot-throne are built on the work of W. Bousset, "Die Himmelsreise der Seele," *Archiv für Religionswissenschaft* 4 (1901), and of G. Scholem, *Major Trends in Jewish Mysticism* (English translation, 1955). For particular details in this book I am indebted to M. Beard, J. North, and S. Price, *The Religions of Rome* (Cambridge University Press, 1998), for the cults of the *lares* and of Augustus; M. Bockmuehl, "The Form of God," *The Journal of Theological Studies* 48 (1997); C. Fletcher-Louis, *All the Glory of Adam* (Brill, 2002), for his treatment of the Songs of the Sabbath Sacrifice;

J. Klawans, *Impurity and Sin in Ancient Judaism* (Oxford University Press, 2000); W. Meeks, "The Image of the Androgyne," reprinted in *In Search of the Early Christians* (Yale University Press, 2002); and C. Rowland, *The Open Heaven* (SPCK, 1985), for his treatment of the four rabbis' journey to heaven.

Adam is the subject of many studies, recently (and with a duly cautious tone) by J. R. Levison, *Portraits of Adam in Early Judaism* (Sheffield, 1988); few such studies focus on Ezekiel's visions or the conditions for the possibility of knowledge. J. Bowker, "Merkabah-Visions and the Visions of Paul," *The Journal of Semitic Studies* 16 (1971) first suggested a tight connection between Ezekiel's vision and Paul's. J. Murphy-O'Connor, *Paul: A Critical Life* (Oxford University Press, 1996) provides a survey of Paul's life; I have gratefully followed the majority of his conclusions. I have named other scholars in the Preface; a glance at their bibliographies on the Internet will show the debt that *The Gospel According to Paul,* Parts I–IV, owes to their work. To these—and to many others—I owe thanks not just for the answers they offer to questions, but for the questions they have raised. Their work provides the earth in which such a book as this can take root and grow to fruition.

If the second half of this book (Parts V–X) is successful, it will itself provide such a setting for future investigation of Paul's letters. A good many scholars in the last thirty years have compared the structure, style, and devices of Paul's rhetoric with those catalogued and recommended by Greco-Roman theorists. I have commented briefly on this comparison in relation to 1 Thessalonians in *The Journal of Theological Studies* 52 (2001). My own concern is with the purposes to which Paul is putting his rhetoric; and we will learn all that we can about these from the letters themselves.

Within the confines of this book I have had to forgo discussion of the enthronement of the heavenly Son of Man or Elect One in 1 Enoch (e.g., 46:1, 61:8), the apparent displacement of God by Moses ("Ezekiel the Tragedian," *Exagoge* 70–82), and the theophany offered by the high priest (specifically in his office as high priest) on the Day of Atonement.

I have summarized in *The Gospel According to Paul* several conclusions about the four gospels; readers will find a full account in my book *The Four Witnesses* (HarperSanFrancisco, 2000).

INDEX OF SCRIPTURAL AND OTHER TEXTS

Old and New Orders (Old and New Testaments)

Other Early Jewish and Christian Texts

Other Greek and Latin Texts

INDEX OF SUBJECTS

Numbers of chapters and verses appear in italics.
Page numbers of maps appear in bold.

presence, 35–40, 313-14; architecture of, 346–47; density, difficulty of letters, 11; function of, summary, 34–40; illumination through, 12, 31; language of the seers, 24; light as image, 83–84, 90; "mercy seat" imagery, 61, 63, 64, 66, 67, 71–72; mirror imagery, 361, 488–89; Old Order imagery in, 83; poetry and metaphors in, 3, 35, 39, 46, 47–56, 116, 319–23; rhythm of, 12; "son of man," 85–86; style and techniques in, 3, 45, 177–78; Temple imagery, 84–85; tone, 35–36; visionary experience and language of seers in, 94–98, 115–16, 118, 468. *See also specific cities and letters*

Pauline scholarship, 8, 115–16, 246–47, 252, 273–74, 283, 347, 349, 413

Paulus, Sergius, viii, 174–76

Perge, viii

Peter, x, 494; apostolic priesthood and, 495–96; assemblies in Jerusalem and, 153, 155, 166, 255; background, 155; Corinth and, 301, 307; as emissary and rival of Paul, 141, 301, 342; on Gentile converts, 221, 226; in the gospels, 238–40; leadership of, 238; Paul and, 229; Second Coming, signs of, 203–4; "sit at my right hand" (Mission 2.22–23, 32–35), 154; statement of belief, Caesarea Philippi, 162–63; vision of Elijah and Moses, 140–41

Pheidias, 50

Philip, 156

Philippi, ix, 177, 204, 448–49

Philippians, 448–76; Anointed and Paul in relationship to, 450, 453–54; commonwealth on earth, 454–58; commonwealth in heaven, 458–60; date of composition, 448–49; division in the assembly addressed, 39; Euodia and Syntyche, 451–52, 453; form of God, 465–68; gift to Paul, 458; "hymn" of, 450, 461–67, 473–76; introduction, 453; Mosaic law and Paul, 253; overall shape, 453; Paul imprisoned and,

454; purpose and function, 451; representation of Jesus and transformation of followers in, 40; rivalry overcome and goodwill sought, 453

Philo, 44, 62, 66, 112–14, 156–57, 281, 282, 295, 300–301, 324

Phoebe, xiii, 274–75, 279–80

Phrygia, ix

Plato and Platonism, 111–14, 295; *sōma sēma*, 116

Porphyry, 11

prayer houses [synagogues], 9–10; in Antioch, 223–24; opposition to Christian assemblies, 35; size of, 275

Qumran: celibacy in, 292–93; community at, 50; Damascus and, 162–63; Dead Sea Scrolls found at, 50; as *elohim* and *elim*, 99–100; hymns of, 88, 98–104; life of heaven in community, 98–104; and sanctuary of God (*miqdash adonay*), 51–52, 61–62; Temple replaced by community at, 51–52, 69

Rapture, 190

Reformation, 391, 497–98, 499

resurrection: baptized in Anointed Jesus and, 104; Corinthians, denial that dead will rise, 104, 327; final, 23, 104; hope of, 426–27; of Jesus, as rose or was raised or roused (*anasteemi* or *egeiro*), 10–11; Mark's gospel, 148; Paul and, 1 Corinthians, 325–28

Romans, 381–444; Abraham story, 413–14, 426; agonized self in, 124–26, 418–19; Anointed is the new Temple, 69; baptism into the death of Anointed, 367, 368; as "circular," 393; classic reading of letter, 386, 388–95; divisions in assembly, 38, 257, 384, 416–18; on faith, 232; form and function of letter, 385–88, 407; greetings in, 9, 383, 385; healing of community in, 31, 431–33, 438–39; heart of the letter (Chapter 7), 421–26; idolatry and pagans targeted, 404–5; Jewish Law, role of, 384, 386, 387, 389–92,

Tribulation, 190
Troas, ix, xiii, 342, 348

Unveiling [Revelation]: Jesus as subject of
worship, 143, 185; New Jerusalem
(22:1–4), 25; Satan, the dragon, 139;
Jesus' own visions in, 108, 138–44
Urban, 385

Vespasian, Emperor of Rome, 180, 181
Virgil, 117–18
visionaries: angels and, 91–93, 95, 96, 97;
authenticity of, 107–14; Daniel,
85–87, 108–9; Enoch, 90–93, 96,
469; Ezekiel, 18, 78–88, 89, 99; final
battle between God and evil, 147;
four rabbis in paradise, 24–28; Isaiah
and, 56, 59–77, 94–98, 346; Jesus as,

138–44, 146–49, 186; mysticism and,
32–33; Paul and the visionary tradition, 89–98, 107–15; Paul's journey to
paradise (Third Heaven), 18, 22–24,
82, 95–98, 108, 287; Paul's converts
and, 32–33; tradition of, 22, 142

Wesley, John, 120
Wisdom: as agent working for or beside
God, 85–86; as the image of God's
goodness, 53–54; the law and, 54–56
women: marriage and equality, 293–97;
relationship with men, 129–30; role in
worship, 126–27, 130–31
Wordsworth, William, 7

Yohanan, Rabbi, and Rabbi Eleazar, story
of, 79, 80